State Territoriality and European Integration

Territorial sovereignty has been fundamental to European states, but does territory still matter for political organisation in a 'Europe without frontiers?' This new book addresses the under-explored concept of political territoriality from historical, analytical and empirical angles, with a particular focus on the European Union.

This book addresses a topic of much contemporary debate: the future of European nation states in the context of European integration and globalisation. Seeking a better understanding of political territoriality in the European Union, the expert contributions to this volume include:

- Historical case studies illustrating how political territoriality gained its prominence in European states since the Peace Treaties of Westphalia (1648).
- Analytical contributions tracing political territoriality in federations and multi-level polities, such as the European Union and the Brussels region.
- Empirical studies on welfare, defence and policing.

This new volume will appeal to a wide variety of audiences, ranging from Europeanists to political scientists, globalisation scholars and historians.

Michael Burgess is Professor of Federal Studies and Director of the Centre for Federal Studies (CFS) at the University of Kent in Canterbury, England. **Hans Vollaard** is Lecturer in Political Science at Leiden University, the Netherlands.

Europe and the nation state
Edited by Michael Burgess
(Centre for Federal Studies, University of Kent)
and Lee Miles
(Europe and the World Centre, University of Liverpool)

This series explores the complex relationship between nation states and European integration and the political, social, economic and policy implications of this interaction. The series examines issues such as:

- the impact of the EU on the politics and policy-making of the nation-state and vice-versa
- the effects of expansion of the EU on individual nation states in Europe
- the relationship between the EU and non-European nation states.

1 **Poland and the European Union**
   Edited by Karl Cordell

2 **Greece in the European Union**
   Edited by Dionyssis G. Dimitrakopoulos and Argyris G. Passas

3 **The European Union and Democratization**
   Edited by Paul J. Kubicek

4 **Iceland and European Integration**
   On the edge
   Edited by Baldur Thorhallsson

5 **Norway Outside the European Union**
   Norway and European integration from 1994 to 2004
   Clive Archer

6 **Turkey and European Integration**
   Prospects and issues in the post-Helsinki era
   Edited by Mehmet Uğur and Nergis Canefe

7 **Perspectives on EU–Russia Relations**
   Edited by Debra Johnson and Paul Robinson

8 French Relations with the European Union
Edited by Helen Drake

9 The Geopolitics of Euro-Atlantic Integration
Edited by Hans Mouritzen and Anders Wivel

10 State Territoriality and European Integration
Edited by Michael Burgess and Hans Vollaard

State Territoriality and European Integration

Edited by Michael Burgess and
Hans Vollaard

Routledge
Taylor & Francis Group

LONDON AND NEW YORK

First published 2006
by Routledge
2 Park Square, Milton Park, Abingdon, Oxon, OX14 4RN

Simultaneously published in the USA and Canada
by Routledge
270 Madison Ave, New York NY 10016

Routledge is an imprint of the Taylor & Francis Group, an informa business

First issued in paperback 2011

© Selection and editorial matter, 2006 Michael Burgess and Hans Vollaard; individual chapters, the contributors

Typeset in Garamond by Wearset, Boldon, Tyne and Wear

All rights reserved. No part of this book may be reprinted or reproduced or utilised in any form or by any electronic, mechanical, or other means, now known or hereafter invented, including photocopying and recording, or in any information storage or retrieval system, without permission in writing from the publishers.

British Library Cataloguing in Publication Data
A catalogue record for this book is available from the British Library

Library of Congress Cataloging in Publication Data
A catalog record for this book has been requested

ISBN10: 0-415-39046-X (hbk)
ISBN10: 0-415-66391-1 (pbk)
ISBN10: 0-203-96960-X (ebk)

ISBN13: 978-0-415-39046-0 (hbk)
ISBN13: 978-0-415-66391-5 (pbk)
ISBN13: 978-0-203-96960-1 (ebk)

Contents

List of contributors	ix
Preface	xii

1 Introduction: analysing Westphalian states in an integrating Europe and a globalising world   1
MICHAEL BURGESS AND HANS VOLLAARD

PART I
Territoriality in history   15

2 The quest for security: the case of the Dutch Republic   17
OLAF VAN NIMWEGEN

3 The metamorphoses of European territoriality: a historical reconstruction   37
BENNO TESCHKE

PART II
Analysing territoriality in multi-level polities   69

4 Area and administration: a multi-level analysis of a multi-layered phenomenon   71
THEO A.J. TOONEN AND FRITS M. VAN DER MEER

5 Territoriality and federalism in the governance of the European Union   100
MICHAEL BURGESS

6 The hyphenated state, multi-level governance and the
   communities in Belgium: the case of Brussels   120
   WILFRIED SWENDEN AND MARLEEN BRANS

PART III
European integration: a changing territorial state of
affairs?   145

7 Territoriality and the EU citizen   147
   GERTJAN DIJKINK AND VIRGINIE MAMADOUH

8 Building the Common Market but preventing chaos: the
   continuing relevance of the principle of territoriality in
   the field of taxation and the limits of a Europe made by
   judges   175
   HERMAN VOOGSGEERD

9 EU social policy beyond national welfare regime   197
   ANTON HEMERIJCK

10 When push comes to shove: the territorial monopoly
   of force and the travails of neomedieval Europe   228
   JÖRG FRIEDRICHS

11 Europe, war, and territory   252
   PETER VAN HAM

12 Conclusion: state territoriality and European integration   274
   MICHAEL BURGESS AND HANS VOLLAARD

   Index   278

Contributors

Marleen Brans is Senior Lecturer in Public Administration and Public Policy at the Public Management Centre, Department of Political Sciences, Katholieke Universiteit Leuven, Belgium. She has published on local government organisation, comparative public administration and policy professionalisation.

Prof. Dr Michael Burgess is Professor of Federal Studies and Director of the Centre for Federal Studies (CFS) at the University of Kent in Canterbury, England. He specialises in comparative federalism, Canadian constitutional politics and European integration and his *Comparative Federalism in Theory and Practice* (Routledge, 2005) has just been published. Currently he is jointly editing (with John Pinder) a project entitled *Multinational Federations* to be published in 2006.

Jörg Friedrichs is Research Associate at the International University Bremen, Germany. He is working on a research project about the internationalisation of the monopoly of the legitimate use of force. His interests include the theory of European integration and European approaches to International Relations theory. Friedrichs has also published articles on new medievalism as a key to understanding the emergent post-Westphalian order.

Dr Peter van Ham is Deputy Head of Studies at the Netherlands Institute of International Relations 'Clingendael' in The Hague, and Professor at the College of Europe in Bruges (Belgium). His latest books are *Mapping European Security After Kosovo* (Manchester University Press, 2002) and *European Integration and the Postmodern Condition* (Routledge, 2001).

Dr Anton C. Hemerijck is Director of the Netherlands Scientific Council for Government Policy (WRR) and Senior Lecturer in the Department of Public Administration, Leiden University. He has published widely on issues of comparative social and economic policy and institutions. Between 1997 and 2000 he has been a research affiliate of the Max-Planck-Institute for the Study of Societies, working on the large comparative project 'Welfare and Work in the Open Economy', directed by Fritz W. Scharpf and Vivien A. Schmidt. He has also been involved in drafting

x *Contributors*

reports on social policy for Portuguese (2000) and Belgian presidencies (2001) of the EU, respectively with Maurizio Ferrera and Martin Rhodes, and Gøsta Esping-Andersen, Duncan Gallie and John Myles.

Dr Frits M van der Meer is Associate Professor in Comparative Public Administration and Management in the Department of Public Administration at Leiden University, the Netherlands.

Dr Olaf van Nimwegen is a historian in the Department of New History at Amsterdam University, the Netherlands.

Dr Wilfried Swenden is a Lecturer in Politics in the School of Social and Political Studies at the University of Edinburgh, Scotland. His recent publications include a monograph, 'Federalism and Second Chambers: Regional Representation in Parliamentary Federations: the Australian Senate and German Bundesrat Compared' (P.I.E-Peter Lang, 2004) and an article in the *Journal of Common Market Studies* (June 2004). He recently completed a textbook on Federalism and Regionalism in Western Europe (Palgrave).

Dr Benno Teschke is Lecturer in the Department of International Relations at the University of Sussex, England. After receiving his PhD from the London School of Economics, he held positions as an Andrew Mellon post-doctoral fellow at the Center for Social Theory and Comparative History at the University of California, Los Angeles and as a lecturer at the University of Wales, Swansea. He has published in *International Organization*, the *European Journal of International Relations* and in *Millennium: Journal of International Studies*. Teschke is the author of *The Myth of 1648: Class, Geopolitics and the Making of Modern International Relations* which was awarded the 2003 Isaac Deutscher Memorial Prize.

Prof. Dr Theo A.J. Toonen is Professor of Comparative Government and Public Administration in the Department of Public Administration, and Dean of the Faculty of Social and Behavioural Sciences at Leiden University, the Netherlands.

Dr Herman Voogsgeerd wrote his PhD thesis on the four freedoms of the European internal market. His research is mainly about the consequences of these freedoms, interpreted by the European Court of Justice in Luxembourg, for the nature of the European construction. He wrote contributions about legal pluralism on the European internal market and about 'special-purpose associations' in Europe. Currently he is working on the role of codes of conduct as an alternative instrument to legislation in the EU, for example, on areas such as corporate governance and the internal market for financial services. He is Lecturer in the Departments of International Organisations/International Relations and of Commercial and Labour law at the University of Groningen, the Netherlands.

Dr Hans Vollaard is Lecturer in Political Science and Coordinator of the EU-Studies Programme of the Faculty of Arts, and a PhD candidate in the Department of Political Science at Leiden University, the Netherlands. He studied political science at the same university between 1995 and 1999. His research project 'Territoriality in the European Union' deals with the impact of European integration on the territorial organisation of healthcare and security in the Netherlands and the European Union.

Preface

The Dutch city of Leiden is situated on the former frontier of the Roman Empire. Perhaps for this reason the most famous Leiden citizen ever, Rembrandt van Rijn, depicted the coronation of an emperor on his first known painting, now displayed in the municipal museum, 'De Lakenhal'. Rembrandt exemplifies the burgeoning international trade in paintings in the seventeenth century that emanated from the Dutch Republic. In this once faraway corner of the Roman and Carolingian Empires, the Republic was one the first polities that enjoyed some sort of sovereignty. Its declaration of independence was used later in both the French and American Revolutions to create, respectively, a fully sovereign nation-state and the first modern federation. The Dutch Republic remained for long however a curious combination of confederal, consociational and state-like authority structures.

Leiden fulfilled a heroic role in the Dutch struggle for independence against Habsburg imperialism. As an expression of thanks, the Dutch Republic granted the city a university in 1575. One of its first professors, Justus Lipsius, taught Roman history. Meanwhile, the victims of nation-state building and imperial rule across Europe fled to the safe haven of Leiden, peoples such as Flemish and Walloon, Protestants, Jews, Huguenots and the Pilgrim Fathers.

Consequently Leiden's own history contains many concepts currently used with respect to the *territorial* nature of the European Union (EU) and of its member states: Does the Council of Ministers situated in its Justus Lipsius Building in Brussels work towards a political entity resembling an empire, a consociation of sovereign states or a confederation? Leiden has clearly been an excellent location for a conference on political territoriality in the EU. Thanks to the generosity of the European Studies programme of the Leiden Faculty of Arts and the Leiden University Foundation, it has been possible to organise such a conference during the Autumn of 2003. With the help and support of Richard Griffiths, Peter Mair, Leony van der Splinter and Anna Little together with the paper givers, the conference has been a stimulating and reflective encounter, resulting in this collection of contributions on political territoriality in the EU.

Leiden's own history reveals and underlines just how much concepts regarding political territoriality in the present-day EU are infused by past experience. Understanding how certain territorial configurations have emerged and functioned may be of considerable use in helping us to grasp the current territorial arrangements. Accordingly, this volume of essays provides the reader with the key concepts designed to analyse and explain territoriality and its changing expressions in the EU from a number of different scholarly perspectives. We believe that the issue of territoriality has been the subject of only cursory examination in the general political science literature so that a fresh exploration of this important area from a variety of different disciplinary approaches is long overdue.

Michael Burgess and Hans Vollaard

1 Introduction

Analysing Westphalian states in an integrating Europe and a globalising world

Michael Burgess and Hans Vollaard

In the early twenty-first century the territorial nation-state in Europe is delicately perched between two historical processes that are intimately interconnected, namely, European integration and globalisation. Contemporary pressures on the modern state as primarily a territorial association, whose integrity, stability and legitimacy derive from its capacity and effectiveness to provide physical security and general welfare for its citizens, have served to call into question its fundamental role and relevance to the needs of a new age. The principal purpose of this book is to shed new light upon the evolving relationship between the territorial state in Europe and the process of European integration in a way that both re-examines and reappraises the territorial basis of the state itself. While the contentious issue of globalisation is not part of our main remit, it has been nonetheless an intermittent subject of brief attention in some of the chapters that follow.

Questions that immediately spring to mind include the following: Is the state as a territorial association any longer adequate to provide physical security, welfare and effective socio-economic management? Is it the appropriate problem-solving unit to deal with issues of environment, economic prosperity, finance, migration and terrorism? Do experts' functional networks transcend the territorial limits to states' jurisdictions? Does the era of European integration and globalisation herald the end of citizens' attachment to national territories and do mobile citizens look for better performance from non-state providers of security, material benefits and services regardless of conventional state borders and boundaries? One of the fundamental characteristics of the image of the Westphalian state is the territorial demarcation of its supreme authority, as the famous nineteenth century German sociologist, Max Weber, emphasised in his ideal-type definition: '[der] Staat ist diejenige mensliche Gemeinschaft, welche innerhalb einest bestimmtes Gebietes – dies: das "Gebiet", gehort zum Merkmal – das Monopol legitimer physischer Gewaltsamkeit fur sich (mit Erfolg) beansprucht' (Weber, 1956: 27). But has this enduring image of the state now become an image of the past? Does Weber's ideal-type definition of the state any longer correspond with contemporary reality?

These questions that refer to the viability of the territorial state have repeatedly been raised and discussed in political science. For example, John Herz (1957) initially claimed that *inter alia* nuclear weaponry would make territory irrelevant for the military security of states' populations. And according to Jean Gottmann (1973), espionage from air and space would simply render borders irrelevant as defensive mechanisms, just as in the ancient past mediaeval castles were undermined by guns and cannons. The example of environmental issues has also been used with consistent regularity to demonstrate that a 'world without borders' is increasingly necessary if we are to have an effective response (Brown, 1972). In short, an increasingly interdependent world tends to bypass territorially sovereign borders in economic, social and political perceptions and behaviour (Keohane and Nye, 1977). Indeed, even as stern a realist as Kenneth Waltz has acknowledged that the global scale of environmental problems and overpopulation might change the world's political configuration of territorial states (Waltz, 1979: 39). Sub-state regionalism and incremental European integration affecting different policy issues have been widely construed as erasing the territorial demarcation of state authority by merging state governments into multi-level systems of functional overlapping and non-hierarchical jurisdictions, while global networks of economic-financial metropolitan nodes were destined to replace a world carved up into territorially sovereign states (O'Brien, 1991). Some observers have viewed social constructions and perceptions underlying states' configurations as the result of time–space conceptions due to the image of the global village (Harvey, 1989).

Predictions of an end to the territorial state, however, have generated opposing views. Herz (1968) himself acknowledged that the nuclear threat did not crush the territorial urge of nationalism. Apparently, instrumental 'technical range' in military and political devices did not automatically alter the 'human reach' in politics (Jönsson *et al.*, 2000: 168). Intergovernmentalists have claimed that the European integration project is firmly in the hands of the territorially organised Member States, especially in issues of high politics. In work on processes of globalisation, it is acknowledged that territorial states still play a crucial role (Hirst and Thompson, 1995). Penal law on breaching intellectual property rights, for example, is still derived from territorial states. In the 1990s territorial sovereignty has never been more popular as witnessed in the birth of so many new territorial states following the break-up respectively of Yugoslavia, Czechoslovakia and the Soviet Union and the subsequent claims to territorial sovereignty. And the widespread demise of European states as a result of the new sub-state regionalism is also far from becoming a reality (Keating, 1998). Nonetheless, this is not to claim that a certain sense of unease and uncertainty is completely absent in the specific context of European integration. Questions concerning the current and future role of the territorial state in the European Union (EU), together with a conspicuous discourse about what concepts and explanations should be utilised to describe contemporary developments, are self-evidently relevant to the emerging public debate.

It is also interesting to note that so much of this emerging public debate about the purported demise of the territorial state has been expressed in the use and abuse of basic concepts by the prefix 'post'. Consider, for example, the following terms: post-modern; post-Westphalian; post-territorial; and post-sovereign. Such 'post' messages concerning the eclipse of states by processes of globalisation, 'glocalisation', 'fragmentation', and regionalisation have their origins in the fields of international relations, European integration, EU studies and regionalism. Unfortunately they do not directly address in what particular respects contemporary politics has changed nor do they indicate precisely in what direction such 'post-states' are heading. They merely cling to the assertion that we are witnessing the end of the Westphalian epoch of territorially sovereign states. Moreover, states existing from before this so-called 'post-period' have often been misrepresented as if they were fully sovereign, independent, uniform, territorially fixed, clearly demarcated and mutually exclusive when in fact they were nothing of the sort. The Peace Treaties of Westphalia (1648) have often been taken as the decisive turning point in this world carved up into territorial units striving for security, sovereignty and common well being for their inhabitants. The weakness of proclaiming the end or the beginning of an era is that it deflects the eye from what are often subtle, incremental shifts in the nature of politics and polities before, during and after such a putative era (Evans, 1997). Claims about political change and the dawn of a new age can be substantiated only by empirical comparisons across time and place rather than by attempting to compare present-day politics with an image of *the* Westphalian state that never actually existed in reality. And researching incremental shifts also requires an analysis of states as 'composites of institutional variables', focusing upon how these variables are interrelated and how they themselves change across place and over time (Kahler, 2002).

Empirical and historical reflection on the subject of states and their 'territoriality' also alerts us to the need for modesty when making claims for qualitative transformations of political status. After all, we have witnessed large numbers of migrants and open borders before in the nineteenth century, while the subsequent twentieth century certainly did not herald the demise of territorial states. Even if globalisation and European integration might conceivably have reduced the importance of proximity as never before, this in itself does not mean that territory has lost its significance in politics (Ansell, 2004: 4). A similar argument follows for the alleged detrimental effects on nation states caused by a resurgent regionalism: 'The relevance of territory and territoriality in Europe has not necessarily anything to do with a regionalised Europe and new forms of territorial politics do not need to be regionalised politics' (Bartolini, 2000: 22). In other words, anticipated changes to the territorial underpinnings of the nation state should not be taken as assumptions but rather hypothesised, empirically verified and then explained.

Furthermore, the reliance upon historical-empirical analysis enables us resolutely to resist the temptation automatically to introduce new concepts, theories and explanations deemed applicable to these allegedly new political configurations because they are simply not necessary. On the contrary, analyses of past polity formations and different levels of government demonstrate the continuing utility of existing concepts and analytical tools. The introduction of neologisms often obscures rather than clarifies the subject matter. Consequently, even if the EU and its member states do furnish an example of a polity that is historically unprecedented, this does not mean that existing theories developed to explain polities from an earlier age cannot be utilised to help explain and offer insights into contemporary reality (cf. Hix, 1999).

Empirical analysis and historical reflection should not of course be restricted to the enquiry into territoriality and the state alone. Linking insights from different intellectual disciplines in studying states and territoriality also has great merit. For far too long the territorial basis to states was simply taken for granted and served as a division of labour that separated studies of politics *between* territorial states (geopolitics) and politics *within* territorial states (Agnew, 1998). Very few scholars paid close attention to the territorial foundations of states and the varieties of territorial organisation among polities (see, for example, Gottmann, 1973; Sack, 1986; Kratochwil, 1986). Although functional theories of European integration and interdependency theories initially challenged the significance of the territorially demarcated authority of states, the territorial 'gatekeepership' of states between domestic and international politics was soon re-adopted in these theories. Accordingly, a potential qualitative change in the way that political authority is related to territory, functions and the personal characteristics of individuals and groups was left unquestioned and the territorial divide in the theories remained intact. Thorough analyses of differentiation among territorially and functionally organised polities and their mutual relations have been mainly limited to the fields of local administration and intra-federal politics without much theoretical reference to territorial states, globalisation and European integration.

It is important to note that an article written by John Ruggie (1993) on the political configuration of the EU in the mainstream literature on international relations registered a significant intellectual impact by calling attention to potentially qualitative shifts in the territorial organisation of states and supranational organisations. Soon after its publication, contributions from a diverse range of political scientists began to focus upon concepts and processes of re-territorialisation (Forsberg, 1996). An avalanche of newly invented concepts varying in clarity and utility to describe the authority amalgam of the EU followed (see, for example, Caporaso, 1996; Schmitter, 1996). Scholars like Gary Marks, Liesbeth Hooghe and Stefano Bartolini have started to develop explanatory contributions on shifts in territorial patterns in politics, synthesising work in the fields of International Relations, Public Administration, History, Regionalism, Federalism, Comparative Politics and Political Geography. They therefore aim explicitly to link 'islands of theorising' to challenge the issue of territoriality and the state. Taking stock of the state of the discipline of political science, Miles Kahler consequently claimed that 'modelling the institutions of territoriality, which are central in defining state and unit variation, should become a central part of the institutional research agenda on the state' (Kahler, 2002: 79). This volume of essays situates itself firmly in this category, accepting the research agenda and collating diverse perspectives on the incremental shifts in the political territoriality of states, regions and the EU.

The political significance of territoriality

Most accounts of the historical and contemporary significance of territory in West European politics still suffer from a combination of ambiguity and a narrow focus. One basic task of the book is therefore to develop a set of indicators designed to assess the political significance of territory in all of its multi-faceted dimensions. Theoretical explorations of the way that territory first acquired significance in organising and ordering politics, policies and polities are still in their infancy (Ruggie, 1993: 174; Christiansen, 1999: 356; Newman, 2001). In particular, linkages to historical processes of re-territorialisation have been few and far between (Jönnson *et al.*, 2000), while explanations of the mechanisms of territorialisation in history would be helpful for us to understand in what sense territory matters more, less or differently in different contexts in the Euro-polity, its member states and the regions. As we have already stated above, historical analyses furnish an empirical basis for comparison, serving both to moderate the somewhat stereotypical image of *the* Westphalian state and to warn us against making premature and possibly false claims for another critical juncture in political history. We are constantly reminded that the principle of territoriality has been hotly contested ever since it first featured in West European politics (cf. Krasner, 1999).

Another goal of this volume of essays is to provide an historically based set of explanatory notions about the factors and circumstances that make territory matter more, less or differently in organising politics, policies and polities. It therefore focuses on the effect that territorial, personal and functional logics of political organisation might have upon political relations. Since indicators and explanations about territory's political significance are analysed from a diverse range of political science and historical perspectives, it is imperative that we arrive at a preliminary agreement concerning the meaning of the basic concepts that will be used, namely, territoriality, functionalism, extra-territoriality, de-territorialisation and re-territorialisation. The book therefore seeks first to define and refine these concepts in order to provide an analytical vocabulary of political territoriality.

In summary, we intend to arrange historically and empirically grounded concepts, indicators and theoretical notions to denote how and by what measures the political significance of territory changes, as well as what impact such changes might have. The case studies presented are all from polities in Western Europe, the heartland of Westphalia, and from the most developed model of re-territorialisation, namely, the EU, although we should not forget that the concepts, indicators and notions derived from these cases are also, in principle, applicable to the historical processes of globalisation.

Concepts, indicators and theoretical notions

Territoriality is often associated with animal instincts in the territorial demarcation of living space (Ardrey, 1966). In recent years, territoriality has increasingly been perceived as a psycho-social construct that is neither a biological necessity nor an inevitable consequence of anarchy (O'Tuathail *et al.*, 1998). Political territoriality is consequently about 'modes and practices of territorial control for political purposes' such as demarcating polities and dividing political authority (Forsberg, 1996: 362–363). Political territoriality is a much more fluid and dynamic concept or intellectual construct than biological territoriality. This is because it not only refers to fixed, uniform and disjointed territorially demarcated state-like polities, but it also embraces polities deemed to be overlapping, nomadic and parcelled (Kratochwil, 1986; Ruggie, 1993). Clearly the relations between politics, space and place vary and the challenge is to map out precisely how they vary. In this book, then, we must try to meet this challenge and to indicate how territoriality, 'a spatial strategy to affect, influence, or control resources and people, by controlling area' (Sack, 1986: 19), matters in political relations.

An initial point of departure might be to think of the distribution and circumscription of basic competences to indicate political territoriality. The scope of political territoriality may be arranged according to territory, functional occupation or personal characteristics such as language and religion. Jurisdictions might overlap or they may be mutually exclusive depending upon whether supreme authority is rooted in territory (like territorial sovereignty), universalist claims (like empire) or on shared and divided rule (as in federations). A second indicator of political territoriality is the way in which rulers provide their services and allocate values and benefits. Patterns of decentralisation, deconcentration, the planning of public services in centres and socio-economic peripheries all denote the different ways that territoriality still matters in the day-to-day affairs of government.

The loyalties and identities of people who are ruled is a third indicator. The extent to which people feel emotionally attached to a particular territory (regional, national or Europe-wide), or define themselves according to functional occupation or personal characteristics (language, religion, skin colour) regardless of place of residence denote the significance or otherwise of territory related to key issues of legitimacy. Hierarchies among – and the exclusiveness of – identities and loyalties reveal both the strengths and weaknesses of political territoriality in this regard. Moreover, the way that people articulate their interests and demands, support and protest, and generally express their feelings of both political satisfaction and discontent, can be construed as an indicator of political territoriality. The composition, policy aims and operation of interest groups, political parties and social movements is another indicator of the extent to which territory still features prominently in contemporary political systems. It is important to note, however, that patterns in the geographical distribution of certain political groupings and actors should not be viewed as political territoriality *per se*. Only if the geographical distribution gives rise to the issue of organising politics according to a specific delineated geographical area would we properly engage the concept of political territoriality. A fifth and final indicator is the range of action that affects the ruled. Here we are referring to the extent that (territorial) competences and governing patterns feature in the daily practices and movements of people. Van Houtum (1998), for example, has shown that entrepreneurs in Dutch–German and Dutch–Belgian *Euregios* still behaved as if the national borders existed even though they had already been removed, a perception that is reminiscent of the German *Mauer im Kopf* (wall in the head) that persisted despite the collapse of the Berlin Wall in 1989.

The five indicators identified above demonstrate how territory still matters in political relations and why it does not make much sense to speak about de-territorialisation (territory matters less) or territorialisation (territory matters more) in a general, imprecise way. The intricate and complex reconfigurations and reconceptualisations of political relations within states, regions and the evolving Euro-polity merely allow us to utilise the concept of re-territorialisation (territory matters differently). The important point here is to emphasise that territory *always* matters somehow in some way for social and political relations. This means that the key question to ask is how far its significance is changing or has already changed. With regard to the indicator of competences mentioned above, the processes of territorialisation and de-territorialisation have often been conceptualised in terms of 'bundling' and 'unbundling' territoriality (Ruggie, 1993). These terms refer, respectively, to the concentration and centralisation of competences within a single territorial jurisdiction and the break up of a territorially organised polity into separate (functional) units. In fully bundled territorial polities, authority is based upon the principle of territoriality, that is, its politico-legal scope of rule and supreme authority is demarcated by territory. This principle underscores the ideal-type image of what constitutes a state as defined by Max Weber and others. Accordingly, extraterritoriality simply means that certain exceptions and anomalies can exist in the principle of territoriality, such as the role of embassies and the Mare Liberum (Ruggie, 1993). The process of unbundling territoriality on one level might imply that a simultaneous process will occur at another level, as for example in the case of the continuous ceding of competences from the national to the EU level. However, the unbundling of territoriality may also entail non-territorial forms of organisation.

In addition to territory, politics can also be organised according to both function (such as occupation or policy space) and personal characteristics (Forsberg, 1996: 363–364). Personal logic of organisation respects both individuals, such as human rights to be exercised regardless of where someone is or what they are doing (Watson, 1980; Benhabib, 2002) and groups, such as those in Belgium, where a system of 'personal federalism' divides the country according to language (see Chapter 6). The intriguing question is precisely how far these territorial, functional and personal logics of politics differ from each other and also how they are interrelated. Gary Marks and Liesbeth Hooghe (2003) suggest that functional 'task-specific' 'one-purpose jurisdictions' tend to expand towards often territorially organised 'all-purpose associations' for reasons of coordination, accountability and risk-sharing, while the latter have a tendency towards one-purpose jurisdictions for reasons of efficiency (see also Frey and Eichenberger, 1999). These tendencies may feature in the development of corporatist states – one of the well-known examples of functional organisation – inside the territorial boundaries of the EU's Single European Market (SEM) (see Hemerijck: Chapter 9). Differences in organisational logics entail differences in the way that politics operates in polities. This volume of essays will seek to spell out how far empires, networks, unitary states, federations, neo-mediaeval and multi-level polities differ from each other in how territory matters and how the various organisational logics leave their mark upon each respective polity.

The sense in which political territoriality changes is a question that logically follows from that of the various organisational logics that we have just mentioned. Robert Sack (1986) has already furnished us with an extensive description of how territorial strategies facilitate classification, communication, authority enforcement, planning, impersonalisation of authority and reification of power. An all-purpose association therefore often adopts a territorial shape in order to provide an effective and efficient risk-sharing coordination and accountability structure. Consequently, the strategic behaviour of political actors can be analysed from this standpoint. Differences in patterns of conflict and political alliances arise according to how territory and organisational logics matter in polities. For example, interest groups and sub-state regions represent and organise their interests differently in territorially closed states from those in the multi-level EU (cf. Marks *et al.*,1996; Schmitter, 1996). Depending upon what is required in political relations therefore political actors seek either territorialisation or de-territorialisation. Thus Claus Offe (1998) and Jan Zielonka (2001: 527) claim that solidarity, democracy and accountability can be firmly established only in territorially closed systems.

In summary, the way that political actors operate and how their activities are shaped and moulded within territorial, personal or functional polities depends upon their psycho-social 'epistemes' and 'material environment' (Ruggie, 1993). We have to take into account many factors that help to determine both behaviour and outcomes. For example, technological opportunities to communicate, trade or fight, images of how the world is constructed, how property rights are defined and how feelings of (territorial) attachments are expressed can both facilitate and constrain such actors in forging alliances, integrating polities, creating new levels of governance, opening up borders, unbundling territory and generally behaving in ways that determine specific policy outcomes.

The structure of the volume: an historical, analytical, conceptual and empirical focus

The issue of political territoriality in an integrating Europe can be conveniently restated in the double-barrelled question whether and how territory – a delineated geographical area – matters in politics. Section I in this volume comprises two chapters tracing territorialising mechanisms in the formation of national states in Western Europe. Historical examples of military and social–economic mechanisms may offer explanations for the present-day formation of the Euro-polity, and the re-territorialisation of other polities within the EU area. In addition, historical reflection on states' early days also impels us to question and rethink conventional claims about the dominance of the territorial logic in politics from the Peace Treaties of Westphalia (1648) onwards. Since 'Westphalia' is usually still construed as the watershed in Europe's history of political territoriality between mediaeval and modern political formations, the validity of this periodisation of changing political territoriality should be re-evaluated.

The case of the Dutch Republic is explored by Olaf van Nimwegen in order to examine precisely how military security, territoriality and polity formation are interrelated. Officially accepted by the Treaties of Westphalia as a (great) power, and located at the nexus of German, French and English military powers, the Dutch Republic is an excellent case to explore how security issues could bring about a particular political territoriality. After presenting the case of the Dutch Republic, the effect on the Dutch Republic's territoriality of the political organisation and geographical location of the Low Countries, and the military pressures exerted from other military powers are evaluated. The Dutch Republic featured extensive buffer zones and weak centrality, contradicting the Westphalian image of hierarchical rule and clearly demarcated territories. Benno Teschke subsequently sets out the long-term historical alterations in the configurations between territoriality and political power in Europe from the Middle Ages to the present period. His argument is that the social dynamics that derive from historically contested social property relations provide the best guide for a social geography of political space. He rejects the prevalent premise in the globalisation and European integration discourses that equate 'Westphalian' with 'modern' sovereignty because he challenges the idea that the modern state was historically speaking in full control of its territory. Against this, Teschke's chapter provides a revisionist interpretation of absolutist territoriality and argues that the relationship between capitalist states and territoriality is structurally indeterminate, depending essentially on the strategies of territorialisation adopted and enforced by politically dominant classes in the EU and beyond.

Section II discusses different ways to analyse territoriality and organisational logics in multi-level polities. Theo Toonen and Frits van der Meer spell out different levels of analysis to explore changing political territoriality. They argue that the customary use of territoriality is seriously flawed due to the use of the historical construct of the Westphalian nation state in political science. Most European states can traditionally be typified as multi-level governance systems in which changes regarding their multi- and single-purpose nature as well as changes in the geographical scale of politics and service delivery have been the order of the day. They present examples to explain and understand the significance of territoriality in multi-level governance systems by paying attention to the worlds of the intergovernmental constitution (IGC), intergovernmental relations (IGR) and intergovernmental management (IGM).

Michael Burgess reflects on the conceptualisation of political territoriality and relates it to the conceptual bases of federalism and federation before applying these thoughts to European integration and globalisation. He also sets the notion of state territoriality in the specific context of the writing of the Constitutional Treaty for the EU, before concluding that its federal destiny as a union of states and peoples leaves open the question just what *kind* of federal entity it will become. In the intriguing case of the Brussels region, Wilfried Swenden and Marleen Brans explain and describe how principles of territoriality and personality interrelate in the complicated political strategies of minority representation in a multi-level polity. Their contribution explains, first, the position of Brussels within the multi-layered structure of the Belgian state and, second, assesses the recent revisions to the Brussels regional structure that is designed to accommodate both the concerns of the Dutch-speaking minority and non-Belgian residents that live together in the Capital Region. Their chapter also looks at the implications of the Brussels case study for the overall maintenance and stability of the Belgian federation. The Belgian example also serves to demonstrate that a growing European identity can exist alongside – but certainly cannot substitute for – ethno-linguistic nationalism as an important identity-marker.

Section III contains an empirical assessment of precisely how processes of European integration have changed political territoriality in the EU area. It therefore touches upon the neo-functionalist challenge of open borders to the territorial underpinnings of the EU member states, as well as the (perceived) indispensability of territorially closed systems to organise solidarity, security and general welfare. Gertjan Dijkink and Virginie Mamadouh investigate how the EU affects the everyday lives of its citizens. Since political territoriality has been deeply entrenched in the perceptions and loyalties of individuals, current processes of de-territorialisation and re-territorialisation such as European integration and globalisation should also be examined at the level of the citizens. Eurobarometer data are used to analyse how Europeans perceive and identify with these new territorial institutions, through interaction, attachment and information. They also evaluate whether this affects their relation to nation state territories through changing patterns of interaction, attachment and information.

Taxation has been considered as one of the fundamental reasons why polities organised themselves territorially in the shape of states (cf. Tilly, 1975). From a legal perspective, Herman Voogsgeerd considers whether and why the principle of territoriality still dominates in the policy areas of taxation within the EU area. Although EU member states still retain their powers concerning taxation, they have to implement these powers within the framework of the evolving Common Market. In its decisions the European Court of Justice (ECJ) increasingly intervenes in the area of taxation. An interesting element here is that the Court explicitly mentions the fiscal principle of territoriality in its decisions. Evidently the principle is still important since it helps to prevent chaos in levying taxes, but there is no doubt that a conspicuous ambiguity now exists as a result of legal decisions that have some fascinating implications for notions of both territoriality and non-territoriality.

After the Second World War, the European welfare regimes were built within the territorial confines of national states. The creation of an internal market in the territorial area of the EU therefore poses a serious challenge to solidarity within these territorially closed welfare regimes. A combination of both territorial and non-territorial dimensions in the evolving EU social policy profile suggests a potentially significant impact on both the sustainability of these regimes and on the legitimacy that states derive from them. Anton Hemerijck provides a detailed survey that discusses exactly how functional and territorial underpinnings of welfare regimes in the EU are changing due to European integration. The overall implication is that territoriality retains its significance for European social policy but this wide-ranging policy agenda has become much more deeply embedded in an expanding EU economic and social policy space.

Security issues are also perceived as closely linked to the birth and endurance of territorial states (cf. Tilly, 1975). Looking at these issues, respectively, from an internal 'police' perspective, as well as an external 'military' perspective, Jörg Friedrichs sketches out three case studies that underline the extent to which the EU is already moving in the direction of a 'neo-medieval' polity. There is certainly evidence in these empirical cases of a distinct trend towards the trans-territorial management of force, but it is doubtful whether and to what extent this trend will ultimately endure. Friedrichs concludes that this movement has to be construed in the context of the resilience of the territorial state so that the contemporary hallmark of the territorial monopoly of force in the EU is in reality one of overlapping jurisdictions. What we can conceivably expect in the future is a slow stop–go process towards the unbundling of territorial sovereignty.

Peter Van Ham addresses the post-Cold War role of the EU in terms of security and defence policies and postures. He looks at the role war plays in the political, social and psychological process of 'iconising' the space that feels and positions itself as 'Europe'. Given the general acceptance of the ideational and contextual aspects of territory, his key question is less *whether* territory is constructed, but *how*. What part do territory, distance and space take in the shaping of Europe's cognitive framework? Van Ham argues that the EU can emulate the lessons of state-formation by dealing with security and defence matters, even going as far as fighting wars. He analyses the development of the EU's strategic culture and its policies on 'failed states' and 'Weapons of Mass Destruction' proliferation as examples and concludes that there may be nothing like a 'good' European war to generate a European identity.

The concluding chapter draws together the main conceptual and empirical threads that serve to hold the book together. It sums up the historical lessons, analytical reflections and empirical insights that can be drawn from the variety of contributions emphasising the key indicators and theoretical notions used to scrutinise the political territoriality of states and other polities in an era of European integration and globalisation.

References

Agnew, J. (1998), *Geopolitics: Revisioning World Politics*. London: Routledge.
Ansell, C. (2004), 'Territoriality, Authority, and Democracy', in C. Ansell and G. di Palma (eds), *Restructuring Territoriality: Europe and the United States Compared*. Cambridge: Cambridge University Press, 225–245.
Ardrey, R. (1966), *The Territorial Imperative: A Personal Inquiry into the Animal Origins of Property and Nations*. New York: Atheneum.
Bartolini, S. (2000), 'Old and New Peripheries in the Processes of European Territorial Retrenchment versus Expansion/Integration'. Unpublished paper.
Benhabib, S. (2002), 'Political Theory and Political Membership in a Changing World', in I. Katznelson and H.V. Milner (eds), *Political Science: State of the Discipline*. 404–432.
Brown, L. (1972), *World Without Borders*. New York: Random House.
Caporaso, J. (1996), 'The European Union and Forms of State: Westphalian, Regulatory or Post-Modern?' *Journal of Common Market Studies*. 34(1).
Christiansen, T. (1999), 'Territorial Politics in the European Union', *Journal of European Public Policy* 6(2): 349–357.
Evans, P. (1997), 'The Eclipse of the State: Reflections on the Stateness in an Era of Globalisation'. Unpublished paper.
Forsberg, T. (1996), 'Beyond Sovereignty, Within Territoriality: Mapping the Space of Late-Modern (Geo)Politics', *Cooperation and Conflict* 31(4): 355–386.
Frey, B. and Eichenberger, R. (1999), *The New Democratic Federalism: Functional, Overlapping and Competing Jurisdictions*. Cheltenham: Elgar.

Gottmann, J. (1973), *The Significance of Territory*. Charlottesville, VA: University Press of Virginia.
Harvey, D. (1989), *The Condition of Postmodernity: An Enquiry into the Origins of Cultural Change*. Oxford: Blackwell.
Herz, J. (1957), 'Rise and Demise of the Territorial State', *World Politics* 9(4): 473–493.
—— (1968), 'The Territorial State Revisited: Reflections on the Future of the Nation-State', *Polity* 1(1) 11–34.
Hirst, P.Q. and Thompson, G. (1995), *Globalization in Question: The International Economy and the Possibilities of Governance*. Cambridge: Polity Press.
Hix, S. (1999), *The Political System of the European Union*. Basingstoke: MacMillan.
Jönsson, C., Tägil, S. and Törnqvist, G. (2000), *Organizing European Space*. London: Sage.
Kahler, M. (2002), 'The State of the State in World Politics', in I. Katznelson and H.V. Milner (eds), *Political Science: State of the Discipline*. New York: Norton/Washington, DC: APSA, p. 79.
Keating, M. (1998), *The New Regionalism in Western Europe: Territorial Restructuring and Political Change*. Cheltenham: Edward Elgar.
Keohane, R.O. and Nye, J.S. (1977), *Power and Interdependence: World Politics in Transition*. Boston, MA: Little Brown.
Krasner, S. (1999), *Sovereignty: Organized Hypocrisy*. Princeton, NJ: Princeton University Press.
Kratochwil, F. (1986), 'Of Systems, Boundaries, and Territoriality: An Inquiry into the Formation of the State System', *World Politics* 34: 27–52.
Marks, G. and Hooghe, L. (2003), 'Unraveling the Central State, but How? Types of Multi-level Governance', *American Political Science Review* 97(2): 233–243.
Marks, G., Hooghe, L. and Blank, K. (1996), 'European Integration from the 1980s: State-Centric v. Multi-level Governance', *Journal of Common Market Studies* 34(3): 341–378.
Newman, D. (2001), 'Boundaries, Borders and Barriers: Changing Geographic Perspectives on Territorial Lines', in M. Albert, D. Jacobson and Y. Lapid (eds), *Identities, Borders, Orders: Rethinking International Relations Theory*. Minneapolis, MN: University of Minnesota, pp. 137–151.
O'Brien, R. (1991), *Global Financial Integration: The End of Geography*. London: Pinter Publishers.
Offe, C. (1998), 'Demokratie und Wohlfahrtsstaat: Eine Europäische Regimeform unter dem Streß der Europäischen Integration', in W. Streeck (ed.), *Internationale Wirtschaft, Nationale Demokratie: Herausforderungen für die Demokratietheorie*. Frankfurt: Campus Verlag, pp. 99–136.
O'Tuathail, G.O. and Dalby, S. (eds) (1998), *Rethinking Geopolitics*. London: Routledge.
Ruggie, J.G. (1993), 'Territoriality and Beyond', *International Organization* 47(1): 139–174.
Sack, R.D. (1986), *Human Territoriality: Its Theory and History*. Cambridge: Cambridge University Press.
Schmitter, P.C. (1996), 'Imagining the Future of the Euro-polity with the Help of New Concepts', in G. Marks, F.W. Scharpf, P.C. Schmitter and W. Streeck (eds), *Governance in the European Union*. London: Sage Publishers, pp. 121–150.
Tilly, Ch. (ed.) (1975), *The Formation of National States in Western Europe*. Princeton, NJ: Princeton University Press.

Van Houtum, H. (1998), *The Development of Cross-Border Economic Relations*. Dissertation KUB Tilburg.
Waltz, K.N. (1979), *Theory of International Politics*. Reading, MA: Addison-Wesley Publishing Company.
Watson, Ph. (1980), *Social Security Law of the European Communities*. London: Mansell Publishing.
Weber, M. (1956), *Staatssoziologie*. Berlin: Duncker and Humblot.
Zielonka, J. (2001), 'How New Enlarged Borders will Reshape the European Union', *Journal of Common Market Studies* 39(3): 507–536.

Part I
Territoriality in history

2 The quest for security
The case of the Dutch Republic

Olaf van Nimwegen

This chapter focuses on the different ways in which the Dutch Republic tried to cope with territorial defence from 1590 until 1750, the period in which it played a major and from 1672 onwards a pivotal part in European power politics. Its strategic location made the Low Countries – the modern Netherlands, Belgium and Luxemburg – the cockpit of North-Western Europe. The epic conflicts with Spain (1568–1648) and then with France (1672–1748) forced the Dutch to find different ways to preserve their independence. First, from the 1590s until 1648, they sought security through expanding their territorial base. Second, in the 1660s–1690s, through maintaining the Spanish Netherlands as a buffer zone against Louis XIV of France. Third, starting around 1700, the Dutch maintained a system of barrier towns with Dutch garrisons along the border with France. This was the Dutch Barrier which became the cornerstone of a defensive alliance between the Austrian Habsburgs, the Dutch Republic and Great Britain. The 'Old System' as this balance-of-power system was called, lasted from 1715 to 1755.

The staying power of the early modern state depended on three closely related factors: money, fortresses and army size. Tax revenues and credit on the money market were indispensable fund raising instruments for hiring soldiers, undertaking of sieges, and recovering from losses in men and material. Credit was so essential because developments in fortress design around 1500 had turned warfare into wars of attrition. The 'trace italienne' with its thick walls and protruding artillery platforms, the 'bastions', and deep ditches could only be taken after a long and bloody siege. Especially in Northern Italy and the Low Countries the new fortress design proliferated. Early modern warfare was as a consequence of this dominated by siege-operations. The fortresses were often situated on or near rivers blocking possible invasion routes, its garrisons controlled the surrounding countryside, and they could also be used as secure foundations for offensives. Developments in French army organization and logistics around 1670 seemed to tip the balance between offensive and defensive again in favour of the former. Whereas the military establishments of states rarely exceeded 80,000 troops before 1650,[1] Louis XIV (1638–1715), King of France effectively from 1661 to 1715, had at his disposal an army of no less than 250,000 to 340,000 effectives (i.e. troops present for service; the paper establishments were even higher).[2] The French military build-up subsequently forced neighbouring countries to augment their armed forces. As a result the opposing sides in the War of the Spanish Succession (1701–1713) – France and Spain on the one hand and an alliance of Austria, the Dutch Republic, Great Britain and a host of smaller powers, mostly German, on the other – each paid for about half a million men.

Even more spectacular than the growth of army establishments, was the rapid increase in the size of field armies. Until 1648 troop concentrations of more than 30,000 men had been very rare. The armies which were pitted against each other in the Netherlands theatre in the 1670s numbered 50,000 to 60,000 men and more than 100,000 men in the 1690s. During the War of the Spanish Succession field armies of more than 120,000 men became a common occurrence. A quarter of a century later, during the War of the Austrian Succession (1740–1748), field armies were a little smaller, but still numbered 70,000 to 80,000 men or even 100,000 men.[3] Battles and sieges were bloodier than ever before.

Wars of attrition were especially dangerous for smaller states, such as the Dutch Republic, because in contrast to France, Austria or Spain they could not risk defeat in battle as this would jeopardize the entire country. In 1625, during the Spanish siege of Breda, a Dutch official remarked that all great generals were reluctant to fight battles because the outcome was often unpredictable. This consideration was of especially great importance for the Dutch Republic, which was 'very small in comparison to the greatness and power of her enemy.'[4] A century later the Dutch political and military leaders were still confronted with the same problem. The territorial base of the Dutch Republic was simply too small 'to wage a defensive war within her own borders'.[5] The risk that the Dutch Republic would be overrun, however, was much greater around 1700 than at the beginning of the seventeenth century because of the already mentioned enormous increase in army size.

The Dutch at war with Spain (1590–1648)

During the 1590s the Dutch rebels expanded their territorial base extensively. Under the command of Maurice of Nassau (1567–1625) and his cousin William Louis of Nassau (1560–1620) Groningen and the greater part of Gelderland and Overijssel, were added to Holland, Zeeland, Utrecht and Friesland. By 1597 the *tuin* (garden) of the Republic had been closed: the rebellious northern provinces of the Netherlands formed a defensible block of territory, extending the frontier further southward, however, turned out to be very difficult. The famous battle in the dunes of Nieuwpoort (2 July 1600), although a Dutch tactical victory, was a strategic draw. It forced Maurice to forgo the planned siege of Dunkirk. In 1602 the Dutch army was expanded so that a force of about 20,000 men could take the field, but this military might was still not sufficient for invading the Spanish Netherlands. Also, the simultaneous Dutch effort to hold Ostend against Spanish attack – the siege lasted from July 1601 until September 1604 – put an enormous strain on Dutch finances.[6] Following the fall of Ostend, the Spaniards concentrated their war effort on the Dutch Republic's eastern front. The Spanish offensives of 1605 and 1606 revealed to the Dutch leaders, and in particular Johan van Oldenbarnevelt (1547–1619), *landsadvocaat* ('secretary' and 'chairman') of the States of Holland from 1586 to 1618, and as such the informal leader of Dutch foreign policy, their state's vulnerability. As long as the rebels had been locked in their aquatic fortress of Holland and Zeeland, the Spaniards could not make much headway against them. But after 1597 the rebels were faced with the daunting problem of defending a greatly extended frontier under circumstances which favoured a Spanish counter-offensive. The Dutch were forced to disperse their troops in numerous garrisons, leaving Maurice with too few troops to take the field with a powerful army. In 1605 and 1606 the Spanish commander-in-chief Ambrogio Spinola (1569–1630) took four Dutch strongholds on the Rhine and in Gelderland and Overijssel: Oldenzaal, Lingen, Groenlo and Rijnberk.

Spinola's successes did not pose a mortal threat to the Dutch, but it made Van Oldenbarnevelt realise it would take many more years to defeat the Spaniards militarily. This strategy of attrition[7] was beyond the Republic's capabilities. Luckily for the Dutch Spanish financial exhaustion made Madrid willing to work out a tempory suspension of hostilities. In April 1609 the Dutch and Spaniards concluded a cease-fire that lasted 12 years, the Twelve Years' Truce. Van Oldenbarnevelt was its major Dutch architect. Maurice of Nassau totally disapproved of the armistice, but he agreed with Van Oldenbarnevelt about the vulnerability of the eastern frontier. However, in contrast to the *landsadvocaat* he wanted to remedy the situation not with diplomatic but with military means. The Jülich-Cleves Succession War (1609–1614) which began that same year gave him the opportunity to repair the weak points in the east.[8] In 1610 Maurice captured Jülich (Gulik). The supply lines to the Spanish garrisons in Oldenzaal, Lingen, Groenlo and Rijnberk were seriously hampered as a result. When war between Spain and the Dutch Republic was resumed in 1621, Spinola conquered Jülich (1622) and Breda (1625), but the Dutch under their new commander-in-chief Frederic Henry of Nassau (1584–1647), Prince of Orange, Captain and Admiral-General of the Union, took Oldenzaal (1626), Groenlo (1627), Bois-le-Duc (1629), Maastricht (1632) and Rijnberk (1633). In contrast to his late brother, who only waged defensive warfare during the campaigns of 1621–25, Frederic Henry concurred with the late Van Oldenbarnevelt: the Dutch Republic could not sustain a long-drawn conflict and an offensive war was necessary.[9] Consequently he considered a French offensive alliance imperative. Only if Spanish resources were drained by French operations on the border of the Spanish Netherlands, could the Dutch make new conquests. The inroads created would then serve as a springboard for a simultaneous Dutch–French invasion of the Spanish Netherlands. In the opinion of Frederic Henry the security of the Republic would be served by a combination of a major Dutch military effort and an offensive alliance with France. By the 1630s the Dutch army had been strengthened to more than 80,000 men on paper, about 60,000 actual fighting men.[10]

In the end, however, it was the French not the Dutch who gained the most from the alliance of 1635. Although Breda was retaken by Frederick Henry in 1637, the main prize, Antwerp, turned out a nut too hard to crack. The French in contrast captured a whole string of Spanish strongholds. The loss of Dunkirk (1646) to the French, whose infamous privateers had seriously harmed the Dutch fishing fleet for many years, caused a lot of alarm in the Republic. Especially because earlier in that same year the imminence of a marriage between Louis XIV and a Spanish princess had become public. Although this turned out to be false – the marriage was not concluded until 1659 – the rumour that her dowry consisted of the Spanish Netherlands, and possibly even the Northern Netherlands, led to an outburst of unrest. In the province of Holland suspicion about French–Spanish collusion grew, 'and one started to be more apprehensive of the vicinity of France, through the occupation of Flanders together with the other Spanish Netherlands, than to fear the [exhausted] Spaniard', wrote Alexander van der Capellen, an influential Dutch regent from Gelderland.[11] In violation of the alliance with France the leading Dutch politicians decided – without Frederic Henry who had died 14 March 1647 – to achieve a separate peace with Spain. As a consequence the Spanish King acknowledged the independence of the Northern Netherlands in the Treaty of Münster (1648), part of the Peace Treaties of Westphalia.

The Spanish Netherlands as the cornerstone of Dutch defence (1650–1668)

The year 1646 was a turning point in Dutch strategic thinking. Until this year the Dutch war effort was aimed at the annihilation of Spanish power in North-Western Europe in close cooperation with the French, which seemed to serve the Republic's best interest. The 1640s, however, gradually revealed the exhausted Spaniards no longer posed a real threat to Dutch independence. The bellicose French, on the other hand, seemed intent on continuing the war until they were more powerful than any of their neighbours. During the 1650s and 1660s Dutch–French relations remained cordial, but rather out of necessity than a mutual feeling of friendship and trust. This necessity arose due to a series of sea-wars with England in the second half of the seventeenth century. The First Anglo-Dutch War (1652–1654) was a victory for the English. The armed Dutch merchantmen were no match for the English battle fleet. Clearly the Dutch also needed to create a fleet of specialised warships. The enormous costs involved in this enterprise meant less available funds for the army. An alliance seemed the best way to provide the necessary security against an attack on the Dutch eastern frontier. In 1662 France and the Republic concluded a defensive alliance, notwithstanding the Dutch had in 1648 infringed on the 1635 treaty. During the war between the Republic and Münster (1665–1666) – which was waged simultaneously with the Second Anglo Dutch War (1665–1667) – Louis XIV sent a corps to help the Dutch counter the attack by the bishop of Münster, but the French arrived late and the cooperation of their general with the Dutch commander-in-chief left much to be desired.[12]

In 1667 the French–Dutch alliance was dealt a decisive blow by Louis XIV's decision to invade the Spanish Netherlands under pretext of a legal dispute with Madrid. The War of Devolution (1667–1668), as it was called, prompted the then leader of Dutch foreign policy, Johan de Witt (1625–1672), Grand Pensionary (*raadpensionaris*) of Holland since 1653, to make peace with England and to organize an offensive alliance against France. The Triple Alliance, concluded in January 1668 between the Dutch, the English and the Swedes, threatened Louis XIV with military intervention if he did not cease his invasion. De Witt believed that the Spanish Netherlands had to be protected against French aggression even if this meant war. In 1667 his advisor wrote: 'I believe that one can suppose, without mistake: 1. that the proximity of France is the greatest disaster that could befall this State, and 2. that this [disaster] is unavoidable if one does not oppose it immediately.' Surely, admitted the advisor, the carelessness of the Spaniards 'merite punition', but, he warned, the Dutch Republic would suffer even more, if the Spanish Netherlands fell into French hands.[13]

The first Peace of Aix-la-Chapelle (May 1668) saved the Spanish Netherlands from French occupation at a severe price to Spain: 12 fortresses in the Southern Netherlands were annexed to France. Johan de Witt had gained an important diplomatic victory. Although he was right that the Republic's security against France depended totally on the preservation of the Spanish Netherlands, he failed to see that a forward defence could not be based solely on diplomatic securities. It also required substantial military backing. More specifically, since the Spaniards could not protect the Spanish Netherlands alone, Dutch troops were permanently required in Spanish fortresses so that the first French onslaught could be delayed long enough in order for reinforcements to reach the theatre of war. Surely a new French attack on the Spanish Netherlands was simply a matter of time. The decision in August 1668 by the States of Holland to reduce the Dutch army from a wartime strength of 69,000 men to 33,000 men, 6,000 men less than the 'security of the State' in peacetime required, was therefore unsound.[14] With approximately one hundred Dutch fortresses and forts to be guarded,[15] only a very small number of troops were left for service in the Spanish Netherlands. Johan de Witt was very knowledgeable in matters of sea warfare, but not in land warfare. He was convinced that if the need to augment the army should arise again, the Republic would always have the time to hire fully equipped troops from neighbouring German princes. As Herbert H. Rowen in his very extensive biography of the Grand Pensionary points out, De Witt 'failed to see ... the importance of a specific army esprit developed over time; for him an army was a relative simple apparatus, something to be bought, used, and dismissed, as the occasion required'.[16]

Only two years after the conclusion of the Peace of Aix-la-Chapelle it dawned upon De Witt that the reduction of the Dutch army had been a mistake. French diplomatic activity and military preparations on an unprecedented scale made it obvious that Louis XIV was preparing to resume his offensive in the Netherlands. In response the Dutch army was increased to 64,000 men in 1671. The following year the decision was taken to hire 60,000 additional troops, but before these latest augmentations were completed the *Guerre de Hollande* or Dutch War (1672–1678) began.[17] On 12 June 1672 Louis XIV invaded the Dutch Republic with 80,000 to 100,000 men. William III (1650–1702), Frederic Henry's grandson who just a few months before had been appointed commander-in-chief of the Dutch army, retreated to the province of Holland. With at most 22,000 field troops at his disposal William III would have been very foolish to challenge the superior French forces in the open field. By inundating a tract of land spanning from the Zuyder Zee (i.e Ijsselmeer) to the Rhine, the French army's approach to Holland was closed off, and their invasion came to an abrupt halt. In July William III was elected stadtholder of Holland and Zeeland. He used his capacity as political and military leader of the Republic to reorganize and discipline the Dutch forces. Late in 1673 the Dutch in alliance with the Austrian and Spanish Habsburgs and many German princes, began a counter-offensive. This resulted in the evacuation of the occupied Dutch provinces by the French. From 1674 to 1678 the Dutch War was waged in the Spanish Netherlands and the Holy Roman Empire.[18] At the Peace of Nijmegen (August–September 1678) Louis XIV returned some of the fortresses captured by his troops in the Spanish Netherlands to Spain. This, however, was not really significant, because in return the French king acquired various important fortresses such as Ypres (Ieper), Menin (Menen), Condé, Valenciennes and Maubeuge. They enabled Sébastien le Prestre de Vauban (1633–1707), Louis's foremost military adviser and *Commissaire Général des Fortifications* to organize a fortified zone along France's northern frontier.[19]

The *frontière de fer* formed the most important part of the *pré carré* – or prepared duelling field – advocated by Vauban. He considered France to be a country under siege needing safeguard from attacks on all sides. As early as January 1673 he wrote to the Minister of War, François Michel Le Tellier Marquis of Louvois (1639–1691): 'Seriously, Sir, the King should think a bit about getting his *pré carré*. This confused mess of friendly and hostile fortresses [along the border of France and the Spanish Netherlands] do not please me at all. You are obliged to maintain three [garrisons] for one'.[20] By straightening out the frontier fewer fortresses would have to be guarded, resulting in more available troops for field service. In 1678 Vauban presented a memorandum further elaborating his idea for a *pré carré*. Along the border with the Spanish Netherlands he envisaged a double line of fortresses, arranged as an army ready for battle. Vauban, however, believed that the *frontière de fer* should not only serve defensive purposes, but offensive ones as well. In addition to closing all points of entry into the kingdom to France's enemies, it intended to facilitate a French attack on the Spanish Netherlands and consequently, also on the Dutch Republic.[21] The *frontière de fer* was actualised about ten years later.[22]

The Spanish Netherlands is transformed into the Dutch Barrier (1678–1715)

William III and the leading Dutch politicians concurred entirely with Johan de Witt's dictum that the greatest evil for the Dutch Republic would be to see France in control of the Spanish Netherlands. However, whereas De Witt thought Louis XIV could be countered mainly by diplomatic means and military means should only serve as a last resort, the new realities of warfare – unprecedented troop numbers and the collection of tons of foodstuffs to supply armies with bread for the men and fodder for the horses – convinced William III that an initially passive response to French aggression was no longer adequate. At the start of a new war immediate military action was imperative to delay the French advance as long as possible, providing time to organize a massive counter-offensive.[23] Given Spain's weakness it was clear that the Dutch would have to bear the brunt of the Spanish Netherlands' defence.[24] William's decision to invade England in 1688 was prompted by his desire to use British wealth and manpower in the fight against Louis XIV. The Stadtholder hoped that the Dutch and English together could withstand the French until German help arrived – 'the first chock [of the French onslaught] being the most formidable'.[25] The Emperor and the German princes would need many months to mobilize their cumbersome armies.

The Nine Years' War (1688–1697) again demonstrated French military superiority. However, the capture of Namur (Namen) by William III in 1695, revealed the First Grand Alliance's capability of matching the French war effort. In 1697 the belligerents concluded the Peace of Rijswijk. This was, however, more a truce than a peace settlement, because everyone expected the resumption of fighting upon the death of the ailing Charles II (1661–1700), the last of the Spanish Habsburgs. Both France and Austria claimed the Spanish inheritance. To prevent the French from making rapid headway in the Spanish Netherlands Brussels agreed to garrison eight Spanish fortresses along the French frontier with 8,000 to 9,000 Dutch troops in 1698.[26] With this decision the Spaniards openly acknowledged their military impotence, and that the safety of the Spanish Netherlands depended upon the military power of the Dutch. Just two years later, however, this defensive arrangement was unsettled. In November 1700 Charles II died. In his will he named Philip of Anjou (Philip V), one of the

Sun King's grandsons, as the successor to the Spanish throne. Through the night of 5/6 February 1701 French troops, in collusion with the government of the Spanish Netherlands, occupied the towns with Dutch garrisons and sent the troops home. The loss of the Spanish Netherlands showed to William III that a system of forward defence against France would only be viable if the Dutch Republic obtained a firm footing in the Spanish Netherlands. The Second Grand Alliance, concluded on 7 September 1701 between Austria and the Maritime Powers (the Dutch Republic and England), clearly stated in article V that the allies, as far as the war in the Low Countries was concerned, would do their utmost 'to recover the provinces of the Spanish Low Countries, that they may be a fence and rampart, commonly called a barrier, separating and distancing France from the United Provinces'.[27] William III died in March 1702, but the Dutch Republic, England and the Emperor continued to cooperate closely to fulfil the goals of the Second Grand Alliance.

After 11 years of fighting the Maritime Powers and France made peace at Utrecht on 11 April 1713. The peace treaty confirmed the Dutch right to a barrier. The details, however, had to be worked out with Vienna, because the Spanish Netherlands belonged to the Spanish inheritance allotted to Emperor Charles VI (1685–1740) of Habsburg. Two years of difficult negotiations followed until finally on 15 November 1715 the Third Barrier Treaty was signed. It was called so, because two preliminary ones between the Dutch and the English, dated 1706 and 1709, had preceded it. Article II stated that the Spanish – now Austrian – Netherlands would remain an inalienable possession of the House of Habsburg. To protect it a permanent peacetime force of 30,000 men (18,000 Austrians and 12,000 Dutch troops) would be stationed there. In times of crisis this force would be increased to 40,000 men and more if necessity demanded so (article III). Article IV listed the fortress towns that would be handed over to the Republic: Namur, Tournai (Doornik), Menin, Warneton, Ypres, fort Knokke and Furnes (Veurne). Dendermond would have a mixed Austrian–Dutch garrison (article V). Two fortresses on the Lower Meuse (Venlo and Stevensweert) were ceded to the Dutch (article XVIII). Finally, the Austrian Netherlands had to pay the Dutch an annual subsidy of 1,500,000 guilders for maintenance of the barrier towns and as a partial compensation for the 12,000 Dutch garrison troops.[28]

The conclusion of the Third Barrier Treaty was a very important event in both Dutch and European history. It cemented a defensive alliance between the Maritime Powers and Austria aimed at containing France. As such, the treaty was designed, to preserve the balance of power in Europe. Although the barrier towns served a specific Dutch interest, namely protection against an attack from France, the Dutch political leaders had embedded this defensive arrangement in a balance-of-power system. This was exactly what Johan de Witt and William III had strived for. Neither of them had wanted to annex the Southern Netherlands to the Republic because guarding it and the territory of the Dutch Republic proper would be cumbersome. In times of peace, the territories would require at least 80,000 troops; in war, they would demand no less than 117,500 men to defend the most threatened fortresses of the Spanish Netherlands alone. Even if Dutch finances had not been strained to the utmost by 40 years of almost continuous conflict with France (1672–1712), the Republic could not be expected to upkeep an army on a war footing indefinitely.

Influential Dutch politicians such as Anthonie Heinsius (1641–1720), Grand Pensionary of Holland from 1689 to 1720, Simon van Slingelandt (1664–1736), secretary of the Council of State, Sicco van Goslinga (1664–1731), deputy to the States-General for the province of Friesland, and Adolf Hendrik Count of Rechteren and Almelo (1657–1731), a regent from Overijssel who had performed many diplomatic and military missions, all agreed that the Barrier (i.e. the mass of the Southern Netherlands) should be defended by the Dutch in conjunction with Austria and Great Britain. In the event of a new war with France, the French army would take at least two years to reach the Dutch frontier. Hence, the Republic had 'at least always two years to prepare [for defence] . . ., and to conclude alliances, augment its forces, and hire them from the [German] princes'.[29] As such the Barrier performed a task comparable to France's *frontière de fer*. But whereas the fortresses along the French frontier performed a purely military function – to prevent an enemy from advancing to Paris and to open gateways through which French forces could enter into the Southern Netherlands – the barrier towns also served political ends. The Barrier enabled the Republic to partake in European power politics even though its territorial base had become much too small for the new scale of warfare by the 1660s.

Great Britain depended on the Barrier for its security almost as much as the Dutch Republic. A French dominance of the Flemish coast would pose a constant threat to English stability. Although a French invasion was unlikely – such a move would involve extensive preparation giving the English time to ready their fleet, call on the Dutch for help, and strengthen their own army – the French could muster a small expedition relatively easily and send it into action on the spur of a moment. In addition, French privateers could create havoc for the English merchant fleet by controlling the narrow stretch of sea between the Austrian Netherlands and Great Britain. Ostend would serve as a perfect refuge haven. Moreover, George I (1660–1727), King of Great Britain 1714–27, and the Whigs, the political group who on the accession of the Hanoverian George had acquired most government posts, gave a high priority to preventing the Dutch Republic from being driven into the arms of France. George I, and also his son, the future George II (1683–1760), were first and foremost Hanoverians and the Republic constituted the surest link between Hanover and Great Britain. To the Whigs, a close alliance with the Dutch was of great value, because it assured them of prompt military assistance against the Jacobites, the supporters of the exiled Stuarts. In addition an alliance with the Dutch also legitimized their foreign policy. Parliament was wary of sanctioning international commitments without participation of the Republic due to the commercial rivalry between the Maritime Powers. Particularly if Great Britain was to be at war with Spain while the Republic remained neutral, Dutch merchants would prosper at the expense of the English.[30]

Although the importance of the Barrier may be less obvious with regard to Austria, it was no less real. Clearly the Dutch garrisons infringed on the Austrian Netherland's sovereignty and the 1,500,000-million guilder barrier subsidy posed a heavy financial burden. This was, however, commensurate with the enormous advantages Vienna derived from its permanent alliance with the Maritime Powers. The Barrier assured the Habsburgs of Anglo-Dutch military support in case France should attempt to eliminate them as an important political factor. Moreover, in such a situation, Vienna could employ the Austrian Netherlands to draw French armies away from the Danube, the Upper Rhine and the Austrian possessions in Italy.

The Dutch Barrier and the Old System (1715–1755)

After the conclusion of the Third Barrier Treaty the Dutch temporarily stayed aloof from European entanglements, provided their commercial interests were not threatened. When, in the 1720s, Charles VI supported the commercial aspirations of the Flemish who strove to compete with the Dutch and English East India Companies, the States-General increased the Dutch army to an effective strength of 50,000 men in 1726–1727, and prepared for a siege of Ostend. Whenever commerce was threatened, the 'hartader' (artery) of the Dutch Republic, even allies were not safe from its wrath. Charles VI stepped down. The charter of the Ostend Company was suspended in return for an Anglo-Dutch guarantee of the integrity of the Habsburg possessions upon the death of Charles VI (second Treaty of Vienna 1731/1732). The Emperor only had daughters which meant his death was bound to result in disputes with other claimants. France would not let this opportunity slip to weaken its arch enemy, Austria. Concerned with preserving the balance of power and especially the Barrier, Simon van Slingelandt, who had been elected Grand Pensionary in 1727, was convinced Dutch interests were served by guaranteeing the Habsburg inheritance. However, he certainly did not feel this meant the Dutch should support Charles VI in whatever he undertook, as the Emperor discovered to his great dismay in 1733. In this year the War of the Polish Succession (1733–1735) started in which France and Austria supported rival candidates. Charles VI acted under the assumption that the Maritime Powers would campaign on the border of the Austrian Netherlands with France, giving him free rein in Poland. Van Slingelandt, however, worked out a treaty with Paris in which both parties agreed to declare the Austrian Netherlands neutral for the war's duration. Van Slingelandt had achieved a major diplomatic victory. War with France was averted, and the Barrier remained intact. Furthermore, Austria was unequivocally given to understand that the Republic would not be pressured into a war unless its own vital interests and the preservation of the balance of power dictated it. Seven years later, in 1740, this was indeed the case.[31]

In 1740 Charles VI died. In accordance with the Pragmatic Sanction his eldest daughter, 23-year-old Maria Theresa (1717–1780), inherited all his possessions. That same year Prussia, under its newly crowned king, Frederick II, better known as Frederick the Great (1712–1786), attacked the Austrian duchy of Silesia. In 1741 the French also entered the conflict and turned the War of the Austrian Succession (1740–1748) into a European power-struggle. At first Great Britain and the Dutch Republic only aided Maria Theresa financially. But when her situation became more desperate, they found ignoring her pleas for troops very difficult. Grand Pensionary Anthonie van der Heim (1693–1746) – Van Slingelandt had died in 1736 – was convinced the maintenance of Austria as a great power was necessary. Hence, he worked diligently to strengthen the Dutch army in the hope that this would signify to Paris that the Republic would not remain idle while France and its allies – Prussia, Spain and Bavaria – dismantled the Habsburg Empire. In 1743 the Dutch Republic had 70,000 to 80,000 effective troops at its disposal. In the summer of 1743, a Dutch corps of 14,000 men marched into the Holy Roman Empire of the German nation to aid Maria Theresa.[32] However, the decision to augment the army and to send an auxiliary corps had not been uncontested. On the contrary, it had been accompanied by very intensive political disputes. The opponents of army augmentation were worried this would cause the conflict to spill over into the Austrian Netherlands, and the Dutch, once again, would have to bear the brunt of the fight against France. As said before, the Barrier system rested on the cooperation between Austria, the Republic and Great Britain. Under the circumstances Maria Theresa was surely not expected to send additional troops to defend the Austrian Netherlands. They were all needed to retain her heartland and her rich possessions in Italy. Although the British government was very bellicose, the army was not large and the duplicity of George II made the Dutch doubtful about British steadfastness. The British King as Elector was very concerned about the safety of his electorate Hanover. Both the French and Prussians could easily overrun it. Consequently, the British government pressured the Dutch in agreeing to send an Anglo-Dutch army into France. However, at the same time George II started negotiations in Paris concerning Hanover's neutrality. Van der Heim clearly indicated to London that he was not prepared to risk war with France unless the British *and* George II made a firm commitment to defend the Barrier together with the Dutch to their utmost capabilities.[33]

In 1744 the French attacked the Austrian Netherlands. Not because they were worried about an Anglo-Dutch attack on their *frontière de fer*, but for reasons of *gloire*. Just as his great-grandfather before him in 1667 and in 1672, Louis XV (1710–1774) wanted to prove himself a warrior-king. Although the decision to attack the Austrian Netherlands was criticized at the French court as a useless act which would only serve to antagonize the Dutch, the King could not be dissuaded. René Louis de Voyer de Paulmy Marquis d'Argenson (1694–1757), who would become secretary of state of foreign affairs in November 1744, wrote in his memoires: 'Flanders was chosen as the theatre of war, because it is the most illustrious, and one can say that from that moment on, reasons of politics no longer presided over reasons of war'.[34] The French did not meet much resistance in their advance. The Dutch and Austrian generals were at loggerheads with the British commander who was solely concerned with preserving his communications with Ostend, which enabled him to send his troops back to England as soon as their presence there would be required. The British government was very concerned about the possible outbreak of a Jacobite rebellion supported by the French.[35]

The year 1745 promised to be more successful for the allies. The campaign of 1744 had instigated a political crisis in London. A group of ministers under the leadership of the Pelham brothers – Henry Pelham (1696–1754) and Thomas Pelham-Holles, first Duke of Newcastle (1693–1768) – demanded that George II restore relations of confidence between the Republic and Great Britain. For them this was an absolute condition 'of going on with the present burdensome measures.'[36] The King reluctantly agreed and as a sign of good faith appointed his favourite son, William Augustus Duke of Cumberland (1721–1765), commander-in-chief of the British forces in the Low Countries. Although 1745 started promisingly, it turned out to be even more disastrous for the allies than 1744. They lost the battle of Fontenoy (11 May 1745) and the much feared Jacobite rebellion broke out paralysing the British war effort on the continent for two years. D'Argenson believed the time had come to reach a settlement with the Dutch and finish the war once and for all to the advantage of France and its allies. Since the Republic shouldered most of the allied war effort in the Austrian Netherlands – in 1745 for example, the Dutch contingent outnumbered the British one 60,000 to 40,000 men[37] – the French Foreign Secretary was convinced that the road to peace was to be found in The Hague. He believed: 'If the English advise [i.e. pressure] the Queen of Hungary [i.e. Maria Theresa], this princess will always find very considerable [territorial] sacrifices ... but it is to the States-General to get the King of Great Britain to speak with the necessary firmness to the court of Vienna. In short peace cannot be achieved without the will of the Maritime Powers'.[38] Van der Heim, however, was not prepared to consider separate French–Dutch peace negotiations. Considering the enormous discrepancy in French and Dutch military might, the Republic would be seriously disadvantaged. Instead, he was only prepared to work out a settlement with the approval of Great Britain. The settlement would then, as a last resort, be forced upon Austria. D'Argenson stuck to his policy notwithstanding the Dutch answer. To increase the pressure on the Dutch he agreed to dismantle the fortifications of the captured barrier towns. But then, in 1746, d'Argenson went a step too far. He demanded the Dutch agree to a treaty transforming the Southern Netherlands into a neutral buffer in return for the French withdrawal from the Austrian Netherlands. If Austria and Great Britain refused to abide by the treaty, the Dutch would have to forcibly prevent the Austrians and British from continuing the war in the Austrian Netherlands. This was an anathema for Van der Heim. Neutralization of the Barrier would destroy the Old System's foundation, and fatally undermine the Dutch Republic's security. By depriving the Austrian Netherlands of its strategic importance, Vienna would no longer retain its interest in the area. Without the Austrians the Dutch would have to retreat into a neutrality destroying their influence on the European political stage. The much troubled Van der Heim died of a heart attack on 15 July 1746.[39]

The French attack continued. Against d'Argenson's protests, who was dismissed in January 1747, Louis XV decided to menace the Republic directly in the hope of forcing it to a separate peace settlement. The invasion of States-Flanders (modern Zeeuws-Vlaanderen), however, resulted in a political upheaval that bestowed all political power in the Dutch Republic into the hands of William IV (1711–1751), Prince of Orange-Nassau. Willem Count Bentinck (1704–1774), his most influential adviser, was an ardent believer in the Old System that he wanted to maintain at all costs. As a result, the Dutch army was strengthened to about 90,000 effective men in early 1748, but, as was clear to all, except Bentinck, the reconquest of the Austrian Netherlands was an impossibility. A demonstration of Dutch military force should only seek to convince the French that they refrain from demanding the Austrian Netherlands' absolute neutrality. By this time, the British concurred with this view.[40] Louis XV was prepared to forsake his demand for absolute neutrality. The 1747 campaign had revealed his gamble to force the Dutch into a separate peace was a failure. Moreover, the very bloody siege of Bergen op Zoom (July–September 1747) had shown that the Dutch army was still a force to be reckoned with. An attack on the province of Holland would prove even more costly. Inundations had turned it into a vast *forteresse aquatique et continuelle*.[41] On 30 April 1748 Great Britain and the Dutch Republic concluded a separate peace with France. The French agreed to vacate the Austrian Netherlands and to return the barrier towns to the Dutch. The second Peace of Aix-la-Chapelle left the Austrians isolated and forced Maria Theresa, as d'Argenson had predicted, to cease fighting as well.

Shortly after peace had returned, the Dutch Republic and Great Britain sought to persuade Vienna to bear the partial costs involved with repairing the destroyed fortifications of the barrier towns. This was to no avail, however. The experiences of the previous eight years had convinced Maria Theresa and Wenzel Anton Count von Kaunitz-Rietberg (1711–1794), her most influential minister, that the Old System had outlived its usefulness to Austria. The Maritime Powers had only reluctantly joined Maria Theresa's fight against France, and had not hesitated to abandon her and conclude a separate peace when the war did not proceed favourably. The disagreement between the Maritime Powers and Austria over the reconstruction of the barrier towns had extensive consequences. Without the Barrier, the Dutch had no alternative but to abstain from future European commitments. The British were consequently forced to turn their backs on the Continent and concentrate upon maritime operations in the Americas and India. In January 1756, Prussia and Great Britain concluded a defensive alliance, but this could never be a substitute for the First and Second Grand Alliance in which the Republic had been the pivot. The Prussians were helpful only for protecting Hanover. On 1 May of the same year, the former arch enemies, Austria and France, also concluded a defensive alliance. The *renversement des alliances* was the logical result of the end of the Old System.[42]

Conclusion: historical summary

During the eighty years' struggle (1568–1648) against the Spanish King, the Dutch rebels first sought security through expanding their territorial base, and then, starting in 1635, through the annihilation of Spanish power in the Southern Netherlands. Pivotal in this effort was the conclusion of an offensive alliance with France. During the 1640s, however, the Dutch came to realize that not they but the French profited the most from this undertaking. Moreover, they discovered that by eliminating the Spaniards, who by then no longer posed a real threat to Dutch independence, the Republic was facing a much greater danger. Instead of the exhausted Spanish monarchy the Dutch would have the largest and most populous kingdom of Europe as their direct neighbour. The States of Holland declared in February 1646: 'Having superior neighbours has always been judged very dangerous for all states.' And this dictum was even more true with regard to France: 'the nature of the French nation being ticklish and restless'.[43] Two years later, in violation of the 1635 alliance, the Dutch signed a separate peace with Spain. The outbreak of hostilities between the Dutch Republic and England in the 1650s led to a renewal of the French–Dutch alliance in 1662. Johan de Witt believed that the Republic would be in a better position to fight England with French military backing. At first the war with Münster (1665–1666), which was waged simultaneously to the second Anglo-Dutch War (1665–1667), seemed to prove him right. But in 1667 Louis XIV invaded the Spanish Netherlands. The prospect of a French conquest of the Southern Netherlands was even more daunting than in 1646 due to the impressive growth in French army size. De Witt considered halting France more important to the Republic than continuing the war with England. The conclusion of the Triple Alliance between the Dutch Republic, England and Sweden compelled Louis XIV to retreat. Clearly, however, this suspension of the French offensive was only temporary.

The Forty Years' War between the Dutch Republic and France started in 1672 when Louis XIV invaded the Republic with an army of unprecedented size: 80,000 to 100,000 men. The Dutch War (1672–1678) and the subsequent Nine Years' War (1688–1697) both involved all major European states. For the Dutch and, from 1688 onwards also the English, the conflict was about control of the Spanish Netherlands. If Louis XIV became master of the Southern Netherlands, the Republic would be lost consequently overturning the European balance of power. William III and the leading Dutch politicians knew that even if a peacetime army of about 100,000 men was financially viable, the Dutch could not possibly preserve their independence. The French army exceeded it by a factor of three to four. In light of this, only a forward defence system that would delay the French advance for up to two or three years, could give the Republic its required security. The delay would enable the Dutch and British to augment their forces and make the necessary defensive arrangements in expectation of the arrival of the troops sent by the Emperor and the German princes. During the War of Spanish Succession this system of forward defence evolved into the Barrier concept, a permanent balance-of-power system of the Maritime Powers and Austria aimed at containing France. The common defence of the Austrian Netherlands cemented this alliance. The Barrier not only ensured the Republic's safety, but also helped to maintain the European balance of power. The loss of the Barrier between 1744–1746 had extensive consequences for Europe in general and the Republic in particular. The loss forced the Dutch to retreat into neutrality, which consequently led to the *renversement des alliances*, ending the conflict between the Houses of Habsburg and Bourbon, which had lasted for centuries, and ushering in the great French–British struggle over world hegemony.

Editorial conclusion: territoriality and the quest for security

The shift from conflicts between noble families towards struggles between territorial rulers designates a step from personalized towards territorially organized international/inter-dynastic politics (see also Teschke: Chapter 3). According to the well-known historian, Charles Tilly, this military competition between West-European rulers since the late Middle Ages laid the groundwork for the convergence towards 'modern' state territoriality: mutually exclusive, enduring, impersonal and sovereign entities having clearly demarcated, contiguous, and fixed territories.[44] Out of the medieval politics marked by intricate networks of religious, occupational, imperial and princely powers, war essentially resulted in the territorial consolidation of Europe's polities. From a Realist international relations perspective, the demise of Europe's central authorities, the Emperor and the Pope, after the Treaties of Augsburg (1555) and Westphalia (1648), led polities to adopt a territorial hierarchy in order to secure their survival in an anarchic world. Clearly, this perspective shifts the focus of analysis from political authority to military might, but existing political structures in the Low Countries and local geographical circumstances indicate that these may have been of equal significance for the Republic's territoriality. Consequently, the relative impact of both local and 'foreign' factors on the constitution of the Dutch Republic merits a brief summary here. This chapter has examined the formation of the Dutch Republic and the then existing patterns of military conflict to see how political territoriality changed. Its main purpose therefore has been two-fold: to understand the historical relation between security and territoriality; and to provide insights into the territorializing mechanisms of war and their potential imprints on present-day political organization in Europe.

Tilly's explanation about patterns of state formation is based on the geographies of coercion and capital. As he claimed, '[t]he seventeenth-century Dutch occupied an extreme position on the axis of commercialization'.[45] This concentration of capital must have had certain organizational consequences for the (territorial) constitution of the Dutch Republic. The commercialization and consequent monetization of the Low Countries facilitated taxation to such an extent that a strong administrative structure and coercive means were unnecessary.[46] Moreover, the powerful merchant and financial classes in the Dutch Republic considered a strong state for levying taxes as undesirable.

Thus, the stadtholder had no legitimate basis for expanding his powers and the armed forces mainly remained under control of the provinces. The capital-intensive character of the Low Countries precluded a centralizing chain of state formation of security, taxation, representation and bureaucratization: '[a]t moments, (...) the Dutch state dissolved into the governments of its major municipalities'.[47]

The Dutch commercial oligarchies were predominantly concerned with protecting their trade opportunities on the European and world seas. Naval warfare was much less costly than long-term, massive warfare on land: it did not require a longstanding administrative apparatus to provide the troops with food, salaries and weaponry, and commercial vessels were relatively easy to transform into warships. Very few internal forces in the Dutch Republic favoured territorial expansion on the European continent. As a sea-oriented and geographically small polity, the Dutch Republic therefore formed a ring of internal and external buffers around its commercial centre in Holland. As a trading power, the Dutch preferred to spend their funds on wars at sea while maintaining a large defensive barrier to deter continental intruders.[48] Moreover, foreign policies to maintain a European balance of power were predominantly motivated to keep the 'continentals' out. Hence, the Dutch invented two crucial components of the European society of states: the balance-of-power and the defensive state.[49] The Dutch Republic no longer aimed for territorial aggrandizement, but was a vehicle to maintain and foster its members' wealth. According to the political geographer Peter Taylor, the Dutch Republic initiated Europe's commercial domination over the entire world. Mercantilist and trading states no longer heavily invested in imperial military projects, but clung to their territories, which laid the groundwork for a stable and strong national community of fate.[50]

The Dutch participation in international politics was in particular focused on containing their most powerful neighbour on the continent, France. The maintenance of the Barrier was inspired by the idea to have a role in international politics to protect Dutch interests while the loss of the Barrier was likewise motivated by abstaining from international politics to protect Dutch interests. The strategy pursued by one of the French national state's founding fathers, General Sébastien le Prestre de Vauban,[51] constructed a territorially fixed line of fortresses to control the entry and exit into the French territories from the north, east, and south. He constructed such an enormous defendable border as the scale of warfare expanded and invasions continued that losses of territory were huge, particularly in case of the open fields of northern France. Shortly thereafter, countries facing similar strategic problems adopted the French solution and added a strategy of standing armies to this, expanding and centralizing the soldiers' food deliverance and salary administration. Thus, the changing character of warfare set in motion the change into territorial political structures. However, the Dutch Republic continued to keep the eastern and particularly its southern peripheries as internal buffers, directly under the central jurisdiction of Holland and Utrecht. The loss of the zonal defence barrier was only a small step to allocating borders; the precise and linear delimitation and demarcation of a unified, national territory was not yet made during the French occupation in the late eighteenth century.[52] One of the alleged shifts observed in 'Westphalia' is the carving up of the medieval networks of overlapping and fluid authorities, and replacing them with clearcut 'modern' states marked by linear borders. In conclusion, the (territorial) constitution of the Dutch Republic was a product of various local and 'foreign' forces.

Despite its small size and fragmented sovereignty, and in contrast to empires, city-states, city-empires and religious organizations, the Dutch Republic survived the violent chaos of fifteenth- and sixteenth-century Europe. Its capital resources and policies to protect the cities' commercial interests and the weaknesses of neighbouring enemies facilitated this survival. According to Tilly, the formation and transformation of state organization largely stems from patterns of (military) conflicts which create a need for internal order and external security. However, security and territoriality do not form a one-to-one relationship. Commercial interests also determined the Dutch Republic's formation and these interests were not secondary to security issues. Moreover, 'not all warfare is most efficiently organized territorially and centrally – guerrillas, military, feudalism and warrior bands are all examples of relatively decentralized military organizations'.[53] In the case of the Dutch Republic, naval warfare to protect commercial interests precluded for a long time a clearly demarcated and territorially centralized apparatus in the Low Countries for military purposes.[54] Thus, the internal constitution of the Dutch Republic basically featured commercial and confederal ties, not the territorial imprint of the state's coercive machinery and centralizing administration. The Dutch quest for security basically resulted in a bundle of loosely coupled trading territories left intact by its neighbouring powers.

Though Westphalia usually symbolizes the turning point towards the template of state territoriality, the demarcation and internal organization of the Dutch Republic did not match this template. The distribution and circumscription of competences as well as the provision of security were not territorially based, but were founded rather on commercial or nobility links. Nevertheless, Westphalia did recognize the Republic's independence from the Habsburg Empire and consequently provided a legal protection of its external sovereignty within the society of states. The most significant legacy of the Dutch Republic's formation for the territoriality issue, however, has been the quest for combining diversity and unity within the Dutch confederation. The Republic's emergence was the breeding ground for Johannes Althusius to design the organizational principle for both consociationalism and federalism:[55] in the case of the Low Countries, Westphalia thus set in motion the thinking about internal fragmentation rather than unification.

Notes

1. David Parrott, *Richelieu's army. War, government and society in France, 1624–1642* (Cambridge 2001) 220; John A. Lynn, *The wars of Louis XIV 1667–1714* (London and New York 1999) 50. The Spanish army with an establishment of no less than 300,000 men in the 1630s (albeit on paper), was the great exception to the rule. Geoffrey Parker, 'The "Military Revolution, 1560–1660" – a myth?', in: Clifford J. Rogers (ed.), *The Military Revolution debate. Readings on the military transformation of Early Modern Europe* (Boulder, San Francisco and Oxford 1995) 37–54, at 44.
2. John A. Lynn, 'Recalculating French army growth during the Grand Siècle, 1610–1715', in: Rogers, *The Military Revolution debate*, 117–147, at 125.
3. Olaf van Nimwegen, *De subsistentie van het leger. Logistiek en strategie van het Geallieerde en met name het Staatse leger tijdens de Spaanse Successieoorlog in de Nederlanden en het Heilige Roomse Rijk (1701–1712)* (Amsterdam 1995) 9; Olaf van Nimwegen, *De Republiek der Verenigde Nederlanden als grote mogendheid. Buitenlandse politiek en oorlogvoering in de eerste helft van de achttiende eeuw en in het bijzonder tijdens de Oostenrijkse Successieoorlog (1740–1748)* (Amsterdam 2002) 128.
4. R. Fruin (ed.), 'Gedenkschrift van Joris de Bye [Treasurer-General of the Dutch Republic from 1588 to 1628], betreffende het bewind van Oldenbarnevelt', in: *Bijdragen en Mededeelingen van het Historisch Genootschap*, 11 (Utrecht 1888) 400–459, at 458–459.
5. 'om een defensiven oorlog te voeren op haar eigen grensen'. Nationaal Archief The Hague (NA), Familiearchief Fagel 1331, Letter of the Council of State, 31 May 1715.
6. A. Th. van Deursen, *Maurits van Nassau. De winnaar die faalde* (4th edition; Amsterdam 2002) chapters 7 to 10.
7. De Bye, 'Gedenkschrift', 459, speaks of a 'swaere onversoenlicken oorloge'.
8. Van Deursen, *Maurits van Nassau*, chapters 10–11.
9. J.J. Poelhekke, *Frederik Hendrik prins van Oranje. Een biografisch drieluik* (Zutphen 1978) 128.
10. NA, Rijksarchief in Zuid-Holland (RAZH), Archief Jacob Cats 32, 'Rapport

van de heeren gecommitteert bij haere Ed. Groot Mo. op 't stuck van de mesnage waervan de besoigne is begonnen den xi.en october 1635'.
11 'In Hollant was men vol achterdencken datter een heymelick verstant was tussen Vrancrijck ende Spagnen, ende begon men meer te apprehendeeren de viciniteyt van Vrancrijck, door occupatie van Vlaenderen met d'andre Spaensche Nederlanden, als te vreesen den [uitgeputte] Spagnaert.' Robert Jaspar van der Capellen (ed.), *Gedenkschriften van jonkheer Alexander van der Capellen, heere van Aartsbergen, Boedelhoff en Mervelt*, two volumes (Utrecht 1777–1778) II, 141, 143–144.
12 Jaap R. Bruijn, *Varend verleden. De Nederlandse oorlogsvloot in de zeventiende en achttiende eeuw* (1998) 90–97; F.J.G. ten Raa, *Het Staatsche leger 1568–1795*, V (Breda 1921) 164–169, 172–173, 176–177 and 180.
13 'J'estime que l'on peut supposer, sans se tromper, 1. que le voisinage de la France et le plus grand mal qui puisse arriver à cet Estat, et 2. qu'il est inévitable si l'on ne s'y oppose présentement.' NA, RAZH, Archief Johan de Witt 2725-4, 'Raisonnement op[de] oorloch in[de] Spaensche Nederlanden', without date.
14 Ten Raa, *Het Staatsche leger*, V, 211–216.
15 N. Japikse (ed.), *Notulen gehouden ter statenvergadering van Holland (1671–1675) door Cornelis Hop, pensionaris van Amsterdam, en Nicolaas Vivien, pensionaris van Dordrecht* (Amsterdam 1903) 50–54, entry of 1 April 1672.
16 Herbert H. Rowen, *John de Witt, Grand Pensionary of Holland, 1625–1672* (Princeton, NJ 1978) 599, 601.
17 NA, Archief van de Raad van State 1501, Dutch army size from 1649 upwards.
18 Olaf van Nimwegen, 'De betekenis van Willem III voor de wederopbouw en vorming van het Staatse leger (1672–1678)', in: *Jaarboek Oranje-Nassau Museum 2002* (Rotterdam 2003) 25–39.
19 Chr. Duffy, *The fortress in the age of Vauban and Frederick the Great 1660–1789* (London, Boston, Melbourne and Henley 1985) 12.
20 'Sérieusement, Monseigneur, le Roi devrait un peu songer à faire son pré carré. Cette confusion de places amies et ennemies pêle-mêlées ne me plaît point. Vous êtes obligé d'en entretenir trois pour une.' Anne Blanchard, 'Vers la ceinture de fer', in: Philippe Contamine (ed.), *Histoire militaire de la France*, volume 1, 'Des origines à 1715' (Paris 1992) 449–483, at 476.
21 Henry Guerlac, 'Vauban: the impact of science on war', in: Peter Paret (ed.), *Makers of modern strategy: from Machiavelli to the nuclear age* (Princeton, NJ 1986) 64–90, at 86–87.
22 Werner Gembruch, 'Vauban', in: Werner Hahlweg (ed.), *Klassiker der Kriegskunst* (Darmstadt 1960) 150–165, at 152.
23 Werner Hahlweg, 'Barriere – Gleichgewicht – Sicherheit. Eine Studie über die Gleichgewichtspolitik und die Strukturwandlung des Staatesystems in Europa 1646–1715', in: *Historische Zeitschrift*, 187 (München 1959) 54–89, at 66–67.
24 John M. Stapleton, 'Grand Pensionary at war. Anthonie Heinsius and the Nine Years' War, 1689–1697', in: Jan A.F. de Jongste and Augustus J. Veenendaal Jr. (eds.), *Anthonie Heinsius and the Dutch Republic 1688–1720. Politics, war, and finance* (The Hague 2002) 199–227, at 207–210.
25 'Dat de eerste chocq de formidabelste is.' Ironically it was Johan de Witt who remarked this, just two months before the French assault began. Japikse, *Notulen*, 56, entry of 6 April 1672.
26 J.W. Wijn, *Het Staatsche leger*, VIII, 3 volumes (The Hague 1956–1964) i, 5–6.
27 Quoted in: J.B. Hattendorf, *England in the War of the Spanish Succession. A study of the English view and conduct of grand strategy, 1702–1712* (New York 1987) 78–79.
28 Van Nimwegen, *De Republiek als grote mogendheid*, 25–31.

29 'Du moins toujours deux ans à se préparer ..., & à former des alliances, augmenter ses trouppes, & en louer ches les princes.' Koninklijk Huisarchief The Hague, Archief Willem Bentinck G2–21II, Willem van Haren to Princes Anne of Orange-Nassau, Brussels 20 May 1755, transcript.
30 Hugh Dunthorne, *The Maritime Powers 1721–1740. A study of Anglo-Dutch relations in the age of Walpole*, PhD thesis University of London (London and New York 1986) 10; Adriaan Goslinga, *Slingelandt's efforts towards European peace* (The Hague 1915) 52.
31 Van Nimwegen, *De Republiek als grote mogendheid*, chapter 2.
32 Van Nimwegen, *De Republiek als grote mogendheid*, 103, 174.
33 Van Nimwegen, *De Republiek als grote mogendheid*, 143–153.
34 'On choisit le théâtre de Flandre comme le plus brillant, et l'on peut dire que, de ce moment, la raison politique cessa de présider à la raison de guerre.' E.J.B. Rathery (ed.), *Journal et mémoires du marquis d'Argenson*, 9 volumes (Paris 1859–1867) IV, 233.
35 Van Nimwegen, *De Republiek als grote mogendheid*, 178–180, 187.
36 British Library, Additional Manuscripts 35408, Andrew Stone to Lord Chancellor Hardwicke, Whitehall 6 September Old Style 1744.
37 Van Nimwegen, *De Republiek als grote mogendheid*, 102 and 218.
38 'Si les Anglois consultent la reine de Hongrie, cette princesse trouvera toujours les sacrifices trop considérables ... mais c'est aux Etats-Généraux à porter le roy de la Grande Bret.e à parler avec toute la fermeté nécessaire à la cour de Vienne. Enfin la paix ne peut se faire que par la volonté absolue des Puissances Maritimes.' Archives Ministère des Affaires Etrangères Paris (AAE), Correspondance Politique (CP), Hollande 455, D'Argenson aan Delaville, Versailles 18 April 1745, minute.
39 Van Nimwegen, *De Republiek als grote mogendheid*, 264.
40 Van Nimwegen, *De Republiek als grote mogendheid*, 299–300, 335, 347–352.
41 AAE, CP, Hollande 462, Puysieulx aan d'Argenson, Breda 3 January 1747.
42 Van Nimwegen, *De Republiek als grote mogendheid*, 359–389.
43 'Dat overmachtige gebuuren te hebben voor alle staten altijt gans gevaerlijck is geoordeelt geweest. Dat den nature van de Fransche natie kittelachtigh en onrustigh is.' Quoted in J.J. Poelhekke, *De Vrede van Munster* (The Hague 1948) 256.
44 Tilly, C., *Coercion, and Capital, and European States, AD 990–1990* (Cambridge, MA 1990) 4.
45 Tilly, C. (1990) 90.
46 Tilly, C. (1990) 62, 88–89.
47 Tilly, C. (1990) 53–54.
48 Tilly, C. (1990) 71, 91.
49 Taylor, P.J. 'The State as Container: Territoriality in the Modern World-System', in *Human Geography* (1994), vol. 18, no. 3, 151–162.
50 Taylor, P.J. (1994).
51 Gottmann, J., *The Significance of Territory* (Charlottesville, VA 1973) 59ff; Escolar, 'Exploration, Carthography and the Modernization of State Power', in N. Brenner et al., *State/Space: A Reader* (Malden, MA 2003) 41.
52 Sahlins, P., *Boundaries: The Making of France and Spain in the Pyrenees* (Berkeley 1989) 6.
53 Mann, M., 'The Autonomous Power of the State: Its Origins, Mechanism and Results', in N. Brenner et al. (eds), *State/Space: A Reader* (Malden, MA 2003) 61.
54 Mann, M. (2003) 61–64.
55 Hoetjes, B.J.S., 'The European Tradition of Federalism: The Protestant Dimension', in M. Burgess, A.-G. Gagnon (eds.), *Comparative Federalism and Federation: Competing Traditions and Future Directions* (New York 1993) 117–137.

3 The metamorphoses of European territoriality
A historical reconstruction

Benno Teschke

Introduction

The nature and extent of the current changes in the forms of statehood and their international relations, often portrayed as a shift from traditional sovereignty to 'global governance', 'neo-medievalism', or even, 'empire' is key for making sense of the contemporary international system and the European Union (EU) that exists within it.[1] Some Realist theorists of international relations (IR) understand change in terms of alterations to the distribution of power among states in an unchanging anarchical international political structure. The polarity of the system is changing but there is continuity in terms of the structure of the system and the international conduct of states. In this respect, the European integration process may have altered the *territorial scale* of 'Europe' as a political actor and reduced the number of actors, while replacing them with a re-consolidated single pole of authority on a wider geographical basis, but it has not overcome the territorial foundations of political power and the nature of power politics. The internal elimination of borders has only reinforced the external reconstruction of these very same borders.

Others contend that we are witnessing a fundamental transformation in the structure of the international system. One prominent version of this case is the argument that the classical, or Westphalian, system, rooted in the primacy of the modern territorially bounded sovereign state, is being transcended in favour of a post-modern, post-territorial, indeed, 'post-Westphalian' international order. The history of European integration and the politico-institutional architecture of the EU are singled out to typify this new 'unbundled' configuration between territoriality and political authority (Ruggie, 1993). This shift is variously explained in terms of the subordination of an old geopolitical logic of security to a new world of geo-economic cooperation, the development of multi-level governance, or the demands of a multi-actor international/European civil society – changes driven in one way or another by the end of the Cold War and the intensifying process of globalisation.

One problem in the globalisation literature and in the social-scientific discourse on European integration is the assumption that a possible shift towards a de-territorial logic of the spatial organisation of politics corresponds to a transition from a state-centric Westphalian order – with the nation-state in full control over its territory – to a post-Westphalian European order, where territorially distinct sovereignties are progressively dissolved and then pooled in a new trans-territorial polity. In this perspective, historical development is schematically divided into two distinct phases: first, a Westphalian phase that covers the period between the mid-seventeenth century to either the beginnings of European integration in the 1950s or the full onslaught of globalisation in the 1970s – a golden age of territorial sovereignty; followed by a more recent period of the decline and fall of sovereignty undermined and transformed by de-territorialisation and absorbed into a single post-Westphalian polity – be it either a federal superstate, a consociation, a confederation, a polycentric 'dispersed polity' (Schmitter, 1996), an 'international state' (Caporaso, 1996), or an indeterminate evolving formation 'under the sign of the interim' (Anderson, 1997). Modernity is here equated with territorial sovereignty, whereas postmodernity is equated with a post-sovereign and de-territorialising age.[2]

This chapter argues that these premises of the globalisation/European integration debate are deeply flawed. More specifically, I will argue that we have to start by re-theorising seventeenth-century Westphalian sovereignty to fully establish its fundamental non-equivalence to modern sovereignty. Furthermore, I will suggest that when modern sovereignty emerged and became more generalised in nineteenth-century Europe, it was never master over its territory, but contained already a trans-territorialising logic, expressed in the transnational flows of capitalism that easily crossed borders *without*, however, necessarily challenging the sovereign nation-state. The establishment of the nineteenth century British-sponsored world-market and the consolidation of a worldwide system of sovereign states were mutually co-developing and co-constitutive processes. In other words, while modern sovereignty was never spatially congruent with the activities of its society and economy, transnational flows and territorial statehood were not necessarily opposing forces, but structurally linked and mutually supporting phenomena. In capitalist societies, the activities of civil society always already transcended the territorial confines of 'their' states. This means the restrictive research-defining dichotomy between a state-dominant 'before' (1648–1950/1970) and a state cancelling 'after' (post-1950/1970) needs to be opened up and relaxed if we want to properly understand the current constellation between territoriality and political power in the EU.

What these initial reflections point to is that we need a much wider historical perspective to address the more general question of how to think about the long-term development of the nexus between territoriality and political power in Europe. The recent, though probably premature, obituaries for the classical nation-state, rooted in a fixed, clearly demarcated and evenly administered form of territoriality, have re-opened our awareness of the historically variable, if not contingent, correlation between territoriality and power. What, then, drives the constitution and transformation of territoriality? By tracing the 'social geography of political territoriality', this chapter seeks to explain historical variations in the constellations between territoriality and political authority across European history from the Middle Ages to the present. In a second step, it seeks to contribute to the debate on how European history generated a geopolitical pluriverse – a distinct and complex territorial legacy that the European integration process has been trying to transcend since its inception. The key question of this chapter is thus not so much whether or not the EU is in the process of transforming itself into a novel type of polity, but *how and why* Europe became a multi-state system in the first place, rather than remaining an imperial or feudal formation. In this sense, this chapter reverses the research-organising question of this book: rather than asking whether European integration is dissolving multi-territoriality, we need to know why an inter-state system became a constitutive feature of European history in the first place. Once we have answered this question, we may gain a better perspective on whether this multi-state system is currently being transformed into something else.

If we accept the proposition that political territoriality is dynamic and historically variable, rather than static and fixed, this also implies rejecting the prevalent idea that territory – in its geographical-topological or its geo-strategic positional sense – is a primary determinant of state-formation, statehood and statecraft (foreign-policy). However, this territorial ontology has a long and powerful pedigree in the political and social sciences. The primacy of space and location underwrote both the old German School of *Geopolitik* and its organicist and chthonic conception of the state (Teschke 2001) and, in a different sense, forms one part of the near immutable *longue durée* in the social history of the early Annales School around Fernand Braudel. Fixed territoriality as an essential attribute of the modern state is, of course, also a defining feature of Max Weber's political sociology and has survived in both versions of IR rationalism, namely, neo-realism and neo-liberalism. One way to avoid falling into the 'territorial trap' (Agnew and Corbridge, 1995: 78ff.) and to articulate an alternative socio-political geography is to start from the assumption that territoriality cannot be abstracted from the wider ways in which societies (i) organise their relations with nature, (ii) co-ordinate the relations between the individuals that make up theses societies and (iii) organise their relations with each other – something we are used to calling 'international relations'. In other words, I want to suggest that territoriality is not the 'naturalised' bedrock that constitutes statehood, but that the changing forms of territoriality are intimately related to the ways that polities are *vergesellschaftet* (socially organised) and, in particular, to the kinds of 'strategies of territorialisation' that ruling classes design in order to extend their rule and powers of accumulation. One way to uncover the social logic behind the metamorphoses of European territoriality is by analysing historically different social property relations. Thus, rather than having recourse to conventional IR theories, be they neo-realism, neo-liberalism, or constructivism, my core thesis is that social property relations and the forms of class conflict associated with these play a central role in accounting for different forms of political communities and territoriality, for their historically variable and specific forms of conflict and cooperation with one another, and for large-scale transformations of international systems. By setting out this argument in some historical detail, I want to make the further claim that the history of territory-formation and particularly modern state-formation cannot be adequately understood on the basis of a neo-weberian historical sociology as a result of the war-driven competition between centralising rulers and their bureaucratic-rationalising efforts in the sphere of public administration, either in its military, fiscal, financial or juridical dimensions. I further argue that the equation of the modern state, defined as exercising a legitimate monopoly in the means of violence over a bounded and contiguous territory, with 'Westphalian sovereignty' is historically incorrect. The Peace Treaties of Westphalia did not enshrine the principle of modern sovereignty and their associated international relations (Teschke, 2003). Rather, they remained rooted in dynastic sovereignty, imperial forms of territoriality and pre-capitalist property relations that structured the early-modern system of states. But if Westphalia did not codify modern statehood and if 1648 thus represents a (powerful) myth for the discipline of IR, we will have to rewrite the history of the origins, consolidation and subsequent expansion of the modern international system. This may provide an alternative starting-point for rethinking the nature of the EU.

The chapter is divided into five sections. Section one discusses the concept of 'neo-medievalism' and explores medieval territoriality. Section two sets out the consequences of the demise of the Carolingian Empire for the origins of Europe as a geopolitical pluriverse and the divergent patterns of state-formation in France and England. Section three draws out the implications of these divergent trajectories for the nature of territoriality and international relations during the Westphalian period. Section four looks at how post-1688 capitalist England came to restructure the European System of Old Regimes and what effect this had for the territorial consolidation of the states-system while section five concludes with some general remarks on the relationship between capitalism and territoriality.

Politics, geopolitics and territoriality in medieval Europe

Ever since Hedley Bull's introduction of the term 'neo-medievalism' (Bull, 1977), it has been fashionable to invoke the concept to capture the nature of the EU as a polity of spatially overlapping policy-competencies and of multiple loyalties that erode traditional sovereignty (Friedrichs, 2001). The following section rejects the explanatory utility of this notion by looking more closely at the social production of medieval territoriality. While there may be a certain surface analogy between medieval and 'post-Westphalian' order, neo-medievalism's conceptual power is metaphorical, but not analytical. There could not be a greater gulf between medieval and contemporary forms of territoriality.

The modern state, and states-system, involves a clear distinction between domestic international politics, hierarchically organised within the territorially bounded state and anarchically ordered between territorially differentiated states. At the same time, this system involves a division, defined in law, between the 'public' and the 'private', a central aspect of which is the separation of an economic realm of markets and property rights and a political realm of the state and government. The medieval social order was neither characterised by the typical demarcation between the domestic and the international spheres, nor by the separation of politics and economics. In a medieval world devoid of this double differentiation, the fundamental problem is to determine the spatial nature of the political (and the geopolitical) and to specify the actors that were qualified to conduct 'international' relations at the time (Teschke, 1998).

Medieval politics and geopolitics were neither purely anarchical, nor purely hierarchical, but contained both vertical and horizontal relations of subordination and coordination among highly differentiated carriers of political power. It is, therefore, misleading to subsume the range of these diverse political authorities – pope, emperor, kings, dukes, counts, bishops, cities, lords – under the generic term of state-like 'conflict-units', since none enjoyed a monopoly in the means of violence guaranteeing exclusive control over a bounded territory. Political authority was dispersed, fragmented and overlapping, unlike the bounded, unified and exclusive authority claimed by modern sovereign states.

How can we explain this? Classically, the literature on feudalism follows either the Weber–Hintze tradition (Weber, 1968; Hintze, 1968), that conceptualises feudal politics as a type of patrimonial power within the sociological framework of a typology of domination, or the social historian, Mark Bloch, who studied feudalism as a specific form of agrarian economy, based on a dependent peasantry (Bloch, 1961). Patrimonialism, according to Weber, is a form of rule that is an extension of the ruler's extended household, in which administration and force are under the direct, personal control of the ruler. Feudalism was patrimonial rule that was dispersed geographically among subordinates (vassals), based on personal ties between the overlord and his vassals. A dependent peasantry is one that has access to the means of subsistence, the land and its produce, but from which a ruling class is able coercively to extract a share of the total output.

The challenge, however, is to understand the connections between the political and economic aspects of feudalism. They also explain the specific medieval configuration of territoriality – the distinct relation between the internal and the external. Compared with the modern state, the most striking feature of the feudal world was the absence of a state monopoly in the means of violence. Instead, they were distributed among the members of the dominant class, typically in a pyramid of lord–vassal–sub-vassal relations. The means of violence and the political power they supported simultaneously served as a mode of dominating and exploiting the mass of direct producers, the peasantry, in a pre-dominantly agrarian economy. Since these direct producers were, as a rule, in possession of the means of subsistence, feudal lords had to force access to peasant production by coercive political means, backed up by their personal share in the means of violence. This was how they reproduced themselves as political lords. Karl Marx referred to the connections between the economic and political aspects of this form of society as follows:

> It is clear, too, that in all forms where the actual worker himself remains the 'possessor' of the means of production and the conditions of labour needed for the production of his own means of subsistence, the property relationship must appear at the same time as a direct relationship of domination and servitude, and the direct producer therefore an unfree person.... Under these conditions, the surplus labour for the nominal landowner can only be extorted from them by extra-economic compulsion, whatever the form this might assume.
>
> (Marx 1981, 926)

Robert Brenner (1986; 1987) has argued that this gave rise to a particular set of dynamics in feudalism that were quite different from those characteristic of capitalist societies. Since access to peasant surpluses (that is, output over and above that necessary to reproduce the peasantry) required coercive political means (Marx's extra-economic compulsion) lords engaged 'political accumulation', that is, attempts to build up their political and coercive power, in order to ensure their own reproduction. The class power of lords, the power to extract economic resources from the peasantry, depended on access to political power, which in turn gave access to property rights, including rights over the direct producers themselves. Feudal ruling-class power meant property in the means of coercion. As a rule, the relation between producers (peasants) and non-producers (lords and their vassals) took the form of a 'rent-regime', in which serfs were compelled either to hand over part of their produce to a lord, in cash or in kind, to work for the lord on his demesne, or to rent land. These relations were embodied in the institution of the 'lordship' – at the same time a unit of authority and an agrarian economic enterprise – that constituted the basic building block of the medieval 'state'. Thus, the economic and the political were fused together in the Middle Ages.

This fusion of political domination and economic exploitation had a direct impact on the structure of medieval political authority and territoriality. The sharing of power among the individual members of the ruling class, who presided in their lordships over dependent peasants, implied that the 'feudal state', viewed as an ensemble of lordships, was geographically decentralised, institutionally personalised and inherently subject to inter-lordly competition over their relative share in the control of land and labour. This is expressed in Perry Anderson's notion of 'parcellised sovereignty' (1974). Since land was not owned by lords as private property, but, as a rule, held as a fief from an overlord, the fief-holding lord was obliged to perform certain military and administrative services to his overlord in return. In other words, property rights were never absolute, but *conditional* upon the performance of certain obligations, laid down in a mutual vassalic 'contract', directed upwards to whoever occupied the apex of the feudal pyramid, usually the king. But this relation between lord and overlord – often stretching over various levels – did not imply absolute hierarchy and subordination, precisely because lords were not civil servants or functionaries but arms-bearing land-holders and, in that capacity, full political lords. German medieval historians referred to this phenomenon as 'a state of associated persons' (*Personenverbandsstaat*) (Mayer, 1963; Brunner, 1992; Mitteis, 1975).[3]

As bearer of arms, which were necessary both for the subjection of the peasantry and for the provision of military and advisory services to their overlords, lords had the right to carry out feuds (Brunner, 1992), both against their overlords, if they felt injured, and against rival lords. The peculiar institution of the 'feud' indicates the absence of a separation between the private and the public, the domestic and the international, the legitimate and the criminal recourse to arms. It expressed some of the internal contradictions of the feudal ruling class. In other words, since the means of violence were distributed among lords throughout the feudal pyramid in the context of an agrarian political economy based on a lord/peasant rent-regime, medieval polities were neither internally completely pacified and governed by an impersonal law, nor purely anarchical and governed by considerations of power. Thus, just as the economic and the political were fused together, so too were the 'domestic' and the 'international'. It is not possible to partition feudal politics into a bounded domestic realm of internal hierarchy, on the one hand, and external anarchy, on the other. There was no distinct sphere of anarchical international relations in which power balancing among distinct polities could operate.

What then drove medieval political and geopolitical relations? I noted above that the building block of feudal society was the institution of lordship. Access to property was politically established, and every individual lord stood in a double-edged antagonistic position between a dependent but resisting peasantry and competing rival lords. Because of this, lordly 'strategies of reproduction' required systematic investment in the means of violence, rather than in the means of production, to control land and labour. This is what Brenner means by the phrase 'political accumulation'. This imperative produced a series of military technological innovations, while stalling innovations in economically productive technology. Since peasants produced mainly for subsistence purposes, that is, for their own consumption, their incentives were to diversify production rather than to specialise, and since lords extracted a surplus mainly for non-productive consumption (military equipment and conspicuous consumption), the long-term economic dynamic was relatively static.

However, the systematic built-up of military power was also the precondition for, as well as a consequence of, intensifying the exploitation of labour, the conquest of neighbouring regions, direct internecine warfare with overlords and co-vassals, the reclamation, cultivation and defence of new lands, and the successful conduct of marital policies and inheritance conflicts to acquire land. 'The acquisition of land translated directly into a geographical extension of state territory, and so feudal territoriality was always shifting, contracting and expanding according to the martial and marital fortunes of its noble class.' Not only was its geographical size a function of political accumulation, territoriality was vertically mediated and horizontally perforated by the various layers of sub-infeudation, so that one patch of land could have several political masters with differentiated claims to it.

Moreover, as territoriality stood on shifting grounds, so political space was not clearly delineated by frontiers but by border zones. Precisely because these zones were permanently contested, they also enjoyed special liberties and privileges of military command granted by the king and exercised by marcher lords who thus established semi-autonomous marcher lordships – strongholds that posed as much of a threat to the neighbouring feudal kingdom as to the kingly overlord himself. As the rights to war were not monopolised by the state, but oligopolistically enjoyed by the hierarchy of lords, so was peace a variegated affair, sponsored by differentiated actors in the form of the 'peace of the land', the 'peace or truce of God' or the 'peace of towns'.

To sum up, the political logic of noble reproduction, based on the class division between peasant-producers and noble non-producers, is at the core of the general character of the Middle Ages as a culture of war, a stateless society, and a mobile – fragmented, overlapping and shifting – territorial order. It also reveals a relatively static logic of economic development. Medieval geopolitics was locked in a more or less zero-sum game of political accumulation. Feudal geopolitics, then, can neither be reduced to a mere struggle for security among power maximising actors in a self-help environment (Fischer, 1992), nor to an expression of the ideational self-ascriptions of its key actors (Hall and Kratochwil, 1993). Rather, it expresses lordly competition over their relative share in the rights of domination through political and geopolitical accumulation. In this respect, invoking the term 'neo-medievalism' for understanding contemporary political territoriality is as semantically anachronistic, as it is misleading in explanatory terms.

The break-up of the Carolingian Empire and the making of a territorial pluriverse

So far, I have conceptualised medieval geopolitics and territoriality in general. However, the long-term institutional dynamic of medieval Western Europe followed a trajectory from an imperial formation (*c*.750–950), via the times of feudal anarchy (*c*.950–1150), to the reconsolidation of multiple feudal kingdoms (*c*.1150–1450), until feudalism's final demise in Western Europe in the fifteenth century. I have commented elsewhere on the Carolingian Empire (Teschke, 2003: ch. 3) and limit myself here to summarising some general results. When the opportunities for conquest of the Carolingian 'war-economy' (Reuter, 1985; 1995) dried up around AD 850, a profound crisis of inter-ruling class solidarity led to the successive disintegration of the imperial state. The 'Feudal Revolution' of the Year 1000 (Poly and Bournazel, 1991; Bisson, 1994) established a new mode of political domination and economic exploitation, spawning a series of closely interrelated novel phenomena. Socially, it changed the status of the direct producers from slavery and free peasantry to serfdom (Bonnassie, 1991). Politically, it ushered in a prolonged crisis of public governance resulting in the feudalisation of political power and the rise of the banal regime (Duby, 1974). Militarily, it gave rise to an internal differentiation within the nobility associated with the emergence of the knightly class. Geopolitically, it marked the point of departure for an extraordinary display of noble 'political accumulation', resulting in four expansionary outward movements driving the late Frankish lords over the borders of the Carolingian heartlands into hitherto unconquered regions (Bartlett 1993). In a span of 50 years, the post-Frankish knights asserted their land hunger by setting out to conquer the British Isles (Norman Conquest, 1066), Southern Italy (1061) and the eastern Mediterranean (First Crusade, 1096–1099), the Iberian peninsula (*Reconquista*, 1035), and large stretches of the Slavonic lands east of the Elbe–Saale line (*Deutsche Ostsiedlung*, 1110). Out of the millennial crucible of the 'feudal revolution', lordship-based political communities spread all over Europe with a lasting influence on the various regional processes of state-formation throughout late medieval and early modern times. These knight-led expansionary movements were not completed until the fifteenth century and established the institutional and geographical parameters for the international organisation of the European early-modern system of states.

What are the long-term consequences of this imperial decline, followed by this spectacular wave of conquests? The basic geopolitical configuration of Europe as a multi-actor system was a result of the class conflicts that destroyed the Carolingian Empire around the year 1000 CE. After the inclusion of the European periphery into the feudal world, the recentralisation of feudal authority by late medieval kings laid the territorial basis for the political pluriverse that was consolidated during the early-modern period as the European system of states. Furthermore, the break-up of the Frankish

Empire also conditioned regionally diverging long-term trajectories of European state-formation based on variations in the balance of class forces, especially in the two important cases of France and England. The end result, after the general crisis of the fourteenth century, was the development of two radically different state-society complexes. In the French case, class conflicts between the peasantry, the nobility and the king resulted in a transition from feudalism to absolutism, whereas class conflicts in England resulted in a transition from feudalism to capitalism. These diverging trajectories of state formation in England and France – the two archetypical cases of modern state building that are often (falsely) assimilated to one another – and their consequences for the European states-system, will now be examined. The outcome of these divergent long-term trajectories meant that the French absolutist state-society complex structured the 'Westphalian' system of dynastic states, whereas the English capitalist state-society complex challenged that order and gradually imposed a different logic of international relations on continental Europe during the nineteenth century. There was, therefore, not one system-wide and simultaneous 'medieval-to-modern' shift (Ruggie, 1986; 1993), but two shifts. These were yoked together in a long-term process of geographically combined and socially uneven development. I comment on the second shift in section 4.

Diverging feudal state formations in France and England and the crisis of the fourteenth century

Between the eleventh and fourteenth centuries, feudal state formation in France was driven by weak self-organisation of the ruling class, leading to peasant freedom and the gradual, protracted and imperfect building of a feudal monarchy. Precisely because the concentric expansion of the Capetian monarchy was a gradual, piecemeal and protracted process, the political organisation of the French kingdom never achieved the unitary character of its English counterpart. Most importantly, French 'mediatisation' ('the vassal of my vassal is not my vassal') meant that the authority of the king was far less recognised than in post-Conquest England. Due to this lack of ruling-class self-organisation, the regional French nobility competed with the king for the powers to tax and control the peasantry. These competing claims to final jurisdiction were eventually decisive for the improving status of the French peasantry (Brenner, 1985a, 1985b). The peasantry succeeded in the course of the twelfth and thirteenth centuries in shaking off serfdom – labour rents were commuted to money rents – and in establishing, by the early fourteenth century *de facto* – though not *de iure* – property rights over customary tenures, including the right to inherit. In this process, the king tended to side with the peasants (policy of peasant-protection), for their loss of serfdom was his gain in terms of a new income-base (no longer a rent-base, but a tax-base) and the simultaneous subjection of a noble rival.

In contrast, post-Conquest state formation in England was premised on strong organisation of the ruling class, leading to the imposition and strengthening of serfdom and the consolidation of a unitary, centrally organised feudal monarchy. Lords came to hold their estates 'of the king', in possession and hereditary in character, but not as private patrimonies. The king remained the supreme landowner of the entire territory. Just when Frankish Gaul disintegrated into countless independent banal lordships, England was unified *en bloc*. The 'King's Peace', predicated upon the power of the ban, minimised the continental practices of private feuding by providing recognised and legitimate institutions for the settling of disputes over questions of land, property and privileges among the members of the Anglo-Norman ruling class (Kaeuper, 1988).

During the fourteenth century, large parts of Europe, including France and England, entered into a deep and prolonged period of general crisis. The outcomes of the crisis exacerbated Franco-English divergences and led to two very different kinds of transformation in their respective state-society complexes.

French state-formation: from feudalism to absolutism – from feudal domination to dynastic sovereignty

I have argued that, prior to the onset of the general crisis, there was a gradual decline in the French lords' capacity for surplus extraction, caught between peasant resistance and royal support for petty peasant property. When the crisis struck the French countryside, the *seigneurial* reaction failed due to the persisting pattern of peasant resistance and kingly protection of peasant freehold. As an alternative, lords turned against each other to recover income and increasingly took up offices in the 'state' during and after the Hundred Years' War. Private property in the state's extractive apparatus in the form of venal offices, that is, offices of state sold to the nobility, provided new income opportunities for a de-feudalised nobility. The old sword-carrying nobility (*noblesse d'épée*) turned gradually into the new office nobility (*noblesse de robe*). The result was the consolidation of petty peasant property, now taxed by a centrally organised *noblesse de robe*. The absolutist state now revolved around the kingly court as the centre of intrigue, faction and inter-noble rivalries. Sixteenth- and seventeenth-century France saw the growing consolidation of the absolutist tax/office state (Brenner, 1985b), notwithstanding sporadic waves of noble resistance. The general crisis had accelerated the transformation of a feudal lord–peasant rent-regime into an absolutist king–peasant tax regime.

But can the new absolutist tax/office state lay claim to constitute a modern state, as much of the literature that sees Westphalia as the origin of the modern states-system assumes (Ruggie, 1993; Spruyt, 1994; Philpot, 2001)? The question is crucial, precisely because France is often singled out as the classical case of modern state formation, and precisely because France played, next to Sweden, the leading role in determining the content of the

Peace Treaty of Westphalia and the post-1648 general nature of the Westphalian system of states.

We have seen that the centralisation of sovereignty in the absolutist tax/office state did not entail a separation of public and private realms, of politics and economics, since sovereignty was henceforth personalised by the king, regarding the realm as his patrimonial property. In this context, sovereignty meant proprietary kingship (Rowen, 1980; Symcox, 1974) or 'generalised personal domination' (Gerstenberger, 1990). The transformation of France from a feudal into an absolutist monarchy failed to establish modern sovereignty. While the incorporation of the aristocracy as office-holders into the patrimonial state destroyed its feudal autonomy, office-holding re-created new aristocratic privileges *within* the state apparatus. Absolutism never implied unlimited royal power, but institutionalised a new and unstable *modus vivendi* between king and aristocracy. Recent historical research has shown convincingly that office venality, patronage and clientelism blocked the establishment of a modern bureaucracy in Weber's sense (Beik, 1985; Mettam, 1988; Hoffman, 1994; Parker, 1996; Asch and Duchhardt, 1996). Taxation remained non-uniform. Noble exemption from taxation was associated with a failure to establish permanent representative assemblies. Diverse law codes operated in various regions and for differentiated status groups. No modern system of public finance was set up. The means of violence were not monopolised by the state, but personalised by the king, yet re-alienated to patrimonial officers through the sale of army posts. Mercenarism further undermined royal claims to the monopoly of violence. Mercantilism was precisely the public economic policy of a pre-capitalist state. In short, all the institutional trappings of the modern state were absent in early modern France. The absolutist state was neither, modern, nor efficient, nor rationalised.

But did the absolutist state act as a modernising and rationalising force that balanced the contradictory class-interests of a 'retrograde' nobility with the 'progressive' projects of a bourgeoisie, creating inadvertently the conditions for the rise of capitalism? The absolutist tax/office state failed to establish the conditions for self-sustaining capitalist development and perpetuated the logic of political and geopolitical accumulation, due to the persistence of pre-capitalist agrarian property relations. Punitive peasant taxation in the form of a centralised rent combined with diversified peasant production for subsistence purposes, rather than specialisation on markets, and the subdivision of plots. The proceeds of taxation, in turn, were primarily pumped back into the apparatus of coercion and domination and royal conspicuous consumption, building up the 'permanent war-state'.

State-formation during this period was thus not, as the current neo-Weberian orthodoxy in historical sociology reiterates in various versions (Skocpol, 1979; Mann, 1986, 1988; Tilly, 1985, 1992; Bonney, 1995; Reinhard, 1996), the result of intensified geopolitical competition. In this perspective, military rivalry was the decisive factor in a system-wide chain of causation that led to permanent warfare, cost increases, intensified resource extraction, new modes of taxation and fiscality, military-technological inventions, state monopolisation of the means of violence, and state centralisation and rationalisation. Rather, early modern state-building must be seen as a desperate and ultimately self-destructive attempt by pre-capitalist ruling classes to concentrate their means of exploitation and coercion, to intensify the rates of exploitation, and to increase their relative international share over territory in the context of mostly stagnant productivity rates, and sometimes in the context of a contracting agrarian economy.[4]

When crisis struck again in the early seventeenth century, intensified class conflict over the distribution of income led to peasant revolts, noble unrest and royal repression. This crisis of reproduction may also explain the new system-wide attempts of geopolitical accumulation in the form of the Wars of Religion and the Thirty Years' War, in which France played, of course, a leading role. Domestically, absolutism meant the hypertrophic growth of a parasitic and venal officer class that reproduced itself by owning a share of the means of coercion (offices), trying to extract a surplus from a non-self-sustaining economy. Internationally, it meant the intensification of war understood as geopolitical accumulation, which is, inter-ruling class conflict. Both processes overloaded the system until it finally crashed in a cataclysmic denouement. In the long run, the pre-capitalist French state/society complex, caught between excessive rates of taxation and spiralling military expenditures, underwent a series of fiscal crises during the course of the eighteenth century, until it collapsed during the French Revolution. *Pace* Charles Tilly, but *pre-capitalist states made war, though war unmade states*. In developmental terms, absolutism was not a society in transition, but a dead end. 1789 did not witness the rise of a bourgeois middle class that had slowly matured in the womb of the absolutist state, but was largely carried out by dissatisfied state officials, who were not capitalists and who did not establish capitalism (Comninel, 1987; Doyle, 1999).

England: from feudalism to capitalism – from dynastic to abstract sovereignty

Economic and political development followed a radically different path in England. When the fourteenth-century crisis struck England, peaking in the Black Death (1348), lords tried to recuperate falling income by trying to increase rents despite a fall in the population. However, the *seigneurial* reaction failed due to a long period of peasant resistance that culminated in the rebellion of 1381 (Hilton 1988). The English peasantry removed many of the feudal controls and gained full freedom. However, rather than gaining property rights to their plots (freeholds) and thus security of tenure, as in France, the English peasantry, during the sixteenth and seventeenth centuries, was gradually evicted from its customary lands by landlords. A key mechanism in this process of 'primitive accumulation' was the lords' ability to charge variable and high entry fines on peasant copyholds. Those peasants that were unable to meet these fines lost access to lands, while landlords began to charge market-rents for these plots. Where peasants tried to defend their traditional rights (especially in relation to the common fields), successive enclosure movements undermined peasant subsistence farming. Gradually, landlords drove peasants from their lands, consolidated and enclosed 'their' holdings, and leased them out to large capitalist tenants, who engaged in commercial farming by employing wage-labour (Brenner, 1985a, 1985b). In this process, English peasants were not protected by the monarchy and the French pattern of a peasant/king alliance failed to take hold, derailing the establishment of absolutism in the form of the tax/office state. The result of this process was the destruction of the old lordly powers of political surplus extraction, and the simultaneous subjection of both peasants and landlords to the economic imperatives of the market. The market no longer represented an opportunity, where surplus produce could be marketed, but an economic compulsion in which capitalists and wage-labour had to reproduce themselves (Wood, 2002).

As Robert Brenner argues, the establishment of agrarian capitalism was the unintended outcome of these class conflicts between producers and non-producers over property rights in a specific region of Europe. It was not the result of the gradual and Europe-wide commercialisation and monetarisation of economic life, driven by trade and operated by a nascent bourgeoisie (Brenner 1977, 1989). For present purposes, I define capitalism as a mode of economic production based on a set of property relations in which direct producers are separated from their means of subsistence and forced not simply to produce for the market, but to reproduce themselves in the market. Producers are compelled to sell their labour power to owners of the means of production to make a living. Workers are paid a wage and property owners get to keep any profits generated by the production and sale of goods and services. This type of market represents a compulsion to which both workers and capitalists (property owners) are subjected. This compulsion to survive under the competitive laws of the market produces a series of interlocked phenomena. As a rule, market-dependence entails inter-capitalist competition, engendering systematic re-investment in the means of production (rather than in the means of violence), driving technological innovation, raising productivity and accounting for a dynamic process of economic growth. Out-pricing, not out-gunning, economic, not political, accumulation denotes the dominant mode of capitalist reproduction.

In early-modern England, market success came to depend on economic competitiveness. Cost cutting and innovation became the new mechanisms to increase productivity in commercial farming. Systematic re-investment in the means of production engendered agricultural improvements, the breaking of Malthusian cycles in the countryside, and the beginning of self-sustaining economic development in the form of the 'Agricultural Revolution' (Kerridge, 1967; Beckett, 1990). Dramatic productivity increases in agriculture combined with the development of industry, leading to sustained economic growth, the creation of a home market, and eventually to the Industrial Revolution. While population growth and urbanisation kept apace (Wrigley, 1985), the general crisis of the seventeenth century had relatively little effect on England.

Politically, the transformation of a militarised and de-centralised lordly class into a de-militarised class of capitalist landlords provided the 'social base for the new constitutional monarchy'. A capitalist aristocracy, rather than a commercial bourgeoisie, came to dominate Parliament and determined the affairs of the state (Brenner, 1993). The self-organisation of the entrepreneurial landed aristocracy in Parliament meant that 'sovereignty came to be centralised and pooled in a state that was no longer primarily and directly involved in processes of political accumulation', notwithstanding the fact that many parliamentary acts of enclosure were passed in the eighteenth century. After the anti-absolutist revolutions of the seventeenth century, in which agrarian private property owners came to consolidate their political power over and against the monarchy, sovereignty took on the formula 'King-in-Parliament'. In a series of royal concessions – the 1689 Bill of Rights, the 1694 Triennial Act, and the 1701 Act of Settlement – the 'committee of landlords' that made up Parliament secured essential control over taxation, the army, jurisdiction, foreign policy and the right of self-convocation (Brewer, 1989). This also guaranteed the security of the new private property regime and binding contract. Furthermore, the 'financial revolution' combined a new system of taxation – national, uniform and effective – with a modern system of public credit (National Debt 1693, Bank of England 1694) superior in raising funds (Dickson, 1967; van der Pijl, 1998: 71), while office venality and corruption gave way gradually to a rationalised bureaucracy. Capitalism rose in conjunction with the first modern state – but this was capitalism in one country only.

What are the implications of this for modern sovereignty? The transition from feudalism to capitalism engenders a shift from a regime of political accumulation based on a feudal rent-regime, to a regime of economic accumulation, based on a capitalist wage-regime. Feudalism involves the de-centralisation and personalisation of political power by lords, creating the parcellised sovereignty of the medieval 'state', and absolutism involves the centralisation and persisting personalisation of political power by dynasties. By contrast to both, capitalism makes possible the centralisation and de-personalisation of political power in the form of the modern state. In the capitalist mode of production, the power of the ruling class resides in private property in, and control over, the means of production, and the state is no longer required to interfere directly in processes of production and appropriation. Its central function can be confined to the internal maintenance and external defence of a private property regime. This involves the legal enforcement of what are now civil contracts among politically (though not economically) equal and free citizens, subject to civil law. This, in turn, is consistent with a public monopoly in the means of violence, while enabling the build-up of an 'impartial' public bureaucracy. Political power and, especially, the monopoly of the means of violence, can now to be pooled in a public state set over and above the economy. While these possibilities do not, of course, exhaustively define the role of the modern state, the link between capitalist property relations, operating in a non-coercive economic sphere, and what Marx called the 'purely political' state is a strong one, especially in the English case. The separation between the economic and the political is built into this form of capitalism (Wood, 1995; Rosenberg, 1994; Bromley, 1999). In England, class conflict over property relations generated a dynamic capitalist economy and a new form of political authority, combining as a new state-society complex that was radically distinct compared to its European (and especially French) neighbours.

The Westphalian states-system: the persistence of dynastic territoriality

The account presented above offers a direct challenge to the conventional view of the modernity of the Peace Treaties of Westphalia.[5] My contention is that the Westphalian system remained essentially pre-modern in character, based on political communities and forms of territoriality that were still rooted in pre-capitalist property relations (Teschke, 2002). However, in the seventeenth and eighteenth centuries very different types of state coexisted in the European states-system. France, Austria, Spain, Sweden, Russia, Denmark–Norway, Brandenburg–Prussia and the Papal States were absolutist states. The Holy Roman Empire maintained its status as a confederal elective monarchy until 1806. The Dutch General Estates established an independent oligarchic merchant republic. Poland was a 'crowned aristocratic republic' and Switzerland a free confederation of cantons. The Italian merchant republics struggled against their transformation into monarchies. England turned into a parliamentary and constitutional monarchy presiding over the first capitalist economy. Significantly, as Justin Rosenberg (1994) pointed out, England was the one major European power not represented at the Westphalia settlement. Yet, in spite of the diversity of these polities, the Westphalian system came to be dominated by the numerical and power-political preponderance of dynastic-absolutist states. But dynastic sovereignty, as we established in the French case, had little in common with modern sovereignty. In dynastic states, sovereignty was personalised in the monarch who regarded and treated the state as the private patrimonial property of the reigning dynasty.

Proprietary kingship meant that public policy and, *a fortiori*, foreign policy were not conducted in the name of the interest of state or the national interest, but in the name of dynastic interests. *Raison d'état* meant *raison de roi*. It was precisely in diplomatic and foreign affairs where monarchs were most eager to impose their 'personal rules' in order to negotiate their private titles to sovereignty with fellow monarchs. This reflected the fact that the strategies for expanded economic reproduction of the ruling classes, organised in the absolutist-patrimonial state, remained tied to the logic of political and geo-political accumulation predicated upon investment in the means of appropriation.

Analytically, these strategies can be divided into (1) the arbitrary and often punitive taxation of the peasantry by the king, mediated by (2) the sale of offices to a landless *noblesse de robe*, which was in competition with a defeudalised *noblesse d'épée*. These were matched by (3) geopolitical accumulation through war and dynastic marriage policies, and (4) politically maintained and enforced trade organised through royal sales of monopoly trading charters to privileged merchants. Consequently, the two main contemporary war issues, as has been empirically catalogued by Holsti (1991), were struggles over dynastic territorial proprietary claims and over commercial monopolies and exclusive trading routes.

But precisely because absolutist states remained trapped in the logic of geopolitical accumulation, the tendency towards imperial-territorial expansion remained endemic in international relations. Parity based on sovereign equality was time and again betrayed by imperial designs expressed in the nomenclature of the diverse heads of state. A scale of ranks placed sovereigns on a descending ladder. The Holy Roman Emperor was given pride of first place, followed by the 'Most Christian King', the king of France (Kaiser, 1990). Hereditary monarchs were, as a rule, placed above elective ones and republics ranked lower than monarchies, followed by non-royal aristocrats and free cities. The standing of England was seriously weakened as a result of the various Commonwealth governments, and serious conflict over precedence occurred wherever there was a mismatch between *de facto* importance and title of state as in the Dutch and Venetian cases (Anderson, 1993; Duchhardt, 1997). Peter the Great's adoption of the imperial title in 1721 aroused not only considerable resentment in Vienna, which would not tolerate a second imperial title in Europe, but also in Britain, which recognised the title only in 1742, and in France, which followed suit as late as 1772. Towards the end of the seventeenth century, many German actors sought to gain a royal title on realising that ducal status or *Kurfürsten* (Elector) status tended to exclude them from international politics.

Furthermore, the nexus between centralised public power and patrimonial property meant that the social relations of international intercourse were largely identical with the 'private' family affairs of reigning monarchs. Since sovereignty was transmitted by birth, royal sex, as Marx argued, was directly political. 'The highest constitutional act of the king is therefore his sexual activity, for through this he makes a king and perpetuates his body' (Marx, 1975: 40). The implication was that all the rather biologically determined play of dynastic genealogy and family reproduction – like problems of succession, marriage, inheritance, childlessness – determined the very nature of early modern geopolitics.

Given the persisting personalisation of sovereignty, two conflicting practices dominated early modern patterns of cooperation and conflict. First, proprietary kingship induced systematic policies of 'dynastic inter-marriage' as a political instrument for the aggrandisement of territory as well as for securing and enhancing wealth (Anderson, 1974: 39). Inter-dynastic marriages not only characterised contemporary 'international' relations, they constituted the single most cost-effective and rapid strategy of expanded personal reproduction of absolutist rulers. Consequently, this was a geopolitical order in which 'states' could marry 'states'. Second and inversely, the resulting European-wide web of transregional dynastic family relations and alliances simultaneously contained the seeds of disorder, partition and destabilisation. 'Private' inter-family and intra-family disputes, physical accidents, and pathological calamities were immediately translated into 'public' international conflicts (Kunisch, 1979). Claims to genealogical-hereditary precedence were usually resolved by war. Next to mercantilist trade wars, 'wars of succession' and, more broadly, wars over hereditary pretensions, became the dominant forms of international conflict (Luard, 1993: 149–73). The Wars of the Spanish Succession (1702–1713/1714), the Polish Succession (1733–1738), the Austrian Succession (1740–1748) and the Bavarian Succession (1778–79) patterned early modern international conflict. In each case, precisely because dynastic family disputes, mediated by the web of dynastic family relations, inevitably affected almost all European states, every succession crisis turned immediately into a general European-wide conflict.

What, then, of the balance of power? Conventional IR theories assume that power-balancing – whether as an automatic self-regulatory mechanism (Waltz, 1979) or as a conscious inter-actor strategy designed to regulate geopolitics (Luard, 1993; Gulick, 1967) – stabilises international relations through alliance formation even in systems characterised by a very uneven distribution of power among its constitutive actors. But the history of early-modern geopolitics does not only show the near-permanent frequency of war, it also shows a dramatic decline in the number of polities. Given the imperial drive of pre-capitalist states, power-balancing was not a stabilising mechanism that guaranteed the independence and survival of smaller states, but a predatory foreign policy technique operated by the great dynasties to eliminate smaller polities and to maximise territory and wealth. This technique demanded a consensus among the leading powers – 'convenance' (Duchhardt, 1976) – and invited bandwagoning rather than balancing (Schroeder, 1994). Dynastic power balancing meant 'equality in aggrandisement' (Wight, 1966: 156), leading to a system of eliminatory and compensatory equilibrium among the bigger powers.

The dynastic structure of inter-state relations had consequently direct implications for contemporary territoriality. The politics of inter-dynastic family relations led to supra-regional territorial constructions – especially 'dynastic unions' – which defined the logic of territorial (dis-)order and defied the logic of territorial contiguity and stability. Marital policies and inheritance practices, mediated by violent conflict, led to frequent territorial re-distributions among European princes. Territorial unity meant nothing but the unity of the ruling House, personified in its dynastic head. But the unity of the House was not coterminous with the geographical contiguity of its lands. Although these territories were nominally 'bounded' as they belonged to but one sovereign, they constituted geographical conglomerates, governed by diverse law codes and tax-regimes, criss-crossing the dynastic map of Europe. Early-modern Europe was a states system of 'composite monarchies' (Elliott, 1992). At the same time, the ever-changing territorial size of early modern 'states' intensified the problem of internal administrative cohesion. Austria, Spain, Sweden, Russia or Prussia exemplified the scattered and disjointed mosaic character of early-modern territoriality, combining multiethnic provinces with different law traditions, which had little in common except their rulers.

But while the production of contemporary political space remained a function of absolutist geopolitics – expanding and contracting in line with the martial and marital fortunes of dynasts – the nobility's loss of independent powers of exploitation and its absorption into the patrimonial state had also overcome the parcellised sovereignty and territoriality of feudalism. The internal pacification of the nobility, its incorporation into the patrimonial state apparatus, and the re-definition of sovereignty as proprietary kingship differentiated the internal as a non-military relation from the external. The internal and external aspects of territoriality became increasingly demarcated by boundaries. While absolutist territoriality cannot be likened to the abstract and bounded nature of what we conceive as modern space, it was no longer perforated and overlapping. While the end of inter-noble feuds that expressed the intra-ruling class competitions over territory indicated the domestication of the aristocracy, it also intensified the consolidation of multiple territories headed by dynasts. Henceforth, geopolitical accumulation was primarily defined as a game among central rulers played out in a territorial pluriverse.

In sum, 1648 entailed the end of feudal geopolitics and of the imperial and papal claims to political and moral supremacy. But it did not inaugurate the era of the modern states-system. Westphalia codified the geopolitical relations of dynastic-patrimonial sovereignty. While the Westphalian system was anarchic (though mediated by a hierarchy of princely ranks), this anarchy did not revolve around the security interests of states but around the competitive proprietary interests of kings. Absolutist geopolitical accumulation consolidated Europe as a multi-state system; yet, these plural territories were not organised as abstract, i.e. modern, forms of sovereignty.

Towards a 'post-Westphalian' Europe

How, then, was dynastic, i.e. proprietary and fluctuating, territoriality transformed into what we conceive as 'modern', i.e. de-personalised, homogeneous and fixed, territoriality? In my view, the answer is that this transformation is directly linked to the formation of capitalism and the growth of the modern state in England. In the period between the end of the Glorious Revolution and the accession in 1714 of the first Hanoverian king, George I, the pattern of British foreign policy shifted as a result of the consolidation of a capitalist social property regime, which in turn revolutionised the institutional set-up of the British state (Brenner, 1993; Wood, 1991; Parker, 1996). But precisely because the rise of capitalism and modern sovereignty was not a simultaneous and Europe-wide phenomenon, but occurred first only in England, we cannot conceive of the transition from pre-modern geopolitics to modern international relations as a single system-wide rupture – a 'geopolitical discontinuity' (Rosenberg, 1994) – but have to retrace how the new British state-society complex played a pivotal role in reshaping the European system of states in a long-term process of 'geopolitically combined and socially uneven development'.[6] Furthermore, since the British state did not operate in a geopolitical vacuum, wider international pressures massively inflected its own development. Finally, since capitalism emerged in an international environment that was already territorially prefigured as a political pluriverse, we cannot deduce the states-system (plural territories) from capitalism, but have to understand how the transposition of capitalism to the Continent changed the nature of sovereignty without destroying preexisting multiple territories. However, international relations from 1688 to the First World War and beyond were about the geopolitically mediated and contested negotiation of the modernisation pressures that emanated from capitalist Britain, which put its European neighbours at a *comparative coercive and economic disadvantage* (Teschke, 2003: ch. 8). International relations during this long period of transformation were thus not modern, but 'modernising'.

Post-1688 British foreign policy: blue-water policy and active balancing

If capitalism is not predicated on domestic political accumulation for economic reproduction, then we should also expect to see a decline of external geopolitical accumulation that defined the war-driven conduct during the feudal and absolutist ages. At the end of the seventeenth century, British sovereignty no longer lay with the king, but with Parliament in the context of a constitutional monarchy. The historical presupposition of Britain's new attitude towards Europe was the de-coupling of foreign policy from dynastic interests brought about by Parliament's right – established in the Act of Settlement of 1701 – to co-articulate British foreign policy (Black, 1991).

Great Britain's (since the 1707 Act of Union between England and Scotland) role, strategy and objectives in European politics changed decisively as a result of its new domestic arrangements (McKay and Scott, 1983: 45–47). Parliament adopted a unique 'dual foreign policy', based on the blue-water policy in overseas and on power balancing in the continental theatre. 'For almost three centuries (from about 1650 to 1920) Great Britain had available to it a highly distinctive system of national security' (Baugh, 1988: 33). Blue-water policy meant opposing European powers by technologically and numerically superior naval forces, withdrawing from continental territorial ambitions, and establishing oceanic commercial hegemony overseas. The old dynastic tie between the Hanoverians and their German stemlands was seen as a disturbing legacy by Parliament. It stood in direct contradiction to Britain's overall strategic interests – its 'national interest' (Brewer, 1989: 174; Baugh, 1988: 34, 47). In addition, post-1688 Britain adopted an active policy of balancing the powers of the European sub-system (Duchhardt, 1989; van der Pijl, 1996: 61–2, 1998: 86). After the Treaty of Utrecht in 1713, British foreign policy no longer operated on the principle of 'natural allies' – what was known as the 'Old System' which allied England, the Dutch Republic and Austria against France – but on the fluid principle of rapidly changing coalitions which earned it, on the Continent, the epithet 'Perfidious Albion'. This nickname was as much due to a failure by dynasts to grasp the nature of changing majorities in a parliamentary system, as it was due to a failure to understand the logic of a post-dynastic foreign policy of active balancing in the context of an overwhelmingly dynastic states-system.

This meant that during the eighteenth century, a very specific balancing-regime came into operation in Europe. While Old Regime states continued their policies of imperial expansion driven by geopolitical accumulation, parliamentary Britain sought to manage the balance of the European sub-system by indirect interventions in the form of subsidies and pensions to smaller powers, while also operating a balance of threat to counter any imperial-hegemonic ambition. The objective was to prevent the rise or contain the imperial aspirations of any European hegemon, notably France, by keeping it militarily occupied on the Continent while defeating her overseas by means of superior naval forces. This demanded a policy of divide and rule. In other words, Britain became the balancer of the balance based on a productive capitalist economy that financed naval supremacy. Britain was not the accidental insular exception of dynastic rivalry, but the conscious regulator of a system of European politics from which she was socio-economically, but not geographically, set apart. This also explains why the balance of power was not the flip side of capitalism – both systems being automatically self-regulated by invisible hands. It was activated and manipulated in a mixed-actor international system by a highly visible hand: Britain's hands holding the scales.

Balancing, passive revolutions, and the transformation of Old Regime Europe

In Europe at any rate, the fundamental break with the old territorially accumulative logic of international relations came about because of the rise of capitalism in England. The onset of agrarian capitalism in sixteenth-century England, the conversion of dynastic into parliamentary sovereignty in the late seventeenth century, and the adoption of a new foreign policy, resulted in the gradual de-territorialisation of British interests on the Continent. At the same time, Britain began to manipulate the old inter-dynastic rivalries by a new conception of active balancing.

Yet, developmentally, the eighteenth-century world was not yet a capitalist system. As long as the majority of the dominant European powers were non-capitalist dynastic states, Britain remained engulfed in a hostile world of politically accumulating states. This explains why Britain's struggle overseas with Spain and France retained a military-mercantilist character. It also explains why Britain was, willy-nilly, centrally involved in all major eighteenth-century conflicts, from the War of the Spanish Succession (1702–1713) to the American War of Independence (1775–1783). Likewise, geopolitical pressure also reacted back on and massively inflected post-1688 British state formation in that a smooth transition to a minimalist liberal state was not possible (Brewer, 1989). There never was a pristine culture of capitalism. The key difference with contemporary continental states, however, was that the eighteenth-century British build-up of a 'military-fiscal' state could be sustained based on a productive capitalist economy and its increasingly rationalised state apparatus that operated a superior and relatively conflict-free system of taxation and public finance. In contrast, the financing of the permanent war state on the continent led to recurrent and deep fiscal, social and political crises (and finally collapse) – most notably in France (for figures on taxation and military expenses see Bonney, 1995, 1999).

In terms of the operation of the absolutist inter-dynastic system, Britain was the power that consciously balanced the respective imperial pretensions of largely pre-capitalist states. Powered by its expanding capitalist economy that allowed high public revenues and due to its new dual foreign policy – commercial interests overseas and security interests in Europe – Britain established itself during the eighteenth century as the world's major power. But while active balancing was initially a defensive measure, designed to safeguard the power of Parliament, the new constitutional settlement, and the Protestant Succession against the absolutist Catholic powers, the policy of playing states off against each other had increasingly the effect of undermining the military and financial viability of the Old Regimes. British superiority revealed their domestic mismatch between spiralling military costs and over-taxation in the context of relatively stagnant pre-capitalist economies. In this sense, 'power balancing had the unintended side effect of forcing continental states to respond to and finally adjust to the superior British socio-political model, especially under the impact of the Industrial Revolution'. In this process, balancing became the major conduit for distributing pressure on continental states that had, in the long run, a transformative effect on the political and economic organisation in 'backward' state-society complexes. In the case of conflict between France and Britain, the result was a militarily defeated and bankrupt state, which faced dramatic class conflicts at home, eventually forcing a transformation of property relations. While thriving on its expanding capitalist economy, Britain continued to play off pre-capitalist actors against each other, until they were financially and economically exhausted. The most dramatic result of this was the French Revolution of 1789, the Napoleonic experience, and the modernisation pressures this created for large parts of Europe, notably Prussia. Across Europe further wars and revolutions went hand-in-hand with agrarian reform, peasant liberation, and transformations in the basic character of the state, turning dynastic into modern sovereignty. Capitalism was externally induced. These processes are conventionally termed 'revolutions from above'. Antonio Gramsci theorised them as 'passive revolutions', in which state classes transform their political and economic structures either to pre-empt domestic social unrest or to remain internationally competitive, both militarily and economically (Gramsci, 1971: 114–116; van der Pijl, 1998: 82, 105). Only after the series of European revolutions during the late eighteenth and nineteenth centuries and the 'freeing' of markets in favour of a world market, did the new logic of British-sponsored free trade among capitalist states impose a non-territorial logic of international surplus appropriation, based on economic contracts between private citizens.

The expansion of capitalism and the retrenchment of territoriality

As I have argued above, the political organisation of the modern world in the form of a territorially divided system of states is not a function of capitalism. Rather, capitalism emerged in a system of dynastic polities that had consolidated their territories and overcome feudal fragmentation during the absolutist period. However, once agrarian capitalist property relations were institutionalised and consolidated in the British state towards the end of the seventeenth century, a new form of economic and political order emerged and began to reshape the older inter-dynastic order based on logics of political and geopolitical accumulation. 'The making of capitalist (modern) sovereignty, originally in one country, was to reshape Europe and, then, the world.' However, rather than obliterating territoriality, the expansion of capitalism from Britain to the non-British world 'provoked reactions by state-classes that entrenched state-territoriality in their attempts to mediate British pressures'. How did this come about?

Any reconstruction of capitalist expansion must not only register its chronological unevenness, but also start from the premise that this course was geopolitically mediated, i.e. refracted through the existence of societies territorially organised in states. Capitalism did not cause the states-system, but had to 'work itself through' multiple, pre-established sovereignties. The expansion of capitalism was not an 'economic' process in which the transnationalising forces of the market or civil society surreptitiously penetrated pre-capitalist states, driven by the logic of cheap commodities that eventually perfected a universal world market. It was a political and, *a fortiori*, geopolitical process in which pre-capitalist state classes had to design counterstrategies of reproduction to defend their position in an international environment that put them at a 'comparative economic and coercive disadvantage'. These strategies were not uniform; they ranged from the intensification of domestic relations of exploitation and the build-up of an increasingly repressive state apparatus for military and fiscal mobilisation, via 'enlightened' absolutism, policies of neo-mercantilism and imperialism, to the adoption of liberal economic policies. But in one way or another, on pain of extinction, pre-capitalist states had to accommodate, assimilate, or adjust – or invent radical counterstrategies, most notably socialism. But more often than not, these state strategies of adjustment entrenched territoriality by hardening the grip of the state on 'its' territory in efforts to mobilise 'its' economy and society.

Kees van der Pijl conceives of this process as a three-century cycle in which the Anglo-American 'Lockean heartland' is repeatedly challenged by a series of 'Hobbesian contender states' (van der Pijl, 1998: 64–97). Contender states are characterised by the active lead-role of state-classes that assume many of the functions exercised in the Lockean heartland by civil society. Here, state-led projects of centralised and rationalised public planning mobilise society 'hot-house fashion' to catch-up with and challenge the hegemony of the Lockean heartland. Schematically speaking, this cycle opposed eighteenth-century absolutist France and nineteenth-century Napoleonic France and the German Empire against Britain, early twentieth-century Germany and Japan against Britain, the US and France, and the Soviet Union and China against the US-led Lockean West in the second half of the twentieth century. These variations in state responses express the explosive confluence of the different timing of competitive exposure to Britain and other advanced capitalist states and pre-existing domestic class constellations that ruled out certain state strategies while ruling in others. While the initial impetus towards state modernisation and capitalist transformation was geopolitical, state responses to this pressure were refracted through respective class relations in national contexts, including class resistance. In this sense, the world 'alignment of the provinces' generated nothing but national *Sonderwege* (special paths). If Britain showed its neighbours the image of their future, it did so in a highly distorted way. Conversely, Britain never developed a pristine culture of capitalism, since she was from the first dragged into an international environment that inflected her domestic politics and long-term development. The distortions were mutual.

The transfer of capitalism to the Continent and to the rest of the world was riddled with social conflicts, civil and international wars, social revolutions and counter-revolutions. But its essential mechanism was its 'geopolitically combined and socially uneven development'. This concept allows us to avoid repeating the neo-Weberian literature's mistake of externalising military rivalry to a separate and reified level of determination, while at the same time avoiding economic reductionism. Post-1688 international relations were not a continuation of the rise and fall of great powers in an otherwise unchanging structure of anarchy, but expressed the unfolding of this gigantic human drama. It was a long and bloody transformation – a transitional period – in which the processes of capitalist expansion, regime transformation and integration into the 'West' were generalised – schematically speaking – from 1688 to the First World War in Europe, from the First World War via the Second World War and the period of de-colonisation for the rest of the non-socialist world, and from 1917/1945 to 1989 for the socialist world. Thereafter, a fully integrated world economy may be said to have come into existence.

The functioning of a capitalist world market is predicated, at a minimum, on the existence of states that maintain a rule of law, that is, that guarantee contracts and rights, especially pertaining to property, between 'private' firms, as well as the legal security of international transactions so as to maintain open national economies. The key principle of contemporary international relations is no longer the war-assisted accumulation of territories but the political management of an increasingly worldwide capitalist economy and the regulation of an open international economy by the leading capitalist states. A 'private' universalising world market and a transnational civil society can coexist with a 'public' territorially-based system of states. Inter-capitalist relations can assume a pacified form – a zone of peace. The logic of political and geopolitical accumulation, in the form that was systematically built into pre-capitalist dynastic states, was replaced by a world in which, in principle, contracts are concluded across borders between 'private' economic actors without directly infringing political sovereignty.

Conclusion: The indeterminacy of relations between capitalism and territoriality

This chapter has argued that we need a much wider historical perspective to theorise the metamorphoses of European territoriality. This allows us to problematise the general assumption in the globalisation-European integration discourse of a simple conceptual distinction – corresponding to a chronological periodisation – between a modern territorial states-system and a post-modern de-territorialising order. Starting from the critique of the fallacy of fixed geopolitics rooted in the alleged immovability of territoriality as the foundation for timeless relations between states, the chapter demonstrates the changing nature of political territoriality. The history of European territoriality can be broadly conceived as a sequence from feudal personalised and de-centralised, via absolutist personalised and centralised, to modern de-personalised and centralised politico-spatial organisation. These forms of political territoriality are rooted in different social property relations and their shifts can best be understood on the basis of class conflicts. The chapter also shows that the Westphalian state – properly conceived in historical terms rather than as a stylised IR cypher – does not correspond to the Weberian state, but to the period of absolutism in which territoriality was shifting as a result of dynastic strategies of geopolitical accumulation. But the modern sovereign state, pioneered by Britain, always had a much more flexible relation to transnational flows of capitalism than the defenders of the Weberian model would allow. Capitalism's *differentia specifica* is indeed its capacity to extract surplus abroad without directly infringing political sovereignty, since property rights constitute a private and transnational sphere formally separated from political power.

But rather than ending the chapter by re-stating that a capitalist world-market and the states-system are two sides of the same coin, I want to conclude by suggesting that the relation between capitalism and territoriality is theoretically indeterminate. Capitalism emerged in a states-system already territorially prefigured as a pluriverse – a legacy of European history. But if multiple territories preceded capitalism, then there is no theoretical warrant that the latter will necessarily continue to reproduce the former. While it is true to say that capitalism and a territorially fragmented states-system can be compatible, since transnational flows are authorised by states and do not necessarily undermine state sovereignty, it is less obvious that states will not try to overcome multiple territoriality if they *can* do so (although they may not *need* to). Even a cursory reflection on the history of capitalist international relations demonstrates a wide spectrum of different constellations between territoriality and capitalist states – from the establishment of the liberal trade system of the *Pax Britannica* and the 'New Imperialism' with its oscillation between 'formal' and 'informal empire' preceding the First World War, via the subsequent territorially expansive and economically autarchic *Lebensraum* conceptions of German *Geopolitik*, to the US-sponsored (but multilateral) post-war liberal world order, the EU project and maybe even the intimations of a new US-empire, the historical record manifests the immense co-variation in the nexus between capitalist states and their forms of territoriality. To negate these historical fluctuations as aberrations from a 'normal' correlation between capitalism and the classical states-system means reifying a structuralist view of an essentially invariant capitalist states-system. What this spectrum of variations points to is that capitalist states have different 'strategies of territorialisation' at their disposal, ranging from full territorial independence granted to subaltern states, via semi-hegemonic projects like the EU, to full territorial control as in 'formal Empire' and '*Lebensraum*'. The best way to understand these strategies of territorialisation, then, is to relate them to the specific forms of state – and class agency within specific conjunctures of capitalism – its periods of growth, crisis and downturn. It is with a view to this structural indeterminacy in the relation between capitalism and territoriality that the precise nature of the European integration process needs to be explained.

Notes

1 I gratefully acknowledge the helpful editorial comments by Hans Vollaard and Michael Burgess and the very perceptive oral comments by my discussant, Anton Hemerijck, given at the Conference on 'Territoriality in the European Union' at the University of Leiden, Netherlands, 25–6 September, 2003.
2 See, for example, Caporaso (1996: 34, 45): 'The Westphalian state is the Weberian ideal in which monopolies of legitimate violence, rational bureaucracies and centralized policy-making authority correspond to territorially exclusive political orders. (. . .) the Westphalian system refers to the organization of the world into territorially exclusive, sovereign nation-states, each with an internal monopoly of legitimate violence. (. . .) The post-modern state (. . .) is abstract, disjointed, increasingly fragmented, not based on stable and coherent coalitions of issues and constituencies, and lacking in a clear public space.'
3 For a recent re-statement of the anachronistic fallacy that resides in applying the moden term 'state' to the Middle Ages see Davies 2003.
4 I have discussed the role of cities and trade in this process in my critique of Hendrik Spruyt and Fernand Braudel, see Teschke (2003: 32–9, 111, 137ff.). More research needs to be done to fully incorporate the important dimension of state-church relations into the overall narrative.
5 While Krasner doubts the modernity of Westphalia, he provides no alternative theorization of different forms of sovereignty: 'Rulers want to rule.' (Krasner 1993, 1995, 1999).
6 I have drawn out the implications of this argument for orthodox Marxism in Teschke (2005).

References

Agnew, John and Stuart Corbridge (1995), *Mastering Space: Hegemony, Territory and International Political Economy*. London: Routledge.
Anderson, Matthew S. (1993), *The Rise of Modern Diplomacy, 1450–1919*. London: Longman.
Anderson, Perry (1974), *Lineages of the Absolutist State*. London: Verso.
—— (1997), 'Under the Sign of the Interim', in Perry Anderson and Peter Gowan (eds), *The Question of Europe*. London: Verso, pp. 51–71.
Asch, Ronal G. and Duchhardt Heinz (eds) (1996), *Der Absolutismus – ein Mythos? Strukturwandel Monarchischer Herrschaft in West- und Mitteleuropa (ca. 1550 – 1700)*. Cologne: Böhlau.
Bartlett, Robert (1993), *The Making of Europe: Conquest, Colonization and Cultural Change, 950–1350*. London: Penguin.
Baugh, Daniel A. (1988), 'Great Britain's Blue-Water Policy, 1689–1815', *International History Review*. 10(1): 33–58.

Beckett, John Vincent (1990), *The Agricultural Revolution*. Oxford: Blackwell.
Beik, William (1985), *Absolutism and Society in Seventeenth-Century France*. Cambridge: CUP.
Bisson, Thomas N. (1994), 'The "Feudal Revolution"', *Past and Present* 142: 6–42.
Black, Jeremy (1991), *A System of Ambition? British Foreign Policy 1660–1793*. London: Longman.
Bloch, Marc (1961) [1940], *Feudal Society*, transl. by L.A. Manyon. London: Routledge.
Bonnassie, Pierre (1991) [1985], 'The Survival and Extinction of the Slave System in the Early Medieval West (Fourth to Eleventh Centuries)', in Bonnassie, *From Slavery to Feudalism in South-Western Europe*, transl. by Jean Birrell. Cambridge and Paris: CUP and Maison des Sciences de l'Homme, pp. 1–59.
Bonney, Richard (ed.) (1995), *Economic Systems and State Finance*. Oxford: Clarendon Press.
—— (ed.) (1999), *The Rise of the Fiscal State in Europe, c.1200–1815*. Oxford: OUP.
Brenner, Robert (1977), 'The Origins of Capitalist Development: A Critique of Neo-Smithian Marxism', *New Left Review*, 104: 25–92.
—— (1985a), 'Agrarian Class Structure and Economic Development in Pre-Industrial Europe', in T.H. Aston and C.H.E. Philpin (eds), *The Brenner Debate: Agrarian Class Structure and Economic Development in Pre-Industrial Europe*. Cambridge: CUP, pp. 10–63.
—— (1985b), 'The Agrarian Roots of European Capitalism', in T.H. Aston and C.H.E. Philpin (eds), *The Brenner Debate: Agrarian Class Structure and Economic Development in Pre-Industrial Europe*. Cambridge: CUP, pp. 213–327.
—— (1986), 'The Social Basis of Economic Development', in John Roemer (ed.), *Analytical Marxism*. Cambridge: CUP, pp. 23–53.
—— (1987), 'Feudalism', in J. Eatwell, M. Milgate, P. Newman (eds), *The New Palgrave: A Dictionary of Economics: Marxian Economics*. London: Macmillan, pp. 170–85.
—— (1989), 'Bourgeois Revolution and Transition to Capitalism', in A.L. Beier, David Cannadine and James M. Rosenheim (eds), *The First Modern Society: Essays in English History in Honour of Lawrence Stone*. Cambridge: CUP, pp. 271–304.
—— (1993), *Merchants and Revolution: Commercial Change, Political Conflict, and London's Overseas Traders, 1550–1653*. Cambridge: CUP.
Brewer, John (1989), *The Sinews of Power: War, Money and the English State, 1688–1783*. New York: Knopf.
Bromley, Simon (1999), 'Marxism and Globalisation', in Andrew Gamble, David Marsh and Tony Tant (eds), *Marxism and Social Science*. London: Macmillan, pp. 280–301.
Brunner, Otto (1992) [1939], *Land and Lordship: Structures of Governance in Medieval Austria*. Philadelphia, PA: University of Pennsylvania Press.
Bull, Hedley (1977), *The Anarchical Society: A Study of Order in World Politics*. London: Macmillan.
Caporaso, James (1996), 'The European Union and Forms of State: Westphalian, Regulatory or Post-Modern?', *Journal of Common Market Studies* 34(1): 29–52.
Comninel, George (1987), *Rethinking the French Revolution: Marxism and the Revisionist Challenge*. London: Verso.
Davies, Rees (2003), 'The Medieval State: The Tyranny of a Concept?', *Journal of Historical Sociology* 16(2): 280–300.

Dickson, Peter (1967), *The Financial Revolution in England: A Study in the Development of Public Credit, 1688–1756*. London: Macmillan.
Doyle, William (1999), *Origins of the French Revolution*, third edition. Oxford: OUP.
Duby, Georges (1974) [1973], *The Early Growth of the European Economy: Warriors and Peasants from the Seventh to the Twelfth Century*, transl. by Howard B. Clarke. London: Weidenfeld & Nicholson.
Duchhardt, Heinz (1976), *Gleichgewicht der Kräfte, Convenance, Europäisches Konzert: Friedenskongresse und Friedensschlüsse vom Zeitalter Ludwigs XIV. bis zum Wiener Kongreß*. Darmstadt: Wissenschaftliche Buchgesellschaft.
—— (1989), 'Die Glorious Revolution und das Internationale System', *Francia* 16(2): 29–37.
—— (1997), *Balance of Power und Pentarchie: Internationale Beziehungen 1700–1785*, vol. 4 of H. Duchhardt and Franz Knipping (eds), *Handbuch der Geschichte der Internationalen Beziehungen*. Paderborn: Schöningh.
Elliot, J.H. (1992), 'A Europe of Composite Monarchies', *Past and Present* 137(1): 25-47.
Fischer, Markus (1992), 'Feudal Europe, 800–1300: Communal Discourse and Conflictual Practices', *International Organization* 46(2): 427–466.
Friedrichs, Jörg (2001), 'The Meaning of New Medievalism', *European Journal of International Relations* 7(4): 475–502.
Gerstenberger, Heide (1990), *Die Subjektlose Gewalt: Theorie der Entstehung Bürgerlicher Staatsgewalt*. Münster: Westfälisches Dampfboot.
Gramsci, Antonio (1971), *Selections from the Prison Notebooks*, edited and transl. by Quintin Hoare and Geoffrey N. Smith. New York: International Publishers.
Gulick, Edward Vose (1967) [1955], *Europe's Classical Balance of Power*. New York: Norton.
Hall, Rodney Bruce and Kratochwil Friedrich (1993), 'Medieval Tales: Neorealist "Science" and the Abuse of History', *International Organization* 47(3): 479–491.
Hilton, Rodney (1988) [1973], *Bond Men Made Free: Medieval Peasant Movements and the English Rising of 1381*. London: Routledge.
Hintze, Otto (1968) [1929], 'The Nature of Feudalism', in Frederic L. Cheyette (ed.), *Lordship and Community in Medieval Europe: Selected Readings*. New York: Holt, Rinehard, and Winston, pp. 22–31.
Hoffman, Philip T. (1994), 'Early Modern France, 1450–1700', in Ph.T. Hoffman and Kathryn Norberg (eds), *Fiscal Crises, Liberty, and Representative Government, 1450–1789*. Stanford, CA: Stanford University Press, pp. 226–252.
Holsti, Kalevi J. (1991), *Peace and War: Armed Conflicts and International Order, 1648–1989*. Cambridge: CUP.
Kaeuper, Richard W. (1988), *War, Justice and Public Order: England and France in the Later Middle Ages*. Oxford: Clarendon Press.
Kaiser, David (1990), *Politics and War: European Conflict from Phillip II to Hitler*. Cambridge, Mass.: Harvard University Press.
Kerridge, Eric (1967), *The Agricultural Revolution*. London: Allen & Unwin.
Krasner, Stephen D. (1993), 'Westphalia and All That', in Judith Goldstein and Robert O. Keohane (eds), *Ideas and Foreign Policy: Beliefs, Institutions, and Political Change*. Ithaca, NY/London: Cornell University Press, pp. 235–264.
—— (1995), 'Compromising Westphalia', *International Security* 20: 115–151.
—— (1999), *Sovereignty: Organized Hypocrisy*. Princeton, NJ: Princeton University Press.

Kunisch, Johannes (1979), *Staatsverfassung und Mächtepolitik: Zur Genese von Staatenkonflikten im Zeitalter des Absolutismus*. Berlin: Duncker & Humblot.
Luard, Evan (1993), *The Balance of Power: The System of International Relations, 1648–1815*. London: Macmillan.
Mann, Michael (1986), *The Sources of Social Power*, vol. 1: *A History of Power from the Beginning to A.D. 1760*. Cambridge: CUP.
—— (1988), *States, War and Capitalism: Studies in Political Sociology*. Oxford: Blackwell.
Marx, Karl (1975) [1843], 'Contribution to the Critique of Hegel's Philosophy of Law', in K. Marx and F. Engels, *Collected Works*, vol. 3. New York: International Publishers, pp. 3–129.
—— (1981) [1894], *Capital: A Critique of Political Economy*, vol. 3. London: Penguin.
Mayer, Theodor (1963) [1939], 'Die Ausbildung des Modernen Deutschen Staates im Hohen Mittelalter', in Hellmut Kämpf (ed.), *Herrschaft und Staat im Mittelalter*. Bad Homburg: Gentner Verlag, pp. 284–331.
McKay, Derek and Scott H.M. (1983), *The Rise of the Great Powers, 1648–1815*. London: Longman.
Mettam, Roger (1988), *Power and Faction in Louis XIV's France*. Oxford: Blackwell.
Mitteis, Heinrich (1975) [1940], *The State in the Middle Ages: A Comparative Constitutional History of Feudal Europe*, transl. by H.F. Orton. Amsterdam: North-Holland Publishing Company.
Parker, David (1996), *Class and State in Ancien Régime France: The Road to Modernity?* London: Routledge.
Philpot, Daniel (2001), *Revolutions in Sovereignty: How Ideas Shaped Modern International Relations*. Princeton, NJ: Princeton University Press.
Poly, Jean-Pierre and Bournazel, Eric (1991) [1980], *The Feudal Transformation, 900–1200*, transl. by Caroline Higitt. New York: Holmes & Meier.
Reinhard, Wolfgang (ed.), (1996), *Power Elites and State Building*. Oxford: OUP.
Reuter, Timothy (1985), 'Plunder and Tribute in the Carolingian Empire', *Transactions of the Royal Historical Society*, Fifth series, 35: 75–94.
—— (1995), 'The End of Carolingian Military Expansion', in Peter Godman and Roger Collins (eds), *Charlemagne's Heir: New Perspectives on the Reign of Louis the Pious (814–840)*. Oxford: Clarendon Press, pp. 391–405.
Rosenberg, Justin (1994), *The Empire of Civil Society: A Critique of the Realist Theory of International Relations*. London: Verso.
Rowen, Herbert (1980), *The King's State: Proprietary Dynasticism in Early Modern France*. New Brunswick, NJ: Rutgers University Press.
Ruggie, John Gerard (1986), 'Continuity and Transformation in the World Polity: Toward a Neorealist Synthesis', in Robert O. Keohane (ed.), *Neorealism and its Critics*. New York: Columbia University Press, pp. 131–157.
—— (1993), 'Territoriality and Beyond: Problematizing Modernity in International Relations', *International Organization* 47: 139–174.
Schmitter, Philippe C. (1996), 'Imagining the Future of the Euro-Polity with the Help of New Concepts', in G. Marks, F.W. Scharpf, P.C. Schmitter and W. Streeck (eds), *Governance in the European Union*. London: Sage, pp. 121–150.
Schroeder, Paul (1994), 'Historical Reality vs. Neo-realist Theory', *International Security* 19(1): 108–148.
Skocpol, Theda (1979), *States and Social Revolutions: A Comparative Analysis of France, Russia, and China*. Cambridge: CUP.

Spruyt, Hendrik (1994), *The Sovereign State and its Competitors: An Analysis of Systems Change*. Princeton: Princeton University Press.
Symcox, Geoffrey (ed.) (1974), *War, Diplomacy, and Imperialism, 1618–1763*. London: Macmillan.
Teschke, Benno (1998), 'Geopolitical Relations in the European Middle Ages: History and Theory', *International Organization* 52(2): 325–358.
—— (2001), 'Geopolitik', in Wolfgang-Fritz Haug (ed.), *Historisch-Kritisches Wörterbuch des Marxismus*, vol. 5. Hamburg: Argument-Verlag, pp. 322–334.
—— (2002), 'Theorising the Westphalian System of States: International Relations from Absolutism to Capitalism', *European Journal of International Relations* 8(1): 5–48.
—— (2003), *The Myth of 1648: Class, Geopolitics, and the Making of Modern International Relations*. London: Verso.
—— (2005), 'Bourgeois Revolution, State Formation and the Absence of the International', *Historical Materialism: Research in Critical Marxist Theory* 13(2): 3–26.
Tilly, Charles (1985), 'War Making and State Making as Organized Crime', in Peter B. Evans, Dietrich Rueschemeyer and Theda Skocpol (eds), *Bringing the State Back In*. Cambridge: CUP, pp. 169–191.
—— (1992), *Coercion, Capital, and European States, A.D. 990–1990*. Oxford: Blackwell.
Van der Pijl, Kees (1996), *Vordenker der Weltpolitik: Einführung in die internationale Politik aus ideengeschichtlicher Perspektive*. Opladen: Leske + Budrich.
—— (1998), *Transnational Classes and International Relations*. London: Routledge.
Waltz, Kenneth N. (1979), *Theory of International Politics*. Reading, MA: Addison-Wesley.
Weber, Max (1968) [1922], Guenther Roth and Claus Wittich (eds), *Economy and Society: An Outline of Interpretive Sociology*. New York: Bedminster Press.
Wight, Martin (1966), 'The Balance of Power', in H. Butterfield and M. Wight (eds), *Diplomatic Investigations: Essays in the Theory of International Politics*. London: Allen & Unwin, pp. 149–175.
Wood, Ellen (1991), *The Pristine Culture of Capitalism: A Historical Essay on Old Regimes and Modern States*. London: Verso.
—— (1995) [1981], 'The Separation of the "Economic" and the "Political" in Capitalism', in E. Wood, *Democracy against Capitalism: Renewing Historical Materialism*. Cambridge: CUP, pp. 19–48.
—— (2002), *The Origins of Capitalism: A Longer View*. London: Verso.
Wrigley, Anthony (1985), 'Urban Growth and Agricultural Change: England and the Continent in the Early Modern Period', *Journal of Interdisciplinary History* 15: 683–728.

Part II
Analysing territoriality in multi-level polities

4 Area and administration
A multi-level analysis of a multi-layered phenomenon

Theo A.J. Toonen and Frits M. van der Meer

Introduction

As depressing as it may be, all human endeavours are confined to the dimensions of space and time. Even in the realms of politics and public administration these limitations are hard to overcome. As such, territoriality has always been, and will remain, an enduring feature of politics and public service provision. In the introduction to this volume it is argued that one basic task of this book is to develop a set of indicators designed to assess the political significance of territory in all its multi-faceted dimensions. This chapter aspires to contribute to this aim, among other things, by pointing out that the argument that: 'the importance of territoriality in the European Union (EU) is diminishing', is in fact an ahistorical contention. It is based on a false reconstruction of the historical meaning of territoriality in everyday political and administrative life in the European nation state. In short, territoriality is here to stay. Consequently, we have to develop a framework for analysing what is essentially a multi-layered system of governance operating and positioned on various levels of geographical scale. This creates a better understanding of the place and position of the territorial dimension in politics and administration, while avoiding simple generalisations about what is called the 'changing' significance of territoriality in politics and public service delivery in the European nation states and the EU.

In formulating our framework of analysis, we will revisit some rather basic, if not, classical comparative insights and experiences from comparative public administration (PA) analysis of West European countries. These insights will illustrate our point: that (political) territoriality (still) matters. This argument uses concepts derived from American federalist and intergovernmental theory and research to organise the study of this multi-layered phenomenon, which requires a configurative mode of multi-level analysis. An effort is made to identify the nature of the analytical 'problem' at hand. As a point of departure, some general meta-theoretical issues in studying administrative reform in central Europe are identified. The next step is to suggest a general perspective from which to analyse and assess ongoing developments and reforms. After that, the analysis will be narrowed to focus on the institutional dimension of the adaptive capacity of intergovernmental systems. Various institutional factors influence the adaptive capacity for stable reform. On the basis of this discussion, we will formulate a framework consisting of three separate but interrelated worlds: the intergovernmental constitution (IGC), intergovernmental relations (IGRs), and intergovernmental management (IGM).

This framework will be applied to some Western European cases, sometimes with special reference to the consociational format of Dutch politics, service provision and identity. This in order to indicate the relevance of including civil society institutions in the analysis of territoriality. The Netherlands is often characterised as a decentralised unitary state as far as the formal distribution of authority is concerned. In reality pillarised society includes different, rather informal, organisational logics, in which the often-stressed functional and personal dimensions are completed with a territorial (regional) perspective.

Administrative reform: some meta-theoretical considerations

The debate on territoriality and multi-level governance is rooted in the quest for the institutional identity of the political and administrative system. We know – at least we think we know – where we are coming from, but we do not know where we are headed, at least in an institutional sense. The position of the nation state is said to be eroding, or at least changing, as a consequence of the processes of Europeanisation, internationalisation and globalisation. Europe is claimed not to be a federal system; although nobody knows what federalism exactly means without reference to the particular structure of a given country. The same applies for unitarianism, for many a simpler but in fact equally complex concept. As yet, nobody would claim that the emerging EU institutional order is aiming at a 'unitary state system'. However, claims for the identification of subsidiarity, neo-corporatist and cross-national network systems as features of the emerging institutional European order may quite well be reconciled with the consensual unitary political systems. These are characteristic of several of the consociational democracies identified in the study of comparative politics.

The institutional EU development, in many respects, can be viewed as a 'post'-development. We know what has ended; we do not know what is coming. We are inventing and reinventing Europe in the process. Former Eastern Germany is probably the only example where the transition from 'socialist' to 'post-socialist' has and is still being tried in a comprehensive, synoptic way, by a *de facto* 'buy out' and subsequent 'reorganisation'. All other countries and the EU institutions themselves will be required to make the transition in a more incremental, step-by-step way. This process may speed up and slow down from time to time. Many incremental steps easily amount to relatively quick and far-reaching changes. The analytical principle, however, is that the best prediction of what happens tomorrow is offered by the situation that exists today.

Conceiving a process of administrative modernisation and reform as an incremental and evolutionary development – albeit one that in its implications might be quite 'revolutionary' – means that any proposed analytical scheme must do justice to the fact that one is dealing with a dynamic, multi-dimensional and multi-level phenomenon. Incremental transitions cannot be centrally organised, if at all, and can be directed only in a restricted manner. One would not expect European constitutions – convention or not – to be 'designed', but to grow and evolve in a process of codification and modification, where formal conventions stand side-by-side with sociological and economic realities, in moulding the basic structures within which policies, politics and administrations operate. Conceived of in such a way, one has to assume that in the ongoing transition process, different levels or layers of government and society do play a role. At the same time, different considerations, values and perspectives have to be blended.

Stated somewhat differently: in evolutionary institutional modernisation processes – even if they are revolutionary in their consequences – there are different 'worlds of action' (Kiser and Ostrom, 1982) at play, each with its own analytical implications and normative concerns. In well-established administrative systems, differentiated institutional and procedural provisions often represent these worlds of actions. The historical institutional development in Western democracies has, over time, produced in each system, a certain division of labour and has matched different perspectives to different institutions and processes. The discovery of the importance of 'multi-level governance' in an internationalisation process is actually only the first and, analytically, a rather primitive step in discovering that the players of the game are not unitary or monolithic entities. This rather bold institutional assumption could long dominate the analysis of international relations, and at least be legitimised by referring to the nation state as the 'sovereign' building blocks of any international order. European integration, not to mention globalisation, has fundamentally opened the 'black box' of the presumed 'unified' (nation) state. It has thereby presented an extensive glance at the bewildering complexities of day to day politics and administration in terms of values, interests, organisations, structures and levels of government and administration which characterise any bureaucratic and administrative system, so far hidden behind the façade of the government or the state.

From a PA perspective multi-layered governance and the existence of intergovernmental and inter-organisational systems and policy networks are the rule of 'government in action' as public administration is conveniently identified. One of the analytical complications of the ongoing institutional reform processes in the EU and the EU member states is that the link between value systems and management perspectives, on the one hand, and administrative procedures and institutions, on the other, needs to be re-elaborated and re-developed. This might very well take a different form than the one we were analytically used to in western liberal democracies.

Many of the problems in the continuing transition processes find their origin in the fact that in one institution, or even in one decision, completely different 'problems' may have to be resolved than in another. Although the crafting of a constitution is a skilful and prudent job (Dahrendorf, 1999), constitutional issues are intertwined with policy and management considerations. This is not necessarily bad (or good), but it means that we are in need of an analytical framework that enables the observer to cope with these 'mixed' situations. That framework is presented below.

PA: multiple perspectives

Kiser and Ostrom (1982) have proposed a meta-theoretical framework for the integration of different theoretical approaches in the area of institutional analysis. They distinguish three interrelated, but analytically separate 'worlds of action' which they perceive as giving rise to separate analytical questions and different levels of theoretical analysis: a constitutional, a collective choice and an operational level of action analysis.

The world of operational choice is the world of day-to-day actions and decisions, within a given framework of rules and institutions. This is what we generally refer to as the administrative practice, where general rules, policies and programmes are applied and enforced with respect to concrete objects and issues. The individual decision-maker – official, civil servant, bureau or agency – is the primary point of reference. The world of collective choice refers to situations of joint decision making on policies and other collective arrangements (laws, rules, plans, collective strategies) which structure the behaviour and decisions at the operational level of decision making and can in principle be enforced against non-conforming individual actors or agencies. The world of constitutional choice refers to processes of collective and joint decision making about the rules and principles guiding operational and collective choices. The world of constitutional choice is about meta-decisions: decisions on how to take collective decisions and conduct joint decision making.

Positive and normative analysis

One and the same empirical phenomenon or object can be approached from three different angles. Each provides a different level of analysis, involving different units of observation and analysis and thus highlighting different aspects and dimensions of the same events (processes, structures, programmes, etc.). Constitutional considerations differ from collective choice and operational concerns and often require an interrelated but different theoretical and analytical approach. This also applies to the question of what role 'territoriality' plays in organising the polity, policies and organisations in the public domain.

The Ostrom and Kiser scheme is primarily intended as an integrative framework for positive analysis. It can easily be expanded, however, to include normative and prescriptive concerns as well. Hood (1991) has provided an early critique treatment of the 'new management' tradition in Public Administration. His main objection was that the neo-managerial approach represented one type of value system at the expense or at least neglect of other administrative values. In order to present his case against the idea of 'a public management for all seasons', he derives three different value systems from the history of administrative doctrine and ideas, which he labels in a more or less neutral way as sigma-, theta- and lambda-type values. Closer inspection gives rise to the idea that these three value systems provide a more or less ready normative complement to the previously outlined analytical 'worlds of action'. Such a complement is necessary in a study which aims at identifying indicators of territoriality in organising politico-administrative systems.

Operational values

The new public management (NPM) approach represents in Hoods terms 'sigma-type values': match resources to defined tasks. The main prescriptive idea is efficiency: 'keep it lean and purposeful'. The underlying value system assesses the quality of public administration in terms of frugality and its ability to match resources to tasks for given goals. Low quality is defined in terms of inefficiency, confusion, muddle, the waste of resources and a lack of responsiveness to the demands of the public and the employees of a given civil service. Clear, fixed and single goals are presumed to be a condition for success, which is generally measured in terms of time and money and in terms of resource costs for producers and consumers of public services. The NPM approach, in Hoods representation, advocates 'hands on management', output orientation and various managerial techniques to avoid 'organisational slack'. Seen from the Ostrom and Kiser perspective, the NPM and the related normative concerns primarily represent the 'world of operational action'. The resulting question regarding territoriality is 'What is the role of territoriality in the operational management of public service delivery?'

Collective choice ('public policy') values

Hood contrasts the value system of the NPM with two other value systems. Hoods 'theta-type' of value system corresponds closely to the concerns at the policy-level or 'collective choice level' of administrative analysis. Hood identifies a stream within the administrative doctrine, which is preoccupied with the importance of values of rectitude in collective and joint decision making. The main idea is to 'keep it honest and fair'. The achievement of a degree of fairness, mutuality and a proper discharge of duties in substantive and procedural terms, among the proper parties is branded as important administrative concerns. In this perspective a low quality public administration system is characterised by altercation: a mobilisation of bias in favour or against certain interests or abuse of offices. The operational question of 'getting the job done', is complemented by concern about 'how the job is done'. Not only the output, but also the process of decision making deserves attention from a viewpoint of generating legitimacy, acceptance and consent to collective decisions in which different political entitlements have to be recognised and secured. From this perspective, a process characterised by adversary agencies serving different goals may need to be more transparent in the process of goal setting, than in the pursuit of a clear and single ultimate objective. This results in the question: What is the role of territoriality in relation to legitimation, administrative accountability, integrity, transparency and control of the bureaucracy?

Constitutional values

From the history of administrative doctrine Hood, finally, derives a set of 'lambda-type' values, which concern questions of robustness, trust and sustainability in the administration. A preoccupation with values to 'keep it robust and resilient' has gradually been regaining attention in the domain of PA, even in such 'operationally oriented', remote corners as emergency management and risk assessment (Douglas and Wildavsky, 1983). This concern with the less visible, constituent factors, which underlie the visible operational decisions, successes and failures, reflects the recognition of the constitutional level of analysis. 'Constitutional' considerations in public administration concentrate on the conditions under which large quantities of varied operational and joint decision-making activities have to be conducted over a longer time period. From this perspective, the resilience of administrative structures becomes a crucial concern in assessing the quality of administrative systems. Social support, reliability, robustness and stable adaptation of administrative systems are important values in designing institutional arrangements for public service delivery. System failure and poor administrative quality are, from a constitutional viewpoint, defined in terms of catastrophe, risk and the breakdown or collapse of administrative systems. Success is measured in terms of confidence in the basic 'constitutional' structure of the system, and the security of life and limb, i.e. the protection of basic human rights. Some important characteristics of a sound constitution are the following: organisational slack, a degree of duplication, overlap and other forms of 'checks and balances', the emergent character of administrative targets and causes and the importance of multiple goals within administrative systems are important characteristics of a sound constitution of the administrative process. Finally, the question at hand is: What is the role of territoriality in constituting systems of governance, which from a PA perspective, by definition have to be multi-actor and multi-level in character?

The appropriateness of different value systems

Hood suggests that the appropriateness of the different value systems is contingent on the type of problems with which administrative systems are confronted. The applicability will be or should be changing from time to time in a sequential manner. The 'three worlds approach', however, suggests that we are dealing with simultaneous or parallel value systems. Every sound administrative system will have to satisfy the different value complexes at more or less the same time. Of course, with respect to any concrete decision or developments, the different value systems might be in conflict. This conflict might be resolved by imposing a compromise, a hierarchy, a priority or a sequent in the pursuit of values. In developed administrative systems more or less separated institutions and procedures exist for dealing with the different worlds of action and their respective value systems. Different actors take the decisions on joint goals and values, and operational management decisions. In a complex and elaborated administrative system, goals will be treated as emergent, developing and constantly changing at one level, contested and set by due process at another and accepted as fixed and given ('ceteris paribus') for the third level of decision making, all at the same time. Constitutional decisions are often taken through different procedures and by different actors, separated from joint policy or operational management procedures. Questions of territoriality may or may not occur at various levels of administrative analysis, or at any moment in time be confronted with different sets of administrative values. They thus give rise to tensions and political dilemmas, which often manifest themselves as paradoxes of reform and institutional development (Toonen, 2000, 2003). Which are the paradoxes of territoriality and how are they being resolved in the institutional development process?

In the long-term development of an administrative system, attention for the different worlds of action and their corresponding value systems may differ. In one episode the trust and reliability of the system may be disputed and attention (may be) directed towards constitutional issues. Territoriality might become part of the strategy to find a solution and stabilise the system. The example of Belgium or the formerly united Czech and Slovak republics spring to mind. Other less peaceful examples of a 'territorial' approach to basically constitutional questions are also easy to find. During the next couple of years in European development the main concern might be the economy or frugality of the system, which directs the attention to the operational levels of the administrative systems. The New Regionalism (Keating, 1998) and the territorial dimension of the knowledge-based economy (EU, 2003) have already been identified as key modules for future economic development and the ambition to become the world's leading 'knowledge-based economy'.

When comparing different systems within the same time period, the proposed analytical scheme should also make one aware of the fact that various administrative systems may address similar topics or issues of territoriality according to completely different concerns. Regionalisation might in one country be addressed for 'constitutional' reasons of sustainability, in another for reasons of rectitude (democratic control over bureaucracy or of functional agencies; supervision and oversight of local governments) and in still another system for reasons of functional efficiency (integration, co-ordination, scale enlargement). Conversely, functionally equivalent territorial issues might be resolved at different levels of administrative analysis. The case of Dutch pillarisation as a regionalised institutional design can be presented as a functional institutional equivalent of federalised arrangements for territorial public service delivery elsewhere (Toonen, 2000).

However elaborated the administrative system and however differentiated the institutions and procedures for dealing with the different value complexes at the different 'levels' of the system may be, empirically, they are always interconnected: the three worlds of action and their value complexes are relatively autonomous, meaning that they must always be understood in relation to one another and, from time to time, they interrelate (with one another). In times of stability their interrelationships are characterised by loose coupling. Questions of territoriality may be 'resolved', remain in the back of day to day politics and may thus may go unnoticed for a long period of time, therefore easily being (mis)perceived as 'irrelevant' in a given case. From a perspective of PA the non-contentious nature of territoriality (Bachrach and Baratz, 1962) is perhaps even more interesting and relevant than the issue of territorialisation.

Critical situations emerge when the value systems are tightly coupled, and each specific decision has to be taken regarding the three different value systems at the same time, without reference as to which value system should have priority. In such a case, the theoretical reflex, that deems constitutional values superior to operational values, is typical for the luxury of a well-developed, stable and established administrative system. It is this luxury, which many transitional administrative systems – like the current contemporary EU system at large – cannot yet afford. It makes the question of territoriality so pertinent at any stage of administrative reform or political transformation. The interwovenness of the different administrative value systems in the current stage of EU institutional development seems to be precisely why the question of territoriality is causing conceptual headaches on how to unravel the central state (Hooghe and Marks, 2003).

Intergovernmental systems: an exploratory comparative framework

On the basis of the previous analysis, intergovernmental systems – European, EU or otherwise – can be compared from different angles. Here we restrict ourselves to a few traditional cases in comparative PA in order to try to identify relevant institutional values, indicators and parameters for identifying the significance of territoriality for organising polities, policies and politics in Western Europe from a PA perspective. Later we will elaborate and pay special attention to the Dutch case in order to be able to illustrate the importance of including the sociological ('informal') dimension into the analysis of intergovernmental systems in addition to the legalist ('formal') characteristics of these systems. A constitutional analysis in the previously defined sense puts intergovernmental systems in a perspective of resilience, adaptive capacity and sustainable institutional development. Although, as spelled out, it is not the only dimension of the ongoing European transformation process, the constitutional administrative analysis concern and preoccupation with 'system maintenance', survival, durability or better: innovative and adaptive capacity in a turbulent environment seems highly relevant for the continuing debate on the European multi-level systems of governance. Insight into deeper, constitutional choice factors which contribute to the role of territoriality in a stable adaptation process, as over and against an unproductive stagnation or even breakdown of the system might be extremely valuable in analysing and assessing the nature and quality of ongoing reforms. Positive theory in this field is not very developed, let alone elaborated, but a systematic comparative analysis might provide some clues.

Lane and Erson maintain that the stability of a political system depends on the capacity of a system as a whole to secure for its relevant component parts an acceptable balance in the trade off between 'autonomy' on the one hand and codetermination or 'access and influence' to relevant collective decision making arenas on the other. Where this trade-off is not in balance, instabilities may occur, which eventually might lead to a disruption, stagnation and breakdown of ongoing developmental processes. Destabilisation of existing orders is a necessary – but not sufficient – condition for progress. The question is whether a political and administrative system allows for constant correction and balancing in turbulent environments. Too much internal stability in the short run, in terms of lack of change and adaptation, might in the long run, even drastically destabilise and threaten the sustainability of the system.

Political and administrative conflicts often have their sources in social cleavages. From a constitutional point of view, the robustness and resilience of political and administrative institutional structures may play an important role in mediating these conflicts, facilitating stabilisation processes and thus contribute to a stable and sustainable adaptation process. Within this overall setting the intergovernmental system plays not the least important role. It is often even formally designated to deal with problems of autonomy and codetermination (access and influence; co-governance) of the component parts of the state. Comparative empirical research since the early 1980s has considerably changed previously well-established, but rather legalistic images of the operation of different European state-systems. It has not yet resulted in generally accepted alternative models or frameworks for comparative institutional research. The mere juxtaposition of federal and unitary systems breaks down in the face of the varieties of administrative systems that need to be addressed. Federalism is generally recognised as an abstract and multi-interpretable concept. Gradually analysts are experiencing that the situation with respect to the concept of 'unitarianism' is not very different: 'Indeed, only God knows what the unitary principle is and he has been remarkably reluctant to let mere mortals into the secret' (Bulpitt, 1989: 62; also Toonen, 1990).

For a more refined analysis of different administrative systems, the concept of 'intergovernmentalism' may provide a useful point of departure. In the European context 'intergovernmentalism' for a long time had a specific meaning and referred to a certain approach of the Europeanisation process. In official EU language the concept still often refers to the formal meetings of the governments of different countries. The national government leaders meet in 'intergovernmental conferences' in order to discuss and decide upon changing the Treaties and institutions of the emerging European order. Questions like the political union, the installation of one European currency, a European central bank, and the outcomes of the European Convention have been the typical subjects of regular intergovernmental conferences. The concept of intergovernmentalism in the past, thus, was largely reserved for the 'constitutional' decision-making process within the EU. In the United States, on the other hand, the constitutional debate is conceptualised in terms of 'federalism'. The concept of intergovernmentalism refers to the relations among the different units and planes of government and administration within the federal system. The European debate could benefit from an extension of the 'intergovernmental concept' in the 'American' direction. Relationships beyond the level of the national state could be included as an integral part of the 'intergovernmental relations', thus abandoning the rather formal and legalistic orientation of the nation state as the primary point of reference. On the other hand, the American debate on public administration might benefit from an extension of the 'constitutional concept' in the 'European' direction. Wright (1988) has summarised existing approaches to the study of relationships among different planes of government in terms of three concepts: (1) federalism, (2) IGRs, and (3) IGM. With two amendments his classification can be used here as a starting point for developing an exploratory framework for the comparative analysis of the issue of territoriality in intergovernmental systems.

First, Wright's category of 'federalism' actually represents approaches, value questions and institutional issues, which also do arise in other, non-federal state formations. His first category actually represents the broader 'constitutional' dimension of the analysis of IGRs. We will therefore speak about the IGC, within which 'federalism' obviously is a key category. Second, there is no need to represent the classification in terms of different approaches, like Wright has suggested. The 'three worlds of action' approach (Kiser and Ostrom, 1982) would suggest that the three levels of (intergovernmental) governance are nested into one and another and operate in a distinct but relatively autonomous, interdependent way.

Interpreted this way, an exploration of the issue of territoriality in intergovernmental systems of PA, has to pay attention to the interrelated worlds of:

1 The IGC,
2 The IGRs, and
3 The IGM.

On the basis of comparative research in IGRs (Lane and Ersson, 1987; 1991; Rhodes and Wright, 1987; Page and Goldsmith, 1987; Dente and Kjellberg, 1988; Hesse and Benz, 1990; Benz, 1995; Keating, 1998) several dimensions can be formulated to further explore these different levels and aspects of intergovernmental systems. These dimensions and the examples as existing in some European nation states will be elaborated in the next paragraphs.

The IGC

The IGC is the complexity of legal, political, social, cultural and economic conditions, rules, norms and values, which constitute the context in which intergovernmental processes and relations take place in an empirical and normative respect. Not only the legal constitution, but also the underlying political, social and economic constellations of a country will eventually have to be taken into consideration for an adequate analysis and comparison of different intergovernmental systems. Here, attention is limited to only the first two components.

The distinction between federal and unitary states is primarily a formal legal distinction. It is useful to make a distinction between federal and unitary states and federal and unitary systems of governance and administrations. From an empirical viewpoint the actual relative subsystem autonomy within a unitary state might be as large or small as within a federal structure. The federalisation process in Belgium, for example, for a long time went hand in hand with a strong process of centralisation in (regionalised) central–local relationships, so that the regional authorities held on strongly to their newly acquired powers. This is changing in recent times, but it illustrates that the process of federalisation should not automatically be equated with decentralisation at the local level of the system.

Scheme 4.1 Intergovernmental constitutions

Federalism versus unitarianism			
Dual federalism	Cooperative federalism	Consensus unitarianism	Westminster/Jacobin Unitarianism

In the past, attention has been given to the fact that a unitary system of governance and administration, for example one controlled by a single party, may be in operation within the (legal) structure of a federal state. Thus politically 'undoing' the formal and legally inserted separation of territorial powers. Due to the legalist overtones in the political debate, it is still much less appreciated that the mirror image is also possible. Namely, unitary states from a sociological, political or administrative point of view may actually operate as federalised systems. This can be a sociological federalism, that Lijphart needed to introduce in order to fit the Dutch case into his comparative analysis. Conversely, 'implementation' federalism is also possible. This characterises the administrative build up of many northern European States, in which local governments play an essential role in actually carrying out and 'administering' nationally agreed upon policies. The main *a priori* difference among unitary and federal states is that, due to the different legal frameworks, the relative autonomy of subsystems has a different legal expression (Lane and Ersson, 1987: 193). In itself this is enough reason to include the distinction in the analysis. It is important to note, however, that territoriality may play an equally important role in both federal and unitary systems. Its impact needs to be assessed through empirical analysis, not merely by assertion.

Forms of federal systems

Federal systems come in different guises. For the analyses of intergovernmental systems, a relevant distinction is made between cooperative or horizontal federalism, and dual or vertical federalism. In the case of vertical federalism, the division of labour among the different governments rests upon assigning different policy areas to different governments. The division of labour is characterised by a more or less exclusive allocation of tasks and competencies in the area of legislation and administration within different policy areas to the different layers of government. The different governments in principle carry out their own rules, regulations and policies. In contrast, a system of cooperative or horizontal federalism is characterised by a division of labour in terms of the functions of legislation, execution and financing. One level sets the rule and another level is responsible for implementation. By and large the distinction between horizontal and vertical federalism is the distinction between the German 'cooperative federalism' and the American 'dual federalism' (Gunlicks, 1986). In the German system functions are shared across different levels of territorial government organisation, thus constituting the need for (national/federal) policy makers and (regional/state) policy-executors to 'cooperate'. In the dual system legislative and executive functions stay in one hand, and are divided across territorial governments at different levels of the system. On the European continent, and in their current stages of development, the Belgian and Spanish efforts to federalise, so far, have displayed particular characteristics of dual or vertical federalism where governmental tasks are allocated to one territorial level or another. Of course, many formal and informal relations exist among these different levels in the territorial organisation of the state, but the nature of the territorial division of labour constitutes a different kind of 'cooperation' (and conflict) within the two systems. We will return to this when addressing the nature of IGRs within a given IGC.

Unitary systems at a constitutional level

Also, unitary states, even at a constitutional level, cannot be treated as an undifferentiated category. The archetypes of a unitary state are the Jacobin French and the British Westminster variety of the unitary state. Discussions about different unitary states have often been couched in terms of a juxtaposition of the French 'centralised' and the British 'decentralised' unitary state, a distinction that in the 1980s came under serious scrutiny (Ashford, 1982; Bullpit, 1989). Lijphart's (1984) analysis of different models of democracy gives rise to a further differentiation. In the domain of public law, the Westminster model of parliamentary democracy is often confronted with the American system of checks and balances, and separation of powers. Lijphart contrasts the Westminster model of democracy with what he calls the consensus model of democracy. This enables him to formulate an alternative for the often hidden presupposition that a monocentric source of state authority, parliamentary sovereignty and a two-party system are the requirements for a sustained, stable democratic development. Lijphart derives his alternative model from research into consociational democracies. These consociational democracies have a system of proportional representation, which results in a multi-party system that in turn necessitates coalition government and therefore a certain degree of separation or, at least, a sharing of power. Nevertheless, these plural, fragmented and strongly divided societies have shown their ability to develop as relatively stable liberal democracies.

Lijphart maintains that the majoritarian Westminster type of government is unitary and centralised (1984: 169), while the consensus model would be inspired by federalism and decentralisation. But the Dutch and (former) Belgium cases present him with some difficulties in fitting into this model. A clear consociational structure is coupled to a unitary state structure. Lijphart tries to save the model by referring to 'the sociological federalism of these countries' (Lijphart, 1984: 186). Belgium, in the meantime, has chosen to accommodate its position to the theory by adopting a federal state structure, thus seemingly leaving the Netherlands in an isolated position. However, many Dutch political scientists have a preoccupation with the centre. And so does Lijphart, which makes him overlook the typical nature of the Dutch administrative system and some peculiar characteristics of the Dutch intergovernmental unitary state structure. Contrary to much of the conventional wisdom, the Dutch system has not been designed from the perspective of parliamentary sovereignty and subsidiary notions of centralised governance and administration. The Dutch principal 'decentralised unitary state' is a concept, which according to many political scientists, theoretically cannot exist ('decentralised centralisation') and is therefore discarded as self-contradictory. Yet from an historical perspective, this principle of a 'decentralised unitary state' reveals characteristics that reflect the constitution of what can more appropriately be called a 'consensus state'. The term 'decentralised unitary state' was not used in the 1840s and 1850s, as the system was constitutionally designed; and did not become a convenient, but misleading, shorthand to characterise the IGR system, until in the second half of the 1950s. By that time many other historical developments had taken place, and partly overtaken the institutional structure as designed.

The basic principle underlying the historical constitution of the Dutch unitary state is not that centralised state authority is necessary to create unity – the Jacobin and Westminster presupposition – but, conversely, that unity – read: a degree of consensus – is necessary to generate state authority (Toonen, 1987, 1990; Hendriks and Toonen, 2001). The term 'decentralised unitary state' is actually a misnomer when referring to the constitutional structure as designed by, the founding father of the current Dutch constitutional design, Thorbecke in 1848. The 'consensus-state' would actually be more accurate shorthand for the designed system. Someone other than a 'centralist' political scientist might perhaps be able to perceive that the principle, design and actual operation of the Dutch 'unitary' intergovernmental and administrative system, actually complements the consociational nature of the political system (Toonen, 1987: 118). Therefore, it seems warranted to further differentiate unitary states in terms of hierarchical Westminster and Jacobin models versus consociational or consensus and exchange models. It will, at least, enable us to do more justice to the varieties of unitarianism, which appear on stage once we extend the scope of analyses beyond the archetypes of France and the United Kingdom to the Netherlands, Denmark, Italy, Greece, Portugal or Ireland.

In the Dutch case the non-centralised intergovernmental design and institutional set up of the Thorbeckian unitary state has facilitated the subsequent institutionalisation of the internationally famous system of pillarisation in the modern Dutch state of the late nineteenth and early twentieth centuries. Groenveld even argues that pillarisation has been a traditional feature of Dutch society long before the nineteenth century. The Dutch Republic of the seventeenth and eighteenth centuries also had its pillarised characteristics (Groenveld, 1995). The build-up of pillarisation took place within the constitutional framework of the Netherlands, laid down in 1813 and revised in 1848. The nature of this constitutional framework's design is not nearly as centralist as we are usually led to believe according to the common interpretation of the concept of a unitary state.

'Pillarisation' is one of the holy grails of Dutch political science, attracting much attention from sociologists and historians. These disciplines have never really bothered to pay much attention to the administrative and public policy delivery dimension implied by the notion of pillarisation. Blom (2000), observes the consequences of pillarisation of the intergovernmental system and the interplay (of) between the political and the administrative complex in terms of multi-level governance:

> it appears that other levels of government than the national one alone were needed to perform the functions of this modern state in an orderly way. The result has been a confusion of local, regional, and national institutions, some administered direct by government and others farmed out to interest groups with a specific basis or purpose. (. . .) Not infrequently things go wrong and have to be put right, and the administrative and political systems get entangled. Especially with the blurring of the typical divisions of political ideology, the administrative and political complex takes on a strong management character as well as a muddled appearance.

Daalder rightly stressed the gradual, historical, institutional development and organisational build-up of the system. The energising powers, in his view, came just as much from the bottom up as from the top down. Many of the initiatives were locally made. Historiography, in this respect, is rather underdeveloped, as most (Dutch) historians are still preoccupied with the national (macro) level. Nevertheless local and regional historians have, for instance, pointed to regional pillarisation and the organisation of social economic interests. Pillarisation was not only a centrally coordinated structure it was also as a process instrumental in forming a centre and the identity of a centre (or nation). In the words of Daalder (1981): 'By aggregating and integrating demands on an increasingly wide front of issues, from widely different parts of the country through increasingly differentiated but also interlocking national organizations, more and more groups became involved with national organs of authoritative decision making.'

The lack of possibilities for direct central intervention, compounded by the consensual nature of the plural political system, has caused an incentive to try to bypass the formal framework. Indeed as Blom (2000) observes: 'The result has been a confusion of local, regional, and national institutions, some administered direct by government and others farmed out' However, the build-up of pillarised structures may easily be interpreted as a successful effort to bypass the formal democratic structures of the intergovernmental system. It may be understood as an institutional development to create direct informal linkages between centre and periphery; at least more than following the formal intergovernmental path would allow for. This development served both 'top down' interests from the centre as well as 'bottom up' interests from the region, at least as long as the pillarised system was able to function properly and maintain its 'executive equilibrium'.

The territorial base of Dutch pillarisation might, at first glance, indeed seem not to be so strong as, for example, in Belgium, but also Wintle observes that there is a strong territorial dimension to pillarisation. There is no need for a one-to-one relationship of 'pillar' and 'region' to still have the pillar structure fulfil 'regionalised' functions. Furthermore, one should indeed realise that there were many Catholics living in several important cities and rural areas 'above the rivers'. The position of cities, city networks and rural regions is an important and integral part of the issue of regionalisation and territoriality in government. The advantage of a pillarised form of regionalisation even has some advantages above the territorial (i.e. a provincial) form of regionalisation. It allows regional leaders to 'hop over' territorial regions and also serve people in areas not immediately adjacent to one another. Within the territorial form of 'regionalisation' – using the provinces as a vehicle for regional politics and policy – some of the Catholic 'city-regions' would not as easily be integrated into the 'Catholic Regionalisation' (or city) networks as under the pillarised system of regionalisation. The same reasoning would apply to the protestant communities. The pillarised system provided virtual corridors among social groups located within different territorial areas of the system.

One may think for a moment of the headaches the Walloon region had in finding a solution for the French speaking community in Brussels, not to mention the economic importance of keeping Brussels an integral part of their regional configuration. The solution is partly found by differentiating between 'regions' (Gewesten) and communities (Gemeenschappen). One could say that the regions deal with the territory-oriented, physical infrastructure and the communities with the people-related, cultural infrastructure. This is admittedly a very crude simplification of the enormous complexities of 'Belgian regionalisation'. However, the main point is that by separating these two components one is able to design a complex but flexible regional governance system. It allows us, in principle, to deal with the very common and sometimes violent regional issues that arise out of a situation in which there is a mismatch between the location of a region's cultural territory and that region's people.

To take an example, the provinces – regional territorial government par excellence – played an unimportant, or rather, an invisible role in Dutch politics for a long time as the territorial government for regional politics. This was not by institutional design or because of a flaw in this design. As a matter of fact, if one were solely to compare the legal-formal status of the Dutch province with other European systems, it would probably come out as one of the 'meso-structures' legally best equipped to deal with the modern regional questions. Pillarisation has – whether intentional or not – provided precisely the kind of institutional bypass, the national governments are nowadays so afraid of in the relationship between the European Commission and 'its' regions, i.e. the regions that are politically important to them. Obviously we have to be aware of the existence of institutional rivals in studying the issue of territoriality in politics at the constitutional level of analysing multi-level intergovernmental systems.

If we return to the more traditional 'formal' concept of intergovernmental relations, the underlying analyses indicate that different types of structures constitute different types of IGRs and processes. These will pose different opportunities and constraints to administrative modernisation processes. Many of these crosscut the formal distinction between federal and unitary systems. Problems of dual federalism will, for example, be that enumerated powers and an existing division of labour at a given moment, among the different 'autonomous' units of government, will no longer hold, in the face of changing circumstances. Changes in the administrative environment will lead to configurations of issues and problems, which are different from those for which the existing division of labour was designed or previously negotiated.

The autonomy of the constituent parts with respect to functionally interdependent policy areas is likely to create problems of coordination and conflict over competencies. Constituent subsystems will have the tendency to underscore their 'autonomy' at the expense of emerging interdependent properties within the larger system. Therefore, these subsystems stress the territorial dimension of the system by demanding ever more regional 'autonomy'. It will require a rather complicated and mostly slow process of (constitutional) reform and intergovernmental reorganisation (federalisation/regionalisation) as we may witness in Spain and Belgium – not necessarily with negative functional consequences in terms of policy performance. Adaptations of subsystems to changing circumstances beyond the degrees of freedom allowed for by an existing division of labour will require a reorganisation of the system's constitutional order. The other side of the coin is that the different constituent parts will be clearly and formally represented in this adaptation process. In principle, this allows for a balanced expression of interest among the constituent national, regional and local units of the intergovernmental system. On the other hand, the issue of territoriality is constitutionally accommodated in the system of co-operative federalism, thus calling for a lesser need to stress the issue in the reform of an otherwise rather complex and interwoven intergovernmental system. Under conditions of change both factors in combination may amount to an innovation deficit or 'Reformstau'.

The inclusive authority model of Westminster or Jacobin unitarism will face somewhat similar problems in administrative adaptation and modernisation processes. The clearly circumscribed division of labour and competencies ('intra vires') among the different levels of the administrative hierarchy has the advantage of relative clarity and transparency. The administrative blueprint of the hierarchical, inclusive and supposedly complementary division of labour between different layers of government will, however, be constantly tested by the requirements of a changing administrative environment. Subsystem adaptation to externally changing circumstances requires previous reforms of the existing division of labour and authority. The British system of 'ultra vires', for example, requires an Act of Parliament to change the existing domain of local government autonomy. In contrast to the federal situation, the hierarchical nature of the reform process is prone to contribute to a rather one-sided, unbalanced and centrally dominated adaptation process. Within this, territoriality comes to play a role depending on the ideological bias regarding local and regional government of any given government in power. The classical example is the Thatcher reforms where 'decentralisation' no longer meant 'local government' but 'the market'. Devolution to territorial entities (at the regional level) became an issue again once a (Blair) government was installed which, with all the continuities of its predecessors, had ambitions to improve government operation and to 'rejoin' an evidently disjointed government apparatus by regionalised agentification. Integration and co-ordination are important concerns when seeking to redraw the territorial map[1] in the United Kingdom, although a great tradition of 'unitarianism' still hinders an explicit, and all out, resolution of the territorial map in the case of England.

Cooperative federalism and consensus unitarianism are characterised by overlapping authorities and competencies. Legally these are expressed by provisions such as 'concurrent competencies' and constitutionally undefined 'general competencies' of the different units of government. The legal provisions constitute a fundamental interdependency and bargaining relationship among the component parts of the intergovernmental system in determining the scope of autonomous and overlapping spheres of jurisdiction. The territorial dimension is there, but embedded in a more continuous and functionalist debate on who should do and pay for what.

Both cooperative federalism and consensus unitarianism are confronted with a rather high and institutionalised need for consensus building and conflict resolution. Specific country systems may strongly vary in their capacity for effective conflict regulation, mediation, joint decision making and mutual adjustment. The centrally coordinated structure of a unitary state might contribute to a more easy control and 'closure' of ongoing negotiation processes. On the other hand, the need for sub-central consensus building might easily be underestimated – under-conceptualised – in a 'unitary' state structure. The legitimate existence of different 'governments' with different territories is more easily acknowledged in a federal state, with its formally more clearly distinguished subsystems. This may contribute to more deliberate attention and sensitivity to arrangements for institutionalised cooperation and consensus building, playing up the issue of territoriality as a constitutional topic.

Both types of systems will be characterised by a tendency towards gradual and incremental adaptation to changing circumstances. The systems are more likely to be changed and reformed in the process, than by an overall administrative reorganisation. The evolutionary modernisation processes might over time drastically change the nature of the system, while largely maintaining the same legal constitutional structure. The constitutional 'crises' and required reforms induced by changing circumstances will refer less to the intergovernmental blueprint and division of labour within the system. They are more likely to concern the realm of 'meta-decision making', i.e. decision making about procedures and institutions for (joint) decision making and conflict regulation among the constituent parts of the intergovernmental system. Consequently, the issue of territoriality is more often redirected and dealt with at the level of IGRs, where not so much the issue of 'territorial autonomy' (right of initiative to legislate) but rather of executive implementation powers is at stake in considering the issue of territoriality.

IGRs

IGRs consist of the configuration of legal, financial, political, administrative and organisational relationships and linkages among the different elements and units, which are distinguished within a state system. Most research suggests two important dimensions along which systems of intergovernmental relations might productively be analysed. First, the question regarding the 'horizontal' or the 'vertical' nature of relations repeats itself at the level of IGRs. The second dimension concerns the degree of administrative and political interwovenness of the different levels, which generally characterises the intergovernmental system of a particular country. In Scheme 4.2 these dimensions are elaborated.

Regarding the 'horizontal' or the 'vertical' nature of relations, the relationships between different levels of government may be characterised by the horizontal principle in which units of government at one level carry out the legal rules and norms, which have been set at another level. This principle applies to systems, which are characterised by regional and local self-administration, and includes countries such as Great Britain, the Scandinavian countries, the Netherlands and Germany. The so-called Napoleonic states (Page and Goldsmith, 1987: 163; Wunder, 1995) are predominantly characterised by the principle of verticality or administrative deconcentration. The public authority, which sets the rule, also takes care of the implementation by means of field agencies in the region. The (former) prefectorial system of France is the most notable example in this respect, but the category also includes countries like Italy, Spain, Greece, Portugal, and characterises the developments in Belgium so far.

Both the horizontal and the vertical principles may lead to different outcomes in terms of the degree of fragmentation and integration of

Scheme 4.2 The nature of IGRs

Local self-administration versus administrative deconcentration			
Horizontal administration	Interwoven administration	Vertical administration	Field administration

services at the subnational level. In some systems, forms of vertical administration have led to a more uncoordinated 'picket fence model' (Wright, 1979: 62) in which national ministries have each, more or less independently, set up their own field agencies and thus functionalised service delivery. The issue of territorial integration is neglected at the expense of territorial fragmentation and a lack of coordination and policy integration. The German system differs from the French system in consequently applying the principle of local self-administration in the relations among Bund and Länder and Länder and municipalities. This contrasts with the French deconcentration of services into the hands of a (prefectorial) field administration, which executes assigned functions under the responsibility of the central government. Both systems, however, either by means of a prefectorial, or by means of a local government field organisation, try to secure a comparable degree of integration of national services in the region. The territorial dimension of the French system has become more political in nature in the course of the decentralisation, and reform processes of the 1980s and 1990s, when the *départements* were granted democratic legitimation by inserting directly elected councils as the major way for democratic legitimation and control. Creating more flexibility in the French intergovernmental system has been an important reason behind this form of enhancing and politicising territoriality in the operation of public service delivery and control.

The second dimension concerns the degree of administrative and political interwovenness of the different levels, which generally characterises the intergovernmental system of a particular country. Some systems are characterised by statutory regulation and a high degree of separation of the different layers of government. One might speak of steering from a distance. The most notable historical example is the 'dual' British system where the principle of 'ultra vires', in joint combination with the emphasis on local autonomy, has led to a system that '... can be called a Dual Polity, a structure of central local relations in which national and local politics, and national and local government, operated, by and large, in two separate compartments' (Bulpitt, 1989: 67; 1983). In a somewhat different way, the separation of the government levels is thus far also characteristic for the Belgium and Spanish forms of federalism in its transitory stage of development. In Belgium, the administrative separation of state and regions is complemented by a situation in which national political parties have ceased to exist and are organised on a regional and linguistic basis.

The relative lack of direct administrative and political linkages, as well as of an intermediate meso-level of government between national and local government of the British system, traditionally contrasts with the administrative and political osmosis of the French intergovernmental system (Ashford, 1982). The French system with its reputation for 'tutelage' and detailed administrative regulation is additionally characterised by a high degree of political interwovenness through a system of *cumul des mandats*.

Politicians may be holding several offices at the same time at municipal, regional, national and even European levels of government (Wright, 2001). The opportunity for an accumulation of offices has been legally restricted in the early 1980s, but it is still a characteristic feature of the French system. It is lacking, if not outright foreclosed by, non-accumulation rules and practices in many other countries.

The political interwovenness of levels of government can take on different forms. The operation of the political party system may be relevant, or elaborate institutional and formalised arrangements for joint decision making across various levels of government, like in Germany. In line of Scheme 2, the rather intense and two-lane mobility of German federal and land politicians – and federal and land civil servants – combined with the constitutional and legal provisions for joint decision making (Bundesrat; Gemeinschaftsaufgaben (Joint tasks of federal and state governments)), places the federal German state system, along the present dimension, in the same category as the French unitary state.

The horizontality principle creates a fundamental interdependency relationship among various levels of government. The tradition of a 'non-executant role' of central government, characteristic for countries like Great Britain, Germany, the Scandinavian countries and the Netherlands, is identified as one of the overriding factors in explaining the variety in the share of local government activity in the overall state activities (Page and Goldsmith, 1987; Rhodes and Wright, 1987). In these systems, local governments are strongly embedded in the overall state structure, often taking a larger share of governmental expenditures out of the overall budget than the national government does.

The Anglo-Saxon system of local government and municipal self-administration creates at least a potential dependency of national upon local governments for the implementation of public services. The national 'Napoleonic' governments in Southern Europe preside over their own deconcentrated field agencies to carry out their policies. As already stated, these are less likely to develop in the more unilaterally arranged deconcentrated systems. The interdependencies potentially allow for the development of meaningful forms of co-governance and intergovernmental exchange relations where local governments may exploit the relative advantages of their 'local presence'. Whether this will actually occur depends upon the characteristics of the system in terms of the degree of interwovenness.

The degree of interwovenness is conventionally being addressed – and criticised – under the heading of centralisation. Practitioners will never tire of stressing the need for complementarity in central-local relations. The model of partnership versus the model of central and decentralised government relationships has equally stressed the desirability of disentangling intergovernmental relations on behalf of the 'lower' governments. If anything, comparative intergovernmental experiences over the past decade have at least contributed to a considerable modification of this conventional wisdom.

The 'new centralism' in Britain may have been a temporary interlude caused by the particular ideology of the Thatcher era. It was surely surprising enough to have a closer look at the possible institutional flaws in this traditional bulwark of local government autonomy. The image of the 'Dual polity' suggests an explanation. The relative lack of direct administrative and political interwovenness of the system allowed the Thatcher government to implement its retrenchment policies at the local level of government, without directly being confronted with the administrative and political counter forces. These would undoubtedly have been mobilised if the institutional arrangements would allow for the bureaucratic and party political access of local interest to the national decision-making centres. Not until the introduction of the 'poll tax' did the national administration become directly involved in 'local' issues, and directly experience the effects of its decisions at the local level of government. The osmosis of the French system provides the contrast. It is more centralist in nature, but has developed into a complex interplay of forces in which more than once, central government has not been able to pursue its stated policy preferences against the interests and will of the local authorities. The inability of one of the supposedly most centralised states, to reform the – to many observers – archaic, French municipal government system is almost legendary. Several other examples could be added to illustrate that the political and administrative osmosis of the French IGRs, creates a vehicle for mutual dependency and, at least, a two-way power and influence relationship (Wright, 2001; Mény, 1987; 1988).

A non-executive role of central government and local self-administration are relevant factors for explaining the potential importance of local public economies in intergovernmental systems as a whole. In addition, a certain degree of interwovenness of levels of government, which connects national and local agencies even against their will, seems necessary to allow for institutional conditions under which local politics and administration may maintain or at times raise its importance to national politics.

This institutionalisation of the 'cooperative state' (Hesse, 1987) may be achieved in the more deliberate way, which is typical for the German 'cooperative federalism'. It may also be achieved in the more pragmatic manner, which is typical for the operation of the French system of IGRs. In both cases, however, it comes down to finding and striking a difficult balance between selective activation and joint decision making on the one hand and the stagnation, conflict avoidance and blockade of complex intergovernmental networks on the other.

One dimension has been excluded thus far from the analysis of the different types of IGRs: IGRs in consociational civil society, and state structures in the context of pillarised interest and service delivery. We have stated that pillarisation has been manifest on different geographical scales ranging from central to regional and local levels. As such, these pillarised structures are to be considered as specific manifestations of *societal* self-administration (Toonen, 2000). Apart from intrapillarised, vertical and horizontal (cross policy field) relations, they maintain relations with central, provincial and regional governments on the relevant policy areas.

In relation to central and provincial governments, the non-executant role of the centre and provinces has depended to a large extent on the existence of these pillarised structures at the regional and local levels. Pillarised service delivery thus worked and works as an alternative to direct intervention by central government organisation and/or the use of field agencies. Field administration in the Netherlands has been historically associated with the French (Napoleonic) system of government. That system, particularly in the nineteenth century, was equated with a coercive and oppressive position of government (Raadschelders and Van der Meer, 1995). Thus at the same time the use of pillarised structures (together with local government) delivered a means to limit the size and power of a single, central government bureaucracy. Interestingly enough the use of this non-governmental mode of service provision by pillarised organisation, did limit (at least nominally) the size of government. Consequently, recent studies of the Organisation for Economic Cooperation and Development (OECD), comparing the size of the public sector staff in various member states, show that the Dutch government personnel are in the very low ranges, as they are only limited to government organisations.

Finally, as argued earlier, the top down interpretation of decision making in the pillarised context is a misinterpretation similar to the presumed vertical and hierarchical nature of decision making in the 'decentralised unitary state concept'. The vertical integration operated much more in a mutual (reinforcing) way, supported by a mechanism of cultural coordination and what can be seen as a pillarised version of the *cumul des mandats*. These mechanisms similarly supported a horizontal (cross local, regional and policy field) coordination.

The IGM

The IGM dimension, finally, refers to the array of problem solving activities, procedures, techniques and forms of steering and control, which persons deploy, which operate at the interfaces of the different governmental agencies. They operate within the given intergovernmental constitutional and relational framework of the intergovernmental system.

Different forms of IGM may result in different, and sometimes counter-intuitive, results as far as the operation of the system is concerned. The Scandinavian countries and the United Kingdom, for example, differ from France, Italy and Spain in that they rely more heavily on IGM by general norms, statutes, regulations and criteria that must be observed by the authorities involved. In contrast to this management, according to

Scheme 4.3 IGM

Statutory control versus hands-on management			
Administrative reform	Statutory regulation	Joint decision making	Administrative regulation

statutory regulation, the other countries tend to rely relatively more on administrative regulation by direct and more detailed guidance, in which many decisions of local authorities involve the intervention of central government officials.

In the northern countries the management, by statutory regulation, is often practised and advocated in the name of 'decentralisation'. The empirical observation of Page and Goldsmith (1987: 162) is that the IGM practices underlying administrative regulation implying close links between centre and specific localities. Page and Goldsmith conclude that local government has much better opportunities to influence central policy making in the southern states that were investigated than in the United Kingdom and Scandinavia in the north: 'In South Europe, not only is the voice of local government as a whole heard at the centre, but also that of the individual municipality'.

Images of the operation of intergovernmental systems derived from an inspection of the IGC and IGR may thus vary from the actual day-to-day operation of the system at the level of IGM. Pragmatic IGM, over time, seems to have turned the original hierarchical conception of the Napoleonic state in France into a complex, but relatively stable and rather flexible institutional osmosis – mutual interpenetration – of centre and periphery. On the other hand, the more 'decentralised' forms of institutional separation and statutory regulation in recent years, often seem to have led to alienated, strained and conflicting IGRs. This is particularly true in those systems where the institutional administrative distance in IGRs is not bridged, or is even widened by the IGM conducted within the political party system. This is the likely event if different political parties dominate different levels of government. Belgium and Britain provide the illustrations.

Hesse and Benz (1990: 141) suggest that Reagan's 'New Federalism' of the early 1980s has merely been a symbolic operation from the viewpoint of structural IGRs reform. However, the symbolic nature of the initiative, at the same time, leads to a revitalisation of regional and local politics. This, in effect, has induced a de facto decentralisation of the system, due to a more self-confident, active and assertive role of state and city agencies and officials. This, in turn, at the level of IGM, leads to a better exploitation of the opportunities, which the existing IGC and IGRs offered to sub-central administrations.

On the European continent one may observe some similar developments. The actual structural results of the 'free local governments' experiments in the

Scandinavian, and several other countries, have been limited, especially against the background of expectations with which they were originally launched and copied. In all countries, however, the experimental establishment of 'free communes' has '... helped to develop an ethos of re-thinking and questioning' (Steward and Stoker, 1989: 140). This observation seems to apply more in general to the decentralist wave that many perceive in the European continent over the past decade. Decentralisation seems to follow instead of creating a more active and self-assured role of local governments in IGRs.

The regained self-confidence of regional and local authorities on the European continent has largely been caused by the conclusion of policy makers in many countries that in coping with the economic crises in West European states of the early 1980s, they were dependent upon an upswing of the local public economies. Given its institutional structure, the British system allowed the Thatcher government to more or less relieve local governments of their responsibility for these functions and eventually almost to bypass existing local government structures altogether. This was achieved, for example, by installing separate Urban Development Corporations, enterprise zones and Task Force and City Action Teams. Like the nationally initiated City Technology Colleges, these were all intended to improve and revitalise the urban economy and infrastructures.

In many other countries the institutional set-up of the intergovernmental system required, in contrast, that the same (national) management response to largely the same economic problems was dependent on the cooperation of local and regional governments. In a supposedly 'centralised' system like, for example, the Netherlands it would be unthinkable that municipalities like Amsterdam or Rotterdam could be bypassed in efforts to revitalise 'their' inner city or the broader urban local public economy.

Instead, the most remarkable development in the Netherlands, over the past decade, has been the rise and development of interactive forms of IGM. Despite a fundamental legal indistinctness on the role and position of these intergovernmental 'agreements', national ministries and municipal governments have increasingly taken refuge to covenants and policy agreements in the intergovernmental intercourse. They provide a way to try and reduce uncertainty and to cope, already in the pre-judicial stages of decision making, with the administrative and intergovernmental interdependencies, which are inherent to the Dutch system of 'home administration'. Generally speaking 'territory' seems to have gained more and more status as a point of reference in the management of IGRs. 'Spatial targeting' of investments in social and physical infrastructures has become an important aim in the management of intergovernmental systems, in order to try to achieve accumulative and reinforcing effects out of various functionally organised initiatives. At the same time, in the Netherlands, there is still a lack of territorial coordination at regional and local levels of the social service delivery by the 'social enterprises'. These once belonged to the integral structure of pillarised social service delivery: education, care, social housing and welfare.

The reconstitution of the Dutch welfare state will be incomplete without some form of reterritorialisation in the intergovernmental structure or the IGM of 'spatially oriented' public service delivery, at the level of neighbourhoods, cities and regions.

These are just some illustrations of the general argument. Different styles of management and underlying administrative cultures may drastically change the way in which the same institutional arrangements, at the level of IGC or IGRs, might actually operate on a day-to-day basis and spill over into questions of territoriality. Supervision powers of one public authority over another might be used in one system as a mechanism for coordination, consultancy, support, mediation and problem solving, among levels of government. In other systems they might vehemently be exploited for trying to settle narrow-minded bureaucratic and political fights and conflicts, or to block or veto developments of adjacent units in the intergovernmental system. The same is true for central–local grant systems, the accumulation of public offices, or the central appointment of local or regional officials (like mayors). These institutional arrangements may 'outwardly' all look the same in different countries. At the level of IGM they may very well be differently deployed. Management responses to pressing problems, within the institutional constraints of a given system, might eventually change the operation of the system while leaving the IGC and IGRs largely unchanged. They may also evoke structural changes at the level of IGR or IGC. Equally, efforts to reform the IGRs or the IGC by governmental reorganisations may be neutralised at the operational level of IGM. Observers of the French system, for example, consistently emphasise that one should not overestimate the actual changes that have followed from the institutional reforms in terms of decentralisation and regionalisation of the 1980s. The French 'notables' in the provinces have not been able to absorb and neutralise the institutional reforms that affected their positions and, perhaps, even to turn them into their advantage. Thus, they had once again 'managed' to turn seemingly radical institutional IGRs reforms into marginal – albeit significant – changes.

In sum, the different experiences with the national European intergovernmental systems over the past decade, seem to indicate that the favourable conditions for a stable adaptation to changing circumstances, are a combination of a general (instead of an enumerated) competence of the principal constituent parts of the intergovernmental system. IGC with 'horizontal' co-governance structures at the level of IGRs. This allows for a staggered and differentiated process of adaptation to changing circumstances: first, a mutual interdependency of different administrative levels, which contributes to a certain degree of equilibrium within the intergovernmental system as a whole. Second, an institutional structure which condemns the constituent parts of the intergovernmental system to a degree of mutual concern for each other's affairs. The outcomes depend on the development of a matching IGM culture.

Conclusion

Already in 1949 Fesler wrote, what still is considered one of the leading handbooks in PA, a study called 'Area and administration'. From the early beginnings the problems associated with the combination of territorial, functional and organisational dimensions of public governance have been at the heart of PA debate. Still the issue of 'territory' is a continuing concern. From this perspective discussions about the changing meaning of territoriality in politics and service delivery can be a little bit bemusing. Nevertheless, a debate is simmering (see the Introduction by Burgess and Vollaard to this volume) on the changing significance of territory in politics and service delivery both in the EU and in European nation states. As has been argued in this chapter, there is a fundamental problem with the concept of territoriality in the way that it is often used. In constitutional law and PA a distinction is made between functional and territorial decentralisation. This suggestion of a separation between function and the territorial principles in politics and administration might be analytically correct, but in practice it is a fallacy from a PA perspective. In the final analysis, all politics and administration is territorial and functional, at the same time. The real opposition is between (ideal type) multi-purpose and single purpose constructions that are demarcated to given territories. A term like (de) territorialisation, as such, is consequently losing its clear meaning because it can include both the changing geographical space and the un- or re-bundling of operations. The construct of the Westphalian nation state impedes a real understanding of the fact that most European states can be typified both in a practical and a formal legal meaning as multi-level governance systems. These are systems in which multi- and single purpose governments and other entities are operating and interacting on various geographical scales in the public sphere. Seen from a dynamic perspective changes from multi- to single purpose nature and vice versa, and changing geographical scales of politics and service delivery, have been the order of the day. This experience might benefit the understanding of (changes in) territoriality, especially in the case of the EU.

The European unification process can be seen, from the national perspective, as an extension of the previous national multi-level system. In the latter part of our contribution we have presented some examples as to how the understanding of the significance of territoriality under (changing) conditions of multi-layered governance in intergovernmental systems, as mentioned above, can be greatly improved by paying attention to the multilevel world of IGC, IGRs and IGM. It is not sufficient to restrict the analysis to the institutional features of a given system at one level, as often occurs. It is often the combination of features at the constitutional, relational and managerial levels of intergovernmental systems that determine the nature of the system and the role territoriality may play. Given the different outlines of the various IGCs, the systems of IGRs and the IGM of European nation states and the problems they are confronting, the territorial base of politics, policy making and service provision will be accordingly redesigned and operations appropriately re- or unbundled.

Note

1 The Dutch word *kaart* translates, in this context, into the English word map. Card in English is, for instance, used to refer to business card, a credit card or even a birthday card, while a map is usually a representation, on paper, of a region of the Earth.

References

Ashford Douglas, E. (1982), *British Dogmatism and French Pragmatism: Central-local Policymaking in the Welfare State*. London: G. Allen & Unwin.

Bachrach, P.S. and Baratz M.S. (1962), 'Two Faces of Power', *The American Political Science Review*, 56(4) December.

Benz, A. (1995), 'Institutional Change in Intergovernmental Relations: The Dynamics of Multi-level Structures', in J.J. Hesse and Th.A.J. Toonen (eds), *The European Yearbook of Comparative Government and Public Administration*. Baden-Baden: Nomos.

Blom, J.C.H. (2000), 'Pillarisation in Perspective', *Western European Politics* 23(3). July.

Bulpitt, J. (1983), *Territory and Power to the United Kingdom*. Manchester: Manchester University Press.

—— (1989), 'Walking Back to Happiness? Conservative Party Governments and Elected Local Authorities in the 1980s', in C. Crouch and D. Marquand (eds), *The New Centralism, Britain Out of Step in Europe?* Oxford: Basil Blackwell.

Daalder, H. (1981), 'Consociationalism, Center and Periphery in the Netherlands', in P. Torsvik (ed.), *Mobilization, Center-Periphery Structures and Nation Building: A Volume in Commemoration of Stein Rokkan*. Oslo: Universitaetsforlaget. Reprinted in H. Daalder, J.Th.J. van den Berg and B.A.G.M. Tromp (eds), *Politiek en Historie: opstellen over Nederlandse politiek en vergelijkende politieke wetenschap*. Amsterdam: Bert Bakker.

Dahrendorf, R. (1999), 'Squaring the Circle: Prosperity, Civility and Liberty', in D. Avnon and A. de-Shalit (eds), *Liberalism and Its Practice*. London: Routledge.

Dente, B. and Kjellberg, F. (eds) (1988), *The Dynamics of Institutional Change. Local Government Reorganization in Western Democracies*. London: Sage Publications.

Douglas, M. and Wildavsky, A. (1983), *Risk and Culture: an Essay on the Selection of Technical and Environmental Dangers*. Berkeley, CA and Los Angeles, CA: University of California Press.

EU (2003) *Third European Report on Science and Technology Indicators*. Brussels.

Fesler, J. (1949), *Area and Administration*. Tuscaloosa, AL: University of Alabama Press.

Groenveld, S. (1995) *Huisgenoten des geloofs, Was de samenleving in de Republiek der Nederlanden verzuild?* Hilversum: Verloren.

Gunlicks, A.B. (1986), *Local Governments in the German Federal System*. Durham, NC: Duke University Press.

Hendriks, F. and Toonen, Th.A.J. (eds) (2001), *Polder Politics: The Reinvention of Consensus Democracy in the Netherlands*. Aldershot: Ashgate.

Hesse, J.J. (1987), 'The Federal Republic of Germany: From Cooperative Federalism to Joint Policy Making', in R.A.W. Rhodes and V. Wright (eds), *Tensions in the Territorial Politics of Western Europe.* London: Cass.

Hesse, J.J. and Benz, A. (1990), *Die Modernisierung der Staatsorganisation. Institutionspolitik im internationalen Vergleich: USA, Groszbritanien, Frankreich, Bundesrepublik Deutschland.* Baden-Baden: Nomos Verlagsgesellschaft.

Hood, C. (1991), 'A Public Management for all Seasons?' in *Public Administration* 60: 3–19.

Hooghe, L. and Marks, G. (2001), *Multi-Level Governance and European Integration.* Boulder, CO: Rowman & Littlefield.

Keating, M. (1998), *New Regionalism in Western Europe: Territorial Restructuring and Political Change.* Cheltenham: Edward Elgar.

Kiser, L. and Ostrom, E. (1982), 'The Three Worlds of Action: A Metatheoretical Synthesis of Institutional Approaches', in E. Ostrom (ed.), *Strategies of Political Inquiry.* Beverly Hills, CA: Sage.

Lane, J.E. and Ersson, S.O. (1987), *Politics and Society in Western Europe.* London: Sage.

Lijphart, A. (1984), *Democracies: Patterns of Majoritarian and Consensus Government in Twenty-one Countries.* New Haven: Yale University Press.

Mény, Y. (1987), 'France', in: E.C. Page and M. Goldsmith (eds), *Central and Local Government Relations: A Comparative Analysis of Western European Unitary States.* London: Sage.

—— (1988), 'France', in D.C. Rowat (ed.). *Public Administration in Developed Countries – A Comparative Study.* New York: Marcel Dekker.

Page, E.C. and Goldsmith, M. (eds) (1987), *Central and Local Government Relations: A Comparative Analysis of Western European Unitary States.* London: Sage.

Raadschelders, J.C.N. and Van der Meer, F. (1995), 'Between Restauration and Consolidation: The Napoleonic Model of Administration in the Netherlands 1795–1990, in B. Wunder (ed.), *The Napoleonic Model of Government.* Brussels: IIAS, pp. 199–222.

Rhodes, R.A.W. and Wright, V. (eds) (1987), *Tensions in the Territorial Politics of Western Europe.* London: Cass.

Steward, D. and Stoker, G. (1989), *The Future of Local Government.* Basingstoke: Macmillan Education.

Toonen, Th.A.J. (1987), 'A Decentralized Unitary State in a Welfare Society', *West European Politics* 10(4) October: 108–129; also in: R.A.W. Rhodes and V. Wright (eds), (*Tensions in the Territorial Politics of Western Europe.* London: Cass.

—— (1990), *Internationalisering en het openbaar bestuur als institutioneel ensemble: naar een zelfbestuurskunde.* Den Haag: Vuga.

—— (2000), 'Governing a Consensus Democracy: The Interplay of Pillarisation and Administration', *Western European Politics* 23(3) July 2000.

—— (2003), 'Administrative Reform Analytics', in B.G. Peters and J. Pierre (eds), *Handbook of Public Administration.* London: Sage, pp. 467–476.

Wright, Deil S. (1988), *Understanding Intergovernmental Relations.* Pacific Grove: Brooks/Cole.

Wright, Vincent (1979), 'Regionalization Under the French Fifth Republic: The Triumph of the Functional Approach', in L.J. Sharpe (ed.), *Decentralist Trends in Western Democracies.* London and Beverly Hills, CA: Sage Publications.

—— (2001), *The Government And Politics Of France.* London: Unwin Hyman.

Wunder, B. (ed.) 91995) *The Napoleonic model of government.* Brussels: IIAS.

5 Territoriality and federalism in the governance of the European Union

Michael Burgess

Introduction

In this chapter I want to engage the question of territoriality in the specific context of the emergent federal polity that is the European Union (EU). This survey is inevitably shaped and moulded by the historically dominant feature of the EU, namely, that it is essentially a union of *states* although increasingly one of *citizens* too. Consequently it is not possible to ignore the empirical reality that the territorial state remains the basic building block, the main (though not the only) constitutive element of European integration. This does not mean that it is the sole actor or agent of integrative forces – economic, social, political and legal – that have succeeded in building a new form of federal union. Nor does it imply that member state governments are the sole determinants of the direction, pace and policy outcomes of the integrative processes that characterise the EU. It merely acknowledges that the state has been the principal driving force behind post-war European integration, that member state governments have made rational strategic political judgements about their constitutional and political futures grounded in changing perceptions of their national interests and that these judgements have created conditions and circumstances over which they are now less able to exert independent control.

The territorial state has not been transcended by European integration. It has not disappeared. It has merely been re-conceptualised and re-constituted as part of a larger whole that is the EU. Consequently the notion of 'territoriality' remains an important socio-economic and psycho-political construct but it exists alongside increasingly important non-territorial dimensions of political representation and policy outcomes. The EU therefore is a new federal polity that is characterised by both territorial and non-territorial features in the era of globalisation.

Territoriality and its characteristics

Territoriality is both a simple and a complex concept. At its simplest level of meaning it refers to land (*terra*) and is fundamental to animal life and existence the most sophisticated form of which is human beings by virtue of their brain size, power of reasoning, complexity of culture and social relationships, and their increasing ability to modify and control their environment. Whether or not human territoriality is instinctive or learned remains something about which scholarly opinion is divided.[1] Depending upon case study and context, it is probably the case that both nature and nurture are inextricably intertwined.

Some scholars prefer to construe territoriality as a 'common sense' concept that suggests it is 'purely cultural, a social construct that humans use to mark their possessions or to get ahead in society'.[2] But what really matters in this subject of enquiry is to put together the basic precepts of political geography and political science. These boil down to concerns about the changing configurations between space, place and political processes in the context of an emerging era of globalisation. Ronan Paddison put it well when he observed that 'the meanings of spatial scales and how they interact through political processes are being redefined so that both the "de- and re-territorialisation of politics" constitute processes "that are challenging inherited spatial structures and the territorial means by which politics is and should be organised"'. Consequently the territorial basis within which political processes are transacted itself undergoes continuous incremental change.

Paddison noted that at the end of the twentieth century contemporary processes of political restructuring differed according to how far they 'problematised institutions and processes which were part of the taken-for-granted world'. Among the constitutional and political implications of these deepening trends were the following: the emergence of new territorially defined social movements, decentralist trends in both advanced and developing economies, the political salience of regionalism, the changing role of international boundaries in new forms of political union such as the EU, the rekindling of nationalism and the redefining of citizenship simultaneously with the development of post-nationalist and global forms of citizenship, the emergence of new forms of resistance politics, both local and those transcending national boundaries, renewed emphases upon old concepts such as the community through the revival of political ideals such as communitarianism and federalism, and multi-level forms of governance and the internationalisation of sub-state governments via the establishment of cross-national alliances networking cities within cooperative programmes of local restructuring. And while these developments mapped out what are fundamental shifts in the ways that politics is organised, 'a common denominator is their changing, often malleable, territoriality'.[3] In a nutshell, the relationships between politics, space and place have become more explicit and diversified.

But what is also interesting for our purposes in this chapter is how scholars have conceptualised territoriality. Historical accounts of the rise of the territorial state and alternative models of state formation and organisation have confirmed the viability of non-territoriality, or at least, the fluidity of territoriality. In the disciplinary field of international relations, for example, territoriality has not always conveyed a sense of fixity. John Ruggie has noted three particular ways in which forms of rule have historically differed from the modern territorial state. First he notes that human relationships need not be territorially based at all. Systems of rule existed whereby spatial extension was demarcated on the basis of kinship. It was only the shift from consanguinity to contiguity as the relevant spatial parameter that elevated territoriality to a new organisational level. Prior to this development, territory was *occupied* in kin-based systems, but it did not *define* them. Second, the notion of movement among tribes refutes the relevance of territorial fixity. The nomadic propensities of some peoples meant that the priority to move, wander and migrate prevailed over the preference to settle. Third, even where systems of rule were territorial and where there was relative fixity the overriding concept of territoriality did not necessarily entail mutual exclusion. In other words, certain rights, duties and obligations criss-crossed territorial boundaries in medieval Europe because 'authority was both personalized and parcelized within and across territorial formations and for which inclusive bases of legitimation prevailed'.[4] In this way medieval and early modern Europe was characterised by asymmetries, pluralities and anomalies that served to differentiate human collectivities rather than by the familiar mode of organising political space according to the system of territorial states.

Ruggie's reappraisal and re-evaluation of hitherto accepted historical interpretations of the origins of sovereignty, the rise of the territorial state, the Peace of Westphalia and the significance of the Holy Roman Empire that underpin much of the mainstream theoretical literature in international relations (IR) and is evident in some aspects of European integration should be viewed as an attempt to confront the conventional wisdom that surrounds territoriality and the territorial state. It is part of the recent intellectual challenge to old, encrusted assumptions and preconceptions about the nature and meaning of contemporary international politics and it reflects a discernible desire to break free from the conceptual straitjacket of the Westphalian territorial state and the sovereignty-centred view of the world.[5] By questioning these received truths that have served to buttress the realist paradigm in IR, it becomes possible to construe the organisation of political authority in much more imaginative terms than has hitherto been possible. Processes of differentiation can be conceptualised in a variety of forms, both territorial and non-territorial, as was the case in medieval Europe and in the Holy Roman Empire.

Today this line of reasoning, with its focus upon institutionalising difference and lauding variety and asymmetry in redesigning political authority, has come to be described as a form of 'neo-medievalism', suggesting complex combinations of territorial and non-territorial functional principles. Clearly the question of the territorial organisation of states and the emergence of new unions of states, especially in Europe and Latin America, brings into sharp focus the study of federal and confederal forms of political organisation. And the huge varieties of federal forms and arrangements that have existed and continue to flourish have an increasing relevance to contemporary politics in the empirical reality of the EU.

Territoriality in federalism and federation

Territoriality is firmly integrated in the mainstream literature on federalism. Indeed, for many of the major contributors to contemporary federal theory it is the key component on which they base their understanding of modern federation. Here, however, I shall explore this relationship from the particular standpoint of the conceptual distinction between 'federalism' and 'federation'. Let us examine these two concepts a little more closely.

Because it is much more familiar, we will begin by defining what we mean by federation. A federation is a state; it is a federal state. But it is a particular kind of state, one that is founded upon a basic contractual constitutional agreement or bargain designed primarily to recognise and sustain diversity. The appeal of the federal idea – and its manifestation in federation – lies in its institutional and structural capacity both to accommodate and reconcile different forms of unity with different forms of diversity. Federations exist because they formally acknowledge, via constitutional entrenchment, the sorts of identities and diversities that constitute that sense of difference so essential to a living, breathing pluralist social and political order. To qualify as a federation, then, it is essential that the state constitute all of the basic paraphernalia required of a liberal democratic state, including a written constitution, an independent judiciary, a sustainable division of powers and competences between at least two levels of government that is constitutionally entrenched, agreed procedures for constitutional amendment, and a range of attributes designed to guarantee the legitimacy, autonomy and integrity of the constituent units of the federation.

Federalism is rather less tangible than federation. It can refer to three particular forms, namely, ideology, philosophy and what I have called 'empirical reality'.[6] For our purposes in this chapter, I shall confine myself to the first meaning, namely, political ideology. Here federalism is the original and persistent driving force of federation. Federalism seeks federation and embodies diversities, having political salience, which can be accommodated only via constitutional entrenchment in a federation. And these diversities, it should be noted, can take many forms whether territorial or non-territorial. In the mainstream literature on federalism, however, there is a marked tendency to assume that the most significant identities seeking federation are territorially based. Let us have a closer look at this particular trend of thought.

The assumption of territoriality in federations is, in one particular sense, to be entirely expected. This is because federations are *ipso facto* composed of clearly demarcated constituent units that are territorial units. The German *Länder*, Swiss cantons and Canadian provinces are all territorially bounded communities that represent the political organisation of space in the occupation of territory. And in many, though not all, of these cases territoriality – the sense of place – plays a significant role in their self-definition. As we will see, however, it is certainly not the only source of such definition. Territorial identity cannot be construed in isolation from other social cleavages that interact with it to forge a distinct identity, a strong sense of self.

Today probably few scholars of federalism would go as far as William Livingston did in his seminal article of 1952 which is worth quoting at length:

> If they [i.e. societal diversities] are grouped territorially, that is geographically, then the result may be a society that is federal. If they are not grouped territorially, then the society cannot be said to be federal. In either case coherence in the society may depend on the devolution upon these groups of the exercise of functions appropriate to the diversities that they represent. But in the first case only can this take the form of federalism [sic federation] or federal government. In the latter case it becomes functionalism, pluralism, or some form of corporativism ... writers who profess to see federal elements in the various forms of pluralism, such as feudalism or corporativism ... have added a meaning that was not there before.... No government has ever been called federal that has been organized on any other but the territorial basis.[7]

But Livingston was certainly not alone in his excessive reliance upon the notion of territoriality in the study of federations. In one of the standard commentaries on the comparative study of federal political systems, published in 1970, Ivo Duchacek confirmed that his survey was about the 'territorial distribution of political authority' and that its central concept was 'the territorial community or the territorial interest group – an aggregate of individuals and groups who share not only common experiences, values, fears and purposes but also an awareness of the territorial dimensions of their collective interests and actions'.[8] For Duchacek the study of federations was limited to 'territorial communities' and federal constitutions expressed what he called 'the core creed of democracy, pluralism, in territorial terms'.[9] His reasoning went along the following lines:

> In all political systems there has always been a problem ... as to which is the best principle of organizing authority: should it be based on territorial divisions or on functional divisions? So far the practice seems to indicate a trend toward a combination of both; the formula is to base parties and governments primarily on territorial divisions with functional specialization within, allowing or encouraging functional interests to exercise their pressures on the territorial units of authority.[10]

Similarly Ramesh Dikshit emphasised the importance of spatial organisation in his own contribution to this particular debate in 1975. His interpretation was that of the political geographer and it came as no surprise therefore when he claimed the study of federalism to be 'the most geographically expressive of all forms of government'; it was 'the complex interaction of spatial differences and similarities' that made possible 'the geographical approach to federalism'.[11] Because the study of federations was based largely upon polities characterised by 'interactions and interrelations of a complex set of regionally grouped diversities (represented by and articulated through the constituent states of the nation), a geographical approach ... with its emphasis on areal integrations and regional interactions' was deemed particularly helpful in this task.[12]

Maurice Vile should also be included here because his emphasis upon territoriality, while slightly different from that of Duchacek, was nonetheless quite categorical about territorial federation as the only legitimate form:

> Federalism [sic federation] is *territorial* in its origins, but it can change into a set of institutions adapted to a *pluralistic* political system, where the territorial element becomes increasingly less relevant to the way in which the "federal" institutions actually work.... The growth of a sense of national identity diminishes the importance within the political system of territorial loyalties, and therefore begins to erode those aspects of the political culture upon which the federal system was originally based.[13]

Vile's attempt to offer a developmental model of the federal political system was part of the wider determination among scholars at that time to escape from the definitional congestion that had descended upon the subject in the 1970s, but he shared Duchacek's belief that non-territorial functional determinants of federations remained subordinate to territorial structures.

This brief sketch outline of how far the notion of territoriality has been firmly anchored in the mainstream literature on federalism and federation suggests an uncritical and excessive reliance upon the concept. In most cases it seems to indicate a somewhat oversimplified preconception about the content of such territorial communities. If we descend from the general to the particular, we can more readily appreciate the complexity implied in the term 'territoriality'; in reality it incorporates an amalgam of socio-economic and cultural elements encapsulated in a spatial organisation. It is therefore wrong to construe territoriality as if it is something akin to an empty container that stands in its own right as an independent variable set apart from other patterns of social cleavages having political salience. Territoriality in federal political systems must be viewed as part of the larger conception of the politics of difference that inheres in discussions of federalism. It interacts with a variety of intervening variables to produce complex forms of political identity.

Territoriality, then, is considerably more complex than Duchacek and others appear to suggest. The nebulous and shifting nature of territory is perhaps best illuminated by adapting Frank Trager's claim: territoriality is not a fixed point on a map.[14] A proper analysis of the social, economic, political and cultural-ideological forces involved in the processes of decision making would demonstrate that the composition of the so-called territorial aggregate – and consequently its concerns – varies from one policy issue to the next.

If we now summarise this section of the chapter, we can state clearly that the concept of territoriality in federal political systems is an extremely complex matter. It can mean much more than the notion of constituent regional political units in a *federation*, such as the German *Länder*, Swiss cantons or American states that enjoy territorial representation in second chambers of government. In terms of *federalism* the focus of the survey shifts to the interaction of a wide range of socio-economic and cultural-ideological factors that interact to produce a distinct sense of territorial identification. This means that 'territoriality' should not be over-simplified, nor should it be spoken about in absolute terms. Unless we are referring specifically to the administrative machinery of the state, it is advisable to construe territoriality as at best an intervening variable that can be extrapolated only in abstract terms.

Contemporary challenges to the territorial state

Before we look in more detail at the EU as a case study of how far the concept of territoriality is played out in an emerging federal polity, let us pause to reflect upon the nature of the contemporary challenges to the territorial state. After all, the EU is itself one of the tangible institutional responses to these challenges.

In his pioneering article entitled the 'Rise and Demise of the Territorial State', published in 1957, John Hertz identified four main threats or challenges to what he called the 'hard shell' of the state. These were, 'in order of increasing effectiveness': economic blockade; ideological-political penetration (psychological warfare); air warfare; and atomic warfare.[15] Hertz was primarily concerned with matters of international defence and security but his references to the changing scope and scale of change itself and to the 'newness of the new' that underlined the 'new condition of permeability' of the modern territorial state conveyed the sense of having already moved into an epoch of its potential obsolescence.[16] In his apparent sense of despair, however, he had (perhaps inadvertently) already arrived at some basic conceptual reformulations that were not very far from becoming the new reality:

> the short-term objective must surely be mutual accommodation, a drawing of demarcation lines, geographical and otherwise, between East and West. . . . May we then expect, or hope, that radically new attitudes,

in accordance with a radically transformed structure of nationhood and international relations, may ultimately gain the upper hand over the inherited ones based on familiar concepts of old-style national security, power and power competition.[17]

Indeed, when this article was first published, it was in the very year that the Treaty of Rome was signed in March 1957 establishing 'an ever closer union among European peoples'. Consequently his sophisticated remarks about 'the juxtaposition of old and new factors, a coexistence in theory and practice of conventional and new concepts, of traditional and new policies' were, in hindsight, remarkably prescient.[18] The territorial state was moving into an era of unprecedented change and the second half of the twentieth century did evolve towards 'the necessity of multilevel concepts and multilevel policies'. If his diagnosis was somewhat limited in identifying the nature of the new challenges, it was certainly correct in pinpointing the need for a radical rethinking of fundamental concepts and policies.[19]

Today the principal interest of many research studies that focus upon challenges to the territorial state can be reduced to one word, namely, 'globalisation'. This is a rather elastic term that remains highly contested and contestable. Nonetheless, it is used by journalists, academics, politicians, military elites, environmental technicians and business executives to signify that something profound is happening, that the world is changing, 'that a new world economic, political and cultural order is emerging'.[20] There seems, in short, to be a popular awareness of deep-seated change; people clearly have a heightened sense of the 'immediacy' of change, that they are somehow touched by forces and pressures that are simultaneously close and remote and over which they have little or no control.

With these thoughts in mind, it would seem that the key to understanding globalisation is to start with the assumption that it is essentially a multidimensional phenomenon. Indeed, David Held has asserted this boldly:

> Globalization is neither a singular condition nor a linear process. Rather, it is best thought of as a multidimensional phenomenon involving domains of activity and interaction that include the economic, political, technological, military, legal, cultural, and environmental. Each of these spheres involves different patterns of relations and activities.[21]

There is much common sense in this position. Globalisation is actually 'a complex and multidimensional phenomenon that involves different levels, flows, tensions and conflicts'. And Douglas Kellner is right when he emphasises that in a sense 'there is no such thing as globalization *per se*'. Instead 'the term is used as a cover concept for a heterogeneity of processes that need to be spelled out and articulated'.[22]

What, then, are these processes – these activities and relations – to which scholars of globalisation regularly refer? Judging by what appears broadly in the mainstream literature on globalisation, the most frequent references are to financial transactions (especially capital markets), information technology (IT), international trade and investment and environmental issues and policies. In this world of global linkages, states, governments and political systems have had to adapt and adjust to the presence of new actors engaged in worldwide activities with connections that form part of a complex bargaining process for resources where companies can provide them with instant access to capital and technology. And these circumstances immediately bring us into direct contact with the structure of the international political economy (IPE). In this fiercely competitive world we can see why Susan Strange should have referred to 'structural power' as the most important form of power in contemporary IR She claimed that structural power gave states the capacity to choose and to shape the IPE within which other states and their economic and political organisations and institutions were compelled to operate.[23] The implication of this analysis at least acknowledged that the *territorial state* still had a role to play in the globalisation game and that it had not, as some have argued, been superseded by new forms of capital, technology and production. Instead the evolutionary structural change in the IPE has been responsible for altering the notion of the state so that it is the character of the state and of the state system that has changed.

Before we turn to look at the implications of globalisation for the territorial state, some of which are disputed, let us pause to consider what all of this means. Globalisation can be described positively or negatively depending upon subjective values, beliefs and interests so what sort of phenomenon is it? And what words do we usually associate with it? The terminology is important because it conveys the particular sense in which it is broadly understood. Terms like linkages, connections, interconnectedness and interdependence, and words like permeation, interpenetration and porousness furnish the sense of a global network of multifarious, multilevel activities that exist independent of states and governments. Indeed, in some respects, they seem powerless either to control or even to exert significant influence upon them. And in turn citizens and mass publics appear increasingly distanced from and marginalised by the growing intensification of global forces.

The conventional observation that is usually made concerning the political impact of globalisation is summarised in the work of Manuel Castells who has claimed that from around the 1970s two fundamental transformations have occurred, one in the technology of information transmissions and the other in the organisation of business and the global economy. These two processes have resulted in what amounts to a reconstruction of space: the nature of space, place and distance has been radically altered. Castells' belief is that a technological revolution – tantamount to a new technological paradigm – of historic proportions is transforming the basic dimensions of human life, namely, time and space.[24] Put briefly, this suggests that these two facets of globalisation – both a feature of the contemporary restructuring of the capitalist mode of production – are in essence a contradictory set of processes which have been responsible for a double movement of integration and fragmentation. This means that the national state has been subjected to global forces and pressures that have propelled it in the direction of regional integration, like the EU, in the world of states, while simultaneously generating new feelings of solidarity, new political linkages and new forms of political behaviour among its own citizens within the state. There has therefore been a notable propensity for states to come together to form new unions at the same time as they have been confronted with new challenges from within by disgruntled social, economic and cultural groups and communities unhappy with their status and welfare, and increasingly willing to utilise territorial politics as a means by which to mobilise common local-regional interests.

None of this sketched out above suggests that territorial politics and the territorial state have been in some sense transcended or that they have been eroded from within and ceased to be politically significant. On the contrary, it is much more the case that, as Michael Keating has argued, we have moved into an era that is witnessing not the demise of the territorial state, or the end of territorial politics much less the disappearance of territoriality as a politically significant social cleavage. Rather what we are now part of is a process involving the re-conceptualisation, reconfiguration and reconstruction of territorial politics and the territorial state.[25] As a result, territorial politics has both increased in significance in some areas and has declined or been displaced in others.

The broad set of challenges encapsulated in the term globalisation, then, suggests that its disintegrative effects prompt a response geared to new forms of territorial cohesion and a search for new political spaces within and without the polity. This leads in turn to new actors, new social movements and new forms of political organisation designed to adapt and adjust to the contemporary challenges to the territorial state. Here we have come back full circle to what Paddison identified above as the deepening processes of contemporary political restructuring. Let us return briefly to the EU as our case study of both territorial and non-territorial politics.

The EU as a case study

Our short survey suggests that it would be wrong to assume that the creation and subsequent evolution of the EU signified the attenuation of territorial politics and the subordination of the territorial state to non-territorial functional activities. In one sense the supranational level of mobilising economic and political resources is just that – an elevated arena of public policy activities for the member states. Territorial interests have therefore merely been elevated to a different arena that has the institutional capacity to accommodate sub-state local-regional, national, European and increasingly international dimensions of public policy. Territorial state interests are represented by the member state governments in the European Council and Council of Ministers, while the EU territorial space is occupied by the European Commission and the local-regional territorial sub-state units have been formally incorporated in the Committee of the Regions (Coreper).[26] Meanwhile the formal representation of non-territorial functional activities in the Economic and Social Committee (ESC) is complemented by the less formal activities of the European Trades Union Congress (ETUC), the Union of Industrial and Employers' Confederations of Europe (UNICE), the European Round Table of Industrialists (ERT) and the Committee of Agricultural Organisations in the EU (COPA) that reflect a variety of socio-economic interests.

In the specific terms of territorial representation in the central institutions of the EU, it is worth pointing out the unique nature and significance of the EU Presidency of the European Council as the dominant mode of intergovernmental bargaining and negotiation in treaty reform. The Presidency is generally regarded as the pivotal central institution of the EU that, in cooperation with the Commission, sets political priorities and shapes the main policy agenda. It is therefore largely responsible for determining both the major institutional reforms and the grand policy issues that serve to shape and reshape Europe's future. The Presidency represents the Council both in the Union's *internal* institutional structure towards other EU institutions and *externally* in acting as the collective voice for the EU in international organisations and towards third countries in the world of states. But it is important to note that the role of the Presidency is not always in practice what it might seem to be in theory. The mainstream literature tends to focus upon its role in promoting the national interests and national policy preferences of the member state governments, but as a central EU institution it also promotes the interests of the union *as a whole*. Consequently it is perfectly legitimate to construe the Presidency as an actor with both national and supranational interests and priorities. In other words, there is a sense in which it represents *both* national and EU interests, especially in external relations in general, which gives it more of a confederal role than many theorists of European integration would care to acknowledge.[27] This means that in practice its role is much more inherently ambiguous — as an extremely sophisticated level of institutionalisation in international relations terminology — than conventional theories of European integration would allow. For our purposes in this chapter, then, the EU Presidency can be construed as having a double role in representing the territorial interests of both the member states as single autonomous *states* and the EU as a unitary spatial actor.

Today it is generally accepted that European integration is driven principally by competing conceptions of the national interest and that in pursuit of these the member states have pooled their power resources and decision-making capacities which in consequence have been channelled and canalised upwards to Brussels. Member state governments have acknowledged that by themselves they are no longer capable of national self-determination in a much more competitive and hostile world. Indeed, many political elites construe membership of the EU precisely as a means of regaining their lost or declining state capacity. Consequently statist terms like 'sovereignty' and 'independence' can have no real meaning in a world where the vast majority of national states simply do not have the economic and political resources to compete not only with other states but also with multinational corporations (MNCs) and the mobility of finance capital. It is not that they have become mere ciphers in the era of globalisation. Some of them are actually the principal agents of different forms of globalisation, but they certainly cannot afford to ignore the harsh realities of another new age. In these ferociously competitive circumstances the best way to describe the position in which the national state finds itself today is that of, at best, a 'relative autonomy' rather than a fictitious independence.

Power in this particular sense, then, has drifted upwards to Brussels. And an institutional structure has been created in the EU the like of which has never before been seen, one which has generated much frustration and anxiety among member state governments and mass publics as well as remarkably innovative and progressive policy initiatives and departures. Looking back in hindsight over the last half-century, the achievements of West European economic and political integration – of the European project – have been quite astonishing. Indeed, it is a measure of its great success that it has come to be taken for granted by so many of its member states, governments and mass publics, and that so many other national states continue to form a queue to join this unique regional international organisation that is a new form of federal union. This, then, is one side of the coin.

On the other side of the coin we encounter the political implications of these developments which have themselves intensified since the Single European Act (SEA) ratified in 1987. The jewel in the crown of the SEA was the Single European Market (SEM) that signalled the formal commitment of Europe's then Twelve to a comprehensive market model and economic strategy that would foster increased trade and capital flows linked later in 1992 to an equally formal commitment to Economic and Monetary Union (EMU) in the Treaty on European Union (TEU), agreed at Maastricht. Both the SEM and EMU served to symbolise the fact that member state governments' capacities to shape economic and monetary decisions had been seriously enfeebled. And as certain power resources and decision-making capacities have been gradually moving upwards to Brussels, the impact of this process has in a certain way marginalised and marooned mass publics and the political institutions that represent them in the member states. They are further away from the sites where decisions that directly affect them are made. Small wonder that their own self-perception is one of voices from the periphery. But this, it must be admitted, is also a perception of reality that needs to be carefully considered. After all, the sense that liberal democratic values, beliefs and institutional practices are being violated can be and often is exaggerated. It is a view that is predicated upon the assumption that conventions and practices like parliamentary scrutiny, public accountability and transparency in decision making already exist and are effective in these member states, an assumption that might be construed as wildly optimistic in most of them. There is, then, an element of mild hypocrisy based upon double standards among such critics of the EU. They often apply standards of judgement to the EU that are much more stringent than those that they apply to the liberal democratic member states that they themselves inhabit.

But the political impact of European integration does not end here. It is not just the national state – the territorial state as a *state* – that has had to adapt and adjust to EU membership. It has become a veritable truism today to point out that integration also has an inherently political backlash against what are construed by many as the inexorable universalising and homogenising forces of a dull, drab uniformity. The backlash, which can take many different forms and can be both violent and non-violent, has usually been triggered by a combination of factors that are perceived as being real: a recognised cultural identity is being suffocated; an established economic interest is being undermined; a distinct minority's rights are being transgressed; or a whole region's political status is simply being ignored. In the EU particular steps have already been taken to try to accommodate this so-called 'political fragmentation' epitomised in the ubiquity of new social movements, the mobilisation of self-conscious regions, the assertion and reassertion of sub-state national identities and the assorted intra-state claims for structural funds to alleviate unemployment and poverty. Nonetheless, it is within the member states themselves rather than the EU that fragmentation has been most challenging. A large body of scholarly literature exists that has chronicled the so-called threat to the national state from within as well as from without. Clearly the EU itself furnishes a convenient platform for these challenges but integral to the survival of the territorial state is its capacity to effectively devolve power and decentralise decision making down to lower levels that can more directly engage these new challenges.

What, then, has been the overall impact of these far-reaching developments on the territorial state? Keating emphasised the traditional features of the sovereign state as a territorially-defined political unit whose authority and legitimacy were bounded and whose citizenship, rights and principles of representation were typically organised by territory, but he also acknowledged that territory was 'a key element in economic exchange and the structure of markets'. 'Spatial proximity' encouraged exchange, facilitated communication and generated complementary activities 'while access to materials, labour and markets' was 'structured by territorial factors'.[28] Territory, as we have already noted, is not reducible to a single factor, but is a relative term that operates as an intervening variable in social science analysis. From the standpoint of the SEM, then, we would be wise to note Keating's observations for what is, after all, essentially an areal construction:

the economic content of territory is given by patterns of territorial exchange, linkages between buyers and sellers and interdependencies in production, by labour markets and travel to work areas. It is also given by the activities of place-based development coalitions, defining territory as the relevant unit for development and constituting territorial lobbies.[29]

This tells us that the SEM did not signify the end of territorial politics much less the demise of the territorial state. The national economy of each member state has not simply ceased to exist, but has been placed within a new economy – that of the EU as a whole. And if the SEM has served effectively to cut across traditional territorial state boundaries in a *Europe sans frontières*, it is itself nonetheless an essentially areal construction with walls and boundaries. In other words, it, too, is a new, albeit moving, shifting, *territorial* space that acts to unite Europeans but also to separate them from the Other.

This thumbnail sketch outline highlights the fact that there is manifestly a double movement of 'governance' both upwards beyond the national state and simultaneously downwards within the state that reflects the impact of new, largely economic, global forces. And as we have seen, it is movement that reflects the need to create new political spaces – new forms of political representation – to accommodate the reassertion of the inherently territorial interests of the state and its mass publics. But this double movement can be construed as essentially contradictory only if these processes are viewed from a particular standpoint. In practice they are also complementary; they are two sides of the same coin, often giving the impression that the state is being squeezed to the point where its very *raison d'être* is brought into question. This is a mistaken impression. What it actually implies is that the state's own position in world affairs and its relationship to its own citizens have both changed in a fundamental way rather than the somewhat facile but frequently voiced conclusion that it is now completely redundant and has already been supplanted.

Let us summarise this section in the following way. Integration and fragmentation are linked in an extremely complex way. But their relationship suggests that states are having to adjust and adapt imaginatively in order to create new constitutional and political spaces that will enable them successfully to reconcile the contemporary forces of global competitiveness (or economic prosperity) with the concomitant need for social solidarity (or social justice). In a particular sense, then, the EU today can be interpreted, at least partially, as a response to globalisation. George Ross has boldly claimed that 'the origins of European integration may best be seen in the light of globalizing tendencies at work at the time, even if the word was not used at the time'.[30] This is a good example of just how elastic the meaning and interpretation of the term 'globalisation' can be. And the substitution of 'globalising tendencies' for 'globalisation' invites suspicion of a good deal of conceptual stretching. But this really takes us back to a conspicuous conundrum: scholars have simply failed to agree upon a precise definition of globalisation and its implications also remain disputed.

Probably a more convincing answer to the question about the relationship between European integration and globalisation is that both phenomena are moving targets – both have changed significantly in meaning, theory and practice since 1945. During the early post-war years European integration could be explained by a combination of internal factors specific to each participating state and external considerations located at both intra- and extra-European or international levels. From around the mid-1970s, however, its resilience and survival cannot be explained without reference to global factors and circumstances that simply did not exist in earlier decades. There has, then, been a qualitative as well as a quantitative change in the nature of the beast.

This section has demonstrated that everywhere the national (territorial) state has begun to experience new economic, political, technological and environmental pressures, both quantitative and qualitative, that are unprecedented in both their scope and intensity. It also suggests that the single focus for citizens' loyalties and identities which the national state model has traditionally promoted with such great success until today has gradually been eroded and undermined but has not yet been replaced by any viable alternative focus for the forging of new identities and loyalties. In Europe the EU is actively seeking to develop a 'European identity' but one that is designed to sit alongside, rather than replace, the national state. In the early years of the new millennium it is much too early to make a serious detailed assessment of this project. However, the democratic problems associated with the emergence of an EU that is 'neo-confederal' – a unique mixture of both federal and confederal elements – are among the most daunting that confront the advocates of institutional reform.[31] And territorial concerns are as prominent as they have ever been. With these thoughts in mind, we will shift our attentions to the most recent, not to say dramatic, instalment in the building of constitutional and political Europe, namely, the constitutional Convention on the Future of Europe.

The convention on the future of Europe

The decision to convene a 'constitutional convention' on the future of Europe was taken in December 2001 in Laeken, near Brussels, during the Belgian presidency of the EU. The opening reference of the so-called 'Laeken Declaration' was entitled 'Europe at a Crossroads' and described the impending constitutionalisation process as 'a defining moment' in the EU's existence – 'a real transformation' that called for 'a different approach from fifty years ago'.[32]

The Convention was chaired by the former President of France, Valéry Giscard d'Estaing, together with Giuliano Amato and Jean-Luc Dehaene as vice-chairmen, and a host of representatives drawn from national governments, national and European parliaments, and the European Commission making in total a 105-strong body of delegates. Beginning on 28 February 2002, the Convention on the Future of the Union held regular monthly plenary sessions, open to the public, together with a series of working groups to look at specific issues in closer detail, and completed their task on 20 June 2003 when the Draft Treaty Establishing a Constitution for Europe was formally presented to the European Council meeting in Thessaloniki, Greece. Judgements about the legitimacy, effectiveness and overall significance of the constitutional document, described formally as the 'Constitutional Treaty', remain controversial as member state governments continue to engage in a wrangle over both policy and principle.

In a nutshell, the new Constitutional Treaty is designed to make the EU more democratic, more transparent and more efficient. The Convention was asked to draw up proposals on three principal subjects: first, how to bring citizens closer to the European design and to the European institutions; second, how to organise politics and the European political area in an enlarged Union; and, finally, how to develop the Union into a stabilising factor and a model in the new world order. Briefly stated, the Convention's response identified the following proposals:

1   A better division of Union and Member State competences.
2   A merger of the Treaties and the attribution of legal personality to the EU.
3   A simplification of the EU's instruments of action.
4   Measures to increase the democracy, transparency and efficiency of the EU.
5   Improvements in the structure and role of the EU's three central institutions.[33]

It is important to note that Giscard d'Estaing presented the original draft treaty as 'the foundation of a future Treaty establishing the European Constitution', thus confirming the pivotal role played by the member state governments that made the key decisions in 2004 before subjecting the result to formal ratification processes.[34] Clearly there remains much to do before the EU acquires a formal constitution.

There can be no doubt that this is a major achievement, marking 50 years since the last draft constitutional text was proposed to establish the European Political Community (EPC) in March 1953. It should be construed at this juncture as another stepping-stone towards the building of Europe in the context of Jean Monnet's political strategy of small steps. Conceivably this might turn out to be the largest step taken so far. And it is another step, it should be noted, that builds upon what already exists, especially the national state as the principal building block. Indeed, the Preamble to the new Draft Treaty proposal formally acknowledged 'national identities and history' and 'the citizens and States' of Europe.

It is not my purpose to present a detailed textual exegesis of the current Constitutional Treaty, but it is, I think, important to underline the extent to which territoriality and territorial politics are firmly ingrained in it. Part One of the document constitutes the main body of the proposed constitution dealing with institutions, policies and jurisdictional competences while Part Two is devoted to 'The Charter of Fundamental Rights of the Union'. In Part One there are at least 14 references to territorial or areal categories/criteria that serve to underline the continued significance of the *territorial state* in the EU. Some selected examples include the following. In its basic objectives, the EU will offer its citizens 'an *area* of freedom, security and justice without internal frontiers' and 'promote economic, social and *territorial* cohesion' (I-3). It will guarantee 'free movement of persons, goods, services and capital, and freedom of establishment ... *within and by* the Union' (I-4) and it will respect 'State functions, including those for ensuring the *territorial integrity* of the State' (I-5). It will also ensure 'the right to move and reside freely within the *territory* of the Member States' (I-8).

In addition to these examples it has to be stressed that political and legal representation in the central institutions remains largely territorial. Both the European Council and the Council of Ministers are representative of territorial state interests while the European Parliament continues to derive its authority and legitimacy from constituent state units whatever electoral system is utilised. Even the composition of the European Commission has typically been drawn from an established member state formula of two representatives from the large countries and one from the smaller countries (a system of equal rotation of Commissioners selected by the member states in a streamlined Commission of 13 members is proposed in the new constitution). The European Court of Justice (ECJ) will also continue to consist of one judge from each member state. And this is to be expected given the essentially intergovernmental or statist conception of the EU. Where it has been diluted by non-territorial functional aspects – as in the case of the social partners or the principles of citizenship – it does not amount to a serious attenuation of territoriality. And as I have already emphasised, the EU itself is a bounded territorially inclusive union in the sense that it excludes those states and peoples outside its areal jurisdiction.

None of this should surprise us. The new constitutional proposal reinforces both the federal and confederal elements in the EU, but it is built largely upon what already exists. There is no genuine attempt to go back to the drawing board. It is not akin to the Philadelphia Convention that created the new American federal model during 1787–1789. Nor should it be. The European project will continue to evolve and progress according to very different circumstances than those that pertained to the late eighteenth century in North America. Europe will be built only in piecemeal, incremental fashion, step-by-step according to Monnet's political strategy that has as its teleology a federal Europe but one equally as unique and unprecedented as that of the United States of America.

Conclusion: territoriality and federalism in the governance of the EU

We are now on the threshold of a federal Europe. The building of constitutional and political Europe has reached yet another crossroads where Hertz's 'coexistence in theory and practice of conventional and new concepts, of traditional and new policies' will produce a new synthesis of ideas, institutions and policies for the new millennium. But this new synthesis will not necessarily witness the decline or disappearance of territoriality as long as the territorial state itself survives. Territoriality will continue to vary in significance according to different policy issues in the EU but it seems clear that – at least in the foreseeable future – we will continue to live in a world of states, even if that world for the EU citizen might consist increasingly of overlapping jurisdictions, blurred areas of competence and multilayered governance. In practice there will be both government and governance.

The key question, then, is not whether the EU will constitute a federal Europe, but what *kind* of federal Europe will it be? With this in mind, it seems appropriate to conclude with a thought-provoking quotation from C.S. Maier:

> Europe may still claim to be a community, but need Europe be a territory? Is it not time for this most inventive of continents to reinvent itself beyond territory and outside of frontiers? Perhaps the moment has come to give up on the idea of territory, to associate our collective enterprises not with place or frontier, but with some other principle of community and association. What unites a people that are organised politically? Is it not these days a commitment to redistribution of resources, an acceptance of a community of risk?[35]

We are limited only by our imagination.

Notes

1. Controversy still surrounds the claims made in Robert Ardrey, *The Territorial Imperative: A Personal Inquiry into the Animal Origins of Property and Nations*, (New York: Atheneum, 1966).
2. See V.L. Mote and W. Trout, 'Political Territoriality and the End of the USSR', *Space and Polity*, Vol.7(1), (April 2003), 21.
3. See the 'Editorial' by R. Paddison in the first edition of *Space and Polity*, Vol.1(1), (May 1997), 5–7.
4. J.G. Ruggie, 'Territoriality and Beyond: Problematizing Modernity in International Relations', *International Organization*, Vol. 47(1), (Winter 1993), 149–150.
5. See, for example, J. Caporaso, 'The European Union and Forms of State: Westphalian, Regulatory or Post-Modern?', *Journal of Common Market Studies* (JCMS), Vol.34(1), (March 1996), 29–52; M. Smith, 'The European Union and a Changing Europe: Establishing the Boundaries of Order', JCMS, Vol.34(1), (March 1996), 5–28; and A. Osiander, 'Sovereignty, International Relations and the

Westphalian Myth', *International Organization*, Vol.55(2), (Spring 2001), 251–287.
6 For further details about the conceptual distinction, see M. Burgess, 'Federalism and Federation: A Reappraisal' in M. Burgess and A.-G. Gagnon (eds), *Comparative Federalism and Federation: Competing Traditions and Future Directions*, (Hemel Hempstead: Harvester Wheatsheaf, 1993), Ch.1: 3–14
7 W.S. Livingston, 'A Note on the Nature of Federalism', *Political Science Quarterly*, Vol.67, (1952), 85.
8 I.D. Duchacek, *Comparative Federalism: The Territorial Dimension of Politics*, (New York: Holt, Rinehart and Winston, Inc., 1970), ix.
9 Duchacek, *Comparative Federalism*, 191–192.
10 Duchacek, *Comparative Federalism*, 11.
11 R.D. Dikshit, *The Political Geography of Federalism: An Inquiry into Origins and Stability*, (New Delhi: The Macmillan Company of India Limited, 1975), x, 10.
12 See his introductory section entitled 'The Geographical Approach to Federalism', Dikshit, *Political Geography of Federalism*, 17–22.
13 M.J.C. Vile, 'Federal Theory and the "New Federalism"' in D. Jaensch (ed.), *The Politics of 'New Federalism'*, (Adelaide: The Australian Political Studies Association, 1977), 4–6.
14 F.N. Trager, 'Introduction: On Federalism', in T.M. Franck (ed.), Why Federations Fail, (London: London University Press, 1968), x.
15 J.H. Hertz, 'Rise and Demise of the Territorial State', *World Politics*, Vol.9.(4), (1957), 486.
16 Hertz, 'Rise and Demise of the Territorial State', 489–491.
17 Hertz, 'Rise and Demise of the Territorial State', 492.
18 Hertz, 'Rise and Demise of the Territorial State', 490.
19 Hertz, 'Rise and Demise of the Territorial State', 491.
20 D. Kellner, 'Globalization and the Postmodern Turn' in R. Axtmann (ed.), *Globalization and Europe: Theoretical and Empirical Investigations*, (London: Pinter, 1998), Ch.2: 23
21 D. Held, 'The Transformation of Political Community: Rethinking Democracy in the Context of Globalization', in I. Shapiro and C. Hacker-Corson (eds), *Democracy's Edges*, (Cambridge: Cambridge University Press, 1999), Ch.6: 92.
22 Kellner, 'Globalization and the Postmodern Turn', 24–25.
23 See S. Strange, *States and Markets*, (London: Pinter Publishers, 1989) and her later work, *The Retreat of the State: The Diffusion of Power in the World Economy*, (Cambridge: Cambridge University Press, 1996).
24 See M. Castells, *The Informational City: Information Technology, Economic Restructuring and the Urban-Regional Process*, (Oxford: Basil Blackwell, 1989).
25 For a detailed analysis of this argument, see M. Keating, *The New Regionalism in Western Europe*, (Cheltenham: Edward Elgar, 1998).
26 See the collection of articles in C. Jeffery (ed.), 'The Regional Dimension of the European Union: Towards a Third Level in Europe?', Regional and Federal Studies, (Special Issue) Vol.6(2), (Summer,1996); and in D. Kennedy, 'The European Union's Committee of the Regions', *Regional and Federal Studies*, (Special Issue) Vol.7(1), (Spring 1997).
27 See M. Burgess, 'Federalism and Federation', in M. Cini (ed.), *European Union Politics*, (Oxford: Oxford University Press, 2003), Ch.5: 65–79. For a survey of the role of the European Council and Council of the Union as both territorial and essentially confederal, see S. Bulmer, 'The European Council and the Council of the European Union: Shapers of a European Confederation', in M. Burgess, (ed.), 'Federalism and the European Union', *Publius: The Journal of Federalism*, (Special Issue), Vol.26(4), Fall, 1996, 17–42.

28 Keating, The New Regionalism, 1.
29 Keating, The New Regionalism, 7.
30 G. Ross, 'European Integration and Globalization', in R. Axtmann (ed.), *Globalization and Europe*, Ch.10: 164.
31 See M. Burgess, *Federalism and European Union: The Building of Europe, 1950–2000*, (London: Routledge, 2000).
32 http://european-convention.eu.int/pdf/LKNEN.pdf.
33 http://european-convention.eu.int.
34 http://european-convention.eu.int.
35 Maier quoted in J. Zielonka, 'How New Enlarged Borders will Reshape the European Union', *JCMS*, Vol.39(3), (September 2001), 530.

6 The hyphenated state, multi-level governance and the communities in Belgium
The case of Brussels

Wilfried Swenden and Marleen Brans

Introduction

In his work on comparative federalism, Ivo D. Duchacek defines a federation as a political system in which 'political authority is *territorially* divided between two autonomous sets of separate jurisdictions, one national [federal] and the other provincial [regional, cantonal]' (Duchacek, 1969: 192; our emphasis). Constitutional lawyers and political scientists agree that Belgium has transformed from a decentralized into a fully fledged federal state. However, Belgium does not entirely comply with Duchacek's understanding of a federation. The concept of Belgian *Regions* (the Flemish Region, the Walloon Region and the Brussels Capital Region) clearly affirms the territoriality principle, but the parallel existence of Belgian linguistic *Communities* (Flemish Community, French Community and German-speaking Community) deviates from it. Language has been the strongest force in the federalization process of Belgium, but not all three regions contain linguistically homogeneous populations.

This chapter is concerned with the *principal* exception to the territoriality principle: the case of Brussels. As the important capital of the Belgian state, Brussels is recognized as a territorial unit (Region) of its own, but it remains the playing field of two linguistic Communities: the Flemish and the French. The share of Dutch-speakers is estimated at only 12–15 percent of its approximately one million strong regional population. However, the relevance of Brussels as a source of employment and recreation for those who live in the adjacent Flemish or nearby Walloon Regions is substantial. The international vocation of Brussels, capital of the European Union and home to NATO, adds to its symbolic value. Arguably, Brussels is the most important hyphen, binding the two most relevant Belgian Communities, the Flemish and the French, together.

This chapter seeks to clarify the multi-level character of policy-making in Brussels. We spell out to what extent the *Community* divide in Belgium and Brussels characterizes daily politics at the various levels that compound the Brussels body politic: the 19 municipalities that encompass the Brussels Capital Region (BCR); the Flemish and French Community governments whose competencies stretch into the territory of the BCR; the BCR itself, and the federal arena.

The institutional anchoring of the BCR within the Belgian federal system can be understood with reference to three important strands of recent political science literature. First, the concept of *Multi-Level Governance* has been defined as a 'system of continuous negotiations among representatives at several territorial tiers, supranational, national, regional and local' (Hooghe and Marks, 2003). Institutional change affecting the BCR can be understood in those terms insofar as many proposals for change also involve negotiations with representatives from the 19 municipalities *and* frequently require the consent of both linguistic Communities in the federal Parliament. Second, we can apply Robert Putnam's terminology for analyzing the negotiation process that leads to institutional reform in Brussels, although its direction is the inverse of his 'two-level game' (Putnam, 1988). Negotiations start at the lower (regional) level, subsequently representatives at the higher, federal parliamentary level, consent. Furthermore, federal MPs do more than just consenting. Negotiations continue at the federal level. Here, the institutional position of the BCR can be linked to institutional reform affecting all Regions or Communities. In reality, changes to the position of BCR are usually made part of such wider package deals, which political pundits have come to describe as 'state reforms'. Consequently, the shape of 'win-sets' at the federal level may be different from the 'win-sets' to which politicians from the level of the BCR initially agreed. Third, the qualified majorities that are needed at the federal level, as well as the *informal* requirement that representatives from both linguistic Communities at the level of the BCR agree to the proposed changes result in many potential veto-points. Unless the presence of a 'critical juncture' upsets the common interests of all 'veto-players' (for instance, the unexpected rise of a right-wing party that is not willing to play the rules of the game), institutional change is likely to follow an incremental path. Drawing from Georges Tsebelis' terminology, we argue that important *institutional* (cf. the requirement of bicommunal consent in a multi-level setting) and *partisan* veto-points (negotiations often comprise representatives drawn from six parties or more) are at work. However, the presence of Community based parties at the federal *and* regional levels of government ensures that the interests of Dutch *and* French-speakers are accommodated whenever proposals for institutional reform affect a policy level in which both Communities take a direct interest. In this sense party-executives and their party presidents are not only veto-players, but they also serve as potential transmission belts between the federal and regional policy arenas. They reduce the likelihood of institutional paralysis, given that the same party elites find themselves around the regional and the federal negotiation tables.

Apart from situating the institutional position of the BCR within the broader framework of the Belgian federation, we also analyse which and how decisions are made *within* the BCR itself. While the parliament and executive of the BCR are responsible for the *regional* i.e. territorially based polities in Brussels, the members of the regional parliament also serve as *Community representatives,* implementing cultural and educational policies of the Flemish and French Communities in Brussels. To that purpose, separate 'Community commissions and colleges' were created within the realm of the BCR structure. In this sense, the territorial (Regional-based) and personal (Community-based) logics can be separated in form, but they considerably overlap in practice. In addition to the regional level, we also analyze the *bicommunal* nature of the 19 municipalities. These municipalities have acquired a bilingual status in time, but the Community-based logic is certainly weaker than at the level of the BCR. This is the case because municipalities predate the creation of the Regions and thus were formed when French was unmistakably the principal administrative language of Belgium. Finally, we seek to relate our analysis to the indicators of territoriality that Michael Burgess and Hans Vollaard specified in their introductory chapter to the book. More in particular, does the creation of the BCR instill a territorial logic, or are citizens more likely to commit their loyalty toward one of both Communities? Furthermore, is the BCR model well suited to reflect the increasingly cosmopolitan character of a region, which for 40 percent of its population is inhabited by citizens of non-Belgian origin, and should we expect these citizens to profess their public loyalty to either of the major Communities?

Defining Brussels and determining a linguistic regime for the capital and its suburbs

In this chapter we have used the term 'Brussels' to refer to the *Brussels Capital Region* (BCR). However, the 19 municipalities that are located within the BCR predate its creation by more than 150 years. Unlike the Flemish and the Walloon Regions, the BCR, as well as the 19 municipalities that are part of it, have a bilingual status. Therefore, demarcating the borders of Brussels and defining the number of municipalities that would be part of it was a contentious issue. The following paragraphs shed light on that process.

Since its formation in 1831, Belgium comprised a predominantly Dutch-speaking population, but until the 1930s a French-speaking political and industrial elite governed the country. French was the only official Belgian language. Dutch was widely spoken in Flanders, albeit not among the highest classes. French had been the only language of significance in Wallonia throughout. By the end of the nineteenth century, French had developed into the most widely spoken language in Brussels too. This was primarily the result of extensive immigration from French-speaking Belgians who filled up leading administrative and financial positions in the new Belgian capital (Witte and Van Velthoven, 1998). Generally, high-skilled jobs were provided in French, whereas Flemish was used by low-skilled laborers only

(Brans, 1993). The position of French was further strengthened by the Frenchification of original Dutch-speakers.

In the second half of the nineteenth century, a so-called 'Flemish Movement' developed from among the lower clergy and middle classes in Flanders. Its members were able to advance socially, but not without acquiring French at a certain cost first. The representatives of this Movement fuelled demands for the recognition of Dutch as the official language of Flanders and campaigned for a bilingual status of Brussels (Wils, 1992). Gradually the overall demographic preponderance of the Flemish population translated into a realization of the Flemish linguistic demands. The gradual extension of the franchise, which provided a political voice to the middle and lower Flemish classes, certainly contributed to this process. A series of language laws, enacted between 1873 and 1932 made Dutch the only official language of Flanders. French received the same recognition in Wallonia. The French-speaking Belgians rejected a proposal to apply a generalized policy of bilingualism, as this, so they feared, would lead to better employment opportunities for the Flemish, who, at that time, were more likely to be fluent in French than French-speakers were in Dutch. Therefore, it was decided that official bilingualism would only apply to the municipalities that made up the Brussels' city-agglomeration.

The development of Flanders and Wallonia into monolingual Dutch and French-speaking zones was made possible because both regions were already homogeneous from a linguistic point of view. For instance, in the last language census (1947), 90.4 percent of the respondents living in Flanders declared themselves as Dutch-speaking (compared with only 4.9 percent who were said to be French-speaking) whereas 90.8 percent of the respondents living in Wallonia reported themselves as French-speaking (compared with only 2.0 percent who claimed to be Dutch-speaking)[1] (Hooghe, 2003: 76). Yet, a clear legal demarcation of the borderlines between Flanders, Wallonia and Brussels and thus also of the linguistic zones was not achieved until 1962, particularly because the language situation in Brussels and its adjacent suburbs that are located in Flemish territory was less clear.

Until 1947, the linguistic borderline was established by means of a language census: municipalities in which 30 percent or more of the population spoke a minority language were offered certain *facilities* in that language.[2] When 50 percent or more of the inhabitants declared to speak the majority language of the other region, the municipality was to be *transferred* to that region (Swenden, 2004). The population numbers of Brussels exploded in the second half of the nineteenth, and in the first half of the twentieth century. As a result, more municipalities were included in the (officially bilingual) agglomeration. A process of suburbanization, which started in the years following upon World War II, had driven a share of the well-off French-speaking middle and upper classes to the green (and predominantly Dutch-speaking) suburbs. The language censuses of 1930 and 1947 documented this increasing 'Frenchification' process of Brussels *and* of its suburbs

(Distelmans and Koppen, 2002). This development increased demands for enlarging the size of the Brussels city-agglomeration and for extending the number of suburban municipalities offering facilities to the French-speakers. The publication of the 1947 census resulted in the enlargement of the Brussels agglomeration (hence formally bilingual areas) and extended linguistic facilities to four suburban municipalities with a French-speaking population of more than 30 percent. Therefore, the Flemish political elites favored a solution which *once and for all* fixed the territorial borderline between the Dutch, bilingual (Brussels) and French-linguistic zones; while the French-speaking political elites preferred a continuation of the language censuses. Eventually, the Flemish political elites pushed through a fixed demarcation of the linguistic borderline.

The 1962–1963 legislation did not come as a priceless victory. Four suburban municipalities that were located within the Dutch-linguistic zone continued to offer *facilities* to their French-speaking populations, whereas a further two suburban facilities were added to this list. The borders of bilingual Brussels itself were confined to the present 19 municipalities; confirming the addition of three municipalities in 1954 that were previously located in the Dutch-speaking zone (Sieben, 1993: 145–147). The demarcation of the linguistic borderline, as well as the number of facility municipalities and the scope of the linguistic facilities are anchored in the federal constitution and in (federal) laws that are approved with special majorities. Changing them requires the consent of both linguistic groups in each of the federal parliamentary chambers (Chamber of Deputies and Senate).

The political discourse that led to the language laws of 1962–1963 is sometimes misunderstood as a clash between two views, the *territoriality* principle (defended by the Flemish) and the *personality* principle (supported by the French-speakers). This vision only works as far as Brussels and its periphery is concerned since, as was indicated above, the French-speakers dismissed a bilingual solution for the entire Belgian state. In fact, as a result of the 1962–1963 linguistic legislation, only 1,250,000 Belgians representing a mere 12.2 percent of Belgium's 10,260,000 strong population do *not* live in a strictly territorial linguistic regime. In popular terms, the 19 municipalities of Brussels, assembling approximately 978,000 citizens, mark the largest exception (NIS, 2002a). Citizens living in this area can communicate with the municipal, regional or federal authorities in the language of their choice (either Dutch or French). A policy of *full bilingualism* applies here. A further 282,000 inhabitants live in municipalities, which, although located within a monolingual zone, provide certain *facilities* to citizens speaking the regional (not necessarily local) minority language. The six suburban facility municipalities located near Brussels are the best known example; they represent 68,000 inhabitants (NIS, 2002a).

The 1962–1963 language laws and their political aftermath

The events which culminated in the linguistic demarcation of the borderline generated three major political developments. First, the political debates that preceded and followed upon the 1962–1963 legislation sent shockwaves through the Belgian political landscape. Significant political parties with a regional profile emerged; in particular the Flemish People's Union (*Volksunie*) and the French-speaking Front of Democratic Francophones (*Front Démocratique des Francophones*). The former campaigned against linguistic facilities in the suburban municipalities and propagated a bilingual solution for Brussels (the size of which should not extend beyond the 19 municipalities). The latter defended an extensive interpretation of French facilities in the suburban municipalities, and initially also protested against the bilingual status of Brussels. The rise of these regionalist parties polarized the traditional polity-wide Belgian parties. Between 1968 and 1978, the Belgian Christian-Democrats, Social Democrats and Liberal Democrats broke up along linguistic lines, partially as a strategy to recapture votes that they had lost to these regionalist parties (Deschouwer, 1999a). Leaving aside Brussels, parties from both linguistic roles would not compete against each other.

Second, the Flemish majority largely succeeded in having its view on language policy pushed through, but the institutionalization of *consociational* practices at the national level prevented the French-speakers from being reduced to the status of a national minority (Lijphart, 1999). As alluded to above, changing the linguistic regime and borderline requires the consent of special parliamentary majorities, a requirement that applies to all Community-sensitive legislation. With the exception of the federal Prime Minister, the national executive is composed of an equal number of Dutch- and French-speakers and decides by consensus. Top administrative appointments, including diplomatic and military positions, are equally divided between French- and Dutch-speakers.

Third, once the linguistic borderlines were fixed and the political parties were split, the federalization process of Belgium itself could begin. The federalization of Belgium is the result of a negotiation process between the political elites of linguistically split parties, occasionally involving representatives of the regionalist parties that were referred to above. The structure of Belgian federalism reflects two different views of the state. On the one hand, the Flemish political elites were keen on gaining autonomy in policy areas that are clearly linked to language, i.e. in particular education and culture. The concept of *Communities* corresponds to this notion, as three language-based Communities were created: the Flemish, the French and the tiny German-speaking Communities. In parallel, a notion of strictly territorially defined *Regions* emerged, primarily out of a strongly felt need in Wallonia to inject its suffering coal and steel industries with substantial state subsidies.

Regional governments and parliaments were created, which by 2002 assumed legislative and administrative responsibilities in territorially bound competencies, among which are regional economic development, industrial restructuring, environment, land-use planning and urban renewal, agriculture, public infrastructure, local and provincial government, agriculture and external trade.

In practice there is a significant overlap between the concept of a Region and that of a Community. If we ignore the special case of Brussels (and of the German-speaking Community) Communities are also territorially structured. For instance, the French Community has *no* authority over the (relatively small group of) French-speakers who live in the Flemish Region, just as the Flemish Community has no say over (the even smaller group of) Dutch-speakers who live in the Walloon Region. Because the group of Dutch-speakers who lives in Brussels as a share of the total group of Dutch-speaking Belgians is so small (approximately 2.5 percent), the Flemish Community and Regions have even merged their institutions. Consequently, there is only one Flemish government and parliament that is responsible for *Regional* (for citizens located in the Flemish region) and *Community* competencies (addressing all inhabitants of the Flemish region and the Dutch-speakers who live in Brussels). Conversely, since the group of French-speakers who live in Brussels, considered as a share of the total group of French-speaking Belgians, is substantially larger (approximately 17.5 percent), the French Community and Walloon Region have *not* been merged. Separate Regional and Community parliaments and governments continue to exist, although the French Community parliament is entirely composed from MPs who have been directly elected to the Brussels and Walloon regional parliaments respectively. The non-merger of the French Community and the Walloon Region is also a consequence of political differences and different sources of territorial identification among the French-speaking inhabitants of Brussels and the Walloons. The French-speaking citizens of Brussels are less likely to vote for the Social Democrats and more likely to vote for the Liberal-FDF (conservatives). While Walloons are likely to define themselves as *Walloons or Belgians (or possibly as a combination of both)*, the French-speaking inhabitants of Brussels perceive themselves as members of the French-speaking Belgian Community or simply as French-speaking *Bruxellois*. By comparison, the voting behavior of the Dutch-speakers who live in Brussels is more akin to that of the Flemish electorate, and it is assumed that the former are also more likely to identify themselves as *Flemish* inhabitants who live in Brussels (*Brusselse Vlamingen*) than as Dutch-speaking inhabitants of *Brussels* (*Nederlandstalige Brusselaars'*).

Since the political identities of French-speaking Belgians have been more divided between those who live in, and those who live outside Brussels, the desire to create a BCR that is distinct from a Walloon Region should not come as a surprise. Nevertheless, it was not until 1989 that Brussels received the status of a (quasi) fully-fledged Region, alongside the Flemish and the

Walloon Regions (which had been recognized as such since 1980).³ This delay was primarily a consequence of Flemish fears: the existence of three Regions, two of which with an exclusively or predominantly French-speaking character, would turn the national demographic preponderance of the Dutch-speakers on its head. Eventually, the Flemish political elites agreed to the regionalization of Brussels because similar consociational devices to those at work at the federal level were to protect the position of the Flemish minority in the BCR. They will be discussed in the next paragraph.

The politics of Brussels: local, Regional, Community and federal politics intertwined

In order to comprehend the working of daily politics in Brussels, one should realize that the various *territorial* components of the Brussels' body politic (the local, regional and federal tiers) are strongly *interconnected*. Chronologically speaking, the 19 Brussels municipalities predate the formation of the Communities (1970–) and of the BCR (1989). In the following paragraphs we will explicate the linkage between the various tiers of government that influence policy-making in Brussels. For analytical purposes, we will start with the lowest tier, and subsequently move on to the Community, Regional and federal levels. Table 6.1 gives a schematic overview of the various levels of government at work in the capital. A personal *fusion* of mandates across the levels *(cumul des mandats)* underscores the institutional linkages that exist between them. For instance, since its first direct election in 1989, the BCR parliament has been made up of politicians, who, with a likelihood of about 70 percent, combined their seat in the legislature with that of a mayor, alderman or municipal councilor in one of the 19 municipalities. Moreover, prominent municipal councilors may even become members of the federal parliament (e.g. Francois-Xavier de Donnéa, mayor of the *city* of Brussels between 1996 and 2000 (i.e. the most centrally located of the 19 municipalities) also served as a national MP.⁴) As we shall discuss, there is an inbuilt institutional linkage between the BCR parliament and the Flemish Parliament and French Community Councils too. Put differently, local, regional and possibly even national political mandates are fused.

Politics at the local level

The BCR encompasses 19 municipalities. These municipalities play an important role in among other things providing construction permits, organizing basic local infrastructure, including basic sports and cultural facilities, offering social services (social assistance) and collecting garbage. Tellingly, in 2002, the budget of the 19 municipalities combined was almost as high as that of the BCR. Municipalities vary considerably in population, income, share and origin of their foreign population. For instance, the smallest municipality (Koekelberg) counts 16,716 inhabitants, the

Table 6.1 Multi-level governance in Brussels (situation in 2003).

	Municipality[+]	Communities	Region	Federal
Number	19	2	1	1
Policy Scope	Basic social, recreational and infrastructural assistance and equipment; garbage collection	Education, culture, preventive health care; integration of immigrants	Environment, agriculture, industrial planning, urban renewal (full list in text) organization and administrative tutelage of municipalities	Social security, foreign affairs and defense justice institutional reform including organization and policy scope of Communities and Regions
Budget (expenditures)	(in 2003): €1,703,791,000	JCC (in 1999): €57,821,164 FRCC (in 1999): €207,432,234 FLCC: N.A.	(in 2003): €2,006,677,000	Cannot be specifically determined for Brussels
Institutions	Mayor; College of Mayor and aldermen; municipal council	Flemish, French and Joint Community Commissions and Colleges	Brussels Regional Parliament and Executive	Federal Bicameral Parliament and Executive
Minority protecting devices At the legislative level (including the method of election of the legislature and procedural rules in the legislature)	Free access to council meetings of at least one Flemish local politician	Certain decisions in Joint Community Commission require Double Majority (e.g. decisions pertaining to bilingual hospitals)	Vote pooling of Dutch-speaking parties* Government designation requires double majority in Council** Double Majority in Council for changes to standing orders and constructive motions of want of confidence***	French and Flemish Community senators are equal in number Language groups in both chambers; majorities in both groups needed for adopting 'special majority laws'
			Alarmbell Procedure	Alarmbell Procedure

At the executive level	Fiscal Rewards in the case of appointment of Flemish alderman	Linguistic Parity in the Joint Community Commission (Minister-President only has advisory role)	Linguistic Parity in the Executive – with exception of Minister-President	Linguistic Parity in the Executive – with exception of the Premier
At the administrative level		Protective Quota for Municipal Administrators	Protective Quota for Regional Administrators (69–31)	Top administrators are equally divided between both language groups (50–50)

Source: Municipal expenditures in *Dexia*, 2002: 100; Regional expenditures at http://www.bruxelles.irisnet.be/FR/1FR_ADMI/1FR_3ADM/budget/Expose2003.pdf; Data FRCC and JCC expenditures in Heremans and Philipsen, 1999: 225.

Notes

+ In 2001 six police zones were created overarching the 19 municipalities, with special representation rights for the Flemish.
* Since the 2004 regional elections a fixed quota of seats is allotted to the Dutch-speakers in the enlarged council (17/89). Consequently, the mechanism of linguistic vote pooling disappears.
** Since the 2004 regional elections, the double majority requirement no longer applies for the designation of the BCR executive.
*** Since the 2004 regional elections, double majorities are required for changes to the organization of the municipalities, a competence that was devolved to the Regions in 2001. However, in the absence of a Dutch-speaking majority, a cooling off period of one month is envisaged. Subsequently, on the occasion of a second vote, only the consent of a third of the Dutch-speaking group is required. The same rule applies for votes on constructive motions of want of confidence and amendments to the standing order of the BCR Parliament.

largest (Brussels city) 136,730 (NIS 2002a). On the basis of the average annual taxable personal income of its working population, the poorest municipality is Saint Gillis (€18,473); the most affluent is Woluwe Saint-Pierre (€30,707). The average for the BCR as a whole is €23,136 (NIS, 2002b). In 1997, the share of non-Belgian inhabitants at the municipal level ranged between 11.4 percent (Ganshoren) and 53.8 percent (Saint-Josse). In the former, Italians make up the largest group of non-Belgian citizens; in the latter the Turkish community is the best-represented non-Belgian group. For Brussels as a whole, the share of non-Belgian citizens was as high as 29.9 percent, and the Moroccans make up the largest foreign group. Unsurprisingly, municipalities with an above average taxable income are more likely to comprise higher groups of non-Belgian European or North American citizens (De Lannoy, *et al.*, 1999: 131–132).

The 19 municipalities of the BCR received a bilingual status long before the Region was created. None of these 19 municipalities are predominantly Dutch-speaking in character, but some contain above average concentrations of Dutch-speakers (particularly the municipalities that are located in the northeast and northwest side of the region).[5]

In general, the Dutch-speaking minority is much better protected at the level of the BCR than at the municipal level. This is so, because the Flemish political elites were much weaker when bilingualism was made the norm at that level. Furthermore, adjusting existing institutions to a new situation (from *de facto* French *monolingualism* to official *bilingualism*) is more burdensome than prescribing bilingualism as the rule for institutions that had to be established from scratch (i.e. the creation of the BCR in 1989). The 'stickiness' of existing institutional configurations has been well documented by political scientists, who have focused on the path-dependent logic of institutional change. Once institutions are in place, incremental rather than profound reform is likely, unless 'a critical juncture' opens up a window for more profound structural reform.

Nevertheless, four mechanisms that protect the minority position of the Flemish at the local level are rooted in the language laws of 1962–1963. First, citizens should receive all official documents in the language of 'their' choice (i.e. Dutch or French). Second, in order to ensure that citizens can be served in Dutch, protective quotas were established for municipal administrators as well as for personnel working in inter-municipal utilities and national decentralized offices (e.g. post offices). Third, the national language laws of 1962–1963 resulted in a higher number of Dutch-speaking schools within each of the municipalities, as well as in an increase in the hours of Dutch as a second language in French-speaking schools (Wils 1992: 269; Luyckx and Platel 1985: 519–525). Finally, even if no single Dutch-speaking municipal councilor has been elected, one Flemish local politician is guaranteed access to the deliberations of the municipal council (i.e. local parliament).

The above guarantees exist on paper but for a variety of reasons they are not always equally well observed. One reason pertains to the lack of personnel that qualifies as being sufficiently fluent in both languages or in Dutch. There may simply be a shortage of candidates who pass the rigorous language examinations or sometimes an excessive number of non-permanent employees are appointed (who do not always observe the language criteria). Occasionally, however, a lack of employees who are fluent in both languages may emerge from a deliberate unwillingness among the local college of mayor and aldermen to observe the language laws. Hence, in 1998, 21 percent of local acts were seen as violations of the language laws, a majority of which pertained to illegal nominations of municipal personnel (Detant, 1999: 426–430). A federally appointed vice-governor can *suspend* such acts, but ultimately the government of the BCR is responsible for *nullifying* them, a step that was taken with regard to only 12 percent of the suspended acts. The low share of nullifications reflects the sensitivity of this issue as the regional executive is composed of an equal number of French- and Dutch-speakers and decides by consensus.

The still rather weak enforcement of linguistic legislation at the municipal level supports Flemish arguments in favor of tackling the problem at its very root. *Guaranteed representation* of the Flemish in municipal executives (college of mayor and aldermen) would put a hold on appointing personnel whose qualifications do not comply with the language laws. It was not until 2001 that the demands of the Flemish were acted upon. As part of a wide agreement, in which Brussels local politics became linked to the politics of the Brussels Region, the Communities and even federal politics, a majority of the French-speaking members of the federal parliament (supported by a majority of the local and regional public officeholders in Brussels) agreed to strengthen Flemish representation rights in the 19 Brussels' municipalities (Chamber of Representatives, 2001; Senate 2001a, 2001b). However, strengthening Flemish representation rights came at a certain cost: municipal executives comprising at least one Dutch-speaking alderman or president of the local council for social welfare receive a fiscal benefit provided by the *federal* government. To this purpose, the federal government, each year sets aside €25 million. In 2002, a majority of the 19 municipalities seized this opportunity, but the solution remains debatable as a Flemish alderman could be appointed 'without portfolio' and the method itself too conveys the impression that Flemish representation rights were bought.

The eagerness with which most of the municipalities accepted federal grants in exchange for appointing a Dutch-speaking alderman is an indication of their precarious budgetary situation.[6] This may seem a paradox as Brussels generates an enormous (and increasing) wealth for the Belgian economy. In 1998 the per capita GRP of the BCR was 2.06 times as high as the Belgian average; in 1988 it was only 1.52 times the national average (Hooghe, 2003). Yet, much of the wealth that is produced in Brussels is consumed elsewhere. Average taxable income is remarkably higher and unemployment figures are lower in the adjacent or nearby provinces of Flemish and Walloon Brabant.

It may come as a surprise that merging the municipalities into larger units has not yet been seriously contemplated, although it could have served a double purpose. First, merging these municipalities into socio-economically coherent units could have reduced the inter-municipal inequalities of income (for instance exemplified by the previously noted difference in average taxable income between Saint-Gilles and Woluwe Saint-Pierre). In addition, a merger would have facilitated a coherent strategy in urban structural planning (which was lacking altogether prior to the creation of the BCR in 1989). As Guy Baeten asserts '... the lack of authoritative higher spatial plans has induced a culture of clientelism and competition among the 19 Brussels municipalities, which, in the end, have only served rather than regulated the interests of property developers' (Baeten, 2001: 126). Second, merging the municipalities could have been perceived as an alternative strategy by the Flemish minority to secure minimum representation rights at the local level. Indeed, merging two municipalities in which the Flemish parties obtain, respectively, 2 and 20 percent of the vote would evidently result in the election of a number of Dutch-speaking councilors who could be perceived as the representatives of all the Dutch-speakers. The failure to do so is primarily the result of the issue of Flemish representation rights, less so of the potential reduction of available local public positions that such a merger would entail.[7]

The major overhaul of the Belgian police system in the wake of the tragic Dutroux scandal resulted in the creation of six police zones in Brussels. It remains to be seen whether these six zones could serve as the basis of a more profound restructuring of the municipalities. Interestingly, the Flemish MPs in the federal parliament only agreed to the creation of these zones in Brussels, on the condition that special representation rights for the Dutch-speakers would be provided for. As for the appointment of one Dutch-speaking alderman, the stronger position of the Dutch-speaking majority at the federal level was instrumentalized to strengthen their minority representation in Brussels.

In the absence of strong devices guaranteeing their representation in the local arena, Flemish politicians may resort to certain electoral strategies. Unlike on the occasion of regional or federal elections, neither the voters, nor the politicians *must* commit themselves to either language community in municipal elections. Therefore, Dutch-speaking politicians could increase their chances of being elected by gaining an eligible position at a – officially – *bilingual* party list. Such a list would link corresponding ideologies from both sides of the linguistic divide. While such bilingual lists may arise out of pure necessity – at least from the viewpoint of the Dutch-speaking politicians –, their presence or absence also serves as an indicator of the strength and/or weakness of the Community principle. Does local politics replicate federal and regional politics, by forcing voters and politicians into monolingual party lists, or is there a more frequent appearance of bilingual lists? One recent example is the formation of a joint PRL–FDF (French Liberal)–VLD

(Flemish Liberal) list prior to the municipal elections in the city of Brussels (October 2000). Whenever 'bilingual lists' are proposed, the positing of the candidates of the minority linguistic group reflects the popular share of the minority group in the local population. Hence, if one fifth of the local electorate is Dutch-speaking and a party thinks it can lay claim on five seats in the municipal council, then, in the most likely scenario, one of five eligible candidates on the party-list is of Dutch-speaking origin. Alternatively, Dutch-speaking local politicians, who fear that they may not stand a chance of being elected to the municipal council, may form a joint list with *other* Dutch-speaking candidates representing different party ideologies. In this case, the Community principle clearly dominates. A typical example of this strategy is the party list VLAAMS (Flemish) in the municipality of Auderghem, assembling candidates who are individual members of the Flemish Social-Democratic, Green and Christian-Democratic parties.

Analyzing the process of list formation for local elections in Brussels between 1970 and 1994, Jo Buelens and Kris Deschouwer noted that local party elites in all 19 municipalities do not have a fixed preference for either strategy. On the occasion of the 1982 and 1988 local elections, Flemish Christian-Democrats campaigned on a *bilingual* list in about 10 percent of the municipalities; the corresponding percentages for the Social Democrats and Liberal-Democrats were 40 and 25 percent respectively. By 1994, these percentages had increased to 25 percent for the Christian-Democrats and even 55 percent for the Liberal-Democrats, but decreased to about 25 percent for the Social Democrats. The data reveal that in 1994, Dutch-speaking parties have even less frequently campaigned under *their own* banner (i.e. without resorting to either of the two options), thus making list formation with candidates from *at least one other* Dutch-speaking party, as (Christian-Democrats) or even *more* attractive (Social-Democrats; see Deschouwer and Buelens, 1997: 91–93).

The BCR (1989–2004)

Since 1989, Brussels has been recognized as a Region in its own right. Unlike at the local level, the Flemish gained much stronger minority protecting rights at the regional level. Such rights were a condition for the much-needed support of the Francophones to establish a third Region. The constitutional round as a result of which the BCR was created also involved the devolution of educational competencies to the Communities (primarily a Flemish demand), and an encompassing increase in the spending autonomy of the federated entities (in which a solidarity mechanism favoring the fiscally weaker French Community was retained, albeit it diminishing in nature). In this sense, the creation and institutional shape was part of a much wider package deal on institutional reform that was concluded by the party leaders representing the Dutch- and French-speaking parties in the national government.

The newly established parliament of the BCR was elected for the first time in June 1989. A combination of *consociational* devices similar to the ones that operate at the federal level, typify the 1989 institutional settlement of the new BCR. Five such mechanisms protect the Flemish minority in the regional institutions in four different arenas: the electoral, the legislative, the executive and the administrative.

The mechanism for *electing* the 75 members of the Council makes use of *monolingual* lists and the pooling of votes for each language group. If seats were divided directly, the Flemish parties would lose several of them because small parties are already disadvantaged by the D'Hondt electoral divider (Lijphart, 1994). The Flemish parties are first considered as a single party after which the seats assigned to this group are divided between the individual parties. This mechanism implies that *unlike* for municipal elections, parties must be filed as belonging to the Dutch- or French-speaking group, ruling out the formation of bilingual party lists.

At the *legislative* level two procedural and two representational power-sharing mechanisms are at work. Government-formation is subject to a double majority vote in the parliament, which is divided in two language groups. By default, these groups can present their own two candidate-ministers. Only the designation of the minister-president then remains subject to an absolute parliamentary majority. The 'double majority requirement' also applies for changes to the parliament's standing orders and for any constructive motions of want of confidence (Clement and Delgrange, 1999: 531). Furthermore, when a language group deems that any legislative or executive proposal substantially harms its interests it can invoke a suspensive veto. This 'alarmbell procedure' postpones the vote until the executive reaches an alternative agreement. If the latter fails to do so, the proposal is relinquished. Representational protection includes a minimal presence of Dutch-speakers in legislative committees and the requirement to appoint a president and vice-president of different language groups.

At the *executive* level power sharing is guaranteed by the usual consensus procedure. There is however representational parity: with exception of the Brussels minister-president, there are as many Dutch as French-speaking ministers in the BCR's executive (2 + 2). By convention the minister-president is a French-speaker. This parity requirement is relaxed for the secretaries of state (junior

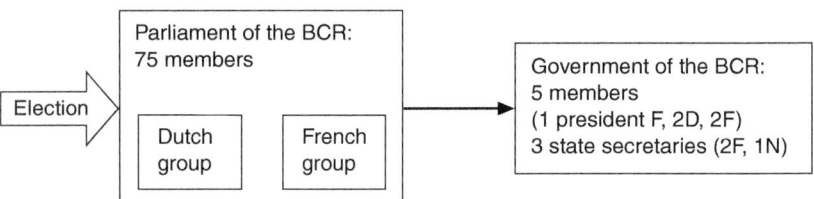

Figure 6.1 The institutions of the BCR (1989–2004).

ministers) to which a two-to-one Francophone preponderance applies. To prevent the occurrence of empty portfolios, ministerial competencies are fixed, as well as subjected to a picking-order in case the language groups disagree.

Finally, at the *administrative* level, representational quotas fix 69 percent for Francophones and 31 percent for Dutch-speakers. At the very top of the administration parity is guaranteed (Detant, 1998: 96).

Brussels as the meeting-point for two Communities

Although the BCR is not a Community in its own right, its institutions make specific allowance for its citizens as members of the Flemish or French Communities. The French and Flemish Communities continue to play a role in Brussels. Unlike decrees from the Walloon and Flemish Regions, to which the territoriality principle applies, Flemish Community decrees affect Dutch-speakers living in Brussels; French Community decrees affect Francophone *Bruxellois*. This calls however, for the participation of Dutch- and French-speakers from Brussels in the decisions of the respective Community institutions. Figure 6.2 illustrates the complex mechanisms which aim at involving BCR inhabitants in Community affairs. Clearly, the structure of

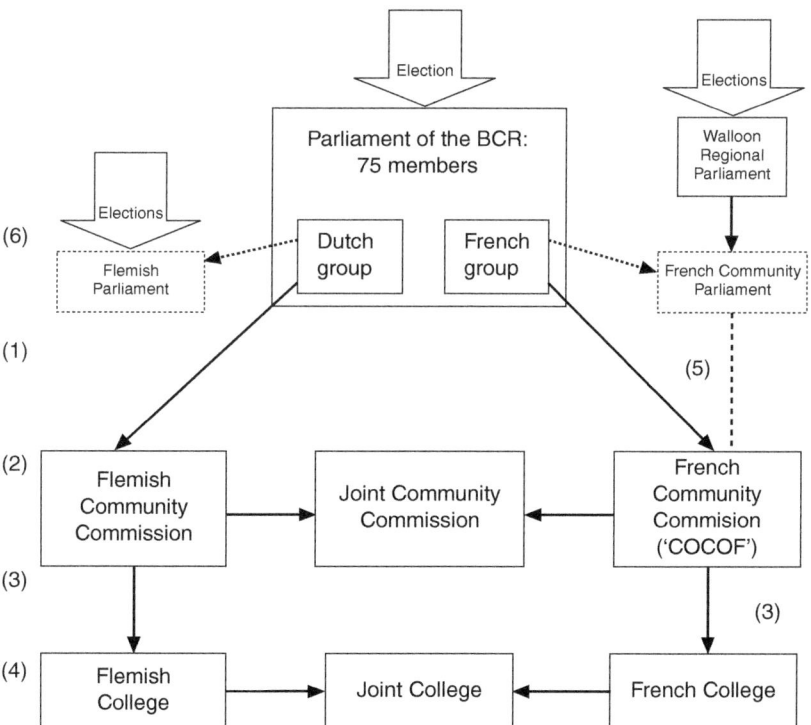

Figure 6.2 The implementation of Flemish and French Community policies in Brussels.

the BCR institutions is used for linking both of the Communities and their capital (indeed Brussels was chosen as their capital by the Flemish and the French Communities).

Earlier it was argued that all 75 directly elected members of the BCR Parliament are split along linguistic lines between a Dutch- and a French-speaking group. A first linkage between Brussels and both of the Communities is *representational*. The first six elected Dutch-speaking members and the first 19 elected French-speaking members of the BCR Parliament are members ex officio of the Flemish Parliament and the French Community Parliament, respectively (the dotted arrows in Figure 6.2).

The important asymmetry between Dutch- and French-speaking Belgians which was alluded to before is reflected in Figure 6.2, insofar as reference is made to only one Flemish Parliament whereas a directly elected Walloon Regional Parliament and an indirectly elected French Community Parliament are mentioned – see Figure 6.2, arrow 6). As one can note, the contingent of Dutch-speaking BCR MPs who are members by virtue of the Flemish Parliament is more than three times smaller than its counterpart in the French Community Parliament. This makes sense too, as the Dutch-speakers in Brussels are already a minority within their Region, and even more so within the entire Dutch-speaking population, whereas the Brussels' Francophones constitute a strong regional majority, and a sizable minority within the total group of French-speaking Belgians.

A second linkage between Brussels and the Communities is *procedural*. The language groups of the BCR Parliament constitute Community commissions who can specify Community legislation. For instance, the Flemish Community Commission (FLCC) can supplement (albeit under tutelage) Flemish cultural policy pertaining to Flemish cultural initiatives in Brussels. Its executive arm, the Flemish Community College, is composed of the same two Dutch-speaking ministers belonging to the BCR-executive. Similar scenarios apply to a French Community Commission (FRCC) and a French Community College (arrows 1 and 3 in Figure 6.2). The Flemish College operates as the executive arm of the FLCC. It is composed of the same two Dutch-speaking ministers belonging to the BCR executive (Figure 6.2, arrow 3). Community policies affecting both Communities (for instance the administering of a bilingual hospital) require the co-operation of both Community Commissions. To that purpose the Community Commissions merge into a Joint Community Commission (JCC – Figure 6.2, arrow 2) of which the Joint Community College is the executive arm (Figure 6.2, arrow 4). The minister-president of the BCR takes part in the deliberations of the JCC, but only plays an advisory role. Decision-making is by two ministers from each language group, totaling four. Finally, in certain cases decisions of the JCC are subject to a double majority requirement, for instance when deciding to establish bilingual hospitals (Alen, 1995: 428–430; Van Orshoven, 1990: 227–264). It is clear that these institutional complexities arise from an intricate combination of group autonomy and power sharing.

The role of the federal government

The competencies, powers and institutional make-up of the Regions and Communities are adopted by the *federal* parliament, either as constitutional amendments or as special majority laws. By entrusting the formal monopoly for adjusting the institutional structure to the *federal* level, the institutional make-up of Brussels (where the Flemish have been the demanding party in terms of increasing their representation rights) could be easily linked to institutional demands that emerged elsewhere. The existence of two parallel linguistically homogeneous party systems means that even federal political elites are only accountable to linguistically homogeneous electorates, and thus take regional interests into account. Consequently, the most recent adjustments to the institutional make-up of Brussels (2001), which responded primarily to Flemish demands, was linked to improving the fiscal position of the French Community (a French-speaking demand). Such intricate package deals, which emerge out of an intense process of inter-Community logrolling, typically link the interests of the Dutch-speakers at the Brussels' level (a 'regional minority') with the concerns of the French-speakers at the federal level (a 'national minority'). This balance between both 'minorities' is an almost unique Belgian phenomenon. It limits the possibilities for institutional transfer of the Belgian and Brussels institutional models to multicultural societies elsewhere.

Assessing the governance structure of Brussels – strengths and weaknesses

Prior to the regionalization of Brussels and the crafting of minority protecting devices, the city-region was in almost complete administrative and urban chaos. Up until 1989, a small nationally controlled ministerial committee whose members considered the regional governance of Brussels to be of relatively little importance exercised the competencies of the Brussels Region. The institutional regionalization of Brussels put decision-making more strongly in the hands of politicians with a direct interest in the well being of the capital.

Notwithstanding these assets, the Brussels' model is not without its weaknesses. Some potential weaknesses are obvious and do not require in-depth clarification. First, the complexity of the system holds a certain amount of institutional spear-head technology in it, but to citizens who live in the region it is not always clear whom they should address when they require a construction permit, wish to attend a vocational training course, or seek to file a complaint about irregular public transport services. Second, from a formal point of view, cultural and educational affairs (Community competencies) and matters that relate to public transport (a Regional competence) can be easily separated. However, in the mind of the individual, disentangling these responsibilities is not always possible, certainly if one considers oneself as more *Community* than *Region* oriented. For instance, the prolonged levying of television and radio surcharges (a regional tax) in Brussels, contrasts with its abolition in the Flemish Region, even if in general Dutch-speakers who live in Brussels watch the same TV programs as their counterparts who reside in Flanders. Or, only a few years ago, the former Minister of Transport in the Flemish government, the flamboyant Social-Democrat Steve Stevaert, announced free public bus transport for all citizens aged above 60 years old. The public transport firm, *De Lijn* organizes bus transport in the Flemish Region, but in Brussels this service is provided by the MIVB. Accepting that local transport is a regional competence is agreeing to the principle that senior citizens who live in Flanders are given certain privileges that their counterparts who live in Brussels are denied. Some buses that are operated by *De Lijn* transport passengers from the Flemish suburbs into Brussels. If the policy recommendations of the minister are acted upon, senior citizens who live in the Flemish Region can travel for free, but Flemish senior citizens who live in Brussels must pay the full fair, even if they are traveling on the same bus. Strictly speaking, asking boarding passengers to show their identity card can only enforce this principle. The alternative – of making public transport free for all Flemish senior citizens, irrespective of their place of living – would not only create a conflict of competence with the BCR, but it would also discriminate against French-speakers who live in Brussels.

Evidently such a problem does not arise with regards to Community services that are provided in Brussels, as they are designed to benefit *all* members of a linguistic Community including those who live in Brussels. Yet, a potential problem of 'intercommunity – free-riding' exists. It is linked to the fact that Communities cannot raise money of their own, a consequence of the legal prohibition for citizens to declare their sub-nationality. For instance, Dutch-speaking children who live in Brussels can be sent freely to French-speaking schools and vice versa. This possibility could (and in the view of the authors should) be favorably assessed, as it fosters a dialog between the Communities. The language of instruction of the school defines the Community under whose public authority the school operates. As far as the funding of education is concerned, the Communities receive a share of *federal* VAT-revenue, and the distribution among the Communities largely derives from the number of schoolchildren following education in that language. However, the lack of any tax-raising capacity of the Communities implies that they cannot influence the price of the services they provide. At present a significant number of French-speaking children attend Dutch-speaking schools in Brussels. From a *fiscal* point of view, the mesmerizing effect of the Flemish Community education system is at best a zero-budgeting operation.[8] By the same token, one could make the case that the current success of Flemish Community schools has an important symbolic and instrumental value, particularly in light of the past Frenchification of the capital.

Third, as is the case at the municipal level, the enforcement of language laws cannot always be guaranteed in institutions that are controlled by the federal or bicommunal levels of government. Hospitals are a case in point. According to the law, doctors or nurses assisting in medical urgencies should always be able to do so in the language of the patient. In practice, there is a significant shortage of qualified doctors and nurses who are bilingual. Dutch-speaking doctors are not interested in moving to Brussels, which has a per capita concentration of medical personnel that is higher than in Flanders. French-speaking doctors and nurses are not knowledgeable enough in Dutch. Fifteen Dutch-speaking municipal councilors, including three mayors representing Flemish *suburban* municipalities, even filed a complaint with the Council of Europe for breach of the federal language laws. The Council has sent out a Latvian MP who is currently conducting some field-research on this matter. A report was presented to the Assembly of the Council, after the regional elections of 2004 (*De Standaard,* 5 September 2003).

Fourth, although individuals must never openly declare their sub-nationality (no language censuses have been held since 1949), in regional and federal elections voters must commit themselves to either language group. One cannot really make the case that parties would refrain from building bilingual lists, should they be allowed to do so. The process of list formation at the municipal level demonstrates that such lists have continued to exist, albeit not in a dominant fashion. Furthermore, it is reminded that a substantial share of the members of the BCR Parliament also serve as municipal councilors, and thus are elected on such bilingual municipal electoral lists.

Fifth, the consociational mechanisms that are operating at the level of the BCR and the bicommunal institutions protect the Dutch-speaking minority. However, they can turn into sharp veto points that may paralyze the entire institutional framework. For instance, until 2004, double majorities were required to install a new regional government. Following the regional elections (1999), the extreme-right wing Flemish Nationalist Party *Vlaams Blok (now Vlaams Belang)* gathered 4.5 percent of the total *regional* vote. This is considerable, given that the percentage of votes that was cast for Flemish parties was below 15 percent. Therefore, the *Vlaams Blok* captured 4 out of 11 or 32 percent of all the Flemish seats and all the other Flemish parties joined forces to provide the Brussels regional government with the looked after majorities. The blocking potential of the *Vlaams Blok* is considerable. As an anti-system and right-wing nationalist party, it openly strives for Flemish independence and propagates the absorption of Brussels into a monolingual Flemish state. In Brussels however, it gives this agenda a much lower profile, instead its entire campaign focuses on anti-immigration policy in order to attract a share of the French-speaking voters. If the party's electoral rise were to continue, its support may well be *needed* (but not likely provided) to form a Flemish majority after the regional elections in 2004. To avoid this scenario, the Flemish agreed to a relaxation of the double majority rule and made the designation of the group of Flemish ministers dependent from the consent of an *enlarged* FLCC. The 'additional members' of this enlarged FLCC would be selected on the basis of the election results for the Flemish Parliament, instead of the election result for the BCR Parliament. The vote share of the *Vlaams Blok* is lower in Flanders than in Brussels (at least as a share of votes that were the case for Dutch-speaking parties in the BCR elections). Consequently, the share of 'enlarged' members who would represent the *Vlaams Blok* would be sufficiently high to provide the democratic parties with the looked-after majority. However, in a landmark ruling, the federal Constitutional Court declared this arrangement as unconstitutional on the grounds that the FLCC cannot possibly assume a role in designating a future BCR executive, when not even all the members of this enlarged FLCC are directly elected to the BCR Parliament (Belgian Constitutional Court, Case 35/2003, judgment of 25 March 2003). No alternative proposal has been suggested to prevent the *Vlaams Blok* from using its 'blackmail potential', should such an opportunity arise after the 2004 regional elections.

Finally, the political structure of Brussels forces its citizens to implicitly declare their loyalty to either Community when seeking to obtain certain services. The reality is more complex. A distinct Brussels territorial identity may exist which transcends a primary identification with either of the Communities. Such a feeling has always been present among the French-speaking *Bruxellois*, even if it was not often accompanied by the recognition of living in a *bilingual* City-region. One wonders whether the presence of strong minority protecting devices may have led Dutch-speakers who live in the BCR to identify more frequently with their region as well? Furthermore, the difficulty of identifying with either Community seems most problematic for two population groups in the region: citizens who were raised in bilingual or mixed Dutch–French families and citizens from non-Belgian origin. Pioneering survey research by sociologist Rudi Janssens has demonstrated that the group of 'bilingual' (Dutch–French) families who live in Brussels is as large as the group of families from Dutch-speaking origin (Janssens, 1999; 2001). Sixty percent of these bilingual (Dutch–French) families pass on *both* languages to the next generation. In addition, 4 out of 10 citizens who live in the BCR are of non-Belgian origin (although a quarter of them have acquired the Belgian nationality by now; Jacobs: 2004). For a majority, neither Dutch, nor French is their native tongue. Janssens' figures somewhat support the thesis of a further Frenchification of Brussels, particularly of these citizens of non-Belgian origin who neither speak French, nor Dutch as their native tongue. However, this does not imply their stronger commitment to identify with the French community. Additional survey research by Dirk Jacobs and Marc Swyngedouw has demonstrated that Moroccan, Turkish and Kurdish community leaders are willing to identify with Belgium or Brussels, but refuse to choose between either of the Communities (Jacobs, 2004). Extending the franchise for regional (and not only municipal) elections to all non-Belgian citizens with legal residence in Belgium could provide a more elegant way of containing the *Vlaams Blok*. While speaking French in public, these new immigrants are not necessarily inclined to vote for French-speaking parties in regional elections. Our reasoning assumes that an extension of the franchise to non-Belgians will not drive too many Belgian citizens to far-right parties and that the Flemish political parties would make a real effort to attract the immigrant vote.

Conclusion

This chapter has provided a brief overview of the politics of Brussels. The politics of the capital offers a unique patchwork in which local, Regional, Community and federal interests closely interact. A distinction was made between the local and non-local arenas. In the former, devices protecting the Flemish political minority are less well institutionalized, but politicians are free to campaign on bilingual lists. In the latter, politics is primarily structured along Community lines, and minority-protecting devices are more strongly entrenched. Demands for improving representation rights of the Flemish in Brussels have been traded against demands for safeguarding the position of the French-speakers at the federal level. The institutional solution that was worked out for Brussels cannot be properly understood without keeping this Belgian equilibrium in mind. Politicians, who are active at the local and regional level, are increasingly involved in negotiations that affect the future development of their region. However, the federal parliament, which itself is almost exclusively composed from representatives of Dutch- or French-speaking parties, and in matters of institutional reform requires the consent of both linguistic groups, ultimately decides. The party leaders as well as the top ministers of the federal and regional governments play an important role in the co-ordination of these multi-level negotiations.

Apart from various institutional linkages that bind the various levels together, a strong personal fusion can be noticed, certainly between local and regional politics, between the BCR regional and Community institutions, as well as between the BCR and the Flemish Parliament and French Community Council. However, the political game is not always structured along similar parameters, as the 'de facto self-determination' of the electorate and the forced identification of politicians at the supra-local level with either Community reduce the potential for inter-Community dialog. This is all the more regrettable, given that the BCR inhabitants may increasingly identify themselves with the BCR as a distinct territorial entity and given that the regional population of non-Belgian origin is not willing to declare its loyalty with either Community, despite their more frequent use of the French language.

Notes

1 In Brussels, the share of Dutch-speakers was still as high as 24.2 percent, while the share of French-speakers amounted to 70.6 percent. Since no language censuses have been held since, the results of regional elections in the BCR are used as the best (but certainly not watertight proxy) for the linguistic composition of the Brussels regional population. On the occasion of the most recent regional elections (1999), the share of the Dutch-speaking vote amounted to approximately 14.1 percent of the total regional vote.
2 Facilities guarantee that citizens who speak the regional (not necessarily local) minority language can receive official documents (e.g. taxation forms) in their language; they ensure that public signposts and messages are also available in the regional minority language and that nursery schools and primary education can be provided in that language if requested for by at least 16 family heads.
3 There are two minor aspects in which the competencies of the BCR are inferior to those attributed to the Flemish or Walloon Regions. First, the BCR's legislative acts (so called ordinances) are not completely identical to those from the regional Walloon and Flemish Councils (so called decrees). They can be subjected to judicial review and to limited administrative control by the federal authorities to protect the role of Brussels as an (international) capital (Alen and Ergec, 1994: 17). Second, the BCR has a more limited 'constitutive autonomy.' Changing the consociational mechanisms underpinning the functioning of the BCR institutions requires a special *federal* majority law.
4 A direct link to the federal parliament may come in handy, because *only* the federal parliament can formally decide on the competencies and funding of the Communities and the Regions, and, in the case of Brussels also on the organization (procedures, numbers of delegates, linguistic equilibrium) of the regional (but not necessarily the local) institutions that are located within the Region. Typically, such decisions require a two-thirds majority in each federal parliamentary chamber (House and Senate) and a majority within each of the linguistic groups in each of the chambers.
5 The largest share of Dutch-speakers can be found in *Anderlecht, Sint-Jans Molenbeek, Koekelberg, Sint-Agatha-Berchem, Jette, Evere and certain parts of Sint-Pieters-Woluwe*. No precise figures can be given, as citizens who live in the BCR must not declare their sub-nationality.
6 Municipalities receive a surcharge on (federal) income-tax and regional property-tax receipts. In addition, they can directly levy garbage collecting, patrimony and company taxes.
7 Given that the national government successfully reduced the number of Belgian municipalities from 2000 to approximately 600 in 1977, notwithstanding a parallel reduction in the number of available local public positions.
8 At present, the Flemish Community schools are in a fiscally less precarious position than their French-speaking counterparts (in Brussels and in the French Community in general). Part of the reason refers to the merger of Regional and Community budgets at the Flemish side, which allows for a more fluid transfer of fiscal resources. In addition, French-speaking children need on average more time to complete their high school courses than their Dutch-speaking counterparts, making education more expensive. Finally, the Flemish education system benefits from economies of scale caused by the dominance of the 'Catholic' school network whereas in French-speaking Belgium the public and Catholic school networks are of comparable size (Nassaux, 2000, 2001).

References

Alen, A. (1995), *Handboek van het Belgisch Staatsrecht*. Antwerp: Kluwer.
Alen, A. and Ergec, R. (1994), *Federal Belgium after the Fourth State Reform*. Brussels: Ministry of Foreign Affairs.
Baeten, G. (2001), 'The Europeanization of Brussels and the Urbanization of "Europe". Hybridizing the City. Empowerment and Disempowerment in the EU District', in *European Urban and Regional Studies* 8(2): pp. 117–130.
Belgian Constitutional Court (2003), 'Arrest nr. 35/2003 van 25 Maart 2003' accessible via http://www.arbitrage.be.
Chamber of Representatives (2001), 'Projet de Loi modifiant la loi du 12 janvier 1989 réglant les modalités de l'élection du Conceil de la Region de Bruxelles-Capitale et la loi ordinaire du 16 juillet 1993 visant à achever la structure fédérale de l'Etat', *Document 50–1247/001*.
Clement, J. and Delgrange, X. (1999), 'La protection des minorités – De bescherming van de minderheden', in E. Witte, A. Alen, H. Dumont and R. Ergec (eds), *Bruxelles et son statut*. Brussels: Larcier, pp. 517–556.
De Lannoy, W., Lammens, M., Lesthaege, R., Willaert, D. (1999), 'Brussel in de Jaren Negentig en na 2000: Een Demografische Doorlichting', in E. Witte, A. Alen, H. Dumont and R. Ergec (eds), *Bruxelles et son statut*. Brussels: Larcier, pp. 101–154.
Deschouwer, K. (1999a), 'From Consociation to Federation: How the Belgian Parties Won.' in K. Deschouwer and R.K. Luther (eds), *Party Elites in Divided Societies: Political Parties in Consociational Democracy*. London: Routledge.
Deschouwer, K. and Buelens, J. (1997), 'De Gemeenten en de Lokale Politiek in het Brussels Hoofdstedelijk Gewest,' *Res Publica* 1: 89–99.
De Standaard (2003), 'Brussel Klaar voor Komst Rapporteur Raad van Europa', in *De Standaard*, 5 September, accessible via htttp://www.destandaard.be.
Detant, A. (1999), 'Kunnen taalvrijheid en officiële tweetaligheid verzoend worden? De toepassing van de taalwetgeving in het Brussels Hoofdstedelijk Gewest', in E. Witte, A. Alen, H. Dumont and R. Ergec (eds), *Bruxelles et son statut*. Brussels: Larcier, pp. 411–438.
DEXIA (2002), *De financiën van de lokale overheden in 2002*, Brussels: Dexia Bank.
Distelmans, B. and Koppen, J. (2002), 'Hoofdlijnen in de Ontwikkling van de Faciliteitenproblematiek', in J. Koppen, B. Distelmans and R. Janssens (eds), *Taalfaciliteiten in de Rand. Ontwikkelingslijnen, conflictgebieden en taalpraktijk*. Brussels: VUB-Press, pp. 15–40.
Duchacek, I.D. (1970), *Comparative Federalism: The Territorial Dimension of Politics*. New York, NY: Holt, Rhinehart & Winston.
Heremans, D. and Philipsen, C. (1999), 'Financiële Aspecten van het Brusselse Model', in E. Witte, A. Alen, H. Dumont and R. Ergec (eds), *Bruxelles et son statut*: Brussels: Larcier, pp. 207–249.
Hooghe, L. (2003), 'Belgium. From Regionalism to Federalism', in J. Coakley (ed.), *The Territorial Management of Ethnic Conflict*. London: Frank Cass, pp. 73–98.
Hooghe, L. and Marks, G. (2003), 'Unraveling the Central State, but How ? Types of Multi-Level Governance', *American Political Science Review* 2: 233–243.
Jacobs, D. (2004), 'Pacifying National Majorities in the Brussels Capital Region. What About the Immigrant Minority Groups?', in A.H. Morawa (ed.), *European Yearbook of Minority Issues*. Leyden: Bril.

Janssens, R. (1999), 'Aspecten van het Taalgebruik in Brussel', in E. Witte, A. Alen, H. Dumont and R. Ergec (eds), *Bruxelles et son statut*. Brussels: Larcier, pp. 283–306.
—— (2001), *Taalgebruik in Brussel – Brusselse Thema's – 8*. Brussels: VUB Press.
Lijphart, A. (1994), *Electoral Systems and Party Systems*. Oxford: Oxford University Press.
—— (1999), *Patterns of Democracy. Government Forms and Performance in Thirty-Six Countries*. New Haven: Yale University Press.
Luykx, Th. and Platel, M. (1985), *Politieke Geschiedenis van België*. Antwerp: Kluwer.
Nassaux, J.-P. (2000), 'Le groupe de travail sur le fonctionnement des institutions bruxelloises. Première phase: octobre 1999–mai 2000', *Courrier Hebdomadaire du CRISP*, no. 1682.
—— (2001), 'Le groupe de travail sur le fonctionnement des institutions bruxelloises. Deuxième phase et accord dit du Lombard', *Courrier Hebdomadaire du CRISP*, no. 1716–1717.
NIS (2002a), 'Werkelijke Bevolking per Gemeente op 1 Januari 2002'. NIS publication accessible via http://www.statbel.fgov.be.
—— (2002b), 'Fiscale Inkomens – aanslagjaar 2001, inkomens 2000 (bedragen in euro)'. NIS publication accessible via http://www.statbel.fgov.be.
Putnam, R. (1988), 'Diplomacy and Domestic Politics: The Logic of Two-Level Games', *International Organization* 42(3): 427–460.
Senate (2001a), 'Ontwerp van bijzondere wet houdende overdracht van diverse bevoegdheden aan de gewesten en de gemeenschappen', *Document 2–709/7*, 23 May.
—— (2001b), 'Wetsvoorstel houdende diverse institutionele hervormingen betreffende de lokale instellingen van het Brussels Hoofdstedelijk Gewest', *Document 2–740/4*, 7 June.
Sieben, L. (1993), 'Gemeenten op de wip tussen Vlaanderen en Brussel', in E. Witte (ed), *Brusselse Thema's – 1: De Brusselse Rand*. Brussels: VUB Press, pp. 145–167.
Swenden, W. (2004), 'Personality vs. Territoriality. Belgium and the Framework Convention for the Protection of National Minorities', in A.H. Morawa (ed.), *European Yearbook of Minority Issues*. Leyden: Brill.
Van Orshoven, P. (1990), 'Brussel anno 1989. Een derde gewest, een enige agglomeratie, drie gemeenschapscommissies en . . . een vierde gemeenschap', *Rechtskundig Weekblad*, jg. 1989–1990, 449–466.
Wils, L. (1992), *Van Clovis tot Happart. De Lange Weg van de Naties in de Lage Landen*. Leuven: Garant.
Witte, E. and Van Velthoven, H. (1998), *Taal en Politiek. De Belgische Casus in een Historisch Perspectief*. Brussels: VUB Press.

Part III
European integration
A changing territorial state of affairs?

7 Territoriality and the EU citizen

Gertjan Dijkink and Virginie Mamadouh

The significance of territory

The notion that human action has been liberated from the bonds of local/national culture and politics has made territoriality a prominent topic in discussions about globalisation and European integration. Yet, minds and feelings change less easily than rules and political practices. In our opinion adaptation to change is even more difficult with territorial matters because (political) territory gets deeply interiorised in the citizen. The dominant story of globalisation has elicited counter-narratives about the persistence of national and local frameworks and the ascendancy of new identities arising in reaction to globalisation. If current territorial attachments are weakening then we should at least expect 'reterritorialisation' behind 'deterritorialisation'.[1] In this chapter we examine whether the European Union constitutes such a level of reterritorialisation for the EU citizen. We will use data from public opinion, voting, protest movements and media research in order to establish if the EU has adopted the same territorial significance as the national state previously.

Behind the discussion concerning shifting scales and identities obviously lurks the theoretical problem of the 'significance of territory', a subject already addressed in 1971 by French geographer Jean Gottmann.[2] According to Gottmann, territoriality was inseparable from the development of the state or from what other writers have called the 'bundling of territoriality'. Robert Sack, a geographer less burdened with European history, proposed a more instrumentalist perspective on territoriality. Starting from the basic meaning of territoriality as a regulating principle he contrasted territoriality with regulation by means of personal authority or enumeration. This opposition sheds some light on the efficiency of territorial strategies: one may list all things a child is not allowed to touch but one may also put these things in a room where the child is denied access.[3] The latter is easier to communicate and to check and it also depersonalises authority by deflecting attention from the person who forbids to the territory that is forbidden. Although this is a rather simplified approach to the phenomenon of political territoriality, it at least has the advantage of clarity.

This approach may suggest that territorial strategies represent a more advanced stage in political history. For example medieval society was dominated by systems of personalised authority in which the relevant authority changed according to the kind of activity concerned (religious, labour, traffic, etc.). Territorial strategies which allow certain people to do certain things, such as hunting, picking berries or levying tolls in a specified area, have a longer history than centralised rule. The control over all rights or obligations of the people living within a particular area did not develop until the late Middle Ages. This new political phase, the rise of kings and absolute power, was not acknowledged until it had already been established for a considerable period of time. Jean Bodin introduced the concept of *sovereignty* in 1576,[4] remarking how amazing it was that the principle had not been formulated earlier. This sixteenth-century example illustrates just how intangible the basic facts of political reality can be.

The fact that political thinkers found it difficult to discuss a basic political principle such as sovereignty, even though it had already been put into practice indicates that political experience becomes part of an individual's way of looking at the world rather than an easily examinable concrete phenomenon. This problem seems particularly pressing in the study of territoriality. It has often been observed that the development of central authority can be compared with the discovery of central perspective (the 'vanishing point') in art.[5] Perspective, in the art of drawing, is created using lines on a flat surface, which nevertheless arouses the sensation of depth. Similarly political territoriality is not merely a way of organizing a system of authority but a concept that appeals to individual feelings of integrity or legitimacy. The historical innovation of territorial sovereignty broadened the legitimacy of rulers because their rule was no longer merely motivated by symbolic (religious) references or by warranting the security of loyal individuals but increasingly by responsibility for welfare in different spheres of life. The new power invested in kings was superficially a matter of conquest but ultimately a consequence of *empowerment* from below as well.[6] Therefore the study of territory must not only focus on the organisational basis but also on the feelings and experiences of citizens.

In order to substantiate the importance of a citizen's perspective the substance of territoriality as experienced by the human individual must be clearly defined. The Finnish geographer Anssi Paasi has paid a great deal of attention to the 'institutionalisation of territory'; the conditions that turn territories into social realities. He distinguishes four dimensions: territorial shape (its geographical delimitation), symbolic shape (its symbols especially its name), institutional practices (not necessarily administrative practices) and identity of the territory within a broader system. In terms of assessable citizen behaviour these elements of territoriality imply that people can address, or are addressed by, territorial institutions (*interaction*), feel attached to the people and things in and symbols of a territory (*attachment*), look at the world from the perspective of a territory (*information*). These distinctions do not directly indicate what territoriality means as an individual fact of life ('seeing in depth'). We suggest that the social construction of territory enters our perception and feelings as *connectedness* and *confidence*. These experiences both provide substance to the human need for belonging; enabling individuals to interact, and thus feel attached; and allowing for information in a territorial setting.

Connectedness means first that items originating from a distinct geographical area, like material articles, official letters and news items have a substantial impact in our daily life. Second, the territory is a distinct area co-ordinated by a central principle, and a common enterprise or destiny. The concept of connectedness has penetrated the production of news and the writing of history books used for educational purposes. Through these texts particular places are connected to a territory by means of stories about the past and places outside the boundaries are connected with the fate of another territory. Thus, through the conversion of time into space the citizen views his or her territory within the confines of constructed boundaries.

Confidence provides citizens with the means to navigate through the thicket of rights and rules within the bounds of a particular territory. Since the formal rules and obligations are 'masterminded' and pass on through a public channel they are easier to accept as legitimate, there is either divine sanctification or the possibility of evaluation and influence (voting). On the one hand confidence is based on citizenship rights, and on the other hand on knowledge of culture, unwritten manners that one must observe in order to enlist the help of other people. The expectation of solidarity, either from the state or from fellow citizens, in times of crisis also contributes to the basic feeling of confidence.

The bundling of territory, which initiated the formation of the European or Westphalian state, caused many indirect effects reinforcing the territorial experience of individuals aforementioned. The direct effect was of course the attribution of all regulation to one actor or 'mind'. A more long-term effect was the material and cultural integration of the territory with the formation of national identities. These processes all contributed to the experience (but not everywhere equally strong) of connectedness and confidence among citizens of the respective European states. In the examination of the reverse process, the unbundling of territory, an equally spectacular effect on the individual outlook of European citizens may be expected. The history of the nation-state should however remind us of the long-term change in such secondary products as a common national culture and material integration. Thus, we can assume that these enduring changes will most likely apply to the reverse process.

If the theme of territoriality arises in the context of European integration, the most obvious association is with the *unbundling of territory* i.e. (state-) authority. Nevertheless material dissolution of state-territories is already running ahead of this process: the formation of multinational corporations, mobility of persons, people owning real estate across boundaries, consumption of products fabricated in a wide range of countries, etc. This suggests that a shift in the territorial outlook of individuals occurs on the two dimensions confidence and connectedness.

The basic litmus test for the unbundling of territoriality is two sided: from the side of (national) policy actors it would have to indicate a decreasing reverberation of events in an exclusively territorial (national) policy network and from the side of the citizen it would have to show a decreasing expectation that only the actors and events within territorial bounds determine ones life. The indication that citizens' orientations towards 'their' particular territory and its politicians is dwindling can be determined by three related factors: (1) the inclination of people to spend longer periods of their lives away from their native land; (2) the decreasing success of national information sources in claiming their sole attention; and (3) the decreasing emotional attachment to their own territory. Internalisation of or identification with a territory is the hallmark of territoriality. This is not to say that citizens could not identify with several (nested) territories at the same time, but the attachment is usually not equally distributed across all levels. A comparison of surveys done between 1971 and 1988 in a community in northeastern Italy (Friuli) revealed that

> people feel attached above all to the primordial 'life-world' of everyday life, the place where they have their homes, property, jobs, primary relations, service structures and infrastructures. But they are also much influenced by the most powerful element of the system in which they are embedded – the Nation State – loyalty to which is the goal of much institutional effort, beginning with school.... In all cases Europe kindles weaker feelings that the State and the World (!)[7]

In spite of the emerging Lega Nord at the time these words were written, the author concludes that there is little evidence of people's attachment to the so-called meso-level (i.e. northern Italy). The term territoriality is appropriate in this context if we can show that it influences an individual's perspectives on the world. The manner in which the state has influenced people's perspective about the world has recently been the subject of various studies mentioning a 'territorial trap' in our awareness of the world.[8] Information systems stopping at the state boundaries have a peculiar influence on the perception of social problems or virtues. However, the need for information has actually influenced the reality within the state's boundaries so as to make it readable and measurable for rulers.[9] Moreover this entailed the neglect of certain types of information. As Peter Taylor remarks:

> This means that the vast majority of publicly accessible data provide attribute measures of areas to the relative neglect of measuring the relations, connections and flows between areas. We are provided with masses of information to describe and analyse spaces of places, but relatively little for serious consideration of spaces of flows.[10]

In the Netherlands a host of governmental information like the publications of the SCP (Social and Cultural Planning Office) and CBS (Central Statistical Office) still show this exclusive orientation to the nation as a spatial container. Such information leads to mis-representations of the world to those that do not realise that nations increasingly are leaking containers.[11]

Representation and territoriality are also closely intertwined in another way. After the period in which the ruler represented divine power, the term representation came to mean the election of delegates and an electoral system became the most concrete embodiment of territoriality. The fact that citizens are not deeply disturbed by the impossibility of narrowly controlling the policy decisions advanced by elected representatives is a sign of confidence in a territory as something that requires its own logic. The vote is foremost a demonstration of allegiance to a territorially bounded system. This is not necessarily a democratic imperfection but it is intrinsic to the principle of representation, which implies that one gives shape to (translates) something in a different universe or medium.[12] We can here draw another analogy to art where similarly representation is not the same as copying something. In the same vein territorial identity is not a geographical mapping of personal values and qualities but an autonomous design satisfying basic human needs like belonging. Emerging dissatisfaction with the way democracy works, the call for referendums and the rise of new special interest parties, all indicate deterritorialisation rather than the perfecting of democracy.

In this light, deterritorialisation seems to crop up in the most unexpected and divergent spheres. But what about reterritorialisation? Here European integration seems to offer the most convincing case of a new bundling of territory. The problem, of course, is that it is only partial and goes along with characterisations as 'multilevel governance' or Europe 'rescuing the nation-state'. Therefore it can probably not be equated with the bundling of territory that occurred during the formation of states. One might expect consequently a weak experience of connectedness and confidence on the level of citizens. In order to further explore this we will look at what the EU has to offer for the production of a clear identification and perspective among its citizens.

The EU as territory

The exceptional character of the process of European integration has often been underlined. It is a dynamic process of deepening and broadening which has experienced numerous setbacks since the establishment of the European Coal and Steel Community in 1952. Still, the EU can be analysed as any territory. However if we measure the institutionalisation of the EU using Paasi's four dimensions[13] it is clear that the process is far from complete.

The territorial shape of the EU has not yet been stabilised. Its territory has been enlarged several times by the adhesion of new Member States

(1973, 1981, 1986, 1995, 2004) and by German reunification (1990). The major reduction caused when the Danish autonomous territory Greenland opted out the European Communities (EC) in 1985 has largely gone unnoticed (although Greenland was larger in size than the rest of the EC). Moreover there is no widely accepted ideal of the definitive territorial shape of the EU, as it is the case for most states not yet established (e.g. Kurdistan, Kashmir or Palestine).

The symbolic shape of the EU is characterised by a recent and unstable name. The distinct European Communities has been encapsulated into the European Union in 1992 (Maastricht Treaty) without disappearing, giving way to misunderstandings. The conflation of Europe and the EU is readily comparable to that between America and the USA. Moreover the symbols of the EU are shared with other territories: the flag and the anthem are also those of the Council of Europe. Europe's day (9 May) in honour of Schuman's declaration on 9 May, 1950 is not an official holiday. The motto adopted in May 2000 by the European Parliament after an EU-wide contest among schools 'Unity in diversity' is hardly specific.[14]

The institutional practices regarding the EU are changing rapidly. Successive treaties have altered the balance between the main institutions (Commission, European Parliament and the Council of Ministers), the role of the Court of Justice and the European Council, and have shaped new agencies such as the European Central Bank. The balance between different levels of government inside the EU, especially between the Member States and the supranational level, and between the states and the regions, is under discussion. Thus, there is a continuing, but contested shift of competences and roles between institutions.

The identity of the EU in a broader territorial system is no less disputed. The institutionalisation of the EU occurred in a territorial system dominated by territorial states, in the birthplace of the modern state system. The new territory cannot be established without affecting pre-existing ones and their relations (e.g. the territorial system).[15] During the Cold War, the European Communities stood for Western Europe, but the post Cold War era brought more blurred margins: in the east with Russia, in the south with the Mediterranean countries and in the west with Northern America. Finally, due to the colonial history of many European states and its heritage in most parts of the world, it is difficult to characterise the specificity of Europe as a territory.

The EU as a state in the making

Although poorly institutionalised, the EU now forms a territory and a new polity. Both proponents and opponents sometimes see it, as a state in the making. Therefore its main territorial characteristics can be compared to those features typical of modern state territoriality: the territory, its borders and its capital city.[16]

While the territory of a state is fixed, the territory of the EU is not only expanding, it is variable for different policies. The Euro-zone contains only 12 of the 15 Member States, while other policies apply to state territories outside the EU, for example through the European Economic Area (EEA), through associations' agreements, and through the successive Yaoundé, Lomé and Cotonou agreements with African, Caribbean and Pacific countries.

While state boundaries are absolute, the meaning of territorial boundaries has been affected by European integration through which the distinction is made between internal and external borders (e.g. borders between Member States versus borders between a Member State and a so-called third country). Furthermore, cross-border cooperation has been encouraged symbolically and financially, transforming border regions in areas of communication, instead of national dead ends.

While state power is represented in the capital city, the EU has spread its institutions among several locations. Despite some discussion of a site for a capital city[17] the European institutions were eventually located in different cities: Luxembourg, Brussels and Strasbourg. The European Central Bank is located in Frankfurt/Main and many agencies in other Member States (such as Europol in The Hague and the European Environment Agency in Copenhagen). Moreover, European Summits are held in the state holding the presidency of the European Council. As a result the EU does not have a capital city, functioning as a showcase of its territorial power. In the Treaty of Nice (2000) the position of Brussels was strengthened as in the future more European summits will be held in Brussels and eventually after the 2004 enlargement the rotating system was abandoned.

EU policies affecting citizens

The EU reaches the inhabitants of its territory through both material and representational manners. However, national authorities mediate most of these encounters. It is therefore interesting to study how citizens encounter the EU in their daily lives and how EU taxes, legislation and institutions and policies affect its citizens.

EU taxes exist but are not visible to the citizens as such (there is no line for EU tax on a receipt, like there is for the Value Added Tax). The primary legislation of the EU consists of treaties adopted and ratified by the Member States. The so-called secondary legislation consists of EU legal acts. Those in force as of 31 May, 1999 include 1,662 directives and 5,587 regulations.[18] Regulations are binding and directly applicable in all Member States, directives are binding but to be implemented in national legislation first.[19]

EU institutions are modestly present in the everyday lives of citizens. Symbolic representations of the EU are found on documents that enhance mobility such as passports, driver's licenses and number plates, but in all three cases they are still delivered by national authorities. Moreover, the harmonisation of these documents is only marginally visible through the mention of the EU, a symbol (the so-called Euroband on license plates)[20] or through multilingualism (in passports).

Since 1979 the European Parliament has been directly elected every five years. Yet, elections are held nationally, national parties are running candidates, and the national media cover the event. The Single European Act (SEA) has brought the single market into being, thereby enhancing people's freedom of movement inside the Union. Still, a minority of EU citizens live outside the Member State of which they hold citizenship. According to Eurostat estimates, about 6 million EU citizens were living in another country of the EU in 1998, about 1.6 per cent of the total population.[21] In 1993, there were slightly less: 5.5 millions.[22] Proportionally Belgium (5.4 per cent) and Luxembourg (28.2 per cent) had the most non-national EU residents. In Germany there were about 1.7 million, in France 1.3 million and in the UK 0.7 million non-national EU residents. The largest group abroad were Italians with 1.156 million, followed by the Irish (498,000). In addition there were about 184,000 documented cross-border workers: the largest group commuting from France to Germany (52,449) or to Luxembourg (27,284).[23]

Since the enactment of the Treaty on European Union (TEU) in 1992, EU-citizenship has been granted to the citizens of the Member States. This citizenship is secondary except for those living in another Member State than the one for which they hold a passport, because they can vote in their state of residence for European and local elections, and for those living outside the EU (as they might be serviced by diplomats from another Member State). Only 303,000 of the EU citizens living in another Member State registered to vote in their country of residence for the 1994 EU elections, that is, 2 per cent of those residents in the UK (Irish citizens excluded) and 3 per cent in Portugal up to 25 per cent in Denmark and 44 per cent in Ireland (British citizens excluded).[24] Fifty-three per cent of these EU citizens were candidates in their country of residence but only one of them was elected. In 1999 the figures were hardly better: 9 per cent of the EU citizens living abroad registered for the election in their country of residence, and of the 62 candidates only four were elected.

Since 2002, the most obvious sign of the presence of the EU, at least in 12 states, is the Euro. The adoption of a single currency and eventually the replacement of national coins and bills by Euro ones is both materially and symbolically influential. The total population of these member states use the Euro for any monetary transaction. Furthermore the introduction of different national coin collections has enhanced the visibility of the common currency, as has been shown in various projects to monitor the spread of foreign coins in particular countries.[25]

Last but not least, EU policies are visible on the ground. Some policies pertain directly to the territory, such as the control of borders and movements of peoples, capital, goods and services. These include the removal of border control in Schengenland, the harmonisation of the visa policy etc. or more modest policies to stimulate cross-border exchange such as the students exchange programmes like Erasmus, Socrates and Leonardo. According to King, around 750,000 university students have spent a period of 3 to 12 months studying abroad since the launch of the Erasmus programme in 1987.[26] For the academic year 1993–1994 the UK followed by France, Austria, Belgium and Sweden were net receivers (the UK had a positive balance of 25,618 students) while Italy, Germany, the Netherlands, Spain and Ireland, sent more students than they received. For the academic year 1999–2000 the differences were smaller, the UK was still the main receiver (with a net surplus of 10,649 students) followed by France, Sweden, and two countries that became attractive: the Netherlands and Ireland.

Other EU policies have been made to promote territorial cohesion through the so-called structural funds. They included the European Social Fund (ESF) adopted in 1958, the European Agricultural Guidance and Guarantee Fund (EAGGF) adopted with the establishment of the Common Agricultural policy (CAP) in 1962, and the European Regional Development Fund (ERDF) adopted after the first enlargement. The regional policy was expanded with the establishment of the internal market with the SEA and after the southern enlargements. Several objectives were set for a regional policy and a cohesion policy was adopted to help the poorer Member States (Ireland, Greece, Spain and Portugal) to compete in the internal market. The priority objectives in the period 1989–1993 included development and structural adjustment (objective 1), conversion of industrial regions in decline (objective 2), struggle against long-term unemployment (objective 3), integration of young people (objective 4), agricultural adjustment (5a) and development of rural areas (5b). The structural funds were supplemented with community initiatives such as INTERREG that stimulates cross-border initiatives. Spain, Italy, Portugal, Greece and Ireland were the largest receivers of such aid, Ireland, Portugal and Greece scoring the highest for figures per capita. For the period 1994–1999, an additional priority was adopted for regions with an extremely low population density (objective 6), following the inclusion of Sweden and Finland. For the period 2000–2006, the policy was more radically reformed, with the reformulation of three objectives: development and structural adjustment (objective 1), conversion of industrial regions in decline (objective 2) and adaptation and modernisation of education, training and employment systems (objective 3). The 2004 eastward enlargement confronted the EU with more disparities than ever.

Territorial cohesion was put on the agenda through the effort to develop a spatial planning at the EU level. This endeavour finally resulted in the adoption of the European Spatial Development Perspective (ESDP) in Potsdam in 1999[27] and the establishment of the European Spatial Planning Observatory Network (ESPON), a research programme addressing the 'basic spatial characteristics of the enlarged European territory'. Territorial cohesion is

156   G. Dijkink and V. Mamadouh

also acknowledged as an important objective of the EU in the Draft Constitution presented in June 2003 by the European Convention (Article 3.3). 'Economic social and territorial cohesion' is an area of shared competence between the Union and the states (Article 13) (see Chapter 5).

Now that the possible reach of the EU in the every day life of its citizens has been sketched out we can address the individual level. The following section will address the question of how citizens perceive and identify with the institutionalising territory that is known as the European Union.

Experiencing the new territory

Here we will address the issues of citizen perception and identification by considering data on the three aspects of individual behaviour we distinguished in our introduction: interaction with territorial institutions; attachment to people, things and symbols; and information. We rely mainly on opinion surveys and to a lesser extent on observable behaviour (such as voting behaviour). Opinions about European integration have been monitored since 1973 in *Eurobarometers* commissioned by the European Commission. This extensive collection features several kinds of surveys (the Standard Eurobarometer held every semester, Special and Flash Eurobarometers), surveys in candidate Member States, and more recently qualitative studies.[28] Despite the many critical comments that can be made about the reliability, the representativeness and the relevance of the surveys, they are the best source we have concerning the opinions of EU citizens.[29] Unless mentioned otherwise, the results described here are based on Eurobarometer 59, for which the fieldwork was done in spring 2003.

As a result of the successive enlargements and of differential impacts of EU policies, attitudes towards the Union and its institutions are not likely to be evenly distributed. Differences are expected between residents of different Member States according to the length of their membership: inhabitants of the core countries, the original Six of Schumania, have been part of the European integration process for half a century, while others live in states that have just completed their adhesion negotiations. People in some places are more exposed to EU policies than others. Those people living in rural areas affected by the CAP of the European Communities and those living in so-called objective 1 regions, the main recipients of structural funds, are the most affected by regional policies. In addition, the EU is more visible in some places than in others: border regions between two Member States, at the external borders of the EU and in cities hosting the main EU institutions (Brussels, Luxembourg, Strasbourg) as the presence of civil servants and politicians affect these localities in various ways (job opportunities, raising rents, European schools, cultural activities etc.). Unfortunately these geographic differences can only be addressed when pertaining to differences between Member States.

Interaction with territorial institutions

The first aspect of a citizen's experience we distinguish is the interaction with territorial institutions. EU residents interact with the EU institutions as citizens but the awareness of this EU citizenship is not very high. In autumn 2002, a Flash Eurobarometer was held on the theme '10 years of EU citizenship'.[30] The results show the poor knowledge of EU citizens about their own position. Only about one third of the respondents (31 per cent) knew what the phrase 'citizen of the Union' meant, 37 per cent had heard about it but were not sure what it meant, and 32 per cent had never heard of the term. Differences between the Member States were huge, with the percentage of unaware citizens ranging from 16 per cent in Denmark to 49 per cent in Belgium. The core six states scored very differently with an above awareness knowledge (55 per cent in Luxembourg and Italy) and below average in the other four. Respondents seemed to be misinformed about the ways one becomes a citizen of the Union. Eighty-seven per cent thought that 'you are both a citizen of the Union and the Member State at the same time' (which is true); while 72 per cent thought 'you have to ask to become a citizen of the Union' (false) and 61 per cent that 'you can choose not to be a citizen of the Union' (false). The British were more aware than others that they cannot escape EU citizenship.

When asked what rights a citizen of the Union has, a large majority thought that the following statements were true: 'to work in any Member State' (89 per cent), 'to make a complaint to the European Ombudsman' (84 per cent), 'to reside in any Member State subject to certain conditions' (84 per cent), 'to petition the European Parliament' (83 per cent), 'to ask for help from embassies of other Member states' (82 per cent). Surprisingly many people supported the false statement that the EU citizens living in their country 'have the right to vote at national elections' (51 per cent) and relatively few knew that 'a work permit is needed to work in another Member State' (43 per cent).

EU citizens are directly engaged with EU institutions as voters for EP elections, thus making turnout for EP elections interesting for our purposes. Turnout is in fact quite low in most countries, with the exception of Belgium where voting is compulsory. In 1999, the lowest turnout was found in the UK (24 per cent), but a founding member, the Netherlands (29 per cent) and 1995-newcomer Finland (30 per cent) also scored very poorly (Table 7.1).

In the Eurobarometer poll, respondents have been asked to estimate the likelihood they will vote in the next national and European elections. It is measured on a scale of 1 (sure not to vote) to 10 (sure to vote). This likelihood is higher for national elections (7.73) than for European elections (6.9). It is even below average in Belgium where voting is actually compulsory. There are differences between the two types of elections, as appears when the two are indexed: Italians, Greeks and Belgians report a probability to vote

158 *G. Dijkink and V. Mamadouh*

Table 7.1 Turnout at EP elections in June 1999

Member states	Electorate 1999	Votes cast 1999	Turnout 1999 (%)
Germany	60,766,241	27,472,760	45.2
Austria	5,847,605	2,865,977	49.0
Belgium	7,343,466	6,686,222	91.0
Denmark	4,012,440	2,021,922	50.4
Spain	32,944,451	21,209,685	64.4
Finland	4,141,098	1,247,685	30.1
France	40,129,780	18,765,259	46.8
Greece	8,912,901	6,712,684	75.3
Ireland	2,836,596	1,438,287	50.7
Italy	49,309,064	34,910,815	70.8
Luxembourg	216,512	185,768	85.8
Netherlands	11,855,000	3,544,408	29.9
Portugal	8,572,953	3,460,777	40.4
United Kingdom	44,499,329	10,689,847	24.0
Sweden	6,664,205	2,588,514	38.8
Total	288,051,641	143,800,610	49.9

Source http://www3.europarl.eu.int/election/newep/en/tctp.htm (consulted September 2003).

for EP elections almost as high as for national elections, while the difference is much higher for Austrians, Finns, Swedes and for the Britons, who are in any case the least likely to vote (Table 7.2). At the individual level, the likelihood to vote for EP elections increases with the self-asserted knowledge of the EU.[31]

Other interactions between EU citizens and EU institutions are rare. About 300,000 persons visit EU buildings each year in Strasbourg, Brussels or Luxembourg. Citizens can petition the EP and the European Ombudsman, first appointed by the EP in 1995. The number of complaints has risen slowly over the year; 2,211 complaints were filed in 2002,[32] the vast majority by individuals (others complainants are associations and companies). This seems negligible compared to the size of the EU population. Indeed, for the sake of comparison, the national ombudsman of the Netherlands received almost five times more complaints (9643 *verzoekschriften*, i.e. requests in 2002).[33] Whether it means that citizens are relatively less affected by the activities of EU institutions and agencies than by national, regional and local ones or that they do not perceive their action as clearly as they do when it comes to other state agencies, remains an open question.

Protests targeting EU institutions are rare. However there have been demonstrations such as the 'EU rot op' campaign (literally 'EU fuck off' in Dutch), at the occasion of the 1997 European Summit in Amsterdam where the Amsterdam Treaty was adopted. The European (Euro top) Marches –

Table 7.2 Reported likelihood to vote at next elections (ranked according to ratio EP/national elections) in Spring 2003

Member state	European elections	National elections	Likelihood elections
Italy	7.62	7.68	99.22
Greece	8.05	8.19	98.29
Belgium	6.58	6.77	97.19
Luxembourg	7.41	7.86	94.27
Portugal	6.45	6.89	93.61
Spain	6.97	7.50	92.93
Germany	7.22	7.98	90.48
Ireland	6.65	7.44	89.38
EU15	6.90	7.73	89.26
France	6.85	7.74	88.50
Denmark	8.22	9.42	87.26
Netherlands	6.92	7.96	86.93
Austria	6.68	7.86	84.99
Finland	6.86	8.15	84.17
Sweden	7.14	8.80	81.14
UK	5.46	7.35	74.29

Source: *Eurobarometer 59* (Spring 2003).

with their Charter of Demands – against unemployment, job insecurity and exclusions have organised marches towards the location of European Summits: Amsterdam in 1997; Cologne in 1999; Nice and Paris in 2000; Brussels in 2001; Seville in 2002; and Thessalonika in 2003.[34] Nevertheless protests at European Summits such as those in Nice in December 2000, in Gothenburg in June 2001 and Brussels in December 2001 did not mobilise more activists than at meetings of other agencies, such as the World Trade Organisation (WTO) in Seattle in 1999, the World Bank in Prague in 2000, or the G8 Summit in Genoa in 2001.

Attachment: affective ties

The second aspect we distinguish is attachment to the people, things in and symbols of the territory. The symbolic shape of the EU is occasionally addressed in Eurobarometer surveys, for example a question regarding the name of the European Union in Spring 2003. As we mentioned earlier, the label was established only a decade ago. Just half the respondents (49 per cent) answered that they thought the name should not change, 14 per cent would have preferred United Europe, 11 per cent European Community, 6 per cent United States of Europe, 6 per cent United Nations of Europe, 2 per cent another name and 12 per cent had no opinion.[35] The Union label is problematic in the Baltic States because of its similarity with the Soviet Union from which these states have seceded only a decade ago.[36]

Eurobarometer 58 (autumn 2002) featured questions about the flag. Eighty-nine per cent of the respondents had seen the flag (from 98 per cent in Denmark and Luxembourg to 86 per cent in Ireland and only 73 per cent in the UK). Eighty-two per cent of those knowing the flag knew that it represented the European Union (from 97 per cent in Luxembourg to 75 per cent in Ireland and only 56 per cent in the UK). Eighty per cent of the respondents agreed with the proposition 'This flag is a good symbol for Europe', 51 per cent with the proposition 'This flag should be seen on all public buildings in (our country) next to the national flag' (highest levels are obtained in Italy (75 per cent), Portugal (67 per cent) and Greece (65 per cent). A third of respondents (32 per cent) were against this proposition with particularly high rates in Denmark, Finland and Sweden (76 per cent, 65 per cent and 62 per cent respectively) and 17 per cent, do not know.

Barely 44 per cent of respondents agreed with the proposition 'I identify with this flag' compared to 40 per cent who did not agree and 17 per cent who did not know. Italy, Ireland, Luxembourg and Portugal were the only four Member States where more than 50 per cent of respondents agree with this proposition (63 per cent, 61 per cent, 61 per cent and 57 per cent respectively). Disagreement is the highest in Sweden (63 per cent) and in the Netherlands (62 per cent).[37]

In the same poll, respondents were asked about several propositions about other EU symbols. Only 27 per cent thought that it was true that the EU had an anthem and 34 per cent that each year 'Europe Day' is observed in common by the Member States, thus proving that these symbols are poorly known.[38] This is obviously different for another powerful symbol, the Euro, as it has materialised in everyday life in the 12 Member States of Euro-land. In spring 2003 the attachment to the Euro was limited to 38 per cent of the respondents in the 12 states using the Euro, ranging from 23 per cent in Germany to 67 per cent in Portugal and 72 per cent in Luxembourg.[39]

Among the questions that refer to affective ties, many addressed the identification with geographical entities, and Europe in particular. In winter 2001, when asked 'To what extent do you feel that you belong to (geographic entity)', 67 per cent of the respondents felt strongly about belonging to their country, 57 per cent to their city or village, 55 per cent to their region, 38 per cent to the world and only 33 per cent to Europe.[40] The feeling of belonging strongly to Europe was the lowest in Finland 13 per cent and the highest in Luxembourg (60 per cent) (Table 7.3).

Among the themes discussed in groups during the qualitative study carried out in 2001 in the EU and candidate countries, were images of Europe and feeling of belonging.[41] The researchers divided Europe accordingly into two: a big South and a very small North. In the big South, which actually consists of most of Europe, what makes Europe is mainly its history and culture; empathy with other Europeans was more or less spontaneous. In the small North, which includes the UK, the Netherlands, Denmark and to some extent Sweden, there seemed to be a more 'deep-seated conviction of

Table 7.3 Strongly belonging to Europe in winter 2001

	<33%	33–50%	>50%
Core 6	Belgium France Netherlands	Italy Germany	Luxembourg
Successive enlargements (1973, 1981, 1986, 1995)	United Kingdom Greece Spain Finland Sweden	Ireland Portugal	Denmark Austria

Source: Eurobarometer 58.

the superiority or specificity of the model of society' and weak empathy with other Europeans. Among the candidate countries, Estonia and to some extent the Czech Republic belonged to the same category. The general image of the EU reflected differences in intensity of belonging to Europe. Knowledge of the EU was generally greater in the pro-European countries of the South, and the countries that had just recently joined while it is weaker in the largest countries (Germany and especially the UK).[42]

In spring 2003, respondents were asked: 'What does the European Union represent for you?' and several choices were offered. The EU top 3 featured: (1) the freedom to travel, study and work anywhere in the EU (mentioned by 49 per cent of the respondents), (2) the Euro (43 per cent) and (3) peace (29 per cent). Four countries had this top 3 (Belgium, Germany, Greece and Luxembourg). In others, the top 3 featured two of these and something else: a more important voice in the world (Denmark, Italy, the Netherlands), economic prosperity (Spain, Ireland, Portugal), cultural diversity (France), waste of money (Austria), or bureaucracy (Finland). In Sweden, (1) freedom of movement was followed by (2) bureaucracy and (3) waste of money, in the UK, by (2) bureaucracy and (3) loss of cultural identity.

Finally the relative importance of the EU in feelings of belonging can be estimated through the question 'In the near future do you see yourself as 'European only', 'European plus Nationality', 'Nationality plus European' or 'Nationality only'. EU-wide, the largest group felt 'Nationality plus European' (44 per cent) followed by 'nationality only' (40 per cent) and, far behind, 'European plus Nationality' (8 per cent) and 'Europeans only' (4 per cent). Very few respondents saw themselves as 'European only' (except in Luxembourg: 20 per cent); a small minority chose 'European plus Nationality' (up to 10 per cent in Italy and Luxembourg). Many picked 'Nationality plus European' (from 24 per cent in the UK to 59 per cent in Italy) while the group of exclusively 'Nationality only' varied between 21 per cent in Luxembourg to 64 per cent in the UK.[43] Those feeling 'European only' (in combination or not with 'Nationality only') were a majority in 9 of the

15 Member States (though not in the UK Ireland, Greece, Sweden, Finland and Austria) and in all the states that joined the EU in May 2004.

When comparing the main categories, 'National only' and 'National plus European', one can distinguish between states where the percentage of 'National only' is higher and vice versa in all categories of Member States (Table 7.4). The occurrence of European-ness along with nationality was not related to the length of membership.

Surprisingly, the ten states joining the EU in 2004 had the lowest percentage of exclusive nationals (34 per cent), while it was 40 per cent for the EU 15 and 47 per cent for the three remaining candidates.[44] In other words, EU citizens displayed a higher level of exclusive national identity than those in the accessing states. It is interesting that the new Member States all had a small proportion of exclusive nationals, and that the core countries also scored moderately, compared to many of the states that joined between 1973 and 1995 (Table 7.4).

Table 7.4 Feeling 'National only' versus 'National and European'

	% National only >% National and European	% National and European >% National only
Core 6	Belgium Netherlands	France Germany Italy Luxembourg
Previous enlargements (1973, 1981, 1986, 1995)	**United Kingdom** Ireland **Greece** Portugal **Austria** **Finland** **Sweden**	Denmark Spain
2004 enlargement	Estonia	Latvia Lithuania Poland Czech Republic Slovakia Hungary Slovenia Malta Cyprus
Remaining candidates	**Turkey**	Rumania Bulgaria

Source: Comparative Highlights, pp. 21, 7.

Note
In **bold** states in which the absolute majority of the respondents answer 'national only'.

Information

Lastly, we come to information, the third aspect we distinguish. Knowledge about the EU is clearly limited. Auto-evaluation of knowledge about the EU is modest: on a scale of 1 (knows nothing about the EU) to 10 (knows a lot), few respondents rank themselves in the top classes. The average estimation in spring 2003 was 4.25 (slightly lower than one year before) ranging from 3.7 in Britain to 5.1 in Austria (and between 3.5 for less educated and 5.1 for more educated respondents).[45] This lack of knowledge was confirmed by the poor answers given to many questions about the existence of specific institutions, agencies and policies or the name of Members of the Commission or Members of the EP. In spring 2003, 91 per cent of the respondents had heard of the EP, 78 per cent of the European Commission, 73 per cent of the Central Bank, 69 per cent of the Court of Justice, but only 33 per cent of the Ombudsman, 30 per cent of the Convention and 26 per cent of the Committee of the Regions.[46] During group discussions held in 2001, the lack of knowledge about the institutions was also startling.[47]

When asked what their preferred methods of obtaining information on the EU were, respondents mentioned traditional media most often. Television came in first place (59 per cent in spring 2003), followed by daily newspapers (35 per cent) and radio (23 per cent). There after came more specific sources of media such as a detailed brochure (19 per cent), a short leaflet giving just an overview (18 per cent) and the Internet (15 per cent). Six per cent did not want information.[48] Still, 75 per cent of the respondents found that 'giving people more information about the EU' should be a priority, although only 59 per cent of the British agreed.

Hardly any Europe-wide media exists. Media sources are generally nationally organised. Meanwhile most transnational media (CNN, Arte, TV5, BBC-World, *The Economist*, *The Financial Times*, *International Herald Tribune*) have a clear national basis and have a global reach rather than a European one, Euro-news being the major exception. When asked to report their information sources on the current situation, respondents in spring 2003 mentioned national TV (82 per cent), national newspapers and magazines (59 per cent), national radio stations (40 per cent) while non-national media were shown to be significantly less popular: 20 per cent continuous TV news channels (which are mainly transnational but not necessarily European), 12 per cent the Internet, 11 per cent news on TV, 5 per cent newspapers and magazines and 3 per cent radio from other countries.[49]

To conclude this section on the citizen's experience of the EU, the individual engagement of EU citizens with the Union is according to our three dimensions rather modest: information is limited, interactions are increasing but rather rare, and attachment is moderate, although affective ties do exist for many Europeans.

Unbundling national territories?

It is clear that competences are being transferred from nation states to the EU and to private bodies. Thus it is obvious that national territories are indeed unbundling. Yet, this does not necessarily mean that the basic idea of (state) sovereignty or (state) territorial legitimacy is breaking up. As long as state governments are the most obvious bodies held accountable for everything that happens on the state territory – irrespective of the fact that they need to consult with external authorities like the European Commission on certain matters – political territoriality at the state level is preserved.

One of the most significant impacts on the integrity of our current territorial framework undoubtedly comes from changed *interaction*: the increasing number of jobs that require a temporary or permanent stay outside one's homeland and rising mobility in general. Although expatriates keep following the media from their native country (aided by satellite TV and Internet), they also take note of the news of the country where they settle and they increasingly rely on international media and international schools. The number of 'de-territorialised' people, including those moving to another country after retirement, is increasing although a certain attachment to the native country is never completely lost. Yet one may doubt if this boundary-crossing feature of a person's life-path will ever characterise the majority of a population (see the figures provided earlier in this chapter). For all that, a more pervasive feature of most European's living environments is the presence of substantial migrant populations from North Africa, Turkey or former colonies that tenaciously cling to their own culture without any intention of re-migration. They may seem to be infringing on the existing pattern of territorial solidarity and rights and in that way affect the territorial attachment and feelings of legitimacy of autochthonous population or, conversely, stimulate new claims on territorial rights and obligations (citizenship) such as the extreme right political movement.

Another way to raise the matter of de-territorialisation with data about interaction is by examining whether boundaries still manifest themselves in the institutions people address to solve their problems. A negative result would be indicated by protests (for example of farmers) directly levelled at the EU headquarters in Brussels or by a tendency to take matters to court rather than to political representatives or institutions. The turnouts for elections could be a useful indicator. Although there is a general diminishing of interest in political participation by voting in Europe, comparative results might say something about the importance of state territoriality.

Solidarity is a manifestation of territorial *attachment*. It is expressed in the acceptance of redistribution of wealth through taxation, in the conscription for military service or – in the more voluntary sphere – the willingness to give money or goods to victims of disasters. Territoriality would be disapproved of if there were significant changes in the arrangements that tie an individual to a territory or in the reactions to events that have been defined as territorially significant.

Finally, territoriality is embodied in the way *information* systems like statistics, education and the media are structured because these express most basically what is deemed important in the life of an individual or its regulation. Language is an intervening factor here that automatically consolidates territoriality. Even if there were no special reason or necessity to attend national schools or read national media, people would do so because accessibility of information still depends on language (in spite of the ubiquity of English). Language difference of course does not necessarily imply different information content. So we should ask if the topics presented in the press or the quantities of facts presented still reveal a clear break at the state boundaries

Changing interaction: mobility and citizenship

In several European countries such as the Netherlands, the UK, Greece and Austria, a reappraisal of multiculturalism is under way, again stressing the necessity of integration in terms of language and education. They connect citizenship with the passing of tests. In recent British proposals such tests not only seem to address integration as a problem of skills for competing on the job-market (How do you pay a telephone bill?) but also as knowledge about dominant national values and history (When was the UK last invaded?).[50] Such movements basically revert to territorial cohesion as an essential source of well being for the migrant groups concerned and of security for the rest of the population. It has been asserted that new integration policies in the wake of New York 9/11 and riots in Northern England (Oldham, Burnley, Bradford) in the autumn of 2001 infringe upon a much broader and deeper trend in the EU geared to separate citizenship from national identity.[51] The spirit of the Maastricht (TEU) and Amsterdam treaties was to associate the problem of assimilation with anti-discrimination measures. Notions of national allegiance have been weakened in favour of multiple membership and supranational (EU) citizenship. In Germany nationality law was changed in 2000 in order to include aspects of *jus soli*, which entailed a less exclusive dependency on the German ethnic background of the migrant. In France, *jus soli*, on the contrary has been attacked by young people of Algerian descent as forced assimilation.[52] This example shows how sensitive the issue of integration is among migrant groups when it is connected to national identity. Thus, European countries have been gradually moving in the direction of multicultural citizenship in order to meet such sensitivities and in agreement with EU policies but at the moment the direction is no longer very convincing.

Changing interaction: representatives

The earliest de-territorialisation of national policy in Europe occurred in agriculture. Few groups have more reason to address the EP or the Commission by demonstrating in Strasbourg or Brussels than farmers. At the same time the EU's CAP was initially set up to meet the basic problems of farming as a mode of production in the modern age. Recent pressure on the EU to agree to market liberalisation has changed this. It particularly came to the fore in French protests against globalisation and Dutch protests against the way different cattle diseases were tackled (mad cow disease, foot and mouth disease, fowl pest). Most of the farmer's protests hit local targets like highways, markets, shops and border crossings. If French protests were aimed at an administrative centre it was Paris rather than Strasbourg (although European farmers gathered there in 1992 and 2002). Since 1995 Brussels has only twice been the scene of farmers' protests. In 1995 a few hundred vegetable and fruit producers protested in Brussels against EU subsidies to Spanish tomato cultivators. Again in 1999 50,000 farmers demonstrated during a meeting of the European Ministers of Agriculture in Brussels. Then, in 2002, Spanish farmers demonstrated in Brussels against the new reductions in agricultural subsidies in the EU.

Obviously farmers still see national governments as the most useful tool for breaking open European policy. The paradoxical fact is that they often protest in defence of European arrangements. In some cases they protest against them (like the vaccination ban with foot and mouth disease or the agreements about the admission on GM crops). Whatever their source of income or rules, farmers are determined to attract the attention of the media which ensures that the message reaches governments on various levels. However, looking at the organisational structure of farmers' interest groups, the national level is the most conspicuous one. The so-called CPE (European Farmer Co-ordination) is an umbrella organisation rather than an association of individuals across the European territory.

Doug Imig and Sidney Tarrow have scrutinised protests in Europe.[53] Based on the Reuters Newswire, between January 1984 and February 1998, they isolated some 33,727 reports of political events in the 12 Member States of the EU (1986–1994). From here they drew a sample of 9,872 discrete contentious political events. Only 490 protest events were in response to EU policies or institutions, a mere 5 per cent although this share was on the rise (30 per cent in 1997). An even more interesting finding is that 83 per cent of the EU-directed protests were examples of 'domestification' in which national actors protest in their homeland against policies of the EU, but the proportion of collective European protest was slightly higher for the period 1993–1997, than earlier. They acknowledge three types of transnational protest: international co-operation (national actors in linked and co-ordinated protest campaigns against a shared antagonist), international conflict (national actors competing with each other, for example, clashes between French and Spanish fishermen) and collective European protest: such as the 1992 farmers demonstration in Strasbourg or the 1997 trade unionists converging to Luxembourg in 1997. These European protests are not necessarily aimed at European policies. For instance, the 1997 Eurostrike was a protest against Renault's decision to close its Vilvoorde plant.

New political parties can be interpreted as another indicator of de-territorialisation, particularly the turn to special interest parties that by definition have cancelled commitments to the overall regulatory problems of a territory. Green parties, most of them emerging in the 1980s, have remained the most striking example although they rarely drew more then 10 per cent of the votes. However, one may disagree with the statement that these parties do not aim at a total conception of life in a territory. Pensioners' parties are a better example but they have remained characteristic of post-communist countries like Poland and Slovenia rather than of the EU countries. Regardless of this they remind us of the other, and perhaps more dramatic, form of de-territorialisation that occurs in this part of Europe. A witness of the reverse is the emergence of anti-EU parties in a few member countries (Danish People's Party and to a certain degree Vlaams Blok in Belgium).

We may also focus on less direct interest-guided political behaviour of individuals as manifested by the turnout at elections for different governmental levels (Table 7.5). For the sake of comparison we have selected five countries, which as initial EU members, have frequently shown a greater willingness to abandon national interest and identities in favour of European integration than other European countries. If unbundling of territoriality on the national level occurs, one might expect its symptoms first in these countries. Turnout for elections indicates a belief of potential voters in the relevance of a certain political field. It is well known that turnouts are generally decreasing in Western democracies, which has been explained as either a consequence of affluence or the sign of an underlying dissatisfaction with representative democracy. However, systematic differences in turnout in a comparison involving different governmental levels can hardly be attributed to this phenomenon. As Table 7.5 shows, turnouts for the elections of national parliaments have decreased with, on average 10 per cent in the past two decades, but the elections for the EP show a much more dramatic decrease of on average 35 per cent in three Member States. Whether one would like to attribute this to the institutional deficiencies of the EP or not, it certainly does not suggest a transfer of loyalties from the nation to Europe.

Something not very well indicated by election turnouts is a subtle shift in the pattern of political issues in Europe involving a slow rise in the importance of the regional issue. Data gathered in studies on comparative politics suggest that in the decades between 1945 and 1990 even a traditional national political issue like the capital–labour cleavage had to leave the field to the regional issue.[54] However, this does not necessarily indicate

168 G. Dijkink and V. Mamadouh

Table 7.5 Change in voter turnout (%) in national and European elections (1978–2003), three countries (Belgium and Italy excluded because of compulsory voting)

	National			European		
	~1979	~2002	% 1979–2002	1979	1999	% 1979–1999
France	71.6 (1978)	65.0 (2002)	−9.2	60.6	47.0	−22.4
Germany	88.6 (1980)	79.1 (2002)	−10.7	65.7	45.2	−31.2
The Netherlands	88.0 (1979)	79.9 (2003)	−9.2	57.8	29.9	−48.3

de-territorialisation of the state. This data actually still identifies the region as a 'national' issue.

Changing attachment

Table 7.6 shows the percentage of people who, when questioned about their territorial identity, put nationality first. This is the great majority of respondents who consequently have not preferred to say 'Europe' or 'Europe and then the nation'. The figures demonstrate that in all five countries the number putting nationality first has increased during the period 1994–2002. The March–April 2003 survey may possibly be biased, based on the strong emotions evoked by the Iraq War, which put Belgium, France and Germany in the international limelight as opponents of US policy. Comparison with November 2002 survey suggests that these events have had somewhat contradictory effects. They appear to have diminished the

Table 7.6 Change in national identification 1994–2003, five countries. Percentage of people answering the question: 'In the near future, do you see yourself as . . .' with 'only as [Nationality]' or '[Nationality] and European'

	December 1994	November 2002	(%1994–2002)	April 2003	(%1994–2003)
Belgium	71	80	(+12.7)	81	(+14.1)
France	74	85	(+14.9)	83	(+12.2)
Germany	72	84	(+16.7)	79	(+8.9)
Italy	80	87	(+8.8)	85	(+6.3)
The Netherlands	83	89	(+7.2)	89	(+7.2)

Source: Eurobarometer 42, 58, 59.

reliance on national identity in Germany. Nevertheless, since 1994 the overall trend points to a stronger identification with the nation.

Changing attachments may also be deduced from citizen behaviour, particularly acts categorised as 'solidarity'. It is difficult to find two comparable events (disasters) arousing acts of solidarity occurring within a certain time interval that would allow conclusions on changing patterns of solidarity. However, we may revert to other indicators such as members and contributors to organisations. The Dutch SCP groups a number of (big) organisations under the heading of 'international solidarity'. This concerns organisations like UNICEF, the Red Cross, Amnesty International and Doctors without borders.[55] In 1996–1997 almost four million people in the Netherlands were registered as a member or contributor (participant) to one of these organisations. However, time-specific data are more relevant here. Between 1980 and 1996–1997 the number of participants in organisations aiming at international solidarity rose by 176 per cent whereas the average rise in participation (to 34.5 million in 1996–1997) was only 35 per cent. The increase in international solidarity was only outstripped by organisations in the category 'nature and environment' (510 per cent) and 'abortion/ euthanasia' (662 per cent). Apart from the general tendency of increasing support for idealistic goals rather than for direct interest organisations, the result fits the assumption of a new solidarity surpassing the boundaries of the national territory.

Another, less voluntary, form of solidarity is military conscription. It was an innovation originating in revolutionary France and its double-edged advantage became very clear during the Napoleonic wars in Europe. Conscription helped to link the (male) individual with the nation and its territory and created armies that were more numerous and motivated than the former militias or mercenary armies. However, the nature of the current weaponry, the need for European co-operation, and governmental budget problems has shifted the balance again in the direction of professional armies. The list of European countries that have abolished conscription (the Netherlands, the UK, France, Spain) or that seriously plan to abolish it (Russia, Italy, Portugal) is becoming longer every year. It implies the loss of an opportunity to get involved in a national enterprise and to mingle arbitrarily with fellow citizens.

Changing information

In terms of supply, information from abroad has become more abundantly available with the rise of satellite communication. Yet this does not correspond to a proportionate growth in foreign news reporting. Domestic newspapers and television programmes have in recent years even enlarged the space devoted to regional news in relation to international news. This is explained as an answer to consumer preferences. Research in Belgium has shown that there is a disproportional attention for neighbouring countries and that the proportion of domestic news has even increased between 1990 and 1995.[56] Kai Hafez concludes that the 'content level of the media globalises much slower than technical and economic aspects of media development making us think that there is no linear process of media globalisation'.[57] Even if blunt figures show a substantial interest in facts from abroad, closer (qualitative) analysis reveals that such facts, just like the protest against EU policies, are domesticated. International news coverage shows how national representatives act and highlights the impact of external events on the domestic political scene. The implication is that a uniform political meaning system covering larger territories does not follow the increased scale of human activity.

Conclusion

A central question behind any discussion about territoriality is what its function or meaning might be in a world that does not limit people's movements anymore or that (hypothetically) offers the same entitlements and rights to anybody. One basic utility of territoriality that might get lost in a globalising world is the allocation of responsibility (one of Robert Sack's arguments). Territorial responsibility means that administrators and citizens have the assignment to cope with any problem, which may arise within the bounds of the territory merely because it occurs *there*. This also entails the challenge of sustainable growth and the development of a way of life that is both meaningful and ecologically functional. Particularly in conditions of catastrophic change, territoriality is a much more effective manner in which to arouse and allocate human energy than forms of professional specialisation. For the citizen territorial belonging means the kind of solidarity that can be compared with an insurance policy. It frees the individual from any liability due to personal weakness or material circumstances because it spreads the risks over a population. Second, territoriality makes it easier to draw on networks of people, things and codes that are required to produce something (like a house). In a discussion on territoriality and the EU the logical assumption is that territoriality will be, at least partly, restored on a new transnational (i.e. EU) level. We have seen that this level is real in terms of institutional practices and symbols. The question to what extent this corresponds with a changing experience of connectedness and confidence in European citizens has been addressed in this chapter. As comparative in-depth analyses of the changing 'life-world' of the EU citizen are still rare, we have resorted to available statistics and expert judgements on changing interaction, feelings of attachment and patterns of information.

It is hard to believe that certain substantial changes in the field of human interaction would have no effect on the experience of territoriality: the introduction of the Euro in most of Europe; the gradual disappearance of military conscription; the exchange of students between European universities; and the availability of products from other countries. These may all weaken the territorial shell of the state as seen from the perspective of classic national centres but they neither contribute to the construction of an unequivocal European territoriality nor do they induce a complete shift in the pattern of confidence. As for the first aspect (connectedness) we should point to the development of a Europe with multiple boundaries and multiple speeds, the second aspect (confidence) suffers from the absence of the EU as an institution in the daily life of citizens.

Confidence in particular seems still to be linked closely to the national territory. Judging from the data on attachment and political participation, the meaning of the national level remains strong and is actually strengthening. Plans for the integration of minorities in some cases revert to (knowledge of) national identity. Protests are staged within the bounds of the national territory even if the decision making body is located in Brussels. Most people believe that the impact of national government on their life is bigger than that of the EU.

How should we characterise the condition Europeans find themselves in at the moment? The most tempting conclusion is that citizens are not in step with the emerging territoriality of the EU. In terms of information and attachment they maintain and reproduce old (state) territoriality. We do not suggest that this is a sign of conservatism or lacking capabilities, it is an inevitable consequence of the material and institutional world as it has developed up until now. Simultaneously people have enlarged their interaction space in such a way that connection and confidence remain confined to interpersonal transnational networks. One may call this a 'virtual EU territory'. Virtual should not be read here as something imaginary but (in accordance with complexity theory) as a possible manifestation. The EU citizen moves in virtual space which, if we account for the changing shape of the EU's body, may be judged a rather appropriate term.

Notes

1 Crucial concepts in the work of French philosophers Deleuze and Guattari, see G. Deleuze and F. Guattari, 1980: *Mille Plateaux*. Paris: Éditions de Minuit.
2 Gottmann, 1971: *The Significance of Territory*. Charlottesville: The University Press of Virginia.
3 D. Sack, 1983: Human territoriality: a theory. *Annals of the Association of American Geographers*, 73: 55–74. D. Sack, 1986: *Human Territoriality: Its Theory and History*, Cambridge: Cambridge University Press.
4 *Les six livres de la République*.
5 Ruggie, 1993: Territoriality and beyond: problematizing modernity in international relations, *International Organization*, 47: 139–174. J. Agnew, 1998: *Geopolitics. Re-visioning World Politics*. London: Routledge.
6 Ruggie, Territoriality and beyond.
7 Strassoldo, 1992: Globalism and localism: theoretical reflections and some evidence, in Z. Mlinar (ed.), *Globalisation and Territorial Identities*. Avebury: Aldershot, pp. 35–37. The difference between the (six) questionnaires presented in that paper makes conclusions about temporal change unreliable. See also

Guntram H. Herb and David H. Kaplan (eds.), 1999: *Nested Identities: Nationalism, Territory and Scale*. Lanham: Rowman & Littlefield.
8 Agnew, 1994: The territorial trap: the geographical assumptions of international relations theory. *Review of International Political Economy*, 1: 53–80.
9 Häkli, 2000: In the territory of knowledge: state-centred discourses and the construction of society. *Progress in Human Geography*, 24: 1–20. James Scott, 1998: *Seeing Like a State. How Certain Schemes to Improve the Human Condition Have Failed*. New Haven, Yale University Press.
10 J. Taylor, Amsterdam in a World City Network (Forthcoming AME, Amsterdam) See also: Peter J. Taylor, 1996: Embedded statism and the social sciences: opening up to new spaces, *Environment and Planning A*, 28: 1917–1928.
11 P.J. Taylor, 1994: The state as container: territoriality in the modern world-system, *Progress in Human Geography*, 18(2): 151–162. P.J. Taylor, 1995: Beyond containers: internationality, interstateness, interterritoriality, *Progress in Human Geography*, 19(1): 1–15.
12 H. Hoogers, 1999: *De verbeelding van het souvereine: een onderzoek naar de theoretische grondslagen van de politieke representatie*, Deventer: Kluwer.
13 A. Paasi, 1986: The institutionalization of regions: a theoretical framework for understanding the emergence of regions and the constitution of regional identity, *Fennia*, 164(1). A. Paasi, 2003: Territory, in J. Agnew, K. Mitchell and G. Toal (eds): *A Companion to Political Geography*, Oxford: Blackwell, pp. 123–137.
14 http://www.cahierseuropeens.net/CEDH001/ang/page35.html. This is a motto in India, Indonesia, South Africa ...
15 V. Mamadouh, 2001: A place called Europe: national political cultures and the making of the new territorial order known as the European Union, in G. Dijkink and H. Knippenberg (eds): *The Territorial Factor, Political Geography in a Globalising World*, Amsterdam: Vossiuspers UvA, pp. 201–224.
16 V. Mamadouh, 2001: The territoriality of European integration and the territorial features of the European Union: the first fifty years, *TESG*, 92(4): 420–436.
17 Stresa, where ministers of finance met in September 2003, as one of the candidates. See: C. Hein, 2000: Choosing a site for the capital of Europe, *GeoJournal*, 51(1/2): 83–97.
18 http://www.censis.it/censis/what/italy per cent20today/italytext2.htm.
19 *Decisions*, binding on those to whom it is addressed, and *recommendations*, not binding. Most common are directives, necessitating the mediation of national legislation.
20 To our knowledge, harmonisation here was limited to the acceptance of the Euroband on license plates as a sign for country recognition inside the EU.
21 P. Muus, 2001: International migration and the European Union, trends and consequences, *European Journal of Criminal Policy and Research*, 9(1): 31.
22 Included the Member States of the 1995 enlargement and their citizens.
23 All 1993 statistics from *Background Statistics Citizens First Phase,* available at 1 http://citizens.eu.int/nl/nl/newsitem-2.htm (consulted September 2003).
24 *Background Statistics Citizens First Phase* at 1 http://citizens.eu.int/nl/nl/newsitem-2.htm (consulted September 2003).
25 For example in the Netherlands and Belgium http://www.eurodiffusie.nl/, in France http://www.ined.fr/publications/pop_et_soc/pes384/PES3842.html, in Germany http://www.mathe.tu-freiberg.de/math/inst/stoch/Stoyan/euro/.
26 R. King, 2003: International student migration in Europe and the institutionalization of identity as 'Young Europeans', in J. Doomernik and H. Knippenberg (eds): *Migration and Immigrants: Between Policy and Reality*, Amsterdam: Aksant, pp. 155–179.

27 A. Faludi and B. Waterhout, 2002: *The Making of the European Spatial Development Perspective: No Masterplan*, London: Routledge.
28 By means of group discussions in the different member states. See *Perceptions of the European Union, A Qualitative Study of the Public's Attitudes to and Expectations of the European Union in the 15 Member States and in 8 Candidate Countries* (January 2001): Summary of results.
29 The results are said to be representative for the population of the Member States (Former Eastern Germany and Northern Ireland are surveyed apart from the rest of their state). The weighted average is supposed to be representative for a European public opinion. All Eurobarometers are available on the webserver of the European union at http://europa.eu.int/comm/public_opinion/index.htm.
30 Flash Eurobarometer 133.
31 Eurobarometer 59.
32 The European Ombudsman, Report 2002, p. 17, available at http://www.euro-ombudsman.eu.int/report02/pdf/en/rap02_en.pdf (consulted September 2003).
33 Jaarverslag 2002, 3.1 De te behandelen zaken, http://www.ombudsman.nl/jaarverslagframe.html (consulted September 2003).
34 The organisation secretariat is based in Paris. http://www.euromarches.org/index.htm.
35 Eurobarometer 59.
36 *Perceptions de l'Union européenne, Attitudes et attentes à son égard: Approche qualitative auprès du public des 15 états membres et de 9 pays candidats à l'adhésion, Rapport général,* 211 pp. Available at http://europa.eu.int/comm/public_opinion/quali/ql_perceptions_fr.pdf.
37 Eurobarometer 58, October/November 2002 available at http://europa.eu.int/comm/public_opinion/archives/eb/eb58/eb58_en.pdf.
38 Eurobarometer 58, p. 23 available at http://europa.eu.int/comm/public_opinion/archives/eb/eb58/eb58_en.pdf.
39 Eurobarometer 59.
40 Flash EB 92 on Governance (Winter 2001) p. 24 available at http://europa.eu/public_opinion/archives/flash-arch-en.htm.
41 *Perceptions of the European Union,* ...
42 *Perceptions de l'Union européenne,* ...
43 Eurobarometer 59.
44 *Comparative Highlights,* p. 7.
45 Eurobarometer 59.
46 Eurobarometer 59.
47 *Perceptions de l'Union européenne,* ...
48 Eurobarometer 59, p. 42.
49 Eurobarometer 59, p. 15.
50 Crick *et al.*, The New and the Old. The report of the 'Life in the United Kingdom' advisory group. Home Office 2003. (http://www.ind.homeoffice.gov.uk/default.asp?pageid=4271).
51 Bertossi, Transforming the boundaries of citizenship in Europe: from nationality to anti-discrimination?. Paper presented at the conference Whither Europe? Borders, Boundaries, Frontiers in a Changing World. Göteborg University 16–17 January 2003.
52 Brubaker, 1992: *Citizenship and Nationhood in France and Germany*, Cambridge: Cambridge University Press.
53 D. Imig, 2002: Contestation in the streets, European protest in the emerging Euro-polity, *Comparative Political Studies*, 35(8): 914–933. D. Imig and S. Tarrow, 2000: Political contention in a Europeanising polity, *West European Politics*, 23(4): 73–93. D. Imig and S. Tarrow, (eds), 2001: *Contentious Europeans: Protest and Politics in an Emerging Polity*. Lanham: Rowman & Littlefield.

54 G. Dijkink and C. Winnips, 1999: Alternative states. Regions and postfordism rhetoric on the internet, *GeoJournal* ,48: 323–335. See also C. Harvie, 1994: *The Rise of Regional Europe*. London: Routledge. G. Dijkink and V.D. Mamadouh, 2003: Identity and legitimacy in the Amsterdam region, in S. Musterd and W. Salet, (eds), *Amsterdam. Human Capital*. Amsterdam, Amsterdam University Press.
55 Social and Cultural Report 1998. Only organisations with 50,000 or more participants were included. The full list is: Rode Kruis (the Dutch Red Cross), Unicef, Artsen zonder grenzen (the Dutch branch of Doctors without Borders), Foster parents Nederland (the Dutch branch of Foster Parents Plan), Memisa, Stichting Vluchteling, Novib, Mensen in nood, Amnesty International, Nederlandse Stichting Leprabestrijding, Terre des hommes, Vereniging Vluchtelingenwerk Nederland (the Dutch Refugee Council).
56 Biltereyst and Peeren (eds), 2003: *Nieuws, democratie en burgerschap: onderzoek over hedendaagse nieuwsmedia*, Gent: Academia Press.
57 Hafez, 1999: International news coverage and the problems of media globalisation. In search of a 'new global-local nexus', *Innovation*, 12: 47–62.

8 Building the Common Market but preventing chaos

The continuing relevance of the principle of territoriality in the field of taxation and the limits of a Europe made by judges

Herman Voogsgeerd

Introduction: taxation, law and the principle of territoriality

To ask a lawyer the question whether the principle of territoriality still matters might seem odd. Of course territoriality matters for lawyers. Rules have a territorial scope, as much as they have a substantive, a personal and a temporal scope. But after 45 years of experience with European Community (EC) law and with conflicts between the national legal systems and this new branch of the law the answer to the question becomes a little less straightforward. In several studies the impact of Community law on the principle of territoriality has been noticed.[1] Indeed, the European Union (EU) has had an impact on this principle.

The principle of territoriality is not a legal principle.[2] For lawyers territoriality means in most cases the scope of a rule. Scope rules are a way to define the field of application of a piece of legislation or a complete national legal system. Normally the rule of a certain state is not valid outside the territory of that state. The Dutch government cannot regulate situations inside Germany. This meaning of territoriality corresponds to the first notion of territoriality used in this volume: territoriality as defining and dividing competencies and the scope of political authority. The second meaning of territoriality, as it is used in this book, is of interest for lawyers as well. The way rulers provide their services, values and goods to the ruled differs in each member state of the EU. Every national tax or social security system has its peculiarities. These peculiarities are the result of a long-term historical process.

Both meanings of the principle of territoriality have indeed to be separated. In the approach of the European Court of Justice (ECJ) in Luxembourg scope rules are treated in a different way from the typical and peculiar ways in which member states provide their services, values and goods to their citizens. While these peculiar, traditional and 'biased' ways of regulating in member states are very often declared to be in violation of EC Treaty principles, scope rules are dealt with in a more subtle way. Scope rules are to a certain extent a technical matter, without which cross-border contacts would become more difficult. Without scope rules there would be chaos. But, as will be shown, scope rules can also hinder cross-border movements in exceptional cases as well.

In the EU cross-border contacts are fundamental. The authors of the EEC Treaty gave an extremely high priority to free movement. This priority was reaffirmed in 1986 with the Single European Act (SEA). Indeed, without free movement of goods, persons, services and capital a common market in Europe is not possible. It is the realisation of the Common Market that has brought about, by way of case law of the ECJ, the greatest encroachments on the principle of territoriality.

In this chapter the focus will be on the consequences of free movement and non-discrimination on the basis of nationality for the principle of territoriality as it is applied in the area of taxation. In this field the 'fiscal territoriality principle' has a very strong legacy. Taxation touches the heart of sovereignty and the relation between governed and governments. A wide definition of this traditional principle is given by Pistone: 'Tax sovereignty is absolute, so that each State is free to levy taxes on any economic event, regardless of where it occurs'.[3] This definition, which still has some influence within national administrations, is too wide. Territoriality suggests at least that there is some link with the territory of the levying member state, be it the person that is normally working or residing there or a property. In adapting Cornelissen, who applied the principle of territoriality to social security, the application of the principle to the field of taxation leads to the following elements: (1) the legislator of a state confines the scope of its national legislation by using territorial elements such as working or residing in that state or earning an income or a profit in that state; (2) the legislator determines whether and to what extent tax benefits are granted to (legal) persons residing in the territory of another state; (3) the legislator determines whether and to what extent costs of a (legal) person in another state are deductable in their own state; (4) the legislator takes into account for the entitlement to benefits only those facts which have occurred under its own legislation.[4] See here some elements which are better compared with the broad definition given before.

The contribution is divided into four parts. In the second part the erosion of the principle of territoriality in the EU will be analysed. The third part deals with the continuing importance of that principle. In these parts an analysis of relevant case law of the ECJ will play an important role. The last part compares the results of the first two parts with developments in the field of social security. The next section will introduce some concepts concerning the political nature of the EU. The most important of these is the dichotomy between a one-purpose association and an all-purpose association. The European Common Market as a supreme one-purpose association has an influence on direct taxation, which belongs to the competence of the all-purpose associations, the member states. What is this influence exactly? Reference will be made to the criteria adapted from Cornelissen and the two mentioned general indicators of territoriality used in this volume.

The EU and its internal market: from a specific-purpose association towards an all-purpose association?

In his enumeration of the main elements of the emerging *acquis constitutionnel* of the EU Chryssochoou mentions in the first place the transcending of territoriality. The other elements are 'minimizing transaction costs', 'facilitating the four freedoms of movement', 'combating cultural (among other forms) of discrimination', 'respecting linguistic equality', 'institutionalizing multiple citizenship', 'creating avenues for subnational representation or the central level' and 'respecting minority rights'.[5] Is this first place in his enumeration at random or on purpose? And what does the word 'transcending' mean in this context? Does this mean that territoriality has become an irrelevant notion in the EU-context?

An answer to these questions can be found in the earlier part of his book, where Chryssochoou stresses the functional imperative of European integration. In the post-war history of the European integration process the 'aterritorial logic of Mitranian functionalism' has had a strong influence on the European institutions and the policies these institutions followed.[6] To undo the harshness of the territorial divide within Europe or better still to go completely beyond territorial affinities was the basic goal behind functionalism.

Among lawyers this functionalist paradigm has been influential as well. Especially the idea of the *Zweckverbände* ('special-purpose associations' in English) has been extremely influential. In a recent article Hooghe and Marks refer to this idea in their discussion of two separate and different types of multi-level governance.[7] The first type is the general-purpose jurisdiction, this would correspond with a federation. The federal as well as the state level in federations are both general-purpose jurisdictions. The second type is the task-specific jurisdiction, quite common in Switzerland at the local level where they are called *Zweckverbände*. The authors mention the regulation of transport as an example. But it is not only at the Swiss local level that these special-purpose associations are relevant. The German lawyer H.-P. Ipsen used this idea as a core element in his famous manual on European Community law.[8] The main elements of these special-purpose associations are non-discrimination on the basis of nationality, the four freedoms and a common competition policy. In fact one could see the common market as a special-purpose association. The main purpose of the *Zweckverbände* is the opening up of member states in relation to each other. This is a process without an end. However, according to Ipsen, the process of opening up may not lead to the destruction of member states' identities. A technocratic construction such as the special purpose associations cannot deal with emotional topics like identities. The member states have to carry the European construction. Article 6, paragraph 3, of the Maastricht Treaty on European Union (TEU) explicitly wants the EU to respect the national identity of her member states.

The separation of territories and functions has inspired others to devise new terms for the emerging polity of the EU. Schmitter's term of the *condominio* has become famous in this respect. A growing dissociation between territorial constituencies and functional competencies would lead to this construction. The EU since the Maastricht Treaty would fulfil the criteria of this 'condominio', a construction characterized by territorial as well as functional variability. The different opt-outs made during the final process of the Maastricht negotiations created a Union of 'bits and pieces'.[9] It is territorially variable because not all member states of the EU participate in all of the policy areas of the EU. It is functionally variable because not all member states participate in all functions. An example is the common currency.

For the purposes of this contribution the idea of a *condominio* is not very helpful, although it has been applauded even by a lawyer. Shaw stresses that Europe is in need of an institutional innovation, because of new problems of control Europe is in need of new institutional constructs.[10] The *condominio* could fulfil this role, according to Shaw. Emerson rightly sees the *condominio* as a weak construction and uses NATO and the euro area and the European Central Bank (in case it remains different from the EU) as examples of the *condominio*.[11] Although Emerson admits that at the functional level the *condominio* a given policy can be operated with rather strong and permanent common mechanisms of law, or finance, or decision-making, his qualification of the Maastricht and Amsterdam treaties as steps towards a confederation or even federation shows that Emerson does not agree with Schmitters' ideas of the EU as a *condominio*. Moreover the concept of a *condominio* is not helpful because taxation in the EU is not yet dealt with as a separate function. Forces to keep taxation an exclusive national competency are still very strong. Taxation is a sensitive area and is very often regarded as a core area of national sovereignty. The European internal market cannot be qualified as a *condominio*, because at least for this topic there is no flexibility. The unity of the common or internal market is like a holy principle enshrined in the *acquis communautaire*.

The Common Market is mentioned by John Gerard Ruggie, too, in his discussion of the 'unbundling of territoriality'.[12] And it is one example of this unbundling. Two other examples he gives are 'extraterritoriality' and 'international regimes'. Ruggie seems to presuppose that the creation and completion of a common or internal market in Europe automatically leads to this 'unbundling', whatever that may mean exactly. But the idea of the *Zweckverbände* is also of great relevance. At least the four freedoms and the principle of non-discrimination on the basis of nationality are common to all member states. These core areas of Community law do influence the freedom of member states to tax. There is no freedom to pick and choose out of these areas, apart from such peculiar examples of the second home protocol in

Denmark.¹³ An important question is whether developments such as the European Convention on the creation of the European Constitution will turn the EU from a 'special-purpose association' in an 'all-purpose association'. Probably the EU is somewhere half-way between these two entities. Almost every policy domain is touched nowadays in one way or the other by EU rules. The original *Zweckverbände*, with the four freedoms and the principle of non-discrimination is still very visible. It is a guarantor of the unity of the internal market. It must have some influence on the principle of territoriality as well. The influence of the special-purpose association (internal market) on the remaining powers and competencies of the all-purpose associations (the states) will be used as a central theme. Although the EU becomes more and more an all-purpose association itself, it is for the field of taxation that the qualification special-purpose association still is valid. Taxation is still the competency of the member states. But the internal market has its influence here.

The EC Court of Justice, the internal market and taxation: the erosion of the principle of territoriality in the case of (direct and indirect) taxation.

The case law of the ECJ concerning the internal market is worth some further analysis. The ECJ is the only institution that can interpret these basic principles as a last resort. Although member states are still competent in matters of direct taxation, it is within the framework of Community law (and of the *Zweckverbände*) that these competencies will have to be implemented. The competency itself of the member states is upheld. The realization of the four freedoms of the internal market entails consequences for the principle of territoriality.

> For the topic taxation not all four freedoms are equally relevant. Very important is the free movement of persons. The right of free movement is recognized for persons, workers as well as self-employed and natural persons. Free movement of workers is regulated in art. 39 EC. Freedom of establishment is dealt with in art. 43 EC. The core of these provisions is the obligation of non-discrimination on the basis of nationality. But in the interpretation of these Treaty provisions by the EC Court of Justice in Luxembourg the content and the substantive scope goes much beyond only a duty not to discriminate on the basis of nationality.¹⁴

First, this fundamental right of non-discrimination has been interpreted widely by the ECJ. Direct discrimination is not difficult to detect. But also more hidden forms of discrimination, so-called indirect discrimination is suspicious in an internal market. Famous in the context of a definition of indirect discrimination is the case *O'Flynn* (C-237/94).¹⁵ Conditions imposed by national law will be regarded as indirectly discriminatory when they affect essentially migrant workers. This 'effect-test' is satisfied very easily. Only a quantitative test is enough: there is indirect discrimination when the great majority of the affected are migrant workers. The Court goes even further. When conditions in national legislation can be more easily satisfied by national workers than by migrant workers a case of indirect discrimination is there. This is so even in case there is a 'risk' that the conditions 'may' operate to the detriment of migrant workers. It is submitted that a wider definition is impossible. This concept of non-discrimination, as developed by the ECJ, has been used to force member states to defend their national legislation and to bring forward objective justifications in order to uphold their legislation. No branch of the law is totally immune to this 'free movement law', not even taxation.

Second, it is not only discrimination on the basis of nationality that is the prime focus of the law of the internal market. It is the right itself of migrant workers, the self-employed or natural persons to move cross-border within the Union that is the prime focus. Every sort of negative influence on the decision to move within the territory of the whole Union is subject to a legal test.[16] Any deterrent effect on the decision to move or stay is now suspicious. The only option national governments have is to bring forward grounds of objective justification. They have to justify their national legislation and to show that there is another ground that takes precedence over the right of free movement. There is no guarantee that this defence will always succeed. The ECJ is very active in testing the grounds of objective justification presented by the national governments. With this case law huge interventions have been made on the 'sovereign' rights to tax or in fields like social security law. We will see some examples in the next chapters.

That this development bears on the application of the principle of territoriality in the EU is clear. There is no unlimited freedom (or sovereignty if you like) for national governments any more to legislate cross-border situations. Community law concerning non-discrimination on the basis of nationality and free movement is a sort of law of perspective. National legislators, national judges and national authorities have to add the perspective of the migrant (legal) person from another member state to their decision-making. Sometimes they are not aware of the fact that their national legislation is working to the detriment of non-citizens. National legislation is very often biased in favour of own national citizens. It is the purpose of free movement law to undo that bias, or at least to force governments to justify their legislation.

Until recently taxation has been regarded as one of the main instruments of national sovereignty. This is why the ECJ in Luxembourg was hesitant at first to intervene in this sensitive field, especially in areas where the EC has no competence. Most of the early case law on tax was about VAT, as the sixth directive on value added tax was for a long time the main piece of EC legislation in this field.[17] Another source of case law was discriminatory taxes on products. The French authorities are for example not allowed to tax wines from other member states heavier than wines from France. These sort of product taxes have to be neutral.

On direct taxes like the income tax and corporation tax, the ECJ used to have a more reluctant approach. This reluctant approach changed during the 1990s. Probably because of the Europe 1992 project and the increased interest for the completion of the internal market, the Court dealt in a more robust way with income tax cases, in which workers who migrated from one member state to another were discriminated in relation to non-migrating workers. The most famous of these cases were *Schumacker* (C-279/93), *Wielockx* (C-80/94) and *Asscher* (C-107/94). Specialists in national law have not received this case law of the ECJ with great pleasure. A title of an article by a former Dutch secretary of Finance is illustrative here: 'The Court of Justice of the European Communities and direct taxes: Est-ce que la justice est de ce monde?' 'Asscher: the European Court and the power to destroy' is the title of an article of another tax specialist, Asscher referring to the name of a case.[18] In Germany one tax lawyer is not able to grasp what the ECJ is doing. According to him the concept of non-discrimination is a political concept and not a legal one, like the concept of non-discrimination in national law.[19] This remark is proof of the mixed feelings with which national lawyers, being used to a certain view concerning the principle of territoriality, receive the outcome of many cases decided in Luxembourg.

The consequences of the case law of the ECJ for the principle of territoriality

What are the consequences of these new developments brought about by European Community Law for the principle of territoriality? At first hand the impact of these cases for the principle of territoriality seems like that of a neutron bomb and not an atom bomb. The principle itself is not 'destroyed' completely but its effectiveness, its application within the EU, is influenced. Member states are not entirely free anymore to apply in a 'sovereign' way their national law. Community law commands a correction of the application of a national rule or practice in a specific case. There is a general or more abstract purpose as well: promotion of free movement. National rules which could operate against the realization of free movement (of workers) are struck down in the sense that they may not be applied. But the principle of territoriality itself has not disappeared in the legal discourse and in case law, not even in the case law of the European Court. Let us look more in depth into the consequences of the internal market for the application of the principle of territoriality in the area of taxation. The four elements discussed in the beginning of this chapter as adapted from Cornelissen will be used.

The legislator confines the scope of its national legislation by using territorial elements

The ECJ in Luxembourg does not hesitate to declare specific elements of a national tax rule a breach of EC Treaty obligations. There is a limit though. Real conflict or scope rules, especially those sanctioned by international tax law, are dealt with in a careful way. International tax treaties, like for example those concluded within the framework of the OECD, are used in the legal reasoning of the Court. Some international tax treaties and some bilateral ones are specifically concluded in order to prevent double taxation of persons. Part of the revenues or income of a migrant worker is attributed to state A, other parts are attributed to state B. These rules in international tax law are pretty consistent. Taxing rights over taxing objects are allocated by way of so-called 'assignment rules'.[20] These assignment rules work with a typical terminology. In the first place there is the separation between source countries and countries of residence, the first one is a country where a taxable object or source is situated. The country of residence is the country of residence of the tax payer. The assignment rules also work with an 'exclusive' and/or a 'limited' competence to tax. For somebody who has a relation with two or more states, it is possible that he will be taxed in one country for his income and in another country for his property. For example it is reasonable to attribute income out of immovable property to the country in which that property is situated, it is also reasonable to attribute dividend and interest income to the state of residence.

In its case law the ECJ has at least tried to be extremely careful with these conflict rules, because the elimination of a situation of double taxation is in the interest of the Common Market as well. Double taxation because of migration is a very sensitive issue from the perspective of free movement of persons, guaranteed by the EC Treaty. That implies that these international tax rules combating double taxation support, by their very nature, the idea of free movement of persons. In case the European Court would like to intervene in these rules it should act with care. Indeed, intervening in conflict rules, which very often take the territory of a state as a starting point, could bring about nothing less than chaos.

That is why the ECJ is taking the position (after some learning by doing from earlier case law) that conflict rules, like those in international tax treaties, do not (*per se*) contravene one of the four freedoms. As one of the judges of the ECJ, José Carlos Moitinho de Almeida, is explaining, the conflict rules of an international tax treaty do not 'cause' the adverse or discriminatory treatment. These rules are 'internationally accepted' and 'neutral' from a fiscal point of view.[21] His remarks were made because of *Gilly* (C-336/96),[22] a case in which the criterium of nationality was used in an international tax treaty in order to assign fiscal competence. Because discrimination on the basis of nationality between nationals of the member states of the EU is a 'core prohibition' of Community law, the thought that this criterium could not be used in such international tax treaties quickly raised. But here there is a mistake, according to Moitinho de Almeida. The favourable or unfavourable fiscal treatment of the tax payers is not a consequence of the choice of a certain connecting factor in order to assign competencies in international tax law, it is the consequence of the level of taxes imposed in a situation without harmonization in the EU.[23]

The principle of territoriality as a means to divide competencies among states is therefore not completely in jeopardy. We are still in need of criteria to divide competencies among member states, at least as long as there is no total harmonization at the level of the European Union (EU). Although some rules of a fiscal nature have been created at the European level, harmonization of tax law is still an extremely sensitive matter. Some governments like that of the UK take a completely hostile position towards this topic. Moreover, there is certainly not a linear road from the robust interpretation of some fundamental EC Treaty articles by the Court in Luxembourg to full harmonization of tax law. As the Court itself reiterates every time, taxation belongs to the competency of the member states. This is something the Court cannot change on its own.

Let us look to a case in which the principle is mentioned explicitly by the ECJ. This is the case of *Cura Anlagen GmbH* (C-451/99).[24] The case is about the compatibility of two Austrian laws with the EC Treaty provisions on free movement of services (art. 49 EC). This is also one of the four freedoms of the common market and of great relevance for taxation too. A German vehicle-leasing company leased a motor car for a period of three years to an Austrian limited company called Cura Anlagen. The German company remains the owner of the car and the Austrian company is not allowed to re-register the car in its own name in Austria because it is already registered in Germany. It is agreed that the motor car is to be used in principle only within Austria. In the case before the European Court several related topics are examined separately. First there is the requirement to re-register the car within three days after its first use in Austria. Then there is also a requirement that a vehicle used in Austria by a person based there must also be registered in the name of that same person. Next the requirement of insurance of a vehicle used in Austria by an insurer entitled to operate in that country is at stake. Fourth, the requirement to satisfy technical and environmental tests in Austria although comparable tests have already been fulfilled in Germany has to be examined. Finally the compatibility of the levying of the Standard Fuel Consumption Tax with European law has to be dealt with.

The first topic about the registration requirement as such is the most interesting one and will be analysed here. It is here that the ECJ mentions the principle of territoriality. Any restriction in a national piece of legislation, which is liable to prohibit, impede or render less advantageous the activities of a provider of services, established in another member state where he provides similar services. With only a restriction to prove, the whole idea of discrimination is not so relevant any more. The facts of the case show that the rule is liable to prohibit, impede free movement of services. The German company provides leasing services to another member state, that company provides similar services in Germany. The requirement to register the same car a second time in Austria is an impediment or at least makes leasing of cars to an Austrian firm less attractive. But is registration in the member state of origin, Germany, sufficient?

The Court confirms that the requirement of re-registration impedes free movement of services. But it looks to whether there is an objective justification for this requirement. First, the Court establishes that taxes concerning motor vehicles have not been subject to a harmonization in the EU. This argument is not convincing on its own, because a lack of harmonization cannot justify an impediment to free movement of services. But the Court continues in affirming that the said taxes differ enormously within the EU between the member states. The member states are free to exercise their fiscal competencies within the limits of European law. Because of these competencies member states are allowed to make agreements between themselves on the basis of criteria such as the area where the motor vehicle is actually used or the place of residence of the driver. It is worth citing the regarding paragraph in full:

> It is lawful for them to allocate those powers of taxation amongst themselves on the basis of criteria such as the territory in which a vehicle is actually used or the residence of the driver, which are various components of the territoriality principle, and to conclude agreements amongst themselves to ensure that a vehicle is subject to indirect taxation in only one of the signatory states (paragraph 40 of the case).

The words 'various components' are interesting, but these words do not make it possible to give a limitative view of all the existing components of the territoriality principle. Concluding agreements in order to ensure that a vehicle is subject to taxation in only one state with the help of these criteria is allowed. Registration of a vehicle is the 'natural corollary' (paragraph 41 of the case) of the execution of these fiscal competencies. The registration facilitates controls in the state of registration as well as in other member states. Registration in one member state is proof of payment of taxes in that state. Actual use of a car in Austria gives Austria the right to require registration in that country as well. But the ECJ still effectuates a control. The term within which a re-registration will have to be made may not be too short. A term of three days after the first use of the vehicle in Austria is too short and too cumbersome. In that case the Austrian legislation cannot be justified. This implies that even a successful use of the principle of territoriality by a government canot prevent the Court from intervening in the application of this principle in an individual case.

The area where the motor vehicle is actually used or the place of residence of the driver are both elements of the principle of territoriality. It is as if the

ECJ would like to suggest that this the core of the principle of territoriality. It is 'natural' and accepted for states to use these sorts of elements in their legislation. On their own they cannot impede the free movement of services. This argument looks a bit like that one used by Moitinho de Almeida. There is no necessity for the ECJ to 'touch' the principle of territoriality.

The legislator determines whether and to what extent tax benefits are granted to (legal) persons residing in the territory of another state

Sometimes the ECJ intervenes in atypical cases. The already mentioned *Schumacker* case is of great relevance in this respect. Schumacker was a migrant worker of German nationality, who lived with his family in Belgium but worked in Germany. He was taxed by the German authorities only on his income arising in that country. German income tax law gives a differential treatment to residents of Germany in relation to non-residents. The authorities presumed that he would have other income parts, like for example interests, in his country of residence Belgium. Then it would be up to Belgium to deal with the rest of his income.

This division of tasks is perfectly in line with principles of international tax law. Germany has the right to tax only his income in Germany under article 15 of the OECD Model Convention, a double tax convention. But the main problem in this case was, that Schumacker in reality had no income parts outside Germany. He wanted Germany to take into account all his income, because that would lead to a better tax position in that country. In case all his income is taken into account, he could profit from deductions in relation to personal allowances. Because Germany only taxes his income in Germany and could not judge his personal situation in Belgium, Schumacker could not profit from tax deductions. In Belgium, his country of residence, he could also not profit from deductions, because of his lack of income there.

The case of Schumacker is therefore an atypical case. Nonetheless, the negative consequences of migrant workers are unacceptable from the view of EC law. Migrant workers may not be discriminated in relation to workers who work *and* reside in Germany. In fact, Schumacker is 'punished' *because* he lives with his family across the border in Belgium. This sort of negative consequence can dissuade potential migrants to go to another member state in Europe and work there. Because of this atypical situation the Advocate General and after him the Court intervened, notwithstanding the fact that direct tax is not yet fully harmonized in the EU and that member states have exclusive competencies in this area of the law. Only in these exceptional cases which frustrate the goals of a common market will sovereignty have to be lifted. Because the result of *the application of* common international tax principles is unacceptable, the negative effect for the migrant worker of this way of taxing is clear, Community law intervenes in this specific situation.

It is not the international tax rules themselves that are in violation of Community law but their application in a specific case. Germany will have to take into account in the case of Schumacker all his income, because in Belgium there is no income at all.

The implication of this is that tax authorities and national courts must look at the personal situation at hand, they must look at facts that happened outside their own territory. They can never automatically apply internationally accepted rules. They have to see whether there is a negative impact on the situation of a migrant worker, that could be qualified as a discrimination. This seems easier than it is. It is a 'specific' Europeanized discrimination concept, with which tax authorities in the member states were not acquainted with. The European non-discrimination concept tries to bring about a certain result, it is result-oriented. It is correct that the free movement provisions in the EC Treaty are not only about non-discrimination. These try to reach a goal as well, the promotion of free movement, the tying together of Europe via its travelling citizens. This makes the discrimination concept in Community law a more radical concept in relation to related concepts developed in national and international law. The mentioned OECD double tax convention itself contains in article 24 a non-discrimination provision. This provision covers only a prohibition of non-discrimination on the basis of nationality. This would not suffice in the case of Schumacker, a German treated differently by the German authorities because of his residence outside Germany. Moreover, article 24, paragraph 3 explicitly states that a contracting State is not obliged to grant personal allowances, reliefs or reductions to residents of another contracting State. This provision is justified by the reason that states do not dispose of relevant information about the situation in the state of residence of the taxpayer. This reason might suffice in international tax relations, but it does not within the framework of a European common market. The authorities of the first member state could at least contact the authorities of the state of residence and try to get the relevant information. Especially in an age where technology makes contacts easier, it is up to such authorities to show more action.

This active duty on the part of the authorities and court of a member state is mentioned explicitly in the famous article 10 EC. This article adds an additional element, which we cannot find in international tax treaties. This is the principle of loyalty. Administrative authorities of the member states have to behave in a loyal way in relation to the duties imposed by Community law. A former president of the European Court called this a 'federal' principle.[25] We can find this principle also in existing federal constitutions. In the Federal Republic of Germany the *'Bundestreue'* is known as an important principle. Article 10 is often invoked by the European Court in its case law in order to make the fundamental freedoms, like the free movement of workers as effective as possible. The authorities and courts of the member states have to do everything to help bring about the goals of the EC Treaty. In each case Community law commands an active duty from the authorities and courts to look to the individual position of a migrant worker or independently active person.[26]

The legislator determines whether and to what extent costs of a (legal) person in another state are deductable in their own state

There is no unlimited freedom for member states of the EU though to invoke the principle of territoriality. In a recent case the principle of territoriality was used as a defence by the Dutch government in *Bosal Holding BV* (C-168/01).[27] The European Court did not accept this defence. The company Bosal, subject to the Dutch corporation tax, carries holdings in nine other member states. In the financial year 1993 the company declared costs of almost four million Dutch guilders in relation to the financing of those subsidiaries. Bosal wanted to deduct these costs in the Netherlands. Dutch tax law admits deducting costs from the taxable profits, but only when it is evident that these costs are 'instrumental in making profit that is taxable in the Netherlands'. According to Bosal this condition is against the rules of the Common Market. According to the Netherlands this condition is in conformity with the principle of territoriality, there is great difference between subsidiaries according to whether or not they carry on business abroad.[28] Whether the subsidiaries make a taxable profit in the Netherlands is a relevant criterium, the costs in connection with activities abroad can only be set off against the profits generated by those activities. Moreover the internationally accepted principle of fiscal territoriality would not resist costs being taken into account at a taxpayer other than the one who actually made these costs.[29]

The ECJ looks to the European level and not at the national level: the grouping together of companies at Community level is a laudable goal.[30] Disadvantages resulting from the fact that tax provisions governing relations between parent companies and subsidiaries of different member states are, in general, less favourable than those applicable to relations between parent and subsidiary companies of the same member state. This is yet another application of a discrimination concept. These disadvantages are unacceptable from the viewpoint of the Common Market. Community legislation is relevant here as well. The so-called parent-subsidiary directive, Council Directive 90/435/EEC, is specifically designed to promote cooperation between companies of different member states. Tax rules governing the relations between parent companies and subsidiaries of different member states are in general less favourable than those applicable to parent companies and subsidiaries of the same member state.

The Dutch government cannot invoke the principle of territoriality here. Parent companies are treated differently according to whether or not they have subsidiaries making profits taxable in the Netherlands. This could dissuade decisions of companies to make groups within the EU. The European Court thinks the Dutch rules are problematic, because the profits of the subsidiaries are not taxable in the hands of the parent companies. It makes no difference, whether the profits come from subsidiaries taxable in the Netherlands or from other subsidiaries. Moreover, the parent-subsidiary directive does not provide in an exception concerning the territory where the profits of the subsidiaries might be taxed.

This case created some confusion about the principle of territoriality.[31] According to Wattel the ECJ gives a strict legal interpretation of the principle. He compares this with the broad economic interpretation defended by the Dutch government and the Dutch supreme Court.[32] The *Bosal* case can certainly be seen as a decision to refocus the principle of territoriality at the EU level.

The legislator takes into account for the entitlement to benefits only those facts which have occurred under its own legislation

The principle of territoriality was mentioned explicitly by the European Court as well in an earlier case: in *Futura Participations* (C-250/95).[33] Futura Participations SA is a corporation established in France operating a permanent branch in the Grand Duchy of Luxembourg. Futura wanted to compensate the losses of its Luxembourg branch during the financial years 1981 and 1982 with the profits of the same branch during the financial year 1986. This so-called carry-forward of losses was allowed by Luxembourg legislation, but only in so far as the losses could be determined by a bookkeeping which was in accordance with the Luxembourg conditions. Furthermore, carrying forward was subject to the condition that the losses had to be related to the profit made by the Luxembourg branch itself. The losses had to be in 'an economic relation' with the profits made by the branch in Luxembourg. Non-resident taxpayers like Futura Participations SA were treated differently from resident taxpayers. That resident taxpayers usually have more income from domestic sources and non-resident taxpayers have more income from external sources is seen as a normal situation.

This specific condition in Luxembourg legislation was accepted by the ECJ because this legislation was 'in accordance with the fiscal principle of territoriality'. This view was also defended by the European Commission in her remarks during the oral proceedings in this case. This different treatment between resident and non-resident taxpayers cannot be qualified as a discrimination contrary to EC law. There is a small but important difference with the *Bosal* case discussed above. In *Futura Participations* there was one taxable entity, the Luxembourg branch of the corporation. In *Bosal* there were two taxable entities: the daughter company and the parent, who both had their separate taxes taken into account by the Dutch legislation. The strict relation between the losses and the profits of the permanent branch itself is in accordance with the principle of territoriality.

It is time to give a short summary of the analysis so far. Did the principle of territoriality change in significance for organising polities, politics and policies in the area of taxation in Western Europe? And if so, why is this so and into what forms did it change? The answer to these question is a mixed one. On the one hand the 'core' of the principle is still upheld, the principle of territoriality therefore remains a legitimate way of assigning tax competencies among (member) states. Member states are allowed to limit the scope of their own tax rules. Scope rules are legitimate rules. But there is on the other hand a control executed by the European Court of Justice that encroaches on full fiscal sovereignty. The Common Market rules as interpreted in the last resort by the European Court operate in a certain direction. 'Atypical' situations like the one in *Schumacker* are corrected by the Court. Invoking the 'territoriality principle' is always under the scrutiny of the Court, as the Dutch government realized after the *Bosal* case. In situations where national rules hinder free movement and the construction of the common market the European Court 'refocuses' the principle of territoriality. I agree with Steyger that there has been a change of focus from coherence within the separate national tax systems towards coherence of the separate systems in relation to the individual taxpayer on the common market.[34] The ECJ does not hesitate to intervene when there is reason to do so because of the construction and operation of the Common Market.

Is it possible this common or internal market can still be seen as an 'ordinary' special-purpose association and that there is the inherent tendency of these associations to expand towards often territorially organized 'all-purpose' organizations? The idea behind the special-purpose associations is that such an association deals with in the words of Marks and Hooghe 'particular policy problems', it is a flexible construction and membership is voluntary. The common market is more than only a particular policy problem, it is a supreme construction that affects almost all other policy fields. There is also nothing voluntary about the rules of the Common Market. The unity of the Common Market is very essential for the European construction. Flexibility is not allowed on the area of the Common Market. The case law of the ECJ is very much task-driven and 'teleologically' inspired. Almost all other policy areas are seen from the perspective of the creation and realization of the Common Market.

Even in areas where the all-purpose associations (the member states) are competent such as taxation, this supreme special-purpose association has its influence. National courts and competent authorities have to take into account facts that happened, are happening or will happen outside their territory, when they deal with the tax position of a migrant worker. The focus cannot be any more only on their own tax system. The position of (legal) persons making use of one of the constitutionally guaranteed rights to free movement is relevant, this person may not be dissuaded from making use of these rights. Occassionally these courts and authorities will have to study the legal position of that migrant worker in another member state.

In the long term this development will lead to far-reaching consequences. Nothing less than an attitude change of national administrations is sought.

A more or less detailed research is sometimes needed into two or more national tax systems that are relevant for the migrant worker and also in international tax treaties that have been concluded by the two governments. This detailed, sometimes comparative research into two or more legal systems is the task for national administrations.[35] The long-term exposure of national administrations to the case law of the ECJ will undoubtedly change attitudes. This will affect the second meaning of the principle of territoriality as used in this book, the way rulers provide their services, values and goods to the ruled. Rulers in any case, but hopefully national administrations too, will react in a different way to the position of migrant workers. This is a slow but continuous process.

A linear road from the special-purpose association to the all-purpose association is not present. The actual discussions on a European constitution could lead to another step in the direction of the European all-purpose association, but the EU will not reach that stadium in the near future. But the creation of the Common Market is not only an economic process. It has and will have deep psychological and even cultural connotations. Member states do not wither away slowly as the neo-functionalists presume, it is more that states themselves change because they have to react to the dynamism of a common market. Ruggie calls this the 'multi-perspectival' role of states[36]. Perspectives change, states remain. States are according to him still on the centre of the stage. They have to combine different roles. They are within the Common Market not only defenders of their own interests but also enforcers of the norms and rules of the Common Market. Ruggie is right in mentioning the Common Market as an example of 'unbundling of territoriality'. The ideal of a common market, strictly applied by the ECJ by way of the provisions in the EC Treaty, has had enormous consequences for the principle of territoriality. The Common Market provisions force authorities and courts of member states to deal with issues that happened outside their own territory. These issues have to be treated with care, the legal position of a migrant worker may not be affected in a negative way without a sufficient objective reason. Developments happening outside the national territory cannot be treated any more as 'strange' or 'unknown of' any more. More regular contacts between the different national tax administrations will be needed in order for the requirements of the Common Market to be implemented in a correct way. Technological devises such as the internet will be helpful here.

Some authors are critical of the position the ECJ in Luxembourg has taken in relation to taxation. Vanistendael is of the opinion that its decisions have to be qualified as 'political decisions'. Legal reasoning is now at its limit. Sovereign taxing powers are already an illusion and the member states lose powers and competencies to market forces.[37] The reason behind this development is not only the four freedoms of the Common Market but also non-binding documents such as the Code of Conduct designed to deal with harmful tax competition between the member states.[38] The member states themselves enforce the norms of this Code. Vanistendael's view leans towards more political integration in Europe: 'No European taxation without European representation.'[39] An economic and monetary union in Europe would hardly leave another option.

Although it is perfectly understandable that the four freedoms of the common market as interpreted by the ECJ in Luxembourg unleashes tax competition, it was submitted in the preceding paragraphs that the principle of territoriality still survives. The influence European law is having on national tax law does not lead yet to a total extinction of the principle of territoriality. The principle is in fact reduced to its hard core and is refocused somewhat. If the core of the principle is at stake and not only its implementation in specific and exceptional cases it can be upheld. The principle has a continuing relevance. In some recent ECJ case law this principle was explicitly mentioned. This is proof of the fact that it now explicitly recognizes the existence and continuing validity of the principle.

By way of comparison: the principle of territoriality and European social security law

Not only in the area of taxation, in the area of social security as well the ECJ has been criticized for its case law. This case law would lead to noting less than breaking the principle of territoriality anchored in national security legislation.[40] Cornelissen submits that it is 'to a certain extent', necessary for European Community law to overrule the principle of territoriality 'in order to guarantee the exercise of freedom of movement as conferred by the Treaty of Rome'.[41] After a short comparison with the principle of territoriality in this field I will return on the item of the continuing relevance of the principle of territoriality.

In the area of social security the ECJ, as in the area of taxation, stresses that 'social matters' belong to the competence of the member states: every state is free to determine the content of its own social security system. Every member state is free to set the level of its social security benefits or the pensionable age. But the approach of the Court in the area of social security is a little more robust. This approach is possible because the main legal text, regulation 1408/71, is a so-called coordination regulation. It coordinates the social security systems of the member states. There is not yet such a comprehensive coordination regulation in the area of taxation. Coordination is not exactly the same as harmonization. Harmonization implies new rules of a substantive nature on a European level. Coordination means that the national legal systems do not disappear, but that these systems have to be adjusted in such a way that the social security position of migrant workers does not suffer because of their migration.

In addition, regulation 1408/71 has as legal basis, article 42 of the EC Treaty. This article is part of the chapter on free movement of workers. In its case law the European Court often refers to these articles in the legal finding process. With the help of these Treaty articles the coordination process gets enriched. Because of this purpose, the realization of the free movement of workers, the dividing line between harmonization and coordination becomes more porous.[42]

By what is this robust approach in the area of social security characterised? The main elements of this approach are the following. In the first place is the freedom of the member states to decide on their own the scope of their social security system is severely limited. Scope rules of one member state are often diametrically opposed to the same rules of another member state. This can lead to very nasty consequences for migrant workers. Suppose member state A imposes as a condition for insurance under its social security system the residence in that member state and member state B imposes the place of work as a condition for insurance under its system. In that case a migrant worker who lives in member state B, but works in member state A would not be insured in either state! This consequence is unacceptable from the viewpoint of the Common Market. The same is true when the migrant worker is insured under two national systems, he has to pay contributions two times but will in the end only get one pension, because the pension he derives from the other member state is deducted.

In the area of taxation there exist international and bilateral tax treaties concerning double taxation. Causing chaos by damaging generally accepted international tax rules is something the European Court wants to avoid. This specific problem is not present in the area of social security. Therefore territorial elements in the national social security legislation will always be under the scrutiny of the European Court.

In the second place, the regulation 1408/71 contains provisions which force member states' authorities to take into account facts or situations that happen outside their own territory, when this might lead to a right to a benefit or pension or a higher benefit/pension. The known principle of acquired rights is of importance here as well. *Because* of the migration a worker may not lose rights he already possessed in his country of origin.

The regulation allows in the third place the exportation of a high number of benefits or pensions, from one member state to the other. Pensioners can live in Spain and still receive their pension from their country of work or country of origin. This possibility to export pensions and benefits has some great consequence for the principle of territoriality.

The strong influence of secondary legislation in this area can also work in an opposite direction. The Community legislator can restore the principle of territoriality to a certain extent. In 1992 the regulation 1408/71 was revised, some important non-contributory or hybrid benefits could from that moment on only be enjoyed in the competent state and not in another member state where the migrant person resided. Until 1992 those benefits were treated by the ECJ like any other benefit. An explicit expression of the Community legislator therefore is of potentially high impact. The freedom of this legislator is however not 100 per cent. Secondary Community legislation has to be in accordance with primary Community rules, the Treaty rules. A provision in regulation 1408/71 was held by the Court to be contrary to the principle of free movement of workers in the Treaty because additional and unnecessary differences between the family benefit systems were explicitly created by that provision.[43] This provision created differences between French family benefits and the family benefits of the other member states. French family benefits were in general higher than those of the other member states. Therefore France wanted to tie the right to a French benefit to residence within the territory of France. It negotiated this wish with success in the regulation 1408/71. For all other benefits the normal rule in the regulation was applicable, the benefit can be enjoyed in the country of residence. Migrant workers, working in France, whose families generally are residing in another member state, would be discriminated by this exception. Therefore the European Court intervened in the work of the Community legislator. But this sort of intervention will not happen very often. It is submitted that in the area of taxation such an intervention is less likely.

Conclusion

The consequences of a maturing Common Market in Europe become more visible. This entails consequences for the principle of territoriality as well. Scope rules, when based on internationally accepted tax principles, are not touched by the Court. This could create too much chaos. An important new perspective is that national authorities have to take into account facts and situations happening outside their own border in order to make decisions concerning taxation and social security. Apart from this development, there is the question of political and legal authority. Is legal authority still based on the principle of territoriality? I would like to answer this question in the affirmative. Legal authority is still derived from a pretty clear construction. There is nothing that looks like Schmitter's *condominium*. National courts in the member states are still the main vehicle through which nationals of member states can claim their rights. By way of preliminary questions national courts ask an interpretation of a Community law provision to the European Court. It is up to the national courts to implement and apply the judgement of the European Court in their national legal orders.

Moreover, the EU has clear borders. A new territoriality is born in 1958 with the Treaty of Rome and this one is superimposed on existing territorialities. The implication of this is that the European Court must be aware of the powers and competencies of the member states, but at the same time must 'build the Common Market'. A layered sort of construction is the result in areas where the member states have retained their competencies, as in taxation. Member states are free to legislate taxation, although such legislation may not frustrate the goals of the Common Market. This core area of the *Zweckverbände* is overriding and supreme.

Of course, is the continuing legal integration in Europe going to affect the territorial underpinnings of taxation. The vehement reactions of national tax lawyers to some of the case law of the European Court proves that this case law is not without some deep consequences. The operation of the Common Market will without doubt lead to more competition between the member states and that might lead in the end to more harmonization. But this is a slow process in which the member states will still have a strong say. The principle of territoriality has survived European legal integration. Only in exceptional cases is the Court intervening in this principle. Territory still matters in the area of taxation. Chaos is not something that is of interest to either member states and the EU. But the unity of the Common Market and its operation is a supreme construction. The European Court is continuing to watch this development. There is no unlimited freedom for the member states any more, not even in the area of taxation.

Notes

1. See for example R. Cornelissen (1996), 'The Principle of Territoriality and the Community Regulations on Social Security (Regulations 1408/71 and 574/72)', *Common Market Law Review* 33: 439–471.
2. See F. Pennings (2001), *Introduction to European Social Security Law*, third edition. The hague, london, New York: Kluwer Law International, p. 4.
3. P. Pistone (2002), *The Impact of Community Law on Tax Treaties. Issues and Solutions*. The Hague, London, New York: Kluwer Law International, p. 175.
4. R. Cornelissen, ibidem, 441.
5. D.N. Chryssochoou (2001), *Theorizing European Integration.* p. 102.
6. Chryssochoou, ibid., at p. 41 and 42.
7. L. Hooghe and G. Marks (2003), 'Unraveling the Central State, but How? Types of Multi-level Governance', *American Political Science Review*, 97(2): 233–243, at 237.
8. H.-P. Ipsen (1972), *Europäisches Gemeinschaftsrecht*. Tübingen.
9. A famous phrase of D.M. Curtin, 'The constitutional structure of the union: A Europe of bits and pieces', see K. Hellingman (ed.) (1993), *Europa in de steigers: Van Gemeenschap tot Unie*, Deventer: Kluwer, p. 1.
10. J. Shaw (2001), 'Postnational Constitutionalism in the European Union', in Th. Christiansen, K.E. Jorgensen and A. Wiener (eds), *The Social Construction of Europe*. London: SAGE Publications Ltd, pp. 74, 75.
11. M. Emerson (1998), *Redrawing the Map of Europe*. London: Macmillan, p. 174. He is one of the few authors that react on the concept of *condominio*.
12. J.G. Ruggie (1998), *Constructing the World Polity. Essays on International Institutionalization*. London and New York: Routledge, p. 190. See especially chapter 7, 'Territoriality at millenium's end'.
13. This is a violation of a fundamental economic freedom, the freedom to buy property in another member state.
14. See R.M. Jeffery (1999), *The Impact of State Sovereignty on Global Trade and International Taxation*. London: Kluwer Law International, paragraph 3.3; and also M. Lehner (2000), 'Limitation of the National Power of Taxation by the Fundamental Freedoms and Non-discrimination Clauses of the EC Treaty', in *EC Tax Review*, pp. 8, 9.
15. *European Court Reports*, 1996, p. I-2617.
16. See for an overview of the case law of the European Court concerning the development from non-discrimination to a protection of the right to free movement

as such M. Lehner (2000), 'Limitation of the National Power of Taxation by the Fundamental Freedoms and Non-discrimination Clauses of the EC Treaty', in *EC Tax Review*, 1: 5–15.
17 Directive 67/227/EEC and 68/227/EEC, 1967 OJ Sp Edn, p. 14.
18 W. Vermeend (1996), *EC Tax Review*, p. 54. The other article is in the same review, 1997, p. 4.
19 M. Lehner (2000), 'Limitation of the National Power of Taxation by the Fundamental Freedoms and Non-discrimination Clauses of the EC Treaty', in *EC Tax Review*, p. 5.
20 See R. Rohatgi (2002), *Basic International Taxation*. The Hague, London, New York: Kluwer Law International, pp. 14, 15.
21 See J.C. Moitinho de Almeida (1999), 'Le droit fiscal national, la libre circulation des travailleurs, le droit d'établissement et la libre prestation de services', in *Mélanges en hommage à Michel Waelbroeck*, Volume II, Brussels: Bruylant, p. 1343. I would really recommend this article for those interested in European Tax Law.
22 *European Court Reports*, 1998, p. I-2793. See for this case K. Eicker (1998), 'Tax Treaties and EC Law: Comment on the *Gilly* Case', in *European Taxation*, pp. 322–327.
23 Ibidem.
24 Not yet reported. The case is from 21 March 2002.
25 O. Due gave a lecture on this topic at the Conference Robert Schuman sur le droit communautaire in Florence, 17 June 1991. See for a Dutch translation of the lecture *Sociaal Economische Wetgeving*, 1992, pp. 355–366.
26 The content of the important principle of loyalty is presented in a pretty clear manner by J. Temple Lang (1997), 'The Duties of National Courts under Community Constitutional Law', *European Law Review*, 22: 3–18. See also Temple Lang (1998), 'The Duties of National Authorities under Community Constitutional Law', *European Law Review*, 23: 109.
27 Case of 18 September 2003, not yet reported.
28 See especially the very critical approach by D. Weber (2003), 'The *Bosal Holding* Case: Analysis and Critique', in *EC Tax Review*, 4: pp. 228, 229.
29 Weber, ibidem, p. 229.
30 Vanistendael takes a positive view of the decision of the European Court, see his editorial in *EC Tax Review* 2003/4, pp. 192, 193, 'the parent cannot be denied a tax benefit just because the subsidiary belongs to the tax jurisdiction of another Member State'.
31 See for example H. van den Broek (2003), 'Bosal Holding and the Confusion Surrounding the Territoriality Principle', in *International Transfer Pricing Journal*, May/June: 116–123.
32 P.J. Wattel (2003), 'Corporate Tax Jurisdiction in the EU with Respect to Branches and Subsidiaries; Dislocation Distinguished from Discrimination and Disparity: A Plea for Territoriality', in *EC Tax Review*, 4: 200.
33 *European Court Reports*, 1997, p. I-2471.
34 E. Steyger (1999), 'The neveneffecten van het vrij verkeer op specifiek nationale beleidsterreinen', in *Sociaal-Economische Wetgeving*, p. 231.
35 In my view this leads to a situation called legal pluralism. See H. Voogsgeerd (forthcoming), 'The European Court of Justice and Legal Pluralism', in I.F. Dekker and W.G. Werner (eds), *Governance and International Legal Theory*, Martinus Nijhoff Publishers.
36 Ruggie, ibidem, p. 195.
37 F.J. Vanistendael (1998), 'European Taxation in the 21st Century: The Road towards Integration', in: *European Taxation*, pp. 331–335, at 334.
38 Code of Conduct, *Official Journal* C 2, 6 January 1998, p. 1.

39 F.J. Vanistendael (2000), 'Editorial: No European taxation without European representation', in *EC Tax Review*, 3: 142–143.
40 See R. Cornelissen, ibidem, p. 439.
41 Cornelissen, ibidem, p. 440.
42 See also F. Pennings (2001), *Introduction to European Social Security Law*, third edition, The Hague, London, New York: Kluwer Law International, pp. 6,7, 225, 226.
43 See the famous case of *Pinna*, case 41/84, *European Court Reports*, 1986, p. 1.

9 EU social policy beyond national welfare regime[1]

Anton Hemerijck

Introduction

European economic integration has a profound impact on the structure of the economy. And as European integration progresses, EU policies increasingly infringe upon the basic (re-)distributive powers of Europe's national, territorially bound, welfare states. As European integration has come to seriously affecting the life chances of European citizens in various ways, since the mid-1990s, employment and social policy concerns have moved progressively towards the top of the European agenda. The completion of the internal market and the creation of monetary union in a period of high unemployment have provided strong incentives for European social policy initiatives. The incorporation of a separate employment chapter in the Treaty of Amsterdam (June 1997) marks a watershed in the Europeanisation of social policy. Up until the mid-1990s, the debate over the future of social Europe was couched in terms of 'good intentions, high principles, and little action' (Lange 1993: 7). Today, EU social policy is no longer the 'stepchild' of European integration. The completion of the internal market and the European Monetary Union made it increasingly difficult to exclude employment and social concerns from the European policy agenda. To be sure, claims with respect to the emancipation of 'social Europe' should not be exaggerated. By and large, the Europeanisation of the employment and social policy agenda is the result of 'spillover' effects arising from the dynamic of single market and monetary integration, as has been suggested by neo-functionalist accounts of the dynamic of European integration. However, it is my firm contention that EU-market spillovers will not bring about, in the foreseeable future, a complete transition of welfare provision from the national political space to that of the EU, turning the Union from a 'special-purpose association' into a 'general-purpose' political federation (Voogsgeerd, Chapter 8 this volume). More likely is the emergence of flexible institutional devices, like the social dialogue, the open method of coordination in employment, pension and poverty policy, complementing rather than replacing entrenched social policy repertoires of now semi-sovereign welfare states embedded in a larger European economic and social policy space.

Any adequate understanding of the state of social Europe, it is my contention, has to be built on the interaction between highly entrenched national welfare regimes and the emergent reality of a deepening and widening EU employment and social policy profile. In this chapter I hope to show how national welfare regimes have over time come to be deeply embedded within a wider EU economic and social policy space. Notwithstanding the increased importance of the EU, the nation state remains the principal site for welfare reform and the cornerstone of European institutions.

Before turning to the historical narrative of the Europeanisation of social policy, this paper starts off (section two) with a theoretical exposition of what I would like to call the 'double bind' of Europe's mature welfare state. It is this joint commitment to domestic social policy intervention and European market integration, which makes it extremely difficult to shift social competencies from the national level to the level of the European Union. Section three deals with the dynamic of social policy Europeanisation resulting from the contingencies of the double bind of social Europe. In sections four and five, I subsequently trace the historical dialectic between path-dependent policy developments at the level of domestic welfare regimes and European economic and social policy initiatives across time, beginning with the period from the Golden Age of self-contained domestic welfare capitalism to the launch of the Single Market Programme. Section six focuses on the 'qualitative turn' of EU employment and social policy making, under the shadow of EMU since the mid-1990s. Recent institutional innovations, I contend, have enabled the member states to strike a balance between the principles of competitiveness and solidarity, based on an explicit recognition of *legitimate diversity*, i.e. respecting differences in policy legacies, institutional arrangements and economic development. The closing section tries to assess the robustness of the EU social policy profile in terms of the institutional complementarities 'hard' community legislation, i.e. enforceable directives and regulation, bi- and tripartite social dialogue, and 'softer' forms of *governance by objectives* open coordination, based on recommendations and guidelines, which together have contributed to a reconfiguration – definitely not the crumbling – of the traditional territorial (welfare) state.

The double bind of Europe's mature welfare states

The development of the European welfare state reached its completion in the post-war decade with the attribution of the social rights. Social citizenship is the key organising principle of mature welfare states. It represents a deeply institutionalised social contract. In the words of T.H. Marshall, social citizenship holds out a promise of the enlargement, enrichment and equalisation of people's 'life chances' (Marshall, 1963: 107). Protecting the vulnerable and preventing the disadvantaged from becoming vulnerable lies at the heart of a European ethos of 'equal social worth'. 'Minimum guaranteed resources' are widely accepted by European publics and deeply entrenched in policy programmes and institutions. The welfare state revolved around three constitutive elements. First, citizenship is about the membership in a nation-state and a 'social contract' between the state and its citizens. Second, it delineates a bundle of universal rights. Third, it refers to a particular collective identity of a political community, within which citizenship rights can be exercised. In other words, social rights not only provide individuals with a sense of material security against the adverse effects of poverty, illness, disability, unemployment and old age in a territorially bound state. In turn, social security encourages a sense of belonging and commitment to a kind of national society within which citizens live.

The welfare state has always had a territorial foundation. Its legitimacy and effectiveness depended heavily on political authority over its citizens and control over economic resources within its territorial jurisdiction for the exercise of social and economic policy. Social rights, defined in substantive terms of need, imply affirmative state action of meeting the needs of the vulnerable. It thus requires state intervention in the economy, both on the demand and on the supply side, from wages to working conditions and from profits to investments, so as to maintain basic social security, but also for reasons of redistribution.

Since the early 1980s the celebration of the welfare state's economic, social and political success has given way to widespread doubts, or even despair over the viability of European welfare states to perform the functions which its citizens had came to expect during the post-war decades. In the wake of the first oil price shock, all the developed welfare states of the EU have been recasting the basic policy mix upon which their national systems of social protection were built after 1945 (Hemerijck and Schludi, 2000). As a result of cumulative changes, the authority of the national welfare state over its own territorial and economics boundaries has been drastically reduced. Especially, the lowering of economic boundaries world-wide has weakened the capacity of the national welfare state for effective social problem solving in an era of intensified economic internationalisation. European economic integration has greatly intensified international competition in the markets for goods and services across Europe. While the Monetary Union has reduced the transaction costs of transnational trade and investment, for national governments presiding over an expensive welfare state, European economic integration has greatly increased the difficulties of managing the national economy, regulating production processes and financing social transfers and public services (Scharpf, 2001).

When social problems can no longer be effectively resolved at national level, it seems logical to look to the European level for a rescue, as Scharpf puts it. But how realistic is it to hope that control over the economy that was lost at the national level could be regained through market-correcting European policies? To be sure, the main motive for the Single Market Programme and the liberalisation of services was to liberate the European Community from 'Eurosclerosis' in the 1970s and 1980s. By the same token, for many Member States the commitment to the Economic and Monetary Union (EMU) appeared as a rescue from shocks their economies had suffered through currency speculation in the late 1980s and early 1990s.

Benign European responses to 'spillover' problems resulting from economic internationalisation cannot be taken for in the areas of social policy making, for both technical and political reasons. First of all, EU Member States not only differ in levels of economic development, also countries at the same level of economic development differ greatly in the levels and the structures of social protection and public service provision, with Ireland spending less than 35 per cent of GDP for social protection and public services and Sweden more than 58 per cent (European Commission, 2002). Moreover, the institutions of the EU which have been principally designed to seek market integration are inadequate and ill-equipped for an expansion of social policy competencies. The transposition of macro-economic regulation from the level of the nation-state to institutions of the EU will not be matched by centralised social policy initiatives. However much domestic reforms are constrained by the Single Market Programme, EMU and the Stability and Growth Pact, the territorial site of welfare reform remains the nation-state. Expanding the reach of 'positive integration' to correct for 'negative integration' of the removal of national barriers to trade and free competition, critically depends on unanimity within the Council of Ministers, which is even less likely to be forthcoming in a Union of 25 or more members with highly variegated social policy repertoires and levels of economic development.

Work and welfare policy issues have since the mid-1990s become ever more intertwined with the Single Market and EMU. In this respect, the EU is no longer a 'single purpose' economic intergovernmental organisation or *Zweckverband*. With integrated markets and a single currency, proper social protection and a healthy labour market is no longer a matter just for national governments. Cross-border interests require policy coordination. The question therefore is not *whether* the EU has to play a role in social and employment policy, decided by some simplistic 'subsidiarity' test, but *how* it can make its most effective and legitimate contribution to the continuous process of (self-)transformation in Europe's mature political economies (Hemerijck, 2002). On the one hand, EU Member States are unlikely to shed their welfare-state obligations, as this would jeopardise the political bases of their legitimacy. On the other hand, EU Member States have, since the late 1970s, become irreversibly committed to a pervasive programme of European economic integration. This double bind confronts national level and EU-level policy makers with a thorny dilemma: common European solutions are desirable, but not feasible on account of national political sensitivities and persistent policy legacies. Moreover, they would surely be ineffective in the face of the immense diversity of social security systems in the EU (Scharpf, 2001: 362). In the face of this double bind, Scharpf argues, EU Member States cannot want to shed their welfare-state function without jeopardising the territorial bases of their political legitimacy, while at the same time they cannot want to reverse the process of economic integration which increasingly exposes their now semi-sovereign welfare states to regulatory competition.

From this pessimistic reading, 'uneven growth' with market-correcting 'positive integration' does not keep up with market-expanding 'negative integration', European integration effectively constrains national sovereignty in the core areas of the welfare state, and thus creates a problem-solving gap (Scharpf, 2001). Stephan Leibfried and Paul Pierson suggest that European integration erodes both

> the sovereignty (by which we mean legal authority) and autonomy (by which we mean de facto capacity) of Member States in the realm of social policy. National welfare states remain the primary institutions of European social policy, but they do so in the context of an increasingly constraining multi-tiered polity.
>
> (Leibfried and Pierson, 1995: 44)

As a result of market integration, the loss of national exchange rate and interest rate policies from EMU and the accompanying budgetary restrictions of the Stability and Growth pact, Member States will increasingly be deprived of their capacity to maintain the kind of protective social citizenship arrangements, as they find themselves in a vicious cycle of deflationary 'beggar-thy-neighbour' strategies of internal devaluation, 'social dumping' and a 'race to the bottom' process of competitive welfare retrenchment. Domestic welfare states are most pressed by the economic pressures of international competition and constrained by the primacy of 'negative' integration over politically salient areas of industrial relations, social security, labour market regulation and redistributive taxation. At the same time, it is in these social and economic policy areas that agreement in the EU is most difficult to reach due to conflicts of interest and of ideological preferences among member governments. Lack of agreement makes it extremely difficult to shift welfare-state responsibilities upward to the European level in an attempt to stave off regulatory competition. Ultimately, through the backdoor, in short, European economic integration will ultimately forge a fully-fledged 'disembedded' neo-liberal European political economy.

I very much question the claim that the primacy of 'negative integration' at the level of the EU will inevitably overrun domestic 'positive integration'. In the dynamic interaction between the EU market-making commitments and domestic social protection arrangements new forms of 'embeddedness' have emerged over the past decades, as a consequence of the 'political', not per se 'functional' spill-over effect of European economic integration. To be sure, European citizens have come to base their life plans on the expectation that certain needs would be provided by their national welfare state. When these expectations are indeed disappointed, as Scharpf correctly intimates, the fundamental 'social citizenship contract' and hence democratic legitimacy of both the national welfare state and the European integration project could be put in jeopardy. With the intensification of economic integration, political elites have come to realise that in order to maintain popular support for the European project, the EU must be able to present itself to its citizens as a credible institution of economic protection, and certainly not as a threat to established social rights (Offe, 2003).

In this contribution I will empirically scrutinise the manner and extent the problem solving gap has been dealt with by national policy makers, introducing new patterns of social and economic policy interaction between the various levels of governance in the enlarging European political economy.

Europeanisation, national welfare regimes and the EU social policy profile

Europeanisation of social policy cannot be understood in terms of a vertical and upward transposition of competencies from the territorial level of the nation-state to functionally bound institutions of the EU, as was the case with the completion of the internal market and EMU. Today national welfare states affect each other as a result of intensified interaction through European economic integration. When national policy makers together agree on supranational economic and social policies, these in turn have a tendency to reconfigure national welfare regimes. Europeanisation in this sense has a double meaning in the sense that Europeanisation reflects, on the one hand, the emergence of distinct EU social policy profile, and a growing awareness of national policy makers of what is happening outside their domestic jurisdictions. This understanding of Europeanisation acknowledges the emergence of European orientations together with the persistence of nationally entrenched welfare regimes, mediated by different interpretations of the shared European social patrimony described above.

For an adequate understanding of the process of Europeanisation of employment and social policy, it is therefore critically important to separate, as suggested by Maurizio Ferrera (2002), two relevant dimensions. In order to bring out the interactive dynamic between very different national welfare systems vis-à-vis ongoing deepening and widening of the EU employment and social policy, we need to set apart, on the one hand (the diversity of) national welfare regimes, and on the other, the characteristic features of the emerging EU employment and social policy profile.

Following Esping-Andersen (1990) and Ferrera *et al.* (2000), three or four distinct types of welfare state are distinguished. But even within each family cluster, there is considerable variability. The comprehensive *Scandinavian welfare states* are characterised by citizenship-based universal entitlements; generous replacement rates in transfer programmes; general revenue financing; a broad supply of social services beyond health and education; active family policy encouraging gender egalitarianism and women's integration in the labour market; low (Denmark) to high (Sweden) levels of employment protection, with a strong emphasis on active policies and training programmes linked to general education; and corporatist industrial relations with peak level bargaining, strong unions and high levels of collective bargaining coverage.

The *Anglo-Saxon welfare cluster* is characterised by a bias towards targeted, needs-based entitlements; low replacement rates in transfer programmes; general revenue financing; underdeveloped public social services beyond health and education; poor family services; low levels of employment protection, largely confined to ensure fair contracts, and no legacy of active labour market policy, nor vocational training and education; uncoordinated industrial relations with moderately strong unions, decentralised wage bargaining and low levels of collective bargaining coverage.

The *Continental European welfare state*, historically influenced by a mix of *etatist*, corporatist and familialist traditions is characterised by occupationally distinct, employment-related social insurance; very unequal levels of generosity in transfer programmes, combining generally very high pension replacement rates; a contribution-biased revenue dependency; very modest levels of public social services beyond health and education and often a considerable reliance on 'third sector' and private delivery; passive family policies premised on the conventional male breadwinner family; generally strict levels of employment protection, meant to protect, once again, the male breadwinner combined with passive labour market policies, but comprehensive systems of vocational education and training, especially in Germany, Austria and the Netherlands; strong social partnerships that extend into the administration of social insurance; and coordinated industrial relations, with a predominance of sectoral wage bargaining, with high levels of bargaining coverage and moderately strong unions.

Finally, the *Southern European welfare family* institutionally resembles the continental welfare states, but provides more chequered and unequal coverage in terms of public services and social insurance, with disproportionately high expenditure on retirement. Holes in the social safety net are patched by family members in countries such as Italy, Greece, Portugal and Spain (Ferrera 1996).

The EU is primarily a community of rights which acts essentially by lawmaking. EU laws apply throughout the territory of the Union. They take precedence over the national laws of the Member States. The competencies of the EU arise from the founding treaties and always relate to a single authorisation as laid down in Article 5(1) EC. As a consequence, EU Member States transfer part of their sovereignty to the European level. The result of this transfer of legal competences has been the development of 'multi-level governance', i.e. co-decision making at different levels: the EU and the Member States, as well as regions and municipalities. Most decisions in primary law are taken by the European Council and the European Parliament, on the basis of proposals put forward by the European Commission. The Council can only act if the Commission sets an agenda with appropriate proposals. Thus a dominant role in the legislative process is delegated to the European Commission. The participatory rights of the European Parliament in the legislative process vary from issue area to issue area, which is separately regulated in the individual chapters of the Treaty. The European Court of Justice (ECJ) has to ensure that the application and interpretation of European Community law is in accordance with Article 220 EC.

The prevailing EU social and employment policy profile consists of four components (Ferrera *et al.*, 2000). First, on the level of *constitutional principles*, Article 2 EC explicitly mentions the promotion of high rates of employment and social protection, equality of men and women, high standards of living for EU inhabitants and social cohesion and solidarity between Member States as tasks of the Union; indeed, as core *normative principles* guiding Community action.

Second, *binding community legislation* (regulations and directives), following the logic of the Community method by which the Commission has the exclusive right of initiative, the Council decides (preferably by qualified majority) with participation of the European Parliament (ideally co-decision), subject to jurisdiction of the ECJ, is now in place in many areas of social policy. The Treaty of Rome's market-compatibility requirement (largely related to the free movement of workers) lies at the heart of an elaborate set of supranational rules and jurisprudence ensuring the transferability across Member States of nationally defined entitlements and promoting the interpenetration of national social security systems. Equal-treatment and gender-opportunities directives – spurred by ECJ case law deriving from them – have consolidated a binding set of rights for men and women across national borders. Various aspects of EU citizenship left their imprint on the Maastricht Treaty in 1992 (TEF Articles 17–22).

Third, a number of *institutional complementarities,* next to the traditional 'community method', have in recent decades emerged to promote Member States cooperation on the politically sensitive aspects of social security and employment policy. The bipartite social dialogue that is now included in the EC Treaty (Article 138 EC), allows the social partners to conclude agreements at the Community level, which may be transformed into (framework) directives. In addition to these relatively 'hard' forms of coordination, many 'softer' forms of cooperation and coordination have recently emerged, including the so-called 'Open Method of Coordination' (OMC) and the looser macroeconomic dialogue known as the Cologne process, bringing together the Council, the Commission, the European Central Bank, and the social partners, together with a representative of the monetary authorities outside the euro zone (1999). The Cologne process is important in order to develop a shared cognitive framework of the emergent EMU macroeconomic policy regime through a dialogue, upon which the social partners can better anticipate the consequences of their strategies of collective action.

Finally, there exists a relatively autonomous *policy network, above and beyond the nation state*, of policy institutions and committees, such as the Social Protection Committee, the Employment Committee, the Economic Policy Committee, the Social Affairs and Labour Council. Many of participants in these four are capable of making alliances with non-governmental actors, such as the European Trade Union Confederation (ETUC) and the European employers organisation (UNICE) in shaping European policy developments (Falkner, 1998; Ferrera et al., 2000; De la Porte and Pochet 2001).

Social Europe in historical perspective

Over the past 50 years, at various stages of the process of European integration, depending on prevailing social and economic conditions, policy actors at various levels of decision making have tried to launch domestic level and EU-level employment and social policy intervention. Moments of fundamental political change, often associated with consecutive waves of enlargement of the EU, provided important windows of opportunity for policy redirection towards further Europeanisation but also, at times, tendencies towards (re)nationalisation. A case in point is the extent to which EMU convergence criteria, a clear example of Europeanisation, acted as a catalyst in the resurgence of national 'social pacts' in the 1990s. Economic conditions, political ambitions, enlargement dynamics, in interaction with the path-dependent imprint of national social policy legacies, thus channel and shape the idiosyncratic institutionalisation of social Europe in the enlarging EU. The interactive dynamic between national welfare arrangements with European social policy constraints and ambitions, in the second half of the twentieth century, can generally be divided into four periods: (i) economic modernisation and expansion of the national welfare state (1950–1973); (ii) social conflict and national crisis management (1974–1983); (iii) economic internationalisation and market integration (1984–1994); and, finally, (iv) matching common concerns with legitimate diversity (1995–2003) (Asbeek Brusse and Hemerijck, 2002). With each wave of enlargement, the institutional diversity of social Europe increased. In this section, we concentrate on the first three periods; in the next section we focus more explicitly on the recent period since the Amsterdam Treaty.

Economic modernisation and the expansion of the national welfare state

During the time of *economic modernisation and expansion of the national welfare state* (1950–1973), the foundations were laid for new ground rules of national unity, economic order, collective action and social citizenship for a large number of Western European countries. In the wake of the reconstruction boom, post-war democratic governments in Western Europe strove for economic growth, full employment (especially for men), and a higher level of social security, health care and education through the implementation of an active and interventionist socio-economic policy. By and large, we observe an expansion of the welfare state from targeted policies for the poor and the needy towards more universal schemes. Moderate forces within the trade unions and business organisations supported the welfare state and the Keynesian mixed economic order, which offered the prospect of a positive spiral of full employment, high wages, rising demand, increased productivity and, finally, a higher standard of living (including social protection) for everyone (Hall, 2001).

The ambitious social policy laid out in the Treaty of Rome was the product of post-war optimism and the 'historical compromise' between the moderate representatives of labour and capital. The preamble of the EC Treaty established economic and social advance and the continual improvement of lives and labour environments as essential goals of the EC (Barnard, 2000: 6). Still, national policy makers, with the exception of the French, believed that European social authorities should be limited to establishing only the basic conditions of free movement of labour and harmonisation of social security rights. The fact that, despite this, the treaty referred to 'closer collaboration between Member States' in the areas of education, employment, labour conditions, labour relations and social security can be explained by the Franco-German compromise that occurred at the last minute during the Treaty negotiations when the French proposal for increased harmonisation of social legislation and regulation encountered resistance from Germany, Italy and the Benelux countries (Hantrais, 2000: 2–3). However, the road towards harmonisation was not cut off by this setback. On the contrary, considering that the first Member States, with the exception of Italy, belonged to the group of 'continental' welfare states, a process of 'spontaneous' convergence as a pendant of economic advance was not considered unthinkable. In this period, it was expected that national welfare states would tend towards uniform, qualitatively high standards of social protection in the long run. At a later stage, positive spillover effects of this partial convergence could still lead to further harmonisation. The belief was that, whatever happened, it would be a 'race to the top' rather than a 'race to the bottom'.

With the Treaty of Rome, the 'European Social Fund' (ESF) was established (Articles, 123–128), whose importance increased with successive rounds of enlargement. Its goal was to simplify the employment of workers, to increase their geographical and occupational mobility within the Community, and to facilitate their adaptation to change, particularly vocational training and retraining. Today, ESF expenditures cover 9 per cent of the EU budget.

In the course of the 1960s European businessmen began to want to develop a level playing field in the social domain within a free internal market. This wish was an important driving force behind the Commission's agendas concerning health and safety in the workplace. With reference to the authority of the Community, as far as working conditions were concerned the Treaty of Rome did little more than require the Member States to promote these aims (Article 117 EC). The Commission was given the task of coordinating the Member States' activities in the social sphere, including working conditions (Articles 51 and 118 EG). Gender equality in wages and workers' freedom of movement was laid down in the Treaty (Articles 119 and 48–50 EC, respectively – Leibfried and Pierson, 2000: 274; Barnard, 2000: 1–3). This implied the abolition of discrimination of workers with respect to employment, remuneration and working conditions. Another crucial item of legislation from this period was Regulation 1408/71. In the Treaty of Rome, it had already been determined in Article 42 that, after the completion of the customs union, the free movement of employees had to be realised. Regulation 1408/71 established the social security rights of migrant workers. Through this regulation, national governments lost a degree of control over 'their' working citizens, so that ever since we can speak of 'semi-sovereign welfare states' (Leibfried and Pierson, 2000).

Social conflict and national crisis management

After 1974, European social integration progressed more slowly. The Member States of the European Community were afflicted by the worst economic crisis since the 1930s. They entered a new phase of *social conflict and national crisis management* (1974–1983), partly because of the continuing high wage demands of the strong national unions. Waves of international recessions led to divergent national responses, in which each member state of the EC pursued its own crisis management policy. The naïve expectations of spontaneous social convergence within the EU, supported by intensified policy coordination, dissipated rapidly.

Regardless of the striking renationalisation of social and economic policy, the Commission creatively used its limited power to promote the social dimension of the labour sphere. Based on the general fundamentals of harmonisation contained in Article 100a EC (now Article 94 EC) several guidelines were agreed upon which pertain to conditions in the workplace. When the governments of the Six decided to put the Werner plan (1970) for monetary union on the agenda against a background of economic decline and industrial conflict in a number of Member States, a window of opportunity presented itself. Starting that year, the Commission launched a series of Social Action Programmes, which served as a launch pad for a boom in their legislative initiatives.

Eventually the aim of harmonisation encountered the strong opposition of three Member States which joined in 1973: the United Kingdom, the Republic of Ireland and Denmark. Because their welfare traditions and institutions differed fundamentally from the dominant continental model, Danish and British policy makers in particular rapidly became outspoken opponents of every form of European legislation that could be seen as detrimental to national autonomy in social policy (Hantrais, 2000: 24). The creativity of the Commission and the Court in the development of the social *acquis* was continuously challenged because of this resistance to further deepening of the Union in the 1970s and 1980s.

Economic internationalisation and the deepening of market integration

Despite economic recovery in the second half of the 1980s, unemployment remained high in most European countries. Many abandoned the neo-corporatist experiments that initially had seemed so effective. One exception to this is the Netherlands, where the Accord of Wassenaar of 1982 ushered in a new period of 'responsive corporatism' (Visser and Hemerijck, 1997). Most continental welfare states combated unemployment in part by lowering the effective retirement age and tolerating an increase in the number of people on temporary and permanent sick leave (Ebbinghaus, 2000).

In the political arena, it is significant that at this time European electorates turned their backs on social democracy to join the supply-side-focused neo-liberal solutions of deregulation and privatisation. The position of trade unions was weakened by processes of de-industrialisation, rapid technological advance, and expansion of the service sector. Keynesian economic policy made way for a more stringent macroeconomic variant, focusing on fiscal stability and hard cash. The ability to influence employment hereby shifted from macroeconomic policy to the adjoining domains of wage, social security and labour market policy. In the sphere of labour relations, a re-orientation took place towards market-conforming wage moderation.

At the EU level, this dynamic period of *economic internationalisation and the deepening of market integration* (1983–1995) found its rejoinder in the launch of the '1992 programme', intended to complete market integration. The completion of the internal market was very much a project of internal economic development and external economic assertiveness with regard to the flourishing Japanese and American economies and decisively not a programme of internal social intervention. The Single European Act of 1986 was based on a political consensus over the twin principles of *subsidiarity* and *proportionality*, stipulating that Community action should only take place where it is necessary or more effective than action at the level of the Member States; and Community action should be as limited as possible and leave as much flexibility as possible. The internal market, which however is far from complete, was made possible not only by QMV but also by the move away from detailed European harmonisation through *mutual recognition* and *framework directive* approaches, such as in areas of health and safety at work, leaving detailed technical specifications to standardisation bodies.

With the EU entry of Greece (1981) and of Portugal and Spain (1986), the Southern European welfare state made its debut in the political arena of the EU, although (southern) Italy already represented this category to some extent. Divergence was facilitated partially because the Member States were able to implement guidelines in very different ways and because the EC could exert little control over whether directives were upheld. In the more developed economies of Northwestern Europe, this led not only to fear of possible objections to decisions regarding new initiatives, but also to a fear of social dumping. The perception was that unequal levels of social protection and the very different traditions among the Member States could make social rights detrimental to competitiveness. Countries with higher standards of social protection would be at a great financial disadvantage compared to those with lower standards. Generous welfare states unable to respond adequately to the extremes of policy and tax competition would have to pay a high price in terms of economic stagnation and unemployment.

The expectation of social dumping was never fulfilled. In the first place, social costs turned out to be only one of many factors considered by enterprises making investment decisions, in addition to productivity, education and training, innovative potential, infrastructure, business climate and labour relations stability. Second, the proclivity of Southern European Member States to engage in a 'race to the bottom' was mitigated by EU cohesion policy as a kind of quid pro quo. The relatively easy expansion of the cohesion policy, compared with the small steps made in the areas of labour market regulation, labour relations and social security, can be partly explained by the fact that the cohesion fund, although costly for those making net payments, did not threaten the policy autonomy of the generous welfare states.

When the Single Market came into force in 1987, national welfare policy, in essence, became subject to the principles of free competition. The Single European Act reflects a confirmation of national as opposed to European responsibility for social policy. One important exception was made for minimum harmonisation concerning health and safety of workers as an escape route out of the unanimity agreement, so as to prevent 'unfair' competition (Article 118a). For the first time in European social policy, it allowed directives to be agreed on the basis of qualified majority voting in the Council. In the wake of the completion of the single market, there were proposals with respect to the unification of social protection in a single European system, through the introduction of an additional shared thirteenth (and what would now be a sixteenth) state system. Yet actual measures were very limited: the two 1992 texts on minimum protection and social protection, respectively, were given merely the status of Council Recommendations, and, as such, remained at the 'softest' end of the legal spectrum (Council, 1992a, 1992b). The Council Recommendation 92/244/EEC of July 1992 on the convergence of objectives and policies in social protection aimed at promoting convergence between the social protection policies of the Member States in order to reduce differences in social protection levels which might inhibit the free movement of persons and to prevent any type of mutual undercutting between the systems of social protection of the Member States.

Near the end of the 1980s, it became increasingly clear that accommodating so many policy traditions, systems of finance and enforcement and decision-making styles was no longer feasible on a European basis. This stimulated the development of more innovative, flexible institutional solutions in the 1990s. Ultimately, it was not the competition between the policies of the Southern European and the Continental and Scandinavian welfare states, but the political confrontation between the European Commission and the United Kingdom (with other 'unwilling' countries in its wake) that forced the issue of the necessity of institutional flexibility in the EU.

Matching social dialogue and legitimate diversity

During the negotiations for the Intergovernmental Conference (IGC) preceding the Treaty of Maastricht, attempts to include the objectives of this Charter as Article 117 in the text of the Treaty failed because of the British veto (Cullen and Campbell, 1998: 264). The final result of the negotiations was a separate binding Protocol for each of the eleven Member States concerning social policy ('the Protocol on Social Policy') relating to work environments and a unanimous vote concerning the development of working conditions and social security (Brinkmann, 1998: 239; Hantrais, 2000: 27). With this compromise over the closer coordination of eleven countries, acceptable to all twelve Member States, it was possible for the group of eleven to impose guidelines concerning labour conditions, consultation of employees, and equal opportunities for men and women by a qualified majority. This constituted a remarkable extension of the competencies of the EU into a wide range of policy issues. Market-correcting interventions remained however dependent on unanimity within the Council. In a sense, the British opt-out marked the first step towards greater differentiation in European social policy development.

A second institutional innovation that sprang from the Social Protocol pertains to the formalisation of the European social dialogue between the social partners at the community level. The idea of anchoring the Social Dialogue date back to the 1985 'Val Duchesse' initiative of Jacques Delors to promote industrial relations at the European level, in which the Union of Industries of the European Communities (UNICE), the European Centre of Public Enterprises (CEEP), and the European Trade Union Confederation (ETUC) participate as representatives of the social partners. The Social Protocol allows the European social partners to sign collective agreements. Through decisions of the Council, these agreements are capable of attaining the status of fundamental guidelines, with minimum standards that permit much freedom of policy at the national and sectoral levels (Brinkmann, 1998: 241–242). According to Article 4 of the Protocol, it is also possible to assign the social partners, at their own request, the task of implementing specific guidelines. Ultimately the social dialogue was introduced into the body of the Treaty (new Articles 138 and 139) of Amsterdam in 1997, stating that 'The Commission shall have the task of promoting consultation of management and labour at Community level and shall take any relevant measure to facilitate their dialogue by ensuring balanced support for the parties.' This new status of the social partners is an example of 'horizontal flexibility'.

The results of the social dialogue (inter-sectoral or sectoral) have not entirely lived up to expectations. Since Maastricht, the social dialogue, an example of horizontal subsidiarity, has led to only four relative meagre accords on parental leave (1995), part-time work (1997), fixed-term work (1999), and more recently telework (2002). With respect to the latter, the European social partners chose, for the first time in the case of an inter-sectoral agreement, to implement the 2002 Framework agreement on telework by the 'voluntary route', rather than through a Council directive, backed by legal force. Also, the Work Programme of the European Social Partners for 2003–2005, presented in November 2002, revealed a preference to develop 'a more autonomous social dialogue', indicating a desire to come out from under the shadow of Community legislation. With the encouragement of the Commission, at the sectoral level some 27 sectoral social dialogue committees have been established. Despite a lack of distinct progress in reaching a better balance between social protection objectives and economic policy considerations in the EU, the Social Dialogue, established in Articles 138 and 139 of the new Treaty, provide an important institutional infrastructure for tripartite co-regulation and bipartite self-regulation as central features of the institutional architecture of social Europe. The framework agreements reached in the EU social dialogue which are transformed into EC directives, are explicitly regarded by the social partners as contributing to social Europe. A pressing political problem that remains is how far the Social Dialogue between non-state representatives of management and labour, consulted by the Commission, is acceptable in terms of democratic legitimacy, since neither European Parliament nor national parliaments have any formal role.

The launch of the EMU prompted new forms of *policy coordination* aimed at convergence of national policy towards common objectives on the basis of non-binding multilateral surveillance. This began with the Broad Economic Policy Guidelines (BEPGs), but soon this method of more open policy coordination spread to key areas of social and employment policy. In the wake of the Maastricht Treaty, at first, the prospects for ambitious EU social policy initiatives were bleak. In their critical assessment of the evolution of EU social policy, Stephan Leibfried and Paul Pierson observed an overriding bias towards market-making, rather than market-correcting policy interventions, endorsed by ECJ ruling, and at the level EU decision making a propensity towards political immobilism and 'joint-decision traps' (Scharpf, 1988). The overall reluctance of the Member States to take social policy measures at the EU level resulted in the paradox whereby the Member States, by asserting their sovereignty, were unwittingly losing their autonomy in social policy (Leibfried and Pierson, 2000). The principle obstacle for effective European employment and social policy undoubtedly was the requirement of unanimous consent over social policy harmonisation. Members States continued to suffer from regulatory 'beggar-thy-neighbour' competition because, at the level of European decision making, they are unable to agree on common European rules. This is most clearly visible when social policy practice clashes with economic, single market objectives that have been brought to the ECJ. The Kohll and Decker, and more recently the Smits-Peerbooms and Vanbraekel rulings were an example of how EU economic legislation on free competition might overrule national social legislation.

From the second half of the 1990s we are, however, witnessing a *quality leap* in EU employment and social policy initiatives, trampling the received wisdom of market-making supremacy over market-correcting policy concerns, ECJ-bias towards negative integration, and political immobilism at the level of EU decision making. The pace of change in European employment policy clearly rebuts the bias towards policy immobilism at the level of the EU (see below). Moreover, recent rulings of the European Court of Justice, i.e. the Brentjens and Albany cases, reveal that principles of national solidarity have become recognised as one of the basic objectives of the EU. This juridical recognition might open the way for more socially inspired case law and, indirectly, for political pressure on the Commission at large and the Council to agree on a political recognition of the principle of national solidarity to protect domestic welfare policies. With respect to gender equality, the European Court of Justice, had already been a central actor as it endorsed a broad interpretation of Article 119 on domestic measures to ensure equal pay, equal treatment, also with regard to social security. In short, we are recently observing a qualitative shift towards taking market-correction policy interventions more seriously. So as to capture the essence of the qualitative shift in social Europe since the mid-1990s, we prefer to phrase the most recent period in terms of 'common concerns and legitimate diversity' (1994–2002).

Central to political controversy over EU employment and social policy in the 1990s was the question to what extent EMU would forge national welfare state and labour market regimes to make way for a fully-fledged neo-liberal policy shift, with the negative effect of eroding the basic foundations of Europe's social policy patrimony, triggering a vicious cycle of deflationary 'beggar-thy-neighbour' strategies of internal devaluation through competitive welfare retrenchment. Many critics feared that the scope for autonomous national welfare policies would increasingly be limited by the loss of national exchange rate and interest rate policies and the budgetary restrictions resulting from participation in EMU. To be sure, with a common monetary policy and the loss of exchange rate flexibility, the burden on adjustment will be shifted onto labour markets and welfare regimes. Moreover, the agreement of the Stability and Growth Pact (SGP) implies that fiscal policy can only play a limited role, as the 3 per cent deficit limit obliges governments to cut social security expenditure during an economic downturn. In addition, free mobility of goods, capital and labour in the internal market has made it easier for economic actors to avoid legal restriction, undermining the tax base necessary to finance national welfare states (Begg, 2002). To many observers, the British opt-out, the limited results of the European social dialogue, and the anchoring of the *subsidiarity* principle in the Maastricht Treaty, already revealed a clear tendency towards 'uneven growth' between the EU's economic and social policies: market-correcting 'positive integration' could not keep up with market-expanding 'negative integration' (Scharpf, 1999; 2002).

At the time of the European Council in Amsterdam, June 1997, no fewer than 13 out of 15 Member States had social-democratic or socialist governments, giving the Europeanisation of social policy a vital impulse. With so many social-democratic parties back in government in the late 1990s, the central question was what the EU could do by way of shelter for national welfare states, given that European solutions could not be adopted for both technical and political reasons (Scharpf, 2002)? While they recognised the need for a flexible approach to social problems (particularly high unemployment, exceeding 10 per cent in 1993), they also knew that, at both the national and the European level, room for uniform strategies was foreclosed. Moreover, effective implementation of Community legislation was seen to demand new forms of implementation, as Community policy increasingly touched on sensitive social policy issues (Best, 2003). At Maastricht, the doubling of resources for the structural funds was already accompanied by new forms of partnership with sub-state and private stakeholders. Technically, one-size-fits-all solutions were considered both ineffective and unnecessary in the face of the immense diversity of national system design and their respective regime-specific social policy problems. Politically, unpopular European solutions violating strongly held preferences of national electorates, were impossible to uphold in national political arenas. EU employment and social policy had to come to terms with the increasing diversity and political sensitivities of welfare provisions in an enlarging Union. As a response to this dilemma a policy approach was adopted which left decision making largely with the Member States, but gave greater weight to EU institutions in goal setting, benchmarking, monitoring and policy coordination. By explicitly recognising the legitimate diversity of national welfare states at the European level, new ways of coordinating national reform trajectories based on broadly formulated common social goals were ventured, following the logic of the BEPGs surveillance procedure. The verdict is still out whether these recent innovations of open coordination do stimulate Member States jointly to mitigate 'negative' integration, through enhanced social and economic policy coordination, while making room for differentiated 'positive' integration, by way of effective joint policy learning (WRR, 2003)?

Regime specific responses

Since the 1990s, employment and welfare policy reform is high on the agenda in most EU Member States. Ironically, EMU provided a significant incentive for the conclusion of social pacts in Ireland, Italy, Finland, Austria, Portugal and Spain, policy initiatives which indicate a tendency towards the 'renationalisation' of the linkage between industrial relations and domestic social policy reform vis-à-vis European macroeconomic policy constraints. From the outset, the introduction of the single currency amplified pressures to reform national welfare states, even for those Member States not initially participating but secondarily tied to a hard currency policy (United Kingdom, Sweden and Denmark). Through participation in EMU, national governments were confronted with the need to reduce debt and budget deficits; at the same time, they faced the medium-term burden of rapidly ageing populations and changing family patterns. The large-scale endorsement of early retirement and other forms of paid inactivity was therefore seen as increasingly destabilising. This is why access to social security was made more selective, social rights increasingly took on a conditional character, and social payments were reduced. Finally, the financial and institutional composition of national welfare states was reformed. Despite EMU pressure for policy convergence and other more endogenous challenges, ranging from the rise of a service economy, and population ageing, policy responses still diverged widely among the four European welfare-state types (Hemerijck and Schludi, 2000).

Continental welfare states found it very difficult to create employment opportunities in the last 20 years in the public or private service sectors (the Netherlands is a positive exception). High gross labour costs combined with the relatively low participation of (married) women and the elderly in the labour force hinder job growth in the private sector and encourage early retirement in a number of different forms. Employment in the public sector is inhibited by the heavy burden placed on welfare state financing by the large group of the inactive. The level and duration of payments are tied to a person's working history and family circumstances. They are also largely financed through premiums and payments from employers and employees. This results in a downward spiral of low productivity, wages and labour inactivity (Esping-Andersen, 1999).

In the *Anglo-Saxon welfare states* the reforms of the last few decades have gone hand in hand with steady growth in the quantity of poorly paid jobs and an enormous increase in income inequality, labour market segmentation and relative poverty. Selective access to social insurance has resulted in an upsurge of private social insurance (especially pensions). Because of the low level of payments to the unemployed, the sick and the elderly, fiscal maintenance problems are limited, despite the relatively low tax rates, labour participation rates are relatively high. The UK in particular, however, lacks adequate childcare for women who (often involuntarily) accept low-paying part-time jobs. The incomes of poorly paid employees and their families are supplemented through wage subsidies (Clasen, 2001). In relatively traditional, Roman Catholic Ireland, this sort of social problem is less acute.

The *Scandinavian model* is confronted by growing fiscal problems due to high capital mobility, budget limitations resulting from monetary union, and political opposition to high tax rates. At the same time – and in contrast to Scandinavian ambitions towards egalitarianism – employment in the private, low-wage service sector is growing. Stubborn pursuit of equality of incomes in combination with strict budget discipline leads to more unemployment. A unique feature of the Scandinavian welfare state is the role of the government as an employer in the labour intensive service sector for families with young children, the handicapped and the elderly: the service-intensive Scandinavian welfare state creates employment opportunities not only for well-educated professionals, but also for the less educated.

Finally, in *Southern Europe* the continental 'inactivity trap' is intensified by strict labour market regulation, as a consequence of which there is a growing gap between job market 'insiders' and 'outsiders', resulting in the social exclusion of the young and women (especially young women with children (Ferrera and Hemerijck, 2003)). Women have few opportunities to combine a career with home care. This explains the low birth rate in Southern Europe and the high financial burden of retirement pensions. More than elsewhere in Europe, the southern welfare state is still based on the traditional 'breadwinner model', with the black market serving as an important additional source of income for family networks.

Thus, similar challenges (such as service sector growth, falling demand for unskilled labour and population ageing) facing existing welfare state models are producing quite different employment and other social policy problems. No single best remedies were available: only welfare regime-specific endeavours, based on national policy legacies, seemed to be adequate. This underscores the continuing importance of national political and socio-economic institutions, in spite of – or perhaps because of – the EU's increasingly prominent role in macroeconomic and social policy. The emphasis on variation in regime specific problems and policy responses should not however distract us from convergent policy thinking across Europe.

Joint problem solving through mutual learning

At the Amsterdam Summit, a renewed European social policy agenda emerged, based on the principle of respect for the integrity and divergence of national systems. The European Council unanimously supported the creation of a separate chapter on employment in the Treaty (Articles 125–130 EG [formerly Article 109n–109s]). In addition, the UK, under 'New Labour', signed the Social Protocol (Articles 136–143 EG [formerly Articles 117–120]), which made it an integral part of the EC Treaty. The adapted social chapter introduced co-decision-making authority for the European Parliament, decision making by a qualified majority in the Council, explicit reference to fundamental social rights and a new provision for the development of social inclusion programmes.

Equally critical to the new EU social policy profile has been the change in tune of the ECJ in recent rulings. In a number of cases the Court has upheld national social regulation against the principles of market integration at the EU level. This has led the Court to develop the 'principle of national solidarity' as a legitimate exemption from competition law (Barnard, 2000). This principle when applied indicates a certain primacy of social protection over market integration. In the Albany case, dealing with compulsory affiliation in a Dutch pension scheme, the Court ruled:

> It follows that the social security schemes, as described, are based on a system of compulsory contribution (...) Organisations involved in the management of the public social security system fulfil an exclusively social function. That activity is based on the principle of national solidarity and is entirely non-profit-making. Accordingly, that activity is not an economic activity.

Apparently, the ECJ ruled that the EU could not turn a blind eye to the social problems competition law created for national welfare states. The ECJ, as a court of last resort, has in its rulings concerning social and the internal market, often shied away from endorsing the legalistic primacy of 'negative integration' in this politically sensitive area, where this was in theory possible.

There has also been progress with respect to the sensitive issue of taxation, crucial for welfare financing. With the introduction of EMU, it was feared that tax competition will intensify, leading to an under-provision of public goods (Genschel, 2001). In order to attract and preserve capital, countries will feel pressed to provide advantageous taxation and/or regulation for internationally mobile firms. Other countries will follow suit, which in the end will cause a lower level of taxation and regulation than was previously found appropriate. Such developments would in the long run severely jeopardise current systems of social protection (Tanzi, 1998). Although the empirical evidence suggests that tax competition has so far been limited, there has been a fierce debate on mitigating 'harmful' tax competition at the level of the EU for more than a decade. Ultimately, in November 2000 the European governments were able to reach an agreement on a future directive concerning minimum taxation of interest (13555/00/EC). In June 2003, the directive on 'taxation of savings incomes in the form of interest payments' was adopted. The directive not only paved the way for the introduction of a withholding tax in Austria, Belgium and Luxembourg so as to curtail unfair taxation practices in these countries, it may well have triggered further positive spillovers in the direction of better coordination of taxation within the EU.

The introduction of a separate employment chapter in the Treaty of Amsterdam has to be understood not so much as a 'functional' spillover, but as an effect of 'political' spillover of EMU (van der Meer and van Riel, 2002). It was forcefully championed by the European Commission and most centre-left governments. Through their combined efforts to tackle unemployment, these governments, in terms of policy content, wanted to show that Europe was about more than just 'a market and money', and that its social dimension is also important to the average European citizen. In a political sense, this employment policy can therefore be seen as a 'correction' of Maastricht. In both institutional respects, the European Economic Space (EES) concerns a coordination process, based on a management by objectives approach with respect to national employment and social policy traditions, which have since come to serve as an example of governance in other areas of European policy making.

Although the EES is clearly associated with the 'social democratic moment' in the EU in the second half of the 1990s, its origins date back to Jacques Delors' *White Book of Growth, Competitiveness and Employment* from 1993 and the Essen strategy of 1994. The EES was accepted on condition that no national authority would be transferred to Brussels, there would be no extra cost, and EMU rules would be fully respected. The EES consists of four priority pillars: employability, entrepreneurship, adaptability and equal opportunities, in a manner consistent with the BEPGs. The aim of the EES is to raise employment participation throughout the EU, allowing for different national strategies to contribute to this aim. All this through a procedure of 'learning by monitoring', bent on strengthening, activating and informing national reform debates and strategies through peer review without binding objectives. Every Member State agreed to develop an annual National Action Plan (NAP) for employment to translate the common guidelines into clear-cut national policy measures, supplemented by – often multi-annual – policy goals. There is also an annual multilateral inspection procedure, in which Member States evaluate each other's NAPs (*peer review* – see Article 128 EG). The social partners on the national and European levels are involved in developing plans to improve employment on their respective levels. The Commission plays a facilitating role by defining indicators, exchanging information and producing comparative analyses. The (Social) Council can make recommendations to Member States based on qualified majority voting and at the proposal of the Commission, but it cannot impose sanctions. The Council can also adjust EES pillars and guidelines on the basis of the insight and suggestions of the Commission. These guidelines have increasingly been made more specific: at the Lisbon Summit, agreement was reached on an overall employment level of 70 per cent (60 per cent for women) by 2010. In Stockholm, the EES was further strengthened by the setting of interim objectives and the introduction of a target employment rate of 50 per cent among older employees (55–64 years of age) in 2010 (Goetschy, 2003). In 2003, the employment guidelines were revised. They now aim at the three overarching and interrelated objectives of full employment, quality and productivity at work, and social cohesion and inclusion.

Based on evaluations of the EES we are able to draw a few tentative conclusions with respect to the effectiveness of the strategy (cf. Best and Bossaert, 2002; Zeitlin, 2003). In general, employment ambitions are now loftier. Much more attention is paid to activation, and there is a strong focus on increasing labour participation and better adjustment between work and household responsibilities in young families. Especially noticeable in practice are processes of institutional re-evaluation under which better horizontal harmonisation between the previously separate areas of labour market policy and social protection, and better vertical coordination between different political and administrative layers, are supported by more flexible labour supply. The effects of this development, however, are difficult to trace back to the EES, since in many countries this policy orientation was already in place before the advent of this strategy (for the Netherlands, see Visser and Hemerijck, 1997). Nonetheless, there is ample evidence of increased *policy direction*, with employment objectives now firmly anchored as a central goal of the Union, *policy coherence* between different policy areas at the national level, together with more *policy coordination* between the Member States, and more *policy integration* between national and EU policies. The Luxembourg process seems to have contributed to the establishment of a *learning network* beyond the borders of national welfare states. EES not only expanded the scope for countries to learn from each other, the benchmarking process was also exploited to reveal weaknesses and thus enhanced the potential for better policy delivery. In addition, EES seems to have contributed to improved *social and economic policy coordination* within the EU. Nonetheless, it remains difficult to identify concrete best practices in labour market and social security instrument and tax policies. Finally, with respect to legitimacy concerns, the 'openness' of EES should be questioned. EES has thus far lacked transparency as technocratic evaluations have primarily involved high-level policy elites and EU bureaucrats, devoid of democratic legitimacy. It enhanced the political importance of the European Council, at the expense the European parliament, national parliaments and the ECJ. Most countries have tried to involve the social partners in formulating the NAPs. However, this has often failed because of lack of time and bureaucratic rigidities.

Since the first employment experiments began in Luxembourg, OMC has quickly spread to other social policy areas. It is now used, for example, in social exclusion (Lisbon 2000), the modernisation of pension provisions

(Gothenburg and Laeken 2001) and the implementation of framework directives on lifelong education and teleworking. The European Council at Lisbon on 23 and 24 March 2000 formally recognised OMC as a legitimate form of European governance. OMC exemplifies, as Jelle Visser and myself put it, a 'contextualised' method of benchmarking, allowing consultation over guidelines and national action plans, with ongoing feedback on implementation (Hemerijck and Visser, 2003). This in sharp contrast to one-size-fits-all 'decontextualized' benchmarks that often characterises OECD and IMF recommendations. OMC facilitates policy progress in areas where EU competencies are relatively weak, where regulation is infeasible and impracticable. Open coordination has the potential to develop into a valuable addition to the modes of governing now available in the European polity. It is imminently more flexible than 'joint decision procedures' or 'inter-governmental negotiations'. Moreover, in contrast to 'mutual adjustment, it can provide useful safeguards against an unintended 'race to the bottom' (Scharpf, 2000). Successes achieved through OMC are likely to enhance the legitimacy of the EU as a social union, which in turn would allow policy makers to translate the much discussed but underspecified 'European social model' into a set of agreed policy objectives. This procedure potentially goes well beyond the 'usual solemn but vague declarations at European Summits' (Vandenbroucke, 2002).

Nonetheless, OMC is fragile in the sense that it is highly contingent on the extent to which national policy makers see themselves as pursuing convergent or parallel goals. Some also fear that 'soft' policy coordination, with its lack of real sanctions, will crowd out 'hard' legislation. Moreover, rushing towards social benchmarking with reference to vague objectives runs the risk of discrediting the entire process. In the absence of sanctions or rewards, the attempt to coordinate social objectives may prove futile. More important, national parliamentarians and policy makers know little about what happens behind the scenes of OMC processes, principally because they seldom discuss European issues in any serious manner. This lack of anchoring of the EES in national political debate, makes it a rather precarious *convergence of objectives* cum *governance by objectives* approach, critically dependent on the willingness of national policy makers to learn from each other and voluntarily coordinate and adapt their policies rather than to sabotage the process by free riding. Nevertheless, with the shift to the conservative right in recent years, employment ambitions were not watered down. A final concern is how much diversity in welfare design, institutional structure and problem loads OMC can tolerate. This issue may become acute with the accession of many Central and Eastern European countries.

The institutional complementarities of social Europe

European social policy integration has come a long way since six Continental welfare states set out to establish a common market. The development of EC social legislation has increased since the late 1950s, with the 1990s being the most active period. With each wave of enlargement, EU employment and social policy initiatives have had to come to terms with the increasing diversity of national welfare states. Although social policy is deeply entrenched in national politics, the social dimension of the EU no longer merely holds a 'Cinderella status' of good intentions (job growth, social dialogue), high principles (improving living standards, working conditions, solidarity and adequate social protection), but little action. However, EC social policy largely remains regulatory in the areas of working conditions; gender equality; health and safety in the workplace. The fundamental economic freedoms entrenched in the Treaty Establishing the European (Economic) Community and European Economic Policies were meant to liberalise markets and to deregulate state intervention in the economy. This surely constrained the autonomy of national governments in macro-economic policy. In addition, European economic integration has reduced the range of Member States' interventionist instruments and limited the spending powers for social policy by demanding strict adherence to the criteria of the Stability pact.

Social Europe is not based on legally enforceable social rights. In comparison to national welfare states, (re-)distributive powers, beyond the Common Agricultural Policy and the Structural Funds, will take a back seat in the foreseeable future. EU employment and social policy will continue to focus on 'regulatory policy'. While social objectives have become more important, especially during the 1990s, they have taken second place behind the pursuit of economic integration. Throughout the course of the past half century, a number of shared orientations have become institutionalised across Europe. These are, in the first place, the recognition of social justice as a policy objective; second, the acceptance of the productive role of social policy and its contribution to economic efficiency; and third, the preference for comprehensive bargaining between the social partners and public authorities over broad issues of social and economic policy.

In retrospect, we are able to observe a distinctive evolutionary process in the Europeanisation of social policy. In the wake of the Treaty of Rome, the failure to achieve agreement over the harmonisation of social insurance schemes among the original six Member States, the majority of social policy initiatives were related to the single market. The legal sovereignty of the EU Member States was restricted with respect to equal treatment of men and women in terms of pay, working conditions and health and safety at work. The Treaty of Rome reflects a confirmation of national as opposed to European responsibility for social policy. The coordination of social security systems for migrant workers was an exception to this rule. The Single European Act extended the European Community's authority to issue regulation to improve the 'working environment', granting the Council to issue minimum requirements for the protection of safety and health at work. Most important, the Single European Act introduced qualified majority voting under the cooperation procedure laid down in the old Article 189c EC Treaty. After the implementation of the Single European Act, it was felt imperative to legitimise the integration process in terms of social policy considerations. This led to new initiatives with respect to minimal standards against the prospect social dumping. Following these considerations, the Social Charter was adopted in 1989. The Charter, despite being a non-legally binding declaration, represented a considerable step in a new direction. The Treaty of the European Union (TEU) and especially its Protocol are the basic landmarks of this period. The Agreement on social policy based on the Protocol on Social Policy and concluded within the realm of the TEU at Maastricht, brought about further extension of EC competences in the social field in so far as the Council was given the right to decide on minimum norms for social policy. Moreover, since Maastricht the European social partners have become more actively involved in EU policy making. The organised interests of labour and industry are now free to agree collectively on social standards that can later be turned into binding Council directives. Wage setting and collective bargaining were, however, exempt from this regulatory competence. Agreement was reached over a rather weak commitment on the part of the Member States to seek convergence on social protection objectives (recommendation 92/442/EEC), in an attempt to bolster the legitimacy of social policy ambitions: from the goal of harmonisation to convergence (1992). The White Book of the Commission (1993) for the first time officially defined the 'European social model' as a combination of economic performance and social solidarity, based on the social partners and tripartite bargaining. Proposals for solutions to the problem of coordination (the 'thirteenth' or 'sixteenth state' and the European social snake), on the other hand, were never enacted due to lack of political support. In the run-up to the Treaty of Amsterdam, we are able to observe timid steps towards the constitutionalisation of social policy. By reformulating Article 117 of the Treaty, the EU has come to embrace the promotion of employment, the improvement of living conditions and combating social exclusion, as core European policy objectives. The Amsterdam Treaty transferred the Social Agreement into the main Treaty. In order to achieve the free movement of workers, and especially to ensure payments of benefits from country to country, the ECJ has interpreted regulations for migrant workers expansively and imposed the principle of non-discrimination in all aspects of social security, except for social assistance. Many more directives were enacted in the 1990s, including those on worker information, on conditions of work contracts, on atypical workers and parental leave.

We live in a period of far-reaching societal and economic transitions. Most European welfare states are in the process of renegotiating the terms of the post-war social citizen contract, including a reconfiguration of the role of government, levels of decision making and actors that are or should be involved in the governance of social policy (see Ferrera *et al.*, 2000; Ferrera and Hemerijck, 2003). One of the most distinctive institutional features of the European welfare *state* has been its public nature: the responsibility of ensuring social solidarity and cohesion lies with the government – ultimately the national (i.e. central) government. Public funds, public schemes and public bureaucracies have traditionally been the main pillars of the welfare edifice. Various developments have been challenging this state-centric paradigm in recent years – a challenge often summarised in the emergence of new forms of 'governance' beyond the traditional territorial state. The ongoing redefinition of the territorial state is apparent in two ways (Supiot, 2003). National government no longer monopolise welfare provision. Increasingly, states and EU-institutions focus on laying the institutional ground rules and social principles shaping multi-level governance. Hereby the state is at once withdrawing, while at the same time reaffirming its role as the guardian of the 'goodness of fit' of economic competitiveness and social solidarity. Striking features in this respect is the resurgence of 'social pacts', agreed to by functional organised interests and domestic policy makers, and widening the scope of a *governance by objectives* approach at the level of the EU, epitomised by the social dialogue, and more so by the open method of open coordination in the areas of employment, social exclusion and pensions, which also – albeit at a distance – engage the social partners. While many countries (especially the larger ones) have been experimenting with decentralisation of competencies to sub-national (regional and local) governments in response to numerous pressures – from increased international competition to fiscal overload at the state-national level, the EU, as we have shown above, has been gradually emerging as an autonomous supranational level of social regulation and to some extent redistribution (through the structural funds), creating a complex system of multi-level interactions that has turned national welfare state from fully sovereign to semi-sovereign entities (Leibfreid and Pierson, 2000). Patterns of decision making in European social policy have been transformed in the process. Qualified majority voting has been introduced in Treaty reforms and has extended into day-to-day practice. Furthermore, at the European level, labour and industry groups have become key players in European social policy, able to decide on the content of new directives. While over time, the 'hard' social *acquis* has surely 'deepened', more recently new, 'softer' forms of EU involvement, such as the social dialogue and OMC, have become institutionalised so as to balance common concerns and *legitimate diversity*, i.e. respect for institutional differences of formerly self-contained territorial welfare states.

In the past, with every wave of enlargement, it was argued that widening the EU would enfeeble the prospects for deepening, especially in politically sensitive employment and social policy areas. With the benefit of hindsight, the notion that widening is at the expense of deepening of the EU cannot be upheld. This is not to say that reaching consensus over fiscal, social and employment policy issues will become more difficult in a more heterogeneous Union of 25 Member States. Today, the EU finds itself at an important constitutional moment. With 25 members since 2004 there is a clear need for a new Constitutional Treaty laying down the ground rules for economic and social policy coordination. Accession of ten more states to the EU in May 2004 brought about an enormous increase in the economic and social heterogeneity among Member States. Therefore, it seems fair to conclude that, in the future, agreement on binding standards will be even more difficult to achieve. At the same time, the social policy consequences of European economic integration will become more poignant. If community legislation is more difficult, social progress will have to rely more on horizontal EU social dialogue and 'soft law' processes of the open method of coordination, where state policy makers remain the central actors embedded in a larger European economic and social policy space.

Conclusion

Two conditions are central to the future legitimacy and effectiveness of the EU social policy profile. On the one hand, the EU should anchor the institutional conditions that would protect market-correcting social employment and social policy at the national levels limiting the reach of unfair 'negative integration' while at the same time stimulating mutual accommodation. By way of constitutionalising the ECJ's jurisdiction on the 'principles of national solidarity', exempting national welfare policy from first pillar competition law, national regulatory autonomy in social policy would be better protected than is now the case. Also the inclusion of the Charter of Fundamental Rights of the EU into the European Constitutional Treaty is an important step in the direction of turning a Union of territorial states into a Union of citizens. And this has been achieved in an orderly and incremental fashion. In particular, the incorporation in the Treaty of the Charter of Fundamental Rights could have serious constitutional significance, as it will mark the acceptance by the EU of the principles of social citizenship, an evolution which could in turn unleash activism on the part of the ECJ.

Restraining European competition law on the basis of 'hard' principles of social solidarity as defensive clauses, however, are not sufficient to ensure the long-term viability of advanced European welfare states. Europe's welfare states in both the West and the East remain in need of reform. Intensified international competition, ageing populations, de-industrialisation, changing gender roles in labour markets and households, and the introduction of new technologies, continue to pose severe strains to welfare programmes designed for previous eras of welfare capitalism and state socialism. As common internal and external challenges manifest themselves in different problem loads from one welfare state to the next, flexible forms of 'positive integration' need to complement protective safeguards against 'negative integration', facilitating closer coordinated action through policy learning across countries based on well-understood common interests and concerns. Less-binding and non-legal modes of governance such as the social dialogue and open coordination should, therefore, not be viewed as *alternatives* to the Community method but as necessary or indispensable *complements*. So to improve upon the balance between 'negative' and 'positive integration', Fritz Scharpf suggests a way to make 'framework directives' a combination of the open method of coordination and 'hard' Community law, which would allow for Member State-specific flexibility while mitigating asymmetry between market-making and market-correcting legislation (Scharpf 2003).

It is arguably a sign of good health that 50 years of European integration has thrown up such a wide range of different modes of governance for European cooperation (Best, 2003). Despite the increased importance of the EU in social policy areas, it is very unlikely, as I have tried to show, that we will witness the emergence of a fully-fledged territorial European welfare state, replacing national welfare regimes in an enlarged EU, even in the long run. Multi-level Europe continues to depend on democratic legitimacy derived from and mediated through national legislatures, which remain the primary focal point of political identity in Europe and the cornerstone for further policy integration.

Note

1 This chapter is a product of a wider comparative study of the future of social welfare in Europe, that I started with Maurizio Ferrera and Martin Rhodes in 1999, in the framework of the Portuguese Presidency of the European Union in the first half of 2000. Our joint collaboration resulted in the book *The Future of Social Europe* (Ferrera, 2000), which will be completely revised for publication in 2005. Separate from Maurizio and Martin, I further elaborated, with Jos Bergman, our ideas of the EU dimension of social policy in a study for the Greek Presidency, published under the title *Connecting Welfare Diversity within the European Social Model* (2004). The present paper constitutes a revised, expanded and updated version of the paper 'The European Social Patrimony – Deepening Social Europe through Legitimate Diversity' written for the Greek presidency, with a clear focus on the question whether or not we are likely to observe the emergence of a European social regime that is likely to transcend the national welfare state. Many colleagues and friends have given me excellent comments on earlier drafts over the past five years. I would especially like to thank Maurizio Ferrera, Martin Rhodes, Wendy Asbeek Brusse, Jos Bergman, Jelle Visser and Jonathan Zeitlin, next to the editors of the present volume.

References

Asbeek Brusse, W. and Hemerijck, A. (2002), 'Deepening Social Europe in an Enlarged Union', in M. Dauderstädt and L. Witte (eds), *Work and Welfare in the Enlarging Euroland*. Bonn: Friedrich Ebert Stiftung.

Barnard, C. (2000), *EC Employment Law*, 2nd edition. Oxford: Oxford University Press.

Begg, I. (2002), 'EMU and Employment. Social Models in the EMU: Convergence? Co-Existence? The Role of Economic and Social Actors', Working paper 42/02, One Europe or Several? Working Papers. Brighton: University of Sussex.

Best, E. (2003), 'Alternative Regulations or Complementary Methods? Evolving Options in European Governance', *Eipascope*, 1: 2–11.
Best, E. and Bossaert, D. (eds) (2002), *From Luxembourg to Lisbon and Beyond: Making the Employment Strategy Work*, Maastricht: European Institute of Public Administration.
Brinkmann, G. (1998), 'Lawmaking Under the Social Chapter of Maastricht', in P. Craig and C. Harlow (eds), *Lawmaking in the European Union*. London: Kluwer Law International, pp. 239–61.
Clasen (2001), 'Managing the Economic Risks of Unemployment in the UK', Paper presented at the Conference 'Welfare systems and the management of the economic risk of unemployment', 10–11 December, Florence: European University Institute.
Council of the European Union (1992a), Council Recommendation 92/441/EEC of 24 June 1992 on common criteria concerning sufficient resources and social assistance in the social protection systems.
Council of the European Union (1992b), Council Recommendation 92/442/EEC of 27 July 1992 on the Convergence of Social Protection Objectives and Policies.
Cullen, H. and Campbell, E. (1998), 'The Future of Social Policy-making in the European Union', in P. Craig and C. Harlow (eds), *Lawmaking in the European Union*. London: Kluwer Law International, pp. 262–84.
De la Porte, C. and Pochet P. (2001), 'Supple Coordination at EU Level and the Key Actors' Involvement', in C. De la Porte and P. Pochet (eds), *Building Social Europe through the Open Method of Co-ordination*, pp. 27–68. Brussels: Peter Lang.
Ebbinghaus, B. (2000) 'Any Way Out of "Exit from Work"? Reversing the Entrenched Pathways of Early Retirement', in F.W. Scharpf and V.A. Schmidt (eds), *Welfare and Work in the Open Economy*, volume 2: *Diverse Responses to Common Challenges*. Oxford: Oxford University Press, pp. 511–53.
Esping-Andersen, G. (1990), *The Three Worlds of Welfare Capitalism*. Cambridge: Polity Press.
Esping-Andersen, G. (1999), *Social Foundations of Post-industrial Economies*. Oxford: Oxford University Press.
Falkner, G. (1998), *EU Social Policy in the 1990s: Towards a Corporatist Policy Community*. London: Routledge.
Ferrera, M. (1996), 'The Southern Model of Welfare in Social Europe', *Journal of European Social Policy* 1: 17–37.
—— (2002), 'The European Social Model and the Open Method of Coordination', *Revue Belge de Securite Sociale* 44(3): 469–472.
Ferrera, M. and Hemerijck, A. (2003), 'Recalibrating Europe's Welfare Regimes', in J. Zeitlin and D.M. Trubek (eds), *Governing Work and Welfare in the New Economy. European and American Experiments* Oxford: Oxford University Press.
Ferrera, M., Hemerijck, A. and Rhodes M. (2000), *The Future of Social Europe: Recasting Work and Welfare in the New Economy*. Oeiras: Celta Editora.
Genschel, P. (2001), 'Globalization, Tax Competition and the Fiscal Viability of the Welfare State'. Working paper 01/01, Max Planck Institut für Gesellschaftsforschung, Cologne.
Goetschy, J. (2003), 'The European Employment Strategy: Multi-level Governance, and Policy Coordination', in J. Zeitlin and D.M. Trubek (eds), *Governing Work and Welfare in the New Economy. European and American Experiments*. Oxford: Oxford University Press.

Hall, P. (2001), 'The Evolution of Economic Policy-making in the European Union', in A. Menon and V. Wright (ed.), *From the Nation State to Europe? Essays in Honour of Jack Hayward*. Oxford: Oxford University Press, pp. 214–245.
Hantrais, L. (2000), *Social Policy in the European Union*. Basingstoke: Macmillan.
Hemerijck, A. (2002), 'The Self-transformation of the European Social Model(s)', in G. Esping-Andersen with D. Gallie, A. Hemerijck and J. Myles (2002), *Why We Need a New Welfare State*. Oxford: Oxford University Press.
Hemerijck, A. and Schludi, M. (2000), 'Sequences of Policy Failures and Effective Policy Responses', in F.W. Scharpf and V.A. Schmidt (eds), *Welfare and Work in the Open Economy*, volume 1: *From Vulnerability to Competitiveness*. Oxford: Oxford University Press, pp. 125–228.
Hemerijck, A. and Visser, J. (2003), 'Policy Learning in European Welfare States', manuscript, Amsterdam: AIAS.
Lange, P. (1993) 'Maastricht and the Social Protocal: Why Did They Do It?', *Politics and Society* 21(1) (March).
Leibfried, S. and Pierson, P. (1995), *European Social Policy: Between Fragmentation and Intergration*. Washington, DC: Brookings Institution.
—— (2000), 'Social Policy: Left to Courts and Markets?', in H. Wallace and W. Wallace (eds), *Policy-making in the European Union*, 4th edition. Oxford: Oxford University Press, pp. 267–292.
Marshall, T.H. (1963 [1950]), *Citizenship and Social Class and Other Essays*. Cambridge: Cambridge University Press.
Offe, C. (2003), 'The European Model of "Social" Capitalism: Can It Survive European Integration?', *The Journal of Political Philosophy* 11(4): 437–469.
Sakellaropoulos, T., Berghman, J. and Hemerijck, A. (eds) (2004), *Connecting Welfare Diversity within the European Social Model*. Oxford: Hart Publishing.
Scharpf, F.W. (1988), 'The Joint-Decision Trap: Lessons from German Federalism and European Union', *Public Administration* 66: 239–278.
—— (1999), *Governing in Europe: Effective and Democratic?* Oxford: Oxford University Press.
—— (2000), 'The Viability of Advanced Welfare States in the International Economy: Vulnerabilities and Options', *Journal of European Policy Studies* 7(2): 190–228.
—— (2001), 'Democratic Legitimacy Under Conditions of Regulatory Competition: Why Europe Differs from the United States', in K. Nicolaidis and R. Howse (eds), *The Federal Vision – Legitimacy and Levels of Governance in the United States and the European Union*. Oxford: Oxford University Press, pp. 355–374.
—— (2002), 'The European Social Model: Coping with the Challenges of Diversity', in *Journal of Common Market Studies* 40(4: 645–670.
—— (2003), 'The Vitality of the Nation State in 21st Century Europe', in WRR, *De Vitaliteit van de Nationale Staat in het Europa van de 21ste Eeuw*, WRR-lecture 2002, Groningen: Stefert Kroese, pp. 15–30.
Supiot, A. (2003), 'Governing Work and Welfare in a Global Economy', in J. Zeitlin and D.M. Trubek (eds), *Governing Work and Welfare in the New Economy. European and American Experiments*. Oxford: Oxford University Press.
Tanzi, V. (1998), 'Globalization, Tax Competition and the Future of Tax Systems', in G. Krause-Junck (ed.), *Steuersysteme der Zukunft*. Berlin: Duncker & Humblodt, pp. 13–27.
Vandenbroucke, F. (2002), Foreword, 'Sustainable social justice and "open coordina-

tion" in Europe', in G. Esping-Andersen (ed.), *Why We Need a New Welfare State*. Oxford: Oxford University Press, pp. viii–xxiv.

van der Meer, B. and van Riel, M. (2002), 'De "advocacy coalition" voor het Europese werkgelegenheidsbeleid: Het Europese integratieproces sinds EMU', *Beleid en Maatschappij* 29(3): 123–33.

Visser, J. and Hemerijck, A.C. (1997), *'A Dutch Miracle': Job Growth, Welfare Reform and Corporatism in the Netherlands*. Amsterdam: Amsterdam University Press.

Wetenschappelijke Raad voor het Regeringsbeleid (2003), *Slagvaardigheid in de Europabrede Unie*. Den Haag: Sdu Uitgevers.

Zeitlin, J. (2003), 'Introduction: Governing Work and Welfare in a New Economy', in J. Zeitlin and D.M. Trubek (eds), *Governing Work and Welfare in the New Economy. European and American Experiments*. Oxford: Oxford University Press.

10 When push comes to shove

The territorial monopoly of force and the travails of neomedieval Europe

Jörg Friedrichs

Territoriality operates in many domains, from public services to economic regulation, and from taxation to citizenship. However, not all of these domains are equally important for the reproduction of territorial statehood. It does not really undermine the territorial state if some electricity is provided from abroad, or if citizenship is granted to resident aliens. But if we follow the tradition of Thomas Hobbes, Max Weber and Norbert Elias, there is one fundamental territorial institution that lies at the bottom of all others: the state monopoly of the legitimate use of force in a given territory.[1]

As long as the territorial monopoly of force remains intact, the story goes, there is no transformation of statehood. There may be a transformation in the way states perform their tasks, but that does not touch the very essence of what statehood is all about. There is still the Leviathan, and there is still the anarchical system within which the old beast is bound to operate. Only when the territorial monopoly of force is transformed into something else, will the foundations of statehood be shaken. Or, in other words: the monopoly of force is the hard case for territoriality in transition.

The monopoly of force operates at different levels, from very abstract questions of definition and discourse passing through the adoption of prosecutorial methods down to the operational execution of the law. Let us take as an example the fight against terrorism. At the level of general definitions it makes a difference whether a state is free to decide who the public enemy is, or whether this decision is taken somewhere else. At the level of methods a state may or may not have the discretion to choose its counter-terrorist strategies without external interference. At the operational level a state may conduct investigations alone or together with other states.

Ideally, a state would have to control all of these levels in order to exercise effectively its monopoly of the legitimate use of force. Conversely, institutionalised cooperation with other states on any of these levels implies a loss of control over the territorial monopoly of force, and thereby a loss of sovereign statehood.

Accordingly, any of the three levels would be an interesting topic for empirical research. It is my contention, however, that operational law enforcement is more difficult to internationalise than the other two levels.

The reason is that at the level of definition and discourse it is mostly sufficient to have an informal agreement on the least common denominator, whereas cooperation on methods is less controversial insofar as states are in the win–win situation of a coordination game. For example it is relatively easy to agree that Islamic terrorists are enemies of open society, and that it is mutually advantageous to have a common policy on the confiscation of their assets. Operative law enforcement, by contrast, involves the *physical* use of force, and according to the classical Weberian doctrine this is the linchpin of the state monopoly of force.

In short, the internationalisation of operational law enforcement is the hardest case for territoriality in transition. The empirical part of the chapter is set to examine whether and to what extent the territorial monopoly of force is in a transformation in the European Union (EU). Due to its unprecedented level of integration, the EU is the likeliest regional forum where an internationalisation of the monopoly of force may occur. It is the easiest venue for the hardest case.

Territoriality and the EU

The EU is often said to be a post-Westphalian polity, i.e. one that transcends the time-honoured institution of territorial statehood. And insofar as the monopoly on the legitimate use of force in a given territory is the constitutive institution of sovereign statehood, the EU does indeed constitute a challenge to the Westphalian order. According to the theory outlined at the middle of the seventeenth century by Thomas Hobbes in his *Leviathan*, the monopolisation of violence in the hands of the ruler puts an end to the war of all against all, and this is the *raison d'être* of absolutist power. The crucial importance of the monopoly of force was confirmed in the early twentieth century by Max Weber in *Wirtschaft und Gesellschaft*, and again in the 1930s by Norbert Elias in *The Civilizing Process*. Following this tradition of political thought, the monopoly of the legitimate use of force can be considered as the *sine qua non* of efficient and legitimate statehood (Grimm, 2002).

This is not to say that the traditional claim of states to have territorial sovereignty should be taken at face value. One can argue that states could never make good their pretension to be the final arbiters of political and civic life on their territory. One may even maintain that sovereignty has always been a form of organised hypocrisy (Krasner, 1999). But this does not alter the fact that even though it may be a legal *fiction*, territorial sovereignty does also have a practical *function* (Badie, 1999). It is constitutive of modern statehood (Werner and Wilde, 2001).[2] Territorial sovereignty is the rule from which the "unbundling" of territoriality is the departure (Ruggie, 1993; *cf.* the introduction to this volume).

The monopoly of the legitimate use of force was the first constitutive feature of the modern European state to emerge (Poggi, 1990). Initially it was established vis-à-vis domestic society, and only later did the external use of force become the exclusive prerogative of the members of the European state system (Thomson, 1994). The physical control of territorial borders was the logical corollary of internal sovereignty, and the crossing of the external borders by foreign armies and foreign citizens came to be regulated by military forces and customs authorities. At least in theory, every modern state claims the monopoly on the legitimate use of force on its territory.

In this chapter I am exclusively concerned with the civilian aspects of the monopoly of force and not with inter-state warfare and military intervention. In very crude terms, nobody is allowed to run around with a gun and hunt other people unless he is publicly authorised to do so. At least in those states that follow the rule of law, the lion's share of the internal monopoly of force is exercised by the police forces (Knöbl, 1998).

The pacification of society is the bottom-line of modern statehood.[3] A state that loses its capacity to enforce the internal monopoly of force and to safeguard public order is a failed state. Any systematic and principled transformation of the way territorial policing is organised, whether domestically or at the border vis-à-vis the citizens of other states, does therefore constitute a compelling case that a fundamental transformation of modern statehood is underway.

At least in the geographical area covered by the EU the internal monopoly on the legitimate use of force is not crumbling. In other parts of the world, there are indeed regions where the state has lost its monopoly of force. The response of the international community to such cases is generally an attempt to re-establish territorial statehood. But as far as the EU is concerned, the question is not whether states are losing their monopoly of force. The question is whether and to what extent in the EU the territorial monopoly of force is in a process of transformation.[4]

Is European integration leading to an internationalisation of the monopoly of force? Is the boundary between the internal and the external, the civil and the military use of force being blurred? Is there a trend towards overlapping police jurisdictions, in contrast to the traditional separation of turfs along territorial lines? What implications would this have for the relationship between state and society in Europe? Will it threaten or rescue democratic accountability?

In Europe there is indeed a certain transformation towards the trans-territorial management of force, exercised not separately by the individual member states on their own territory but jointly within the framework of a system of overlapping jurisdictions. Traditionally territorial jurisdictions are mutually exclusive, that is either they are exercised by one state or by the other. In recent times there is a trend among EU members to share certain parts of their monopoly of force. In the most extreme case, this would lead to a situation where jointly, the EU members were still holding the monopoly of force, but each individual member state had to share its territorial sovereignty with other states. From a system of territorial states, Europe would then have truly transformed itself into a system of overlapping jurisdictions. However, at present this seems to be a remote possibility. The member states of the EU are jealously guarding what is left from their territorial monopoly of force.

In the next section I introduce new medievalism as a diagnostic instrument to account not only for the continuing transformation but also for the resilience of territorial statehood in Europe. After that I will illustrate, and as far as possible substantiate this by virtue of three empirical case studies. First, I discuss the emergent European border control regime; then the move from extradition towards the European arrest warrant; and finally the legal and political conundrum of cross-border hot pursuit. In each of the three cases there seems to be a trend towards the trans-territorial management of force, but it is hard to predict whether and to what extent this trend is going to prevail against the powers of inertia. In the final section I will reflect on the relative impact of interests, institutions and ideas on the decision to internationalise (or not) the physical management of the territorial monopoly of force. The conclusion provides an attempt to relate the empirical findings to the theoretical perspective outlined in the first two sections of the chapter.

The EU: A neomedieval polity?

When looking for a pre-Westphalian precedent of post-Westphalian statehood in Europe, the European Middle Ages is one of the most obvious candidates. Of course one could also draw analogies with other historical periods, but one does not have to go back to the Sumerian empire in order to find a polity that has structural features in common with post-Westphalian Europe (*cf.* Wæver, 1997). The European Middle Ages were discovered in the 1970s by Hedley Bull as a heuristic device to understand how the world might develop after the "demise of Westphalia" (Bull, 1977: 254–276; Wilde, 1994; Wæver, 1996; Rengger, 2000; Zielonka, 2001; Tanaka, 2002).

Of course it would be foolish to say that there is an essential or even spiritual affinity between medieval Europe, on the one hand, and the post-Westphalian Euro-polity on the other. But it does seem reasonable to assume that Europe before the advent of modern statehood may have had some structural similarities with a post-Westphalian Europe that is transcending modern statehood. There may be a structural analogy between the way in which order was preserved in the European Middle Ages and how it is preserved now in the emergent Euro-polity. In the final analysis it is an empirical question whether this is the case or whether it is not. And as I have argued elsewhere, there is indeed a structural analogy between medieval and post-Westphalian Europe (Friedrichs, 2001, 2004).

In the briefest possible formula, a medievalist system is a system of overlapping authority and multiple loyalties, held together by a duality of competing universalistic claims. In the European Middle Ages *imperium* and *sacerdotium*, i.e. the Holy Roman Empire and the Roman Catholic Church, were trying to keep together an otherwise highly fragmented feudal society. Both the Emperor and the Pope were raising claims that went far beyond the territory they could physically control. In neomedieval times the glue to hold together a fragmented post-modernist society is again provided by a duality of universalistic claims: the authoritative allocation of values by political decision making on the one hand, and the decentralised allocation of values via the capitalist market on the other.[5]

Under the banner of globalisation, the capitalist market increasingly disrupts territorial borders. The fact that global capital does not respect territorial borders drags politics and society into a reconfiguration along trans-territorial lines. The neomedieval analogy is helpful to understand what that means. In the neomedieval world, politics and economics represent two fundamentally distinct organisational modes, which by their universalistic claims are keeping together a fragmented society that is characterised by overlapping authorities and multiple loyalties. World affairs in the new Middle Ages are characterised by a complex triangular relationship between Politics, Market and Society.

This chapter is focused on only one side of the neomedieval triangle formed by Politics, Market and Society, namely state-society relationships. I leave aside the relationships between the state and the market, and between the market and society. I will limit myself to an examination of how politics in the EU is striving to keep together a society that is increasingly fragmented and, at the same time, characterised by manifold trans-territorial linkages. In particular I will analyse how the EU member states adjust their monopoly of force in the face of the real and perceived challenges posed by massive labour migration and trans-territorial crime.

To the extent that territorial cleavages are becoming less important in the Common Market area, the functional correlation between politics and society becomes more important. But whereas there is a protean civil society constantly shaping and reshaping itself, the political sphere is still characterised by the constitutional form of the modern territorial state. This divergence makes it increasingly difficult to fix the disjunctures between politics and society.[6]

The institutional design of the EU as a multi-level polity can be interpreted as a relatively successful attempt of politics to become better adjusted to the challenges posed by social fragmentation (Jachtenfuchs and Kohler-Koch 1996; Hooghe and Marks, 2001, 2003). On the other hand, the EU does also create new problems of systemic coupling between politics and society. For example, the individual cannot appeal directly to the European Court of Justice (ECJ), but has to pass through the national legal institutions, which then can submit the case for an advisory opinion to the ECJ. More importantly, it is often held that even if one wanted to democratise the EU, the absence of a European *demos* renders popular legitimacy via the direct election of legislative and/or executive institutions unattainable.

In short, the management of territorial borders is less and less of a problem, whereas the management of the systemic boundaries between politics and society in the EU is an increasing challenge. In the face of this challenge, the EU does both facilitate and complicate the relationship between politics and society. This does not mean that territoriality is no longer an issue. However, territorial segmentation is dysfunctional in the face of social problems that by their very nature transcend borders. One might therefore expect that politics should reconfigure itself as a multi-level system beyond territorial segmentation. And indeed the EU bears abundant evidence of the progressive development of a dynamic multi-level system. But against the optimistic vision that politics will automatically adjust to the challenges posed by society, it is worth recalling the old realist adage: "Can" does not derive from "Ought". Territorial sovereignty is a constitutive feature of modern statehood, and it is likely to persist for a variety of good reasons.

As the Stanford school of political sociology convincingly argues, the encapsulation of politics in a territorially segmented system of nation states is deeply rooted in the institutional culture of the political and administrative classes worldwide (Meyer *et al.*, 1997). A reconfiguration of politics along trans-territorial lines would have to reckon with deeply rooted ideational and institutional obstacles. It is necessary to take the intrinsic resilience of the nation state seriously when discussing the prospects for the EU to become a system of overlapping jurisdictions. As we have seen, it is one of the most difficult challenges for the EU to preserve the systemic coupling between politics as the authoritative allocation of values on the one hand, and an increasingly fragmented and borderless civil society on the other. This is rendered even more difficult by the fact that Europe has a unique heritage of nationalism and statehood, which constitutes the very basis of social order and collective identity. Recognised values such as democracy and self-determination are intrinsically linked with territorial sovereignty, and therefore the legitimacy of unbundling territoriality can be questioned on normative grounds.

Taken together, we can construe this conundrum in terms of the following prediction: on the one hand, there is a functional "pull" for the EU to become a system of overlapping jurisdictions; and, on the other, there will not only be an institutional resilience but also an emotional reluctance on the part of the member states and their ruling classes to let this happen.

This is one of the reasons why the EU seems to be in limbo between the development of a continental super-Leviathan and a relapse into petty national parochialism. It will be interesting to see, in the ensuing empirical sections of the chapter, whether and how this prediction is confirmed. We expect a functional pull towards the unbundling of territoriality, on the one hand, and a strong institutional and emotional reluctance of the member states to cede their exclusive territorial powers on the other.

The external border police force: a glimpse ahead

Almost by definition, the territorial monopoly of force presumes a certain control of territorial borders. In the last 50 years, however, the EU has developed into a common market, now known as the Single European Market (SEM). Not only do goods, capital and services circulate unrestrictedly, but also persons have the right to free movement – and all this implies a relative loss of territorial control for the EU member states. In the context of the inauguration of the SEM in the early 1990s, this has led to experimentation with a new European border regime that cannot but have its repercussions on the territorial management of force. The whole point about the new European border regime is that (a) internal borders become more porous and permeable; (b) external border surveillance is reinforced to compensate for the concomitant loss of control; and (c) this is supplemented by a multi-layered system of immigration control that reaches far beyond the external borders (Anderson, 2000; Pastore, 2004).

However, the physical control of the external borders is still in the hands of the EU member states concerned. This is complicated by the fact that it is not 100 per cent clear where the external borders of the EU are. Between 1985 and 1990, the technical details of the new European border regime were negotiated between the so-called Schengen states: Germany, France and the Benelux countries. In later years, most EU members have adhered to these agreements. By virtue of the Treaty of Amsterdam, ratified in 1999, the Schengen agreements were formally incorporated into the EU legal framework. But despite the formal incorporation of Schengen into the EU legal framework, the spatial extension of the EU and the Schengen area are not congruent. Thus, Ireland is a member of the EU but is not party to the Schengen agreements; the UK has acceded to some parts of Schengen but is not a party to the whole agreement; the non-members Norway and Iceland are closely associated; Denmark has a right to stay out of certain agreements negotiated under Schengen;[7] an association agreement with Switzerland is under way; finally, it remains to be seen when the ten new member states will be fully integrated into the Schengen area.

Following the traditional logic of territorial statehood, one might hypothesise that the EU is in the process of supplanting its member states as the privileged referent of exclusive territoriality. In the 1999 presidency conclusions to the Tampere European Council one does indeed find the expression "our territory" – in the singular! – with regard to the envisaged "Area of Freedom, Security and Justice". Most of the time, however, the EU is not referred to as a "territory" but as an "area". This semantic device helps to avoid an open clash with the principle of territoriality as enshrined in the political culture and legal systems of the member states (*cf.* also the conclusion).

However the external border regime is not just about semantics. It is primarily about the *physical* management of external border control. As the

European Commission has put it, "[s]ome EU member states, owing to their geographical situation, have to perform checks and surveillance in the common interest on highly exposed and very long external maritime or land borders, while some other member states no longer have any external borders except the airports".[8] It is easy to see why particularly exposed member states such as Italy, Spain and Greece are calling for burden sharing.

These countries sometimes demand a European corps of border guards, or European border police force, to support them in the surveillance of their external borders. This applies especially to the maritime border from Gibraltar to the Aegean Sea, which is extremely difficult to control. There is the idea of drawing up joint multinational teams having the full prerogatives of public authority, irrespective of their nationality and their place of deployment. However, this would present legal problems for the territorial sovereignty of the member states. To attribute territorial powers, including the right to use firearms and apprehend suspects, to personnel from other states would certainly present constitutional and political headache to virtually every EU member state.[9]

The solution proposed by the European Commission is worth quoting: "One might envisage confining them [i.e. the powers], for surveillance purposes, to a strip a few hundred metres wide at external land borders and to a portion of the territorial waters. Some land, maritime and air-crossing points could be included for the purposes of checks. These portions of territory, enjoying special status, should be listed exhaustively and be delimited precisely by maps and plans, which could be annexed to the Common Manual for External Borders".[10] This would mean a further unbundling of territoriality, albeit without abandoning the principle of territorial sovereignty as such.

In any case, all this remains speculative. In practice the successful implementation of pilot projects and joint operations is the real challenge. The objective is to build mutual trust and common knowledge among different national border police forces. Another objective is to establish common practices in the management of surveillance activities.

In the early 1990s the European Commission had more ambitious plans when it proposed a "Convention on the Crossing of the External Frontiers of the Member States".[11] However the Convention was blocked by Spain, which objected to its application to Gibraltar. The draft was silently buried after the Italian presidency in 1996, and formally withdrawn by the Commission on 11 December 2001.[12] Apart from this abortive attempt, the efforts of the member states are concentrated on more pragmatic measures including:

- The schengen manual on external border checks;
- The computerised Schengen Information System (SIS);
- networking among high-ranking officials;
- staff exchange and cross-posting of liaison officers;
- common training and reflection on best practices.

In recent years there has been a number of pilot projects (Monar, 2004). For example, in March 2002 there was a joint operation of border guards in Estonia, Latvia, Lithuania and Finland. In 2003, Spain and Greece have led two common naval exercises off the coasts of the Mediterranean Sea (*project Ulysses* and *project Triton*). Germany has signed with Poland, and Italy with Slovenia, an agreement on cooperation among border guards.[13]

All this is a far cry from the high-flown plans of some member states to create a European border police force. Not even financial burden sharing and the exchange of equipment among member states are automatic.[14] National border guards are certainly here to stay, even if a common European border police is not completely ruled out for the distant future. True, a European Border Management Agency is under construction.[15] For the time being, however, the joint management of *physical* control at the EU external border is limited to voluntary ad hoc cooperation among the member states.

The European arrest warrant: a difficult birth

Traditionally states have claimed full autonomy over the decision to extradite, or not, criminal suspects or convicts to other states. Especially in the field of political offences such as terrorism, states persistently used to refute an automatic obligation to surrender suspects to the criminal jurisdiction of other states. Such an obligation was considered as irreconcilable with the idea that a state is the final arbiter of criminal justice on its own territory. Accordingly, extradition used to be seen as a matter of comity among sovereign states. Depending on the specificities of the case at hand, states felt free to decide whether or not to extradite a suspect. For example, France and Belgium were providing a safe haven to Spanish and Italian terrorists over many years. No state was obliged to justify these decisions, since the principle of sovereignty and the logic of *raison d'état* were considered sufficient.

After the Second World War, Europe has seen cautious attempts to put extradition on a multilateral basis: the European Convention on Extradition (1957) and the European Convention on the Suppression of Terrorism (1977).[16] Both of these conventions were concluded under the umbrella of the Council of Europe. The 1957 European Convention on Extradition was designed as a mechanism for bringing offenders to justice across European frontiers. However, in the European Convention on Extradition there are three remaining loopholes for states to derogate from the obligation to extradite. First, a state can deny extradition if it deems that a case is about a political offence. Second, extraditable offences must be pursuable under the laws of both countries. Third, a signatory state can deny the extradition of its own nationals and insist on trying them under its own law.

Article 1 of the 1977 Convention on the Suppression of Terrorism denies a political character both to terrorist acts and to the motivations of their perpetrators. This is meant to take away the first loophole mentioned above. If terrorist acts are declared to be plain criminal, no state can deny extradition with the excuse that the case is about a political offence. It is quite obvious that a strict observation of this provision would have made it easier to apply the 1957 European Convention on Extradition to terrorist acts. On the other hand, however, Article 5 of the 1977 Convention provides an explicit loophole: nothing shall be interpreted as imposing a binding obligation upon a Party to extradite a person if the extradition request is grounded on an intention to prosecute the offender in a discriminatory way. Moreover, Article 13 provides for the possibility of making a reservation on the political exemption clause. Those states that did make such a reservation could continue to reject extradition requests on the grounds that the offence is of a political character, notwithstanding the fact that it is listed in Article 1 of the Convention. They were therefore still not fully obliged to extradite terrorists.[17]

The European extradition regime started to gain new momentum after the end of the Cold War. In the mid 1990s there were two attempts to draw up conventions to foster extradition among the EU member states.[18] These conventions would have required ratification by all member states to enter into force. However, France and Italy failed to ratify. In the absence of ratification by these two countries, the conventions never entered into force. In the late 1990s the European extradition regime seemed once more to be at a standstill. At that point, ETA-plagued Spain launched a series of bilateral extradition treaties on the basis of an entirely new principle: mutual recognition. The idea behind mutual recognition is that among legally homogenous and politically like-minded states judicial decisions, such as an extradition request, can be automatically accepted without further review.

While reaching formal agreement with Italy and the UK, Spain promoted the principle of mutual recognition at the EU level as well. In October 1999, mutual recognition was accepted at the European Council in Tampere as the future principle for European extradition law.

The terrorist attacks of September 2001 worked as a catalyst for the adoption of the mutual recognition principle. After nine months of negotiations, in June 2002 the European Council issued a framework decision on the European arrest warrant.[19] When implemented, the European arrest warrant abolishes formal extradition between member states and replaces it by a system of surrender between judicial and executive authorities. Extradition is handled directly among the agencies concerned, i.e. suspects are surrendered without political review.

Formally, the principle of mutual recognition means a step from international to trans-governmental (not supranational) law (Slaughter, 2000). Practically, it means a step from exclusive territoriality towards overlapping jurisdictions. Among the EU members, political actors who used to grant or refuse extradition are replaced, by and large, by judicial and executive agencies. The EU thereby moves considerably closer to its declared aspiration of becoming an Area of Freedom, Security and Justice. On the other hand, the concomitant loss of territorial sovereignty is considerable.

When the European arrest warrant was negotiated in December 2001, the strongest resistance came from Italy. Although Rome had signed in 2000 a bilateral agreement with Spain on the mutual recognition of arrest warrants, in December 2001 the Italian delegation was fundamentally opposed to the European arrest warrant. An analysis of the Italian press reveals that the government was split over the issue. Whereas the post-fascists did not create any problems, Silvio Berlusconi was against the extensive list of crimes that were to fall under the new legal instrument. In particular the inclusion of financial fraud and corruption into the list created concern to the Italian Prime Minister – *honi soit qui mal y pense!* At the same time, there was even more zealous resistance against the European arrest warrant from one of Berlusconi's coalition partners, the populist Northern League, which had discovered the topic as an ideological battle-horse.[20]

In early December 2001, the European arrest warrant was about to fail due to stout Italian opposition at the Justice and Home Affairs Council in Brussels. Italy insisted that the list of offences covered by the new legal instrument should be reduced from 32 to 6, excluding financial fraud, corruption, racism, and xenophobia. This led to a very tense situation where the Belgian presidency and the French minister of justice, among others, threatened to proceed without Italy. Due to tenacious shaming and blaming, the Italian Prime Minister was finally compelled to accept a formal compromise on the eve of the EU summit in Laeken (14–15 December 2001). However, Berlusconi declared that the Italian accession to the framework agreement would require adaptations in the Italian constitution and judicial system. "We shall see," Berlusconi declared at a press conference, "as far as we are concerned, we will have to modify a constitutional law. We shall see whether we manage to do that within 2004. If not so, nothing will happen."[21]

In the meantime, the European arrest warrant entered into force on 1 January 2004 among an unlikely coalition of eight EU member states: Belgium, Denmark, Finland, Ireland, Portugal, Spain, Sweden and the UK.[22] The other seven EU members were either not willing or not able to keep the agreed deadline. In France, the European arrest warrant became valid in March 2004; in Germany the entry into force was delayed until August 2004, that is for almost nine months. At the time of writing (April 2005), Italy was the only old member state of the EU that had still not ratified the European arrest warrant. In Germany, the Constitutional Court was about to rule on the constitutionality of the German ratification law to transpose the 2002 framework decision.[23]

It is still too early to predict how the new instrument will work and whether Italy will remain the only EU member state to boycott the European arrest warrant.[24] At least in theory, the European arrest warrant is depriving states of their traditional prerogative to decide politically whether or not to extradite a political offender from their national territory. The history of the European extradition regime shows that whenever states seemed willing to put extradition on a more routine basis, there was a reluctance among some of them to surrender the final word on extradition. This is not to deny that the European extradition regime has made remarkable headway over the last fifty years. The density and intensity of that regime is unprecedented if one compares it with the situation in other periods of time or in other parts of the world.[25] Nevertheless, one should probably not expect that all EU member states shall be willing completely to abandon political control over extradition to other member states in the foreseeable future.

Cross-border hot pursuit: a regulatory chaos

Hot pursuit is the immediate following of a wrongdoer, who is aware of police presence, across a border to apprehend him or her. This implies the penetration of one state's police forces into another state's territory, which is at odds with the classical understanding of sovereignty. If a state claims the monopoly of the legitimate use of force, how can it allow another state's police forces to operate on its territory? On the other hand there is the archetypical image of the criminal waving back over the border to his pursuers who cannot follow him into another state. Of course this image is more folklore than reality, but it is part of the collective imagery and can make the regulation of hot pursuit popular both with mass publics and police practitioners. Although hot pursuit is not a frequent scenario, to many people the mere idea of a wrongdoer escaping from punishment by crossing a border is sufficiently outrageous to mobilise support for persevering with international negotiations on hot pursuit.

Up until the 1960s there was no international law on hot pursuit across land borders. To give an example, in 1966 West German policemen pursued an Austrian criminal 60 metres into French territory and were then in turn pursued and arrested by their French colleagues (Poulantzas 1969: 11). In Europe, the Benelux countries were the first to take part in multilateral cooperation concerning hot pursuit.[26] The Benelux Treaty on Extradition and Mutual Legal Assistance in Criminal Matters was concluded in 1962 and entered into force in 1967. Article 27 and 28 of this treaty deal with hot pursuit. Within a zone of ten kilometres, a pursuing officer can apprehend a fugitive within another Benelux country and is even allowed to use firearms according to that country's law.

Twenty years later there was a plan to introduce hot pursuit between France, West Germany and the Benelux countries. This was stipulated in the 1985 Schengen agreement (Article 18c). Hot pursuit was an element in a long list of compensatory measures to make up for the expected loss of border control after the completion of the Common Market in 1992. When persons were allowed to circulate freely across internal borders, it was argued, this was going to allow free movement of criminal elements as well. Along with many other measures, hot pursuit was foreseen as a compensatory device against the undesirable effects associated with the abolition of internal border checks. Although Mitterrand and Kohl may not have been aware of it in 1985, hot pursuit was to become a highly contentious issue in the second half of the 1980s. After several years of tough negotiations, in 1990, five member states of the then European Community finally signed the Schengen Implementing Convention (SIC), namely Germany, France and the Benelux countries. Articles 41 to 43 of the SIC provide for the police of one member state in urgent cases to cross the border of a neighbouring member state for the persecution of wrongdoers.

With the entry into force of the SIC, hot pursuit became legal among the Schengen states. This is not to deny that hot pursuit has its limits. It is limited to land borders[27] and must respect a series of procedural limitations. For example, foreign police officers are not allowed formally to arrest criminal suspects on another state's territory. This remains within the exclusive domain of the state where the wrongdoer is apprehended. An offender must be delivered immediately to the authorities of the state on whose territory he was apprehended. After that, the judicial authorities of the persecuting state must request formal extradition (informal deportation sometimes provides a practical alternative). But the legal subtleties of mutual legal assistance do not concern us here. In fact, the relevance of hot pursuit in the context of the present chapter lies elsewhere: hot pursuit provides an interesting case of the unbundling of territoriality. On the one hand, practical reasons are adduced to make territorial boundaries between states more permeable. On the other hand, this permeability is construed as the exception to a rule that still applies in theory, namely, territorial sovereignty.

As provided by Article 41.9 of the SIC, the details for hot pursuit are to be defined by unilateral declarations. The Schengen members are free to opt for temporal or spatial limitations to hot pursuit; they can (but do not have to) grant foreign police officers a right to apprehend criminals hunted down by hot pursuit; and they can limit hot pursuit either to extraditable offences or to a catalogue of offences specified in Article 41.4.

The unilateral declarations, which are very different from each other, are attached as an appendix to the final text of the SIC. The complexity is further increased by the declarations made by other states such as Italy, Austria, Spain, Greece and Portugal on accession to the SIC. Whenever a new member accedes to the Schengen area, it releases a unilateral declaration concerning hot pursuit. This declaration is mirrored by unilateral declarations by the new member's Schengen neighbours. Moreover, Article 41.10 of the SIC provides for the possibility of extending the scope of hot pursuit by bilateral agreement at any point in time. Over time, all this has created a remarkably complex legal situation.

Let us put ourselves for a moment in the position of a German police officer. In the Netherlands he has only ten kilometres to hunt down a criminal who has committed an extraditable offence in Germany and flees across the Dutch border.[28] In Belgium, by contrast, he would have 30 minutes to apprehend his target; after that he could continue pursuit, although without the right of apprehension. In Denmark he would have to give up after 25 kilometres. In France there is no temporal or spatial limitation at all; however, hot pursuit is illegal unless the wrongdoer has committed one of the offences enumerated in Article 41.4; in any event, our German police officer would have no right to apprehend his target in France. In Switzerland, which is neither an EU member nor a member of the Schengen area, paradoxically he would have more hot pursuit powers than in any other neighbouring state due to a bilateral agreement between Germany and Switzerland.

A French police officer can pursue a criminal who has committed an extraditable offence as deep into German territory as is necessary and apprehend him any time. When driving into Italy or Spain, by contrast, he is granted only ten kilometres, is not allowed to apprehend the wrongdoer, and must check Article 41.4 to confirm whether or not the offence is listed there. At the Swiss border he will have to slam on the brakes because there is no agreement about hot pursuit between Switzerland and France. His Spanish colleague at the Portuguese border would have 50 kilometres or even more, as long as the pursuit does not take more than two hours. An Italian officer can drive ten kilometres into Austria (20 kilometres if it happens to be on a highway), provided that the pursuit is about an extraditable offence. The same limitations apply to an Austrian officer in Italy, except that the offence must be listed in Article 41.4.[29]

Belgium requires a temporal limitation of 30 minutes from German policemen, but a spatial limitation of ten kilometres from police officers from Holland and Luxembourg. For French police officers the offence must be mentioned in Article 41.4, whereas for officers from Luxembourg and the Netherlands an extraditable offence is sufficient. On the Øresund Bridge between Sweden and Denmark either state has the right to pursue any offence according to its own domestic law. Not so in the Dover–Calais Tunnel between Britain and France. The UK has never fully acceded to the SIC, and there is no agreement about hot pursuit between Ulster and the Republic of Ireland. Even at the internal border between England and Scotland hot pursuit was legalised only as recently as 1994 (Bewley 1996).

This blatant diversity of spatial, temporal and procedural limitations is clearly preposterous. Nevertheless the failure to reach a coherent European regime for cross-border hot pursuit illustrates an important point: even when there is a consensus among police practitioners that an agreement is necessary for the purposes of crime control, it is still possible that states are reluctant to surrender even the slightest portion of their territorial sovereignty. More than any other issue, the delegation of the right to use coercion to police forces from other states is anathema to many representatives of European nation states. On the other hand, some states are more ready than others to accept the unbundling of their territorial sovereignty. Germany has been particularly keen on hot pursuit, whereas France has proven to be particularly reluctant. Nevertheless, even Germany would probably have a problem with granting the police forces of other states a formal right of arrest on its territory.

According to the last annual report that was published on the implementation of the SIC, in 1998 there were only 39 cases of hot pursuit.[30] Since then there are no general statistics available. Nevertheless, the figures for Germany are quite revealing: between 13 and 23 cases per year from 1998 to 2002.[31] Although the real figure may be somewhat higher, it seems that hot pursuit is far from being a frequent occurrence. This is interesting because at the time of the Schengen negotiations it was argued that in a Europe without internal border controls hot pursuit was going to be routine for police forces in border regions. With the wisdom of hindsight, however, the empirical record shows that "functional necessity" can be ruled out as an explanation for the considerable attention paid to hot pursuit.

On the one hand, police practitioners often invoke the perceived functional requirement to combat increasingly borderless crime – and whether true or false, this argument was among the driving forces for a European regime of cross-border hot pursuit. On the other hand, the normative ideas and legal institutions embodied by the nation state are putting an important constraint on state preferences and possible bargaining outcomes. As the Schengen negotiations and the evolution of hot pursuit in their aftermath show, it is not an easy task to transform a nation-state system into a system of overlapping jurisdictions. Nevertheless, and against all odds, in the long run there seems to be a move in precisely that direction. If the trend is continued over the next decades, a situation of overlapping jurisdictions becomes a distinct possibility. This is not to deny that there are problems from the standpoint of democratic accountability and citizen rights (or would you accept falling victim of a traffic accident caused by a foreign cop on duty?). It is understandable that the territorial monopoly of force continues tenaciously to survive as a legal norm.

The relative importance of interests, ideas and institutions

As can be seen from the three case studies discussed in this chapter, there is indeed some evidence that the EU is in a transformation towards a neomedieval polity. However, there remains a strong institutional and emotional resistance against the unbundling of territoriality. States are traditionally organised in a segmented system of mutually exclusive territorial jurisdictions that has constituted a stable equilibrium over many centuries. Massive labour migration and trans-territorial crime create functional incentives for policing and judicial cooperation beyond borders. Against this functional pull, however, the traditional institution of territorial sovereignty shows a remarkable resilience. If the system is moving at all, it is slowly moving in the direction of overlapping jurisdictions. But the pace of this movement is relatively slow, unpredictable and far from being automatic.

A review of the case studies shows that there is a series of factors that influence the decision to internationalise (or not) the state monopoly of force in Europe. These factors fit into the following three broad categories: interests, institutions and ideas. I assume that interests, ideas and institutions can operate at the sub-national, national and international level. The relative impact of each category can be illustrated by examples taken from the empirical case studies under examination. Depending on context, it turns out that each of the three categories can either foster or hamper the transition from exclusive territoriality towards a neomedieval system of overlapping jurisdictions.

Let us start with interests. It is normal that not all states have the same interest in the solution of the same problems. Due to their geographical position, Italy, Spain and Greece are very interested in the establishment of a European border police; France and Germany have reservations. Concerning the European arrest warrant, after 9/11 all EU members had an interest in displaying some rapid action against terrorism. This made it possible to accomplish the framework decision on the European arrest warrant within only three months. But now, three years later, it is doubtful whether and to what extent some members of the EU do really have an interest in implementing the European arrest warrant.

Behind national interests as represented by governments there are often other interests. For example, in the case of the European arrest warrant one may speculate whether Italian behaviour during the negotiations was motivated by national interests or by the private interests of some members of Government. On the other hand, one may also follow the Italian Minister of Justice in his allegation that the European arrest warrant is the political project of public prosecutors as a professional group rather than an instrument of efficient crime control.[32] At the Schengen negotiations about hot pursuit there was a broad consensus at the working level (especially among police officers) that cross-border hot pursuit was in the professional interest of police officers. Without this consensus it would have been difficult for the national delegations to negotiate an agreement.

In general, interests can work both as a catalyst *for* and as an impediment *against* cooperation. In virtually all cases under examination, there were interests both supporting and opposing the unbundling of territoriality. At the national level, some states are more jealous about their territorial monopoly of force than others. But even this may vary depending on the issue at stake. Thus, Italy is very much opposed to the European arrest warrant and very much in favour of a European border police. At the sub-state level, there are both supporters and opponents of trans-border cooperation as well.

Interests are not the only thing that makes Europe go round. Institutions and ideas also play an important role (Jachtenfuchs, 2002). Virtually all countries would have legal, constitutional and ideological problems with a European border police operating on their territory. When it comes to the implementation of the European arrest warrant, a civil law country like Italy has different problems than a common law country such as the UK. The latter has to derogate from time-honoured principles guiding extradition practice, which is certainly not an easy thing to accept. Italy, however, would even have to amend its constitutional compact by qualified majority, which is more difficult.[33] The relative prize of institutional adaptation to international agreements differs from country to country. For example, in some countries it is easier to change the constitution than it is in others.

In general, centralist countries like France are said to have a more narrow view of territorial sovereignty than other states. Federal countries like Germany, in contrast, seem sometimes almost ideologically committed to the unbundling of territoriality. For example, at Schengen the German delegation showed an incredibly strong commitment towards hot pursuit. France and Luxembourg, by contrast, were deeply concerned with the irreconcilability of hot pursuit with their understanding of territorial sovereignty.[34] Belgium and the Netherlands did not seem to have any strong preferences on the topic.

In particular, domestic institutions and the normative ideas embodied by them can play an important role in the formulation of national preferences. Let us take again the German bargaining position on hot pursuit as an example. Among the German *Länder*, the problem of hot pursuit has been resolved in the 1950s. Anybody in Germany, even a foreigner, has the right to apprehend a wrongdoer on the spot or to pursue him if he or she tries to escape. Accordingly, to the German delegation it must have seemed unproblematic to introduce cross-border hot pursuit. For the French delegation, by contrast, the situation was quite different. In France only the national police forces have the right to pursue an offender all over the French territory. Criminal police officers from local police forces have to stop at the border of the next policing district. Moreover, the right to apprehend a fugitive on the spot is limited to French citizens. Accordingly, it must have sounded odd to legal specialists in the French delegation that police forces from other countries should be allowed to pursue and apprehend a wrongdoer inside French territory.

In any event, organisation theory shows that a certain degree of inertia is normal for organisational structures (Meyer and Rowan, 1977). Standard operating procedures have an inherent tendency to be defended by the bureaucracies habituated to them. There is often a preference for the maintenance of familiar procedures simply because they are familiar. Moreover, agencies usually have a hard time in trusting other agencies that follow different routines. All this makes it understandable that there are strong bureaucratic reservations to be overcome with regard to inter-institutional cooperation. This must be especially true for international cooperation on justice and police affairs, since organisations in this field are less likely to be compatible across rather than within national boundaries. Moreover, it seems particularly difficult to establish trust among judicial and police agencies, which work at a high level of risk and often deal with confidential information.

However, bureaucracy can also work in favour of international cooperation. First of all there are the transnational bureaucracies at the European level. These European bureaucracies see it as their mission to foster transborder cooperation among national bureaucracies. Their primary resource is the recourse to functional arguments. They appeal to the idea that there are trans-border problems that cannot be effectively solved by the member states acting on their own behalf. According to this logic, transnational crime and massive labour migration must be contained by international cooperation among the competent public authorities. Moreover, as any other conventional bureaucracy the Euro-bureaucracies love to see their competencies increased. Nevertheless, alone they are usually not strong enough to overcome the forces of inertia (or even the resistance) of the national bureaucracies in the member states.[35]

Apart from the brokerage provided by transnational bureaucracies, direct transnational loyalties among lawyers and policemen create another important bond to foster trans-territorial cooperation. In the first place, there is a bounty of more or less informal networks of lawyers and police officers from different European countries. Sometimes these networks are even formally institutionalised, such as the European network of police liaison officers, and the European judicial network. Moreover, there are many problem-related groups of law and police specialists meeting on a more or less regular basis. These bodies are mushrooming especially in the field of terrorism and drug enforcement (Busch, 1995, 1999; Bigo, 1996, 2000; Elvins, 2003).

This may lead to a situation where police officers become aware that they have more in common with their counterparts in other European countries than with other agencies at the national level – the latter being also their competitors for competencies and for the allocation of scarce resources. It seems reasonable to assume that these networks are one of the engines of judicial and police cooperation among the member states of the EU.

Conclusion

This chapter contains many conjectures that deserve closer examination. In any event, the empirical record seems to suggest that one should not be overly optimistic regarding the prospects for unbundling the territorial monopoly of force in Europe. This confirms the theoretical reflections in the first two sections of the chapter. There is little reason to believe that, apart from moderate concessions, the EU member states will give up substantive portions of their territorial monopoly of force any time soon. Nevertheless, the trend is clearly going in the direction of international cooperation and not the other way round. What one should therefore expect for the future is a slow stop-and-go process towards the unbundling of territorial sovereignty.

On the one hand, there are strong functional incentives for states to move towards the joint management of the legitimate use of force. Massive labour migration and trans-territorial crime are problems that cannot effectively be dealt with at the national level. On the other hand, one should not underestimate the forces of inertia. Territorial sovereignty has been for many centuries a constitutive norm of the international system. It is more than just an intellectual task to envisage a functional equivalent to territorial sovereignty beyond modern statehood. Moreover, it is not self-evident on normative grounds that the unbundling of territoriality is necessarily and always a good thing.

If it is true that the legitimacy of the monopoly of force is based on representation, the unbundling of territoriality in this specific area must reckon with serious normative problems. It is easier for me to accept the authority of a German police officer to arrest me, and the authority of a German judge to convict me, because I am a German and these are the legal authorities of my country. In the absence of a European *demos* and a fully developed European democracy, I would not easily accept the legitimacy of supranational authorities to arrest or convict me. In other words, a supranational solution for the problem is out of the question. As the case studies have shown, an intergovernmental and/or transgovernmental approach is already difficult enough.

Before bringing the chapter to a close, it is interesting to insert a small digression on semantics. The principle of territoriality is often invoked by the member states to justify the status quo. Therefore it is remarkable that, in the presidency conclusion to the Tampere European Council, the "Area of Freedom, Security and Justice" was referred to as "our territory" (in the singular).[36] The EU would thereby become the privileged territorial referent ("fortress Europe"). At the practical level, this would imply the creation of something like a federal Euro-state with clear-cut territorial boundaries. Another possible expedient is to use the term "area" instead of "territory". In comparison to a territory, an area is a spatial extension without a clear-cut geographical delimitation, as is revealed by the expressions "danger area" or "area bombing". Moreover, an area is distinguished from its environment by some common characteristic, as for example in "industrial area" or "Area of Freedom, Security and Justice". It is probably not by accident that the supporters of European cooperation are so fond of the term "area". While the exclusionary notion of territoriality is diluted without being completely eliminated, the idea of spatial commonality due to shared values and common rules is unobtrusively introduced.

That said, and radical constructivism notwithstanding, we certainly do not live in a fancy world where it is sufficient to change discursive habits in order to change social reality. When push comes to shove, the monopoly of force is executed at the operative level of enforcement, not at the abstract level of definitions and discourse. But we should not underestimate the generative and transformative power of political concepts either. If the EU really manages to promote the creation of an Area of Freedom, Security and Justice without reclaiming the exclusionary notion of territoriality, this will make it much easier for the member states to accept the further unbundling of their territorial powers. A similar sea-change would be under way for the academic discipline of International Relations if it undertook to re-conceptualise world affairs in general, and European affairs in particular, as a neomedieval system of overlapping authorities and multiple loyalties, held together by a duality of competing universalistic claims.

Notes

1 Research on this paper was carried out in the framework of a research project on the internationalisation of the monopoly of the legitimate use of force. The project, which is based at the International University Bremen, is part of a collaborative research centre and receives funding by the *Deutsche Forschungsgemeinschaft*. Thanks are due to the project director, Markus Jachtenfuchs, and to the Federal Criminal Police Office, which gave me an opportunity to study the protocols to the Schengen negotiations on hot pursuit. The paper has benefited from comments by Friedrich Kratochwil, Ferruccio Pastore, Ulrich Krotz, and the contributors to this volume.
2 The monopoly of force should be seen in combination with the monopoly of taxation that provides the resources for its exercise (Tilly, 1992).
3 This is not to deny the existence of private security services that operate within an explicit legal framework. In some (mainly non-European) states, citizens have also a right to carry arms. However that does not alter the fact that the state raises the claim of being the ultimate arbiter of what constitutes the legitimate use of force.
4 For a sound introduction into European cooperation in Justice and Home Affairs see Monar, 2002; *cf.* also Mitsilegas *et al.*, 2003; Walker, 2004.
5 It is important to keep in mind that the neomedieval analogy does not imply any essential affinity between the old medieval and the emergent neomedieval world. It is meant in purely structural terms and suggests that the relationship of *imperium* and *sacerdotium* with regard to feudal society is similar to the relationship of politics and economics with regard to postmodernist society.
6 *Cf.* Luhmann's notion of systemic connectability (*Anschlussfähigkeit*; see Luhmann, 1996: 168–169, 258–259, 391–392, 494, 590).
7 This allows Denmark to stay in the Schengen area without violating its commitments towards the partners in the Nordic Council.
8 Communication from the Commission to the Council and the European Parliament: Towards Integrated Management of the External Borders of the Member States of the European Union, Brussels 7.5.2002, COM (2002) 233 final, at p. 20.
9 Even an Italian-led feasibility study came to the conclusion that a common European border police should consist in a complex network among national border police forces rather than in an independent institution to be staffed by the EU (Feasibility Study for the Setting up of a European Border Police: Final Report, 2002).
10 Ibid., p. 22.
11 Proposal for a decision, based on Article K.3 of the Treaty of the European Union establishing the Convention on the crossing of the external frontiers of the Member States. In: *Official Journal of the European Communities* C 11/6, 15.1.1994.
12 *Cf.* http://www.parliament.the-stationery-office.co.uk/pa/cm199798/cmhansrd/vo971117/text/71117w12.htm (accessed 25.04.2005).
13 There is now a centre for land borders (*Zentrum Landgrenzen*) in Berlin. Together with other centres, it shall become part of the European Border Management Agency that is presently in the making.

14 Many joint operations were funded by the Odysseus (1998–2001) and ARGO (since 2002–2006) programmes of the European Commission.
15 On 11 November 2003 the European Commission formally proposed the establishment of a Border Management Agency (Monar, 2004: 125). The proposal builds on the already existing Common Unit of External Border Practitioners. The agency, which was formally established by the Council in October 2004, is limited to technical and organisational support. It is set to facilitate, from May 2005, operational cooperation among the member states (see Council Regulation (EC) No 2007/2004 of 26 October 2004, *Official Journal of the European Communities* L 349, 25.11.2004).
16 European Treaty Series, No. 24 and 90, available at http://conventions.coe.int (accessed 25.04. 2005).
17 Similar reasons led to the failure of an attempt by the European Council to implement the principles of the 1977 Convention at least among the members of the EEC (Dublin agreement, 4 December 1979, *Official Journal of the European Communities*, n. 12, 1979).
18 Convention of 10 March 1995 on Simplified extradition procedure between the member states of the EU. In: *Official Journal of the European Communities* C 78, 30.3.1995, p. 2; Convention of 27 September 1996 relating to Extradition between the member states of the EU. In: *Official Journal of the European Communities* C 313, 13.10.1996, p. 12.
19 Council framework decision of 13 June 2002 on the European arrest warrant and the surrender procedures between member states. In: *Official Journal of the European Communities* L 190, pp. 1–18.
20 Minister of Justice Roberto Castelli from the Northern League was the spearhead of Italian opposition against the European arrest warrant. There were basically two reasons for this. First, the Northern League was campaigning against an avowed complot by the "Red Robes", i.e. a suspected attempt by Italian prosecutors and their European colleagues to take control out of the hands of the political class. Second, as an openly racist and xenophobic party the Northern League did not appreciate the inclusion of racism and xenophobia into the list of crimes covered by the European arrest warrant. Both of these motivations were publicly declared in interviews given by high exponents of the party (e.g. in Corriere della Sera, 08.12.2001; *cf.* Padania, 19.03.2003).
21 CNN Italia, 11 December 2001; whereas Berlusconi recently seems to have softened his position on the European arrest warrant, Minister of Justice Castelli and Umberto Bossi from the Northern League remain adamant.
22 Source: Statewatch (http://www.statewatch.org/news/2004/jan/01euro-arrest-warrant.htm, accessed 16.01.2004).
23 By and large, the boundaries of the EU are also the boundaries of the AFSJ. Requests from non-member states such as Russia and Turkey to become parties to the developing extradition regime have been rejected. It is not yet clear whether Norway and Iceland are able to accede to the agreement on the European arrest warrant (Norway and Iceland are parties to the Schengen treaty). Negotiations with the USA on a multilateral agreement on extradition were concluded in June 2003. They were relatively tough and had to be temporarily suspended in 2002. As in other cases, the major problem was a disagreement in principle about the death penalty. The agreement, which has nothing to do with the European arrest warrant, will have to be ratified by the US Congress and by all EU member states to enter it into force. The agreement would simply place the existing bilateral extradition treaties within a multilateral framework, and the principle of automatic recognition is not applied.
24 *Cf.* Darnstadt and Hipp, 2005.

25 On extradition in general see Wagner, 2003; on the European arrest warrant in particular see Friedrichs, 2005; *cf.* Blekxtoon and Bellegooij, 2005.
26 Even before the conditions for hot pursuit were sometimes stipulated in special bilateral treaties. However this was only rarely the case, and a generalised system of bilateral treaties did not exist.
27 There is also a (relatively weak) global regime in hot pursuit in the international law of the sea.
28 An extraditable offence is one that is punishable with at least twelve months of detention.
29 If hot pursuit takes place on a train, Italian and Austrian officers are generously allowed to hang on to the first train station after the border, even if the station happens to be more distant from the border than 10 km (Article 17 of agreement between Italy and Austria on police cooperation).
30 Germany 22, Belgium 13, Austria 2, France 1, Luxemburg 1, Italy 0, Portugal 0, Spain 0, Netherlands N.N. (Source: Statewatch, http://www.poptel.co.uk/statewatch/semdoc/file/NEW/schanrep.htm, accessed 25.04.2005).
31 Source: Bundesministerium des Innern, Schengen Erfahrungsbericht 2002 (ohne justitielle Zusammenarbeit), Berlin: Bundesministerium des Innern, 2003.
32 As a professional group, public prosecutors and police officers do indeed have a vested interest in the enhancement of horizontal cooperation beyond borders (Bigo, 1996). On the special role of the public prosecutor in Italian politics see Pizzorno, 1998.
33 Article 10 of the Italian constitution states unambiguously that "[t]he extradition of a foreigner due to political offences is not permissible".
34 Even today, the UK argues that cross-border hot pursuit would be at odds with territorial sovereignty (although the country has an obvious interest in pursuing suspects into Ireland).
35 One could say that the supporters of internationalisation tend to use functional arguments, whereas the opponents appeal to the time-honoured principles of national sovereignty. The supporters tend to form transnational networks and to populate institutions such as the European Commission and Europol, and this increases their leverage on trans-governmental practice and international bargaining outcomes. But they must reckon with conservative forces, which have their primary stronghold in national administrations and are unlikely to surrender their positions any time soon.
36 Source: http://www.europarl.eu.int/summits/tam_en.htm (accessed 25.05.2005).

References

Anderson, Malcolm (2000), "Border Regimes and Security in an Enlarged European Community: Implications of the Entry into Force of the Amsterdam Treaty", Florence: European University Institute (EUI Working Paper RSC No. 2000/8).
Badie, Bertrand (1999), *Un monde sans souveraineté*. Paris: Fayard.
Bewley, Frank (1996), "Final Frontier: The Anglo-Scots Border, Once the Friend of the Felon, is about to be Plugged", in *Police Review* 23: 27–28.
Bigo, Didier (1996), "Polices en réseaux: L'expérience européenne", Paris: Presses de Sciences Po.
—— (2000), "Liaison Officers in Europe: New Officers in the European Security Field", in J.W.E. Sheptycki (ed), *Issues in Transnational Policing*. London: Routledge, pp. 67–99.
Blekxtoon, Rob and Wouter van Ballegooij (eds) (2005), *Handbook on the European Arrest Warrant*. The Hague: Asser.

Bull, Hedley (1977), T*he Anarchical Society: A Study of Order in World Politics*. London and Basingstoke: Macmillan.
Busch, Heiner (1995), *Grenzenlose Polizei? Neue Grenzen und polizeiliche Zusammenarbeit in Europa*. Münster: Westfälisches Dampfboot.
—— (1999), *Polizeiliche Drogenbekämpfung: Eine Internationale Verstrickung*. Münster: Westfälisches Dampfboot.
Darnstadt, Thomas and Hipp, Dietmar (2005), "Die Leviathan-Frage", in *Der Spiegel* 11/2003: 56–58.
Elvins, Martin (2003), *Anti-Drugs Policies of the European Union: Transnational Decision-Making and the Politics of Expertise*. Basingstoke: Palgrave-Macmillan.
Friedrichs, Jörg (2001), "The Meaning of New Medievalism", in *European Journal of International Relations* 7(4): 475–502.
—— (2004), "The Neomedieval Renaissance: Global Governance and International Law in the New Middle Ages", in Ige G. Dekker and Wouter W. Werner (eds), *Governance and International Legal Theory*. Leiden and Boston, MA: Martinus Nijhoff, pp. 3–36.
—— (2005), "National Policies in Comparison: Germany and the United Kingdom", in Ferruccio Pastore (ed.), *Is there a European Strategy against Terrorism? A Brief Assessment of Supra-National and National Responses*. Rome: CeSPI, pp. 13–21. (Working paper 12/2005, available at www.cespi.it/WP/wp12-terrorismo.pdf.)
Grimm, Dieter (2002), "Das Staatliche Gewaltmonopol", in Wilhelm Heitmeyer and John Hagan (eds), *Internationales Handbuch der Gewaltforschung*. Wiesbaden: Westdeutscher Verlag, pp. 1297–1313.
Jachtenfuchs, Markus (2002), *Die Konstruktion Europas: Verfassungsideen und institutionelle Entwicklung*. Baden-Baden: Nomos.
Jachtenfuchs, Markus and Kohler-Koch, Beate (1996), "Regieren im dynamischen Mehrebenensystem", in Markus Jachtenfuchs and Beate Kohler-Koch (eds), *Europäische Integration*. Opladen: Leske & Budrich, pp. 15–44.
Knöbl, Wolfgang (1998), *Polizei und Herrschaft im Modernisierungsprozess: Staatsbildung und innere Sicherheit in Preußen, England und Amerika 1700–1914*. Frankfurt and New York: Campus.
Krasner, Stephen D. (1999), *Sovereignty: Organized Hypocrisy*. Princeton, NJ: Princeton University Press.
Luhmann, Niklas (1996 [1987]), *Soziale Systeme: Grundriß einer allgemeinen Theorie*, 6th edn. Frankfurt a. M.: Suhrkamp.
Meyer, John W. and Rowan, Brian (1977), "Institutionalized Organizations: Formal Structure as Myth and Ceremony", in *American Journal of Sociology* 83(2): 340–363.
Meyer, John W., Boli, John, Thomas, George M. and Ramirez, Francisco O. (1997), "World Society and the Nation State", *American Journal of Sociology* 103(1): 144–179.
Mitsilegas, Valsamis, Monar, Jörg and Rees, Wyn (2003), T*he European Union and Internal Security: Guardian of the People?* Basingstoke: Palgrave-Macmillan.
Monar, Jörg (2002), "Institutionalizing Freedom, Security, and Justice", in John Peterson and Michael Schackleton (eds), *The Institutions of the European Union*. Oxford: Oxford University Press, pp. 186–209.
—— (2004), "Justice and Home Affairs", *Journal of Common Market Studies* 42(s1): 117–133 (annual review).

Pastore, Ferruccio (2004), "Visas, Borders, Immigration: Formation, Structure, and Current Evolution of the EU Entry Control System", in Neil Walker (ed.), *Europe's Area of Freedom, Security and Justice*. Oxford: Oxford University Press, pp. 89–142.
Pizzorno, Alessandro (1998), *Il potere dei giudici: Stato democratico e controllo della virtù*. Roma-Bari: Laterza.
Poggi, Gianfranco (1990), *The State: Its Nature, Development and Prospects*. Cambridge: Polity Press.
Poulantzas, Nicholas Michael (1969), *The Right of Hot Pursuit in International Law*. Leiden: A.W. Sijthoff.
Rengger, Nicholas J. (2000), "European Communities in a Neo-medieval Global Polity: the Dilemmas of Fairyland?", in Morton Kelstrup and Michael C. Williams (eds), *International Relations Theory and the Politics of European Integration: Power, Security and Community*. London: Routledge, pp. 51–71.
Ruggie, John Gerard (1993), "Territoriality and Beyond: Problematizing Modernity in International Relations", in *International Organization* 47(4): 139–174; revised version (1998), "Territoriality at millennium's end", in Idem, *Constructing the World Polity: Essays on International Institutionalization*. London and New York: Routledge, pp. 172–197.
Slaughter, Anne-Marie (2000), "Government Networks: The Heart of the Liberal Democratic Order", in G.H. Fox and B.R. Roth (eds), *Democratic Governance and International Law*. Cambridge: Cambridge University Press, pp. 199–235.
Tanaka, Akihiko (2002), *The New Middle Ages: The World System in the 21st Century*. Tokyo: International House of Japan.
Thomson, Janice E. (1994), *Mercenaries, Pirates and Sovereigns: State-building and Extraterritorial Violence in Early Modern Europe*. Princeton, NJ: Princeton University Press.
Tilly, Charles (1992), *Coercion, Capital, and European States, AD 990–1992*. Cambridge, MA: Blackwell.
Wæver, Ole (1996), "Europe, State and Nation in the New Middle Ages", in Jaap de Wilde and Håkan Wiberg (eds), *Organized Anarchy in Europe: The Role of Intergovernmental Organizations*. London and New York: Tauris, pp. 107–128.
—— (1997), "After Neo-Medievalism: Imperial Metaphors for European Security", in J. Peter Burgess (ed.), *Cultural Politics and Political Culture in Postmodern Europe*. Amsterdam and Atlanta, GA: Rodopi, pp. 321–363.
Wagner, Wolfgang (2003), "Building an Internal Security Community: The Democratic Peace and the Politics of Extradition in Western Europe", *Journal of Peace Research* 40(6): 695–712.
Walker, Neil (ed.) (2004), *Europe's Area of Freedom, Security and Justice*. Oxford: Oxford University Press.
Weber, Max (1956), *Wirtschaft und Gesellschaft: Grundriss der Verstehenden Soziologie*. Tübingen: Mohr.
Werner, Wouter G. and Jaap de Wilde (2001), "The Endurance of Sovereignty", *European Journal of International Relations* 7(3): 283–313.
Wilde, Jaap de (1994), "(Neo)Medieval (Dis)Integration in Europe: Lessons from the Thirteenth Century". Copenhagen: Copenhagen Center for Peace and Conflict Research (WP 22/1994).
Zielonka, Jan (2001), "How Enlarged Borders will Reshape the European Union", *Journal of Common Market Studies* 39(3): 507–536.

11 Europe, war, and territory

Peter van Ham

Introduction: Look mama, no territory!

Territory is not what it used to be. Globalization upsets the monopoly of the state's bounded space, cyberspace becomes the virtual version of *Lebensraum* and time itself becomes the main focus of attention to the detriment of the mundane, boring two-dimensional soil.[1] Wars are being fought to dominate territory, but as a by-product the Westphalian taboo on intervention has gone through the legal window with the "international community's" military actions in Kosovo (1999) and Iraq (2003). Terrorist organizations like al-Qaida operate from everywhere and nowhere, appropriately and worryingly labelled "non-state actors." The United States' (US) new National Security Strategy (NSS) of 2002, draws the obvious strategic conclusion that the traditional Cold War policies of deterrence and containment no longer apply, since the new enemies are terrorists and rogue states bent on wanton destruction, whose "soldiers seek martyrdom in death."[2] If terrorists hit the United States or Europe, how do they hit back if no obvious territorial target is available? Without territory – be it cyberspace or al-Qaida terrorists – the well-known, modern "rules of the game" are being questioned, upsetting our mental map and undermining the relevance of standard operating policies.

We have seen this coming, of course. It has been decades since the first authoritative papers threw light on "the end of" all the imaginable aspects of modernity, from the irrelevance of territory and the death of distance to the end of war. The Internet and al-Qaida terrorists illustrate the nature of this revolution, perhaps sounding a return to (neo-)Medieval times.[3] But these kinds of claims entered the academic (and policy) debate long before 9/11, sparking a broad and fruitful academic debate between cosmopolitans who foresaw the end of the political system as we know it, and (let's call them) neo-Weberians, who aspired to "bring the state back in." For a very short while, the relevance of territory seemed to be limited to biological studies on the behavior of the stickleback fish engaged in territorial dances while snorting bubbles at each other and then aggressively shoving their noses in the sand, trying to stare each other down. The political equivalent of this kind of behavior remains obvious, even in our allegedly post-Westphalian era. But apart from the occasional political fanfare, how seriously should territory still be taken?

Inside the European Union (EU)-space, our impulses have moved from fighting and the formation of borders to political *Ersatz*-mechanisms which political scientists classify under "multi-level governance" within the world's first "postmodern polity."[4] The social constructivist move regarding territory – the now almost commonsensical notion that "territory and borders, as with other spatial concepts, are to be treated contextually"[5] – implies that space and borders are in and of themselves passive, and it is ideas and normative constructs that give them meaning, both socially and politically. John Ruggie has suggested that within the EU, these cultural understandings of territory may be shifting away from a modern single-point perspective toward a postmodern concept of multiperspectivism.[6] For the state, territory is a homogeneous concept, the space where sovereign power can be exercised, identity constructed, and history continued. As Robert Walker has argued, this perspective implies that outside threats are immediately interpreted as strikes on the state's power, authority and autonomy.[7] Adopting Ruggie's understanding of the nature of the EU, the question arises whether the EU – as a postmodern entity – necessarily follows the same script. Or has the EU invented its own political chemistry ("$N=1$"), leaving power politics behind?

On the surface, Europe seems to have lost what Nietzsche would call "der Wille zur Macht," just as it has lost its drive to conquer, pillage and destroy. Etymologically the word "territory" is presumed to derive from *terra*, which means earth, land, and sustenance. But the *Oxford English Dictionary* also suggests that it may derive from *terrere*, which means to frighten, or to terrorize. William E. Connolly has therefore suggested that these two meanings are closely linked, since "[t]o occupy a territory is to receive sustenance and to exercise violence. Territory is land occupied by violence."[8] Europe has turned this notion on its head, since to join Europe is to enter a land of milk and honey, peace and prosperity, a Kantian paradise, a postmodern permanent *plage* where life should be enjoyed and combat can (and should) only be experienced behind consoles. In this sense, real territory may continue to exist outside the "Real Europe", but within the EU-space different rules and emotional agendas apply.

Given the general acceptance of the ideational and contextual aspects of territory, the key question is less *whether* territory (be it the state or the EU) is constructed, but *how*. This chapter looks at the role war, conflict and violence play in the political process of iconizing the space which feels and positions itself as the "Real Europe."[9] What part do territory, distance, and space take in the shaping of Europe's cognitive framework? Dominique Moïsi has aptly compared Europe's geographical space with "a rapidly growing child. [It] does not know where its body ends."[10] This may explain Europe's current political clumsiness and its unwieldy character. Like this child, the

EU lacks sensory skills, orientation, ossified judgments, and – most relevant for this chapter – "adult" ideas about security and defense. Europe is beginning the new millennium in a slightly disorientated state of mind, feeling its way forward without a clear roadmap. Traditional political and emotional moorings have sunk or themselves become mobile and untrustworthy. Josef Joffe once referred to the US as "Europe's pacifier."[11] But what happens when the Yankees *do* go home, taking their "pacifier" with them? Will it be al-Qaida terrorists shooting holes in the permanent blue sky of Europe's very own Truman Show? And what about the EU's awkward neighbors? Once one leaves the "Real Europe" – passing all those jaded and sticky truck-drivers – should the EU not fall back on its almost forgotten survival-instincts? Or is this border essential to maintain the dream of a "Real Europe," generating similes of anarchy and the imaginary "Other" to reach self-awareness, and perhaps finally setting the EU to develop a more mature "strategic culture"?

This chapter argues that territory and the concept of territoriality continue to play a role in establishing the EU as a security and defense actor, and that war (and the idea of war) will be indispensable to that process. Historically, war and violence have played a major part in state-formation. Without war, "we" would hardly know who "we" were. The EU likes to portray itself as a postmodern entity that does not require war to establish itself as a political player. This is, however, a doubtful claim. This chapter therefore poses the uncomfortable question whether the "Real Europe" may need war to get real, to grow up? This is (as Ole Wæver formulated it), "simply a restatement of the classical prejudice that war is the true 'rite de passage' for an international subject."[12] But it is certainly no mere rhetorical question, just for theory's sake. There are clear indications that the EU and its member states are shedding their military inhibitions and are preparing the Union for a more active, interventionist role where coercion and military force are essential components of a carefully calibrated "policy-mix" of instruments of statecraft. The EU's first-ever European Security Strategy (officially endorsed in December 2003) is witness to this European move toward an assertive strategy based on *Realpolitik* and a new European zeal for liberal imperialism.

During the coming years, the EU (to continue Moïsi's metaphor) may well reach geopolitical maturity, becoming more aware and self-conscious of its place and role in the world. In this process, the EU's borders – both political and territorial – will become more important, not less so.

Wollt ihr den europäischen Krieg?

With a few minor exceptions, Europe's borders are not disputed. When there are skirmishes, they tend to assume a comical character, like the Spanish–Moroccan fracas over the Persil Island, in July 2002. Turkey and Greece may still claim each others rocks and, yes, Russia's direct access to

Kaliningrad through the new EU member state, Lithuania, remains precarious. But that is about it. The only territorial questions that remain are bureaucratized within the EU's Enlargement-file: EU-space continues to grow into adolescence. But unlike teenagers, the EU is not picking fights and shows few signs of rebellion against anyone or anything. The EU seems a pretty satisfied power, avoiding life-cycle's silly-season.

The EU is relaxed about territoriality. The European Commission's official aim is "to develop a zone of prosperity and a friendly neighborhood – a 'ring of friends' – with whom the EU enjoys close, peaceful and co-operative relations."[13] It is not obsessed by geopolitics and not tainted by rigid "single-point perspectival forms to the spatial organisation of politics."[14] One could therefore argue that the EU has not been developed from the classical premise of a "sphere of influence," but of a "sphere of affluence": the idea that Europe's stability and peace derive from prosperity and development.[15] The EU has long been a *Zivilmacht* with no authority over the foreign, security, and defense policies of its members. It has developed a political model in which power has been stripped from its coercive, military connotation. This implies, according to the European Commission, that "Europe's model of integration, working successfully on a continental scale, is a quarry from which ideas for global governance can and should be drawn."[16] Although the EU also argues that Europe should "show genuine leadership on the world stage," this remains of a normative nature, especially by benchmarking and emulating "best practices." For the moment, the EU lacks a geopolitical prism and its policies of enlargement have less to do with a Kjellénian quest to establish a European *Großraum*, than with the inward-looking objective to achieve and consolidate Franco-German pacification.[17]

Rudolf Kjellén, and other geopolitical philosophers writing in the first half of the nineteenth century, proposed that a territorial entity is not merely a "living space," but a living organism that could expand and contract depending on its health and strength. The German thinker, Karl Haushofer (who was close to the Nazi-elite) saw this *Lebensraum* as the "battle zone" between cultures, reflecting the strength of competing cultural entities.[18] Due to its associations with fascist ideology, the term "geopolitics" fell into disuse. In the light of this politically tainted history of *Geopolitik*, the EU has carefully avoided a geopolitical discourse, working its texts around disreputable notions like "balance of power"; "control over/access to natural resources"; "the differential impact of size"; and "the impact of topography on foreign policy." In a sense, the European integration project has been designed to thwart this geopolitical impetus.

But it has always remained questionable whether this lofty objective was realistic. Could the nation-state change its spots and reinvent itself on a European level as a postmodern political performer? The EU has certainly tried, and with some success. But as a quintessential modern notion, territoriality remains a necessary ingredient of the contemporary system of international relations. It is not only coded as collective identity, constituting the essence of a "people," it is – perhaps first and foremost – an epistemological principle, a lens through which the outside world is observed and understood. This happens in two ways.

First, without the notions of boundary and border, without discrete territorial spaces, it would be difficult to imagine integrity and to make a clear distinction between the Self and the Other. In many ways, "being" (based on the notion of identity) implies contact and communication, which in turn intimates the crossing of borders, real or imagined. This aspect deals with the phenomenality of territory, or the "territory-ness" of space. Borders are the political and ideational skin of the EU as a political organism; not in a geopolitical sense, but due to the increasing porosity of statal perimeters. One could therefore argue that the EU needs borders, it needs those truck drivers and those desperate immigrants flooding the northern Mediterranean basin, day in, day out. These are the irritants and sensations without which the EU's political antennas would not work. The EU proves itself to its citizens by dealing with these annoyances in a determined and effective manner. This is what states have done for centuries; this is what the EU does (or needs to do) as well.

Second, territorial borders set states apart from other actors on the world's stage. This aspect understands territoriality as a fundamental characteristic of the Westphalian state, turning it into an essential asset of modern statehood. Multinational corporations, global financial markets, non-governmental organizations (NGOs), and terrorists, may all be important players with Chief Executive Officers (CEOs) and Headquarters (HQs), but they have one thing in common: they lack territory. Territory and often well-developed domestic control and disciplining mechanisms, are the state's 'unique selling point' (USP). As is well known, the monopoly of force is another defining element of statehood. As Alexander Wendt suggests, "this means that the potential for organized violence is unified in the sense that those controlling its exercise cannot make decisions independent of each other, but always operate as a 'team.'"[19] Although private military companies are gnawing at this monopoly[20] (and the EU is taking a serious bite too!), war (and the threat of war) remains a key border-drawing concept, setting "us" apart from "them," guarding the boundaries of identity and territory. Like house-owners, states turn conservative status quo-actors, not only keen to keep up with the Jones', but also keen to preserve the existing modern state-system. No intruders are wanted, with the EU as the only exception.

The territorial, down-to-earth aspect makes "the state" unique and relevant, both as a reality and as a concept. Despite debunking efforts of historians and political scientists, the myth of the primordial and eternal state endures. Eugen Weber's *Peasants Into Frenchmen*, among many others, has carefully described how nation-states are made and maintained.[21] Charles Tilly has claimed that states not only make war, but that war also makes (constructs and justifies) states.[22] Benedict Anderson, in turn, has suggested that nation-states are "imagined communities," open to change and adaptation.²³ Given the EU's identity deficit, it seems logical to ask whether (and, if so, how) the EU could/should emulate the lessons of state-formation by dealing with security and defense matters, perhaps even going as far as fighting wars.²⁴

The EU's Eurobarometer opinion poll indicates that across the EU, the general populace already favors (with an impressive 74 per cent majority in April 2003) a clear European security-cum-defense role.²⁵ Rationally, the continental organization of European defense is advantageous, since the economies of scale derived from EU-level military R&D, defense procurement, planning, and operations, are impressive.²⁶ The EU now restricts itself to peacekeeping and peace-support operations, not only in European areas like Macedonia, Bosnia and Herzegovina, but also "out of area" as in the Democratic Republic of Congo (DRC). These are piecemeal steps toward changing the EU's identity (and imago) from a purely "civilian actor," to a fully-fledged statal entity on a continental scale.

The EU's "military" operations, however, are not of the masculine, heroic kind.²⁷ Or, to play on Gordon Gekko's words: "Peacekeeping is for wimps!" And so is nation-building, economic and political reconstruction, and post-conflict reconciliation.²⁸ These are activities that involve the deployment of unarmed (or, at most, lightly-armed) forces in a peaceful environment. Peacekeepers are impartial, relatively passive, seeking consensus and stability. On the opposite end of the spectrum we find armed conflict in war, involving combat operations. War is only "war" when precision-guided missiles are fired and special forces engage in network-centric warfare. Clearly, the EU has not yet embarked upon "war," but has limited itself to the so-called "lower echelon" of the conflict resolution spectrum, leaving the more heroic action to the US and NATO. This seems to corroborate the maxim that the US is from Mars and the EU from Venus.²⁹ Such a gendered analysis makes us appreciate why the EU lacks confidence and status in the military arena. No matter how many body bags return from peacekeeping missions around the globe, as long as the EU is in the business of caring, showing compassion, building, and creating, it will remain unimpressively pedestrian.

The EU's moderation and modesty may be ethically, or morally, preferable and even superior. As suggested earlier, geopolitics and *Realpolitik* were considered past stations of little relevance to postmodern Europe. But this attitude has proven only partially justified. Gareth Evans was speaking for western democracies as a whole when he claimed that "[i]t took us most of the [1990s] to re-learn that war can be a progressive cause."³⁰ In a similar vein, Christopher Hill indicated, "[s]tudents of the European Union have for too long neglected geopolitics, either because they could not see its relevance to a 'civilian power' or because they were uneasy with that kind of discourse for normative reasons."³¹ This state of denial may continue to give pleasure to those who subscribe to the idea/l that the EU constitutes a security community – where members of the system must no longer perceive each other as threats, and hence expect to settle their disputes peacefully.[32] But this idyll only goes so far in solidifying Europe as a *Gemeinschaft*.[33] The EU is now reaching the limits that its civilian integration project has set to the process of identity-formation. And these same Eurobarometer polls also indicate that EU citizens just do not want to feel more "European" over time, preferring to recognize their national and/or regional roots instead.

The inevitable – be it equally uncomfortable – conclusion may be that what is necessary for the EU to mature, is for it to engage in military interventions, preferably without a United Nations (UN) Security Council mandate. This would signal to the EU's international partners that "Europe" had reached the status of an international unitary actor, and at the same time signal to "its" citizens that the EU (and *not* the state) should take responsibility for security and defense matters. Cynthia Weber therefore argues, "intervention is understood to be the flip side of sovereignty," turning "sovereignty and intervention {into} the boundary of a sovereign state's authority." The bottom-line is that "to speak about intervention practices is to imply the existence of sovereign states (...) One way to assert the existence of something (sovereignty) is to insist upon the existence of its opposite (intervention)."[34] Just playing with guns does not a soldier make; the EU has to make its mark, collect scalps, and earn respect. The EU has to undergo the initiation rite of intervention to shed its civilian, feminine image and join the exclusive rank of Superpowers. As Tuomas Forsberg argues, "whereas power is masculine, space is often feminine. Territorial invasion by the other is penetration that equals rape."[35] As this unpleasant metaphor indicates, an intervention-prone EU that is trying to prove its *machismo* will be a mixed blessing. But this is a normative judgment, and not an academic one.

Following this line of argument, the EU may take the next step and prove its "manhood" (or its "actorness"),[36] to itself and the rest of the world by ignoring and violating the sovereignty of others, and it has to mark its territory by illegally trespassing into the territory of others.[37] As will become evident in the discussion on the EU's new Security Strategy (see below), Europe's attitude toward intervention and "pre-emptive strikes" to address threats emanating from "failed states," remains ambivalent and hesitant. This reflects the different strategic cultures represented within the EU, where countries like Sweden and Ireland have long-standing traditions of neutrality, and France and the UK consider themselves global actors in their own right whose military obligations come naturally. But it is testimony to the changing strategic culture within Europe that Germany is reforming its *Bundeswehr* to develop a "35,000-strong '*intervention force*' for fighting and a 70,000-strong 'stabilization force' for peacekeeping, with 'support forces' of 137,500."[38] These intervention forces will under no circumstance serve a national, German cause, but be strongly embedded within the EU (or NATO)-framework (preferably) with a UN-mandate.

As a strategic actor, the EU starts off as a *tabula rasa*, whose institutional record still has to be set. This is not only a discursive process, but also a performative one.[39] In itself, this would hardly be new. As Erik Ringmar argues (taking Sweden's interventions during the Thirty Years' War as a case-study), states can fight wars mainly to get recognition for a different identity, to be taken "seriously" as a Great Power, rather than for objective, rational, Realist reasons of pre-established national interests.[40] For the nation-state, this offers new, heroic narratives based on wars of national defense, national liberation, and the customary glorification of the individuals who sacrificed themselves out of loyalty to their *Heimat*, Motherland, or whatever anthropomorphic characterization of territory is chosen.[41] It will be difficult to imagine a nation whose identity has not been (at least partially) framed by its conflicts and wars.

The centrality of war as a state-builder and identity-congealer is not only a political phenomenon with a long history; it remains lurking in the nature of Europe's postmodern society. Within the EU's Kantian space war has been exorcized and delegitimized, turning the political game into collective nit picking over voting-rights and subsidies; European politics has become domestic politics. But within Europe's Postmodern Man[42] still lingers a Nietzschean desire to glorify war as the greatest of all mental and physical stimulants. It is part of Nietzsche's notion of the duality within individuals, the dynamic between their Apollinian and Dionysian sides. In his *Die Geburt der Tragödie* (*The Birth of Tragedy*), Nietzsche claims that the Apollinian principle exemplifies self-knowledge and moderation (Europe's civilian, reflexive mode), whereas the Dionysian element is a symbol of primal unity where "each one feels himself not only united, reconciled and fused with his neighbour, but as one with him"[43] (Europe's new role as a military actor).

The Dionysian notion of "war" is therefore the flip-side of the "Real (Apollinian) Europe," a psychological urge to experience the danger of life on the "wild side," because the "splendours of freedom are at their brightest when freedom is sacrificed at the altar of security."[44] Without war and anarchy as the ultimate "Other," the appreciation of Europe's peaceful and domesticated "Self" would be less real, and ultimately would decline. War is the Jungian "shadow" which gives Europe's *Persona* its depth, and – although Europeans won't easily admit to it – also a foundation, and a sense of community. As Chris Hedges has argued, "The enduring attraction of war is this: even with its destruction and carnage it can give us what we long for in life. It can give us purpose, meaning, a reason for living. Only when we are in the midst of conflict does the shallowness and vapidness of much of our lives become apparent."[45]

This presents an uncomfortable reading of the EU Eurobarometer's continued appeal for a more European approach to security and defense. Following the call of the likes of Joseph de Maistre and Ernst Jünger, a European war (or better: a war *fought by the EU, as the EU*) offers opportunities for redemption and emancipation of salvation and regeneration. This is a myth, of course, but arguably a powerful and persistent one. It is a myth whose

Dionysian assumptions will upset those desirous to cling to the EU's model as a civilian power. But since the history of nation-building points to the centrality of war to solidify identity and territory (both its "territory-ness" and "Westphalian" qualities), taking this next step has a good chance of resuscitating the EU, giving it a new lease on political life.

Failed states and failed policies

All this is anathema to many, if not most, European policymakers since "Good Europeans" are not supposed to talk about these sort of things and see the EU in a Dionysian light. The discourse on "Europe" is restricted to rose-colored fairytales which, like all linguistic constructions and narratives, shape our knowledge of reality.[46]

The EU's founding myth goes as follows: "Once upon a time, there were nasty states who didn't like each other much, even fighting bloody wars. Then the EU-Fairy showed them the way to cooperate, first on coal and steel, afterwards on other things as well. Today, Euro-people look back in wonder on their ignorant and aggressive forefathers, and they live happily ever after." This is, of course, an abridged version of the EU-discourse. But in all stories on European integration, overcoming narrow-minded nationalism and avoiding war among member states are attributed to the EU's strategy of pooling sovereignty and consensus-based policymaking. Bad states make war; Good (and "Real") Europeans make compromises. This is closely linked to the argument for EU enlargement, which is extending the zone of stability eastward, opening up the "sphere of affluence," and giving less-privileged peoples the opportunity to join Kantian paradise.

But the novelty of the post-9/11 strategic environment and the nervousness about the rapidly deteriorating transatlantic relationship, has forced the EU to rewrite this text.[47] The EU is now reconsidering the relevance of its own fairytale, brainstorming on its strategic options. This is required since the EU wants to close the transatlantic gap in threat perceptions which has opened up after 9/11. The Bush administration's NSS (corroborated by the invasion of Iraq in 2003) indicates that the US is now prepared to embark upon pre-emptive military interventions, even without the UN Security Council green light via a mandate. As President Bush formulated it in his 2004 State of the Union Address: "America will never seek a permission slip to defend the security of our country."

The change in EU-thinking has been encouraged by the thought-provoking ideas from Robert Cooper, who works as Director-General for Common Foreign and Security Policy (CFSP) in the European Council in Brussels. Cooper – who has the ear of Javier Solana, the EU's High-Representative for the CFSP – suggests that while inside the EU's postmodern space Kantian peace prevails, outside a vast array of security threats by both modern states and premodern areas lie in waiting. In particular, the premodern world of so-called "failed states" poses problems, since drug cartels, crime syndicates, and terrorists use this anarchical territory as bases to attack and/or destabilize Europe's postmodern harmony. Cooper is clear in his policy-prescription: The EU needs to intervene. Cooper argues that

> the challenge to the postmodern world is to get used to the idea of double standards. Among ourselves, we operate on the basis of laws and open cooperative security. But when dealing with more old-fashioned kinds of states outside the postmodern continent of Europe, we need to revert to the rougher methods of an earlier era – force, pre-emptive attack, deception, whatever is necessary to deal with those who still live in the nineteenth century world of every state for itself. Among ourselves, we keep the law but when we are operating in the jungle, we must also use the laws of the jungle.[48]

Cooper suggests the EU should be prepared to undertake an enlightened form of colonialism under the label of "liberal imperialism." He realizes the hazards involved, but argues, "the risks of letting countries rot, as the West did Afghanistan, may be even greater." Hence the EU has the duty to intervene, to spare itself future attacks from premodern "failed states," and to "export stability and liberty."[49] Such an assertive foreign policy would not only be in the EU's interest, but also be in line with the US Bush administration's strategy of pre-emptive (or even preventive) strikes against terrorists and their supporters.

An EU-led military intervention should be considered the military equivalent to introducing the EU's single currency, the euro. But just as EU member states have been understandably reluctant to hand over their monetary sovereignty to "Frankfurt," they are loath to let go of this other crown jewel of modernity: their monopoly of violence. This reluctance illustrates the Realist assumption of International Relations (IR) theory that states are jealous guardians of their privileges and powers.

For the record, member states will claim that they are unsure the EU has the competence and capabilities to execute a complex, dangerous, and controversial military operation. But it is more intricate than that. The territorial differentiation of politics is not a "given," but needs to be produced, proven, and imagined on a regular basis. Like male dogs, states endlessly mark their territory; even neutered dogs/states continue this habit, to the annoyance of many. European states used to have a plethora of these sociospacial markers, from passports and visas, to asylum rules and citizens' rights. They still have many left, but some nervousness has crept in now that monetary sovereignty is pooled and the state's USP starts to lose its allure. In this volatile political context, delegating the business of "war" to the EU is seen as a possible transformative moment. Recalling Max Weber's modernist definition of statehood as the coupling together of the principles of territoriality, administrative, and military monopolies, as well as the legitimacy to use them, one can understand the anguish of EU member states. With intra-EU (statal) borders crumbling and EU-governance flourishing, delegating the use of (external) violence to "Brussels" may just be a bridge too far. Following Cynthia Weber's logic, an EU-led intervention would substantiate the Union's authority over defense matters, elevating it into a league of its own.

Rationally, this may not make too much sense, especially since many European states already support the US and NATO in their military operations. But institutional power-envy seems mainly reserved for the EU. European states realize that only accumulated EU power challenges their legitimacy and status; only a strong, "masculine" EU courts European citizens' favors, to the detriment of conceited European states.

And the EU still has much courting to do if it wants to be successful, since participation in "European defense" remains voluntary (only new members have little choice but to accept the Union's *acquis stratégique*). The EU's confused and confusing territoriality in the area of defense is reflected in its so-called "variable geometry," where member states can "opt out" if they wish. Austria, Denmark, and Ireland have special arrangements on defense, exonerating them from any EU-activity with military connotations that do not suit their political and/or moral tastes. The parallel with the early stages of European state formation imposes itself, since (as Mary Kaldor has argued) during this epoch "monarchs raised armies to fight wars from coalitions of feudal barons rather as the UN Secretary General, today, has to mobilize voluntary contributions from individual states in order to raise a peacekeeping force."[50] The EU's velcro-forces are organized in a similar way.

In the current debate on the future of the EU (the so-called "Convention") proposals to insert a collective defense-clause in Europe's embryonic constitution were rejected. Several EU member states do not see the need to accept the avowal that "an armed attack against one or more of them shall be considered an attack against them all." This may indicate unwillingness to subscribe to the very idea of territorial defense, but it also points to a lack of solidarity and a refusal to adopt a geostrategic view on Europe's security.[51] The absence of a standing European army under control of the EU also indicates that "Brussels" cannot yet apply the Clausewitzian dictum that war is a rational tool for the pursuit of European interests as a "continuation of politics by other means." There are no signs that the EU will copy the state's process of consolidating its authority. Whereas the European state levied burdensome taxes to finance its standing armies (which, in the eighteenth century, accounted for three-quarters of the state budget) the EU continues to pay for its military operations on an *ad hoc* basis.[52]

This is not surprising. Europe's "old" wars of the twentieth century were total wars involving mass-mobilization (and conscription-based armies), mass-production, and mass-communication. Instead, the "new" wars still to come are decenterd and deterritorial, where power is not in mass but in speed, not in power but in flexibility. Like the US, the EU strives for a postmodern military with relatively small professional armed forces trained to deal effectively with diverse, but probably subnational (ethnic or terrorist) threats. This implies that, unlike modern times, no mass-mobilization is required. Germany is among the few major powers clinging to military conscription, and unlike the US, most European countries do not have so-called "Reserve Forces." This means that ordinary citizens no longer have to ask "Why die for Brussels?" Instead, postmodern warfare is turned into a high-tech spectator sport "in which audiences will have been reduced to postmodern Romans watching bloody spectacles in the electric arena comprised of televised images."[53] This may make ad-hocery and a high level of voluntarism on EU-defense tolerable, but it also holds back Euro-jingoism and obstructs the accumulation of shared formative (military) experiences at an EU-level.

Europe's emerging strategic culture

The power-envy of EU member states indicates that their national identities remain sticky, and do not change easily, let alone often. But change is possible, particularly during critical junctures which can be defined as *"perceived crisis situations occurring from complete policy failures, but also triggered by external events."*[54] European examples are the change in Germany's national identity after World War II, the UK's post-colonial identity after the dissolution of its Empire, as well as, more recently, Russia's shift toward a post-imperial identity after the end of the Cold War and the demise of the USSR. Obviously, war is such a critical juncture, making it both necessary and easier for political elites to promote different ideas about political order and the role of their own state in a novel power constellation. War – won, lost, or merely endured – often confronts states with a new territorial reality (see the examples of Germany, the UK and Russia), making a commensurate identity-move appear reasonable, almost natural.

Europe's identity as a mainly civilian power was severely dented by the Balkan wars of the 1990s, and the Kosovo imbroglio in particular. The informal institutional division of labor – whereby NATO fights, the EU funds, and the UN feeds – gnawed at Europe's self-image as enlightened, superior Kantians-with-a-mission: to enlarge their postmodern space for others to benefit. In Europe's security discourse, "Kosovo" stood for the looming prospect of a Balkanization of Europe, the ultimate metaphor of chaos and disintegration antithetical to the "Real Europe" of peace and stability. As Wæver argues, "Balkanisation is a tool for legitimising an international order *without* a named enemy (...) 'Security' thus becomes shorthand for the argument: We have to do everything to ensure that integration, and not fragmentation, is the outcome."[55] To speak of Milosevic's Serbia as the ultimate threat to "European security" therefore implied the very existence and strategic relevance of Europe's fairytale on "security through integration."

But the EU missed this unique and timely chance to use "Kosovo" as an alibi to stabilize the meaning of "European security" through military intervention. It was not the EU that intervened, but NATO. Or, more precisely, it was the US with its military superiority and its "just do it!" – mentality which enabled it to muscle in and bring the internecine conflict to a halt. The Kosovo-episode was devastating to Europe's continental dignity and pride. Europe – and the EU in particular – was humbled, even humiliated. As the crow flies, Kosovo is a mere hundred miles from Italy, Greece, and Austria. As such an obvious part of geographical Europe, ending this conflict was flatly on Europe's policy-plate. Moreover, the *Schindler's List*-like TV-scenes reaching European homes were uncomfortably reminiscent of Europe's not-too-distant past. Mr Solana (in his capacity of NATO secretary-general) argued in 1999, that the contest was "between two visions of Europe. One vision – Milosevic's vision – is of a Europe of ethnically pure states, a Europe of nationalism, authoritarianism, and xenophobia. The other vision – that of the NATO allies, the European Union and of our Partners – is a Europe of integration, democracy and ethnic pluralism."[56]

And while Europe's historical "Other" (vision) resurfaced in Kosovo, the EU experienced a *déjà vu* all over again: impotent in the face of evil, long on rhetoric, short on political courage and military power. For the EU, "Kosovo" embodied a critical juncture, a war not fought but merely "seen on TV."[57] It showed that there were still people in Europe who failed to believe in the Euro-fairytale, who defined survival not in terms of ego-comfort, but in valleys and hills occupied, not expressed in comitology but in ethnic cleansing.

"Kosovo" has been a key challenge to the EU's ego and nascent masculine security identity. The ensuing European discourse on the Balkans/Kosovo has reformulated the EU's feebleness into a mythical "wake-up call," sparking a *jetzt erst recht*-mentality in the face of its embarrassing military weakness *vis-à-vis* the US. Indeed, Lord Robertson argued in 1999: "The division of labour we saw in the Kosovo air campaign was militarily necessary, but it is politically unsustainable in the longer term. The European Security and Defence Identity is no longer just an attractive idea; it has become an urgent necessity."[58] Much of the dynamic in the EU's defense ambitions and plans can be traced back to Europe's experiences in the Balkans.[59] The atrocities on the EU's doorstep indicated to most European policymakers that a wait-and-see-approach was not acceptable. If necessary, even military intervention had to be considered as a viable option. As British Prime Minister Tony Blair argued in 1999, "[Kosovo] is a just war, based not on any territorial ambitions but on values. We cannot let the evil of ethnic cleansing stand. We must not rest until it is reversed. We have learned twice before in this century that appeasement does not work. If we let an evil dictator reign unchallenged, we will have to spill infinitely more blood and treasure to stop him later (...) That is the basis for the recent initiative I took with President Chirac of France to improve Europe's own defence capabilities."[60]

Trying to live up to this test, the EU has issued two important new security documents reflecting the impact of Cooper's "liberal imperialist" ideas on European strategic thinking. In Spring 2003, EU Foreign Ministers prepared an initiative to formulate a comprehensive European strategy to halt the proliferation of weapons of mass destruction (WMD), which was officially endorsed by EU leaders at their June summit in Thessaloniki. In this document – entitled "Basic Principles for an EU Strategy Against Proliferation of Weapons of Mass Destruction" – European states argue that treaties, dialog, and international inspections should form the first line of defense against WMD proliferation. But, when this method fails, "coercive measures under Chapter VII of the U.N. Charter and international law (sanctions, selective or global, interceptions of shipments and, as appropriate, the use of force) could be envisioned." This is widely regarded as a first – and remarkable – step by the EU toward accepting the logic of America's new security doctrine.

At the Thessaloniki summit, the EU also issued its first-ever Security Strategy (as a draft paper), which was accepted at the December 2003 European Council.[61] Echoing the US strategy, the EU Security Strategy identifies WMD-proliferation as "potentially the greatest threat to our security." And although the EU still maintains that "our security and prosperity increasingly depend on an effective multilateral system," it makes a few path-breaking statements: "With the new threats, the first line of defence will often be abroad. The new threats are dynamic (...) left alone, terrorist networks will become ever more dangerous." It continues that "[a]ctive policies are needed to counter the new dynamic threats. We need to develop a strategic culture that fosters early, rapid, and when necessary, robust intervention." The EU also carefully accedes to America's judgment that "the gravest danger to [our Nation] lies at the crossroads of radicalism and technology."[62] Obviously, it is this concoction of premodern barbarity and postmodern high-tech which poses the greatest threat to modernity's institutional framework.

The EU's discourse of danger

The EU now recognizes that outside its space, in the "barbarian," premodern world and on the territory of "failed states," new threats lie in waiting. The EU's Security Strategy adopts the US's "evangelism of fear," combining a close knit Realist discourse with a quasi-religious claim that threats and sins lurk everywhere and security and salvation are only possible by relying on the EU church. This is what David Altheide calls the "discourse of fear"[63] and is novel to the EU, whose nomenclature was hitherto focused on challenges, risks, and possibilities. Clearly it is too early to judge how this new discourse will impact on the EU's reading of itself, its policies, and its influence. What is clear, however, is that the EU now unequivocally considers the use of (military) force a natural, legitimate, viable, and potentially effective policy-response.

For the EU, this discourse of fear/danger has a number of advantages. Following David Campbell's analysis, the EU's efforts to beef up its CFSP can "be rethorized as one of the boundary-producing practices central to the production and reproduction of the identity in whose name it operates."[64] Campbell argues that foreign policy and security documents (like the EU's Security Strategy) tell us what to fear, and why. He claims that the constant (re)writing of the nature of (in this case) the EU's character in foreign policy texts, serves to "enframe, limit, and domesticate a particular identity." The new discourse of "9/11" is, like the Cold War, a "coded struggle between the civilized and the barbaric (. . .) a conflict of epic proportions in which the future of 'civilization' [is] at stake."[65] Although the EU has not officially declared itself in a state of war, terrorism is certainly considered a war on the state, as well as a war on the state of Europe's Union.

For the EU, the added bonus of this policy is that it aims to "repair" failed states that are anomalies in the modern world system, and, by their very existence, question other states' status and authority. Following the logic of *horror vacui*, failed states either have to go (for example by absorbing them in "successful" federations), turn themselves into a UN protectorate, or reform and thrive. By identifying the "Indians" and putting on war paint, the EU prepares itself for defending its frontiers and civilizing that anarchic wilderness, subjugate its wild nature and convert the savages to accept the Kantian gospel.

Given the EU's civilian strategic culture, the shift toward a more martial, assertive foreign policy is gradual and erratic. Still, change is already visible, most notably in the EU's approach toward Iran, a founding member of the so-called "axis of evil."[66] The EU is unlikely to endorse the use of force against Tehran, but its policy of "positive engagement" and a "comprehensive dialog" has now been reconsidered. For the past two decades, the EU tried a "soft" approach assuming this would strengthen both Europe's influence and the hand of reformist factions in the Iranian government. While not halting the dialog with Iran, the EU now makes it clear that continued financial and trade relations will be conditional upon concrete, verifiable, and sustained improvements of Tehran's conduct in the human rights field as well as its cooperation on political issues.[67] This is new, since the EU has traditionally been reluctant to make use of its economic and financial leverage for strategic purposes.

This Euro-evangelism has the further benefit that it legitimizes a broadening of the scope of EU-policy into previously restricted, or even forbidden, territory. As Seyla Benhabib has argued, "The presence of an enemy who is neither a military adversary nor a representative agent of a known state creates confusion as to whether it is the police and other law enforcement agencies or the military who should take the lead in the investigation and struggle; the lines between acts of crime and acts of war are blurred."[68] Benhabib makes the point that this invents a new category of "internal enemies," terrorists who are among us, violating our sense of community, and undermining our sense of normalcy and domestic order. Jef Huysmans claims that these "undecidables" are like "strangers [who] pose a hermeneutic problem because they do not fit the categories." In this reading, al-Qaida terrorists are expressing the possibility of chaos from within the existing order, making them "a rest product of the activity of categorizing."[69] Since the EU's internal (state) borders have become less sanguine and relevant, it is now up to the EU to take on this "new" challenge. It has to offer "deliverables," and show what it's worth to its "European citizens."

And so it has, with great zeal even.[70] The EU has strengthened its role in the internal security and intelligence area by introducing a European arrest warrant to supplant the current system of extradition between EU member states; a common definition of terrorism and related penalties; numerous measures against cross-border organized crime (including terrorism); joint investigation teams of police and magistrates from throughout the EU; routine exchanges of information about terrorism between member states and Europol (the EU's nascent FBI); a specialist anti-terrorist team within Europol; a new coordination body composed of magistrates, prosecutors and police officers, called Eurojust; and a cooperation agreement on terrorism between Europol and relevant US authorities. The EU is now also dealing with public health and civil emergency issues related to the coming terrorist atrocities on EU-territory. It is scrutinizing dubious financial transactions on the look-out for money-laundering and links to terrorist organizations. All these efforts are officially aimed at the creation of an "Area of Freedom, Security and Justice in the European Union", originally promised by the EU in October 1999, and achieved in May 2004.[71]

This proliferation of EU-policies indicates the domestication of the security debate by shaping a security-space as well as a security-society. Networked computers and the Schengen Information System (SIS) monitor suspicious events and patterns. External borders are hardened, openness and transparency are under siege by control measures and security-related codes of secrecy. Danger is largely externalized, but control and discipline is exercised following a European design. It indicates that (what Ken Booth labels) "the Cold War of the mind" has returned in full glory: "an eschatological outlook on world affairs (...) fuelled by ethnocentrism, political realism, ideological fundamentalism and strategic reductionism."[72] As in the Cold War, terrorism assumes the tropes of barbarity, neighborhood-watches, and deception. It follows a Foucaultian approach to power, introducing a new post-9/11-governmentality which not only affects the EU and its member states, but also their citizens. Citizens are, and increasingly expect to be, under surveillance, by computers, closed-circuit camera systems and high-tech biometrical systems.

This means that the EU offers a new rationale for further integration, which, since 9/11, has turned into a *raison de nation*.[73] What is at stake is societal security, the basic right of EU-citizens to live their life without fear. The paradox, of course, is that the EU seems to buy into the argument that it has to adopt a discourse of danger to achieve this laudable objective.

Conclusion: war, space, and persuasion

Robert Walker has rightly reminded us that it is a grand cliché of modernity to claim that we live in an "era of rapid transformations": "Ever since the possibility of a progressive history was elaborated during the European Enlightenment, modern thinkers have struggled to grasp the succession of events as an unfolding of a more or less reasonable, even rational process."[74] Europe's post-9/11 fairytale follows a similar narrative: We live in a different era, with new threats and new actors, which "Europe" can only control by continuous integration at home, and a new style of fierceness abroad.[75] It will take some time and many incantations to make this story stick.

What is essential in this process is a dual effort to act strategically (by military intervention) and discursively (by the EU's Security Strategy), encouraging a process of elite and popular socialization toward an heroic European identity within a circumscribed EU-space. EU-led war as the "right thing" to do involves practical adaptation (moving toward European armed forces and defense planning) as well as socialization through discourse, emphasizing communication, argumentation, and persuasion.[76] For the EU, military action should be adopted as a "persuasion," an *habitus* (Bourdieu), or a *Hintergrundkonsens* (Habermas), which shines through over time, be it erratically, and whose meaning we recognize only in retrospect. For the EU to reach this goal, it will take time and will only be realized through deeds and achievement.

It will also mean that the EU – which is always referred to as a process, rather than a condition – is reaching adolescence. After the absorption of Central Europe into the European body politic, the EU will have a clearer appreciation of its territorial shape. The lines of impatient truck-drivers will be moved further eastward. But the flood of the world's poor will continue, reminding the swollen "Real Europe" of its "real" tasks and the permeability of its borders. The EU will (have to) realize that (its) territory is no longer the basis of (its) power; nor is it a sufficient guarantee of (its) security. The prospect of a "Fortress Europe" – emulating the gated communities of opulence dotted across the US – is unrealistic, while unsustainable. Threats to Europe's security know no inside/outside dichotomy; "terrorists" of all feathers have cells, rather than bases, use the Internet, rather than classical diplomacy.

The EU's embrace of the persuasion of power adds a masculine side to its increasingly androgynous persona, inevitably turning diversity into internalized schizophrenia. What Cooper calls a "policy of double-standards" means accepting a legitimate role for war to annihilate (or convert) failed states, and terrorist "undecidables", whose very existence cannot be tolerated. By using the practice and language of violence, the EU makes a discursive move which offers it state-like qualities and state-like authority. Again, this will take time. Taking a Braudelian perspective, our interest goes to the evolution of the fundamental structures and the *mentalités* that define a specific era, rather than mere events or medium-term time spans.[77] In this *longue durée*, the EU will take on "imperial" qualities, and many of the neo-medievalist fantasies may come true. Within this European *Großraum*, people live the experiences of (regional) globalization, informatization, and risk society, in the unsettling awareness that the postmodern geostrategic condition is gnawing at all boundaries, between inside/outside; domestic/foreign; West/rest; us/them. Perhaps even between good/bad. It is in this context that the EU's ambitions of fighting necessary but "just wars" should be situated. Despite all the horror and suffering, war remains the most forceful signifier of all.

Notes

1 Timothy W. Luke (1998), "Running Flat Out On the Road Ahead: Nationality, Sovereignty, and Territoriality in the World of the Information Superhighway," in Gearóid Ó Tuathail and Simon Dalby (eds), *Rethinking Geopolitics*. London: Routledge; James Anderson and Liam O'Dowd (1999), "Borders, Border Regions and Territoriality: Contradictory Meanings, Changing Significance," *Regional Studies* 33(7).
2 Quoted in Joseph Cirincione (2003), "Can Preventive War Cure Proliferation?," *Foreign Policy* 137(July-August): 67.
3 For example, Stephen J. Kobrin (1998), "Back to the Future: Neomedievalism and the Postmodern Digital World Economy," *Journal of International Affairs* 51(2) (Spring).
4 John G. Ruggie (1993), "Territoriality and Beyond: Problematizing Modernity in International Relations," *International Organization*, 47(1): 139–174; Peter van Ham (2001), *European Integration and the Postmodern Condition: Governance, Democracy, Identity*. London: Routledge.
5 Tuomas Forsberg (2003), "The Ground Without Foundation? Territory as a Social Construct," *Geopolitics* 8(2) (Summer): 11.
6 Ruggie, "Territoriality and Beyond."
7 R.B.J. Walker (1993), *Inside/Outside: International Relations as Political Theory*. Cambridge: Cambridge University Press.
8 William E. Connolly, "Tocqueville, Territory, and Violence," in Michael J. Shapiro and Hayward R. Alker (eds) (1996), *Challenging Boundaries: Global Flows, Territorial Identities*. Minneapolis: University of Minnesota Press, p. 144.
9 John A. Vasquez (1993), *The War Puzzle*. Cambridge: Cambridge University Press; Daniel S. Geller and J. David Singer (1998), *Nations at War: A Scientific Study of International Conflict*. Cambridge: Cambridge University Press; and Lawrence Freedman (ed.) (1994), *War*. Oxford and New York: Oxford University Press.
10 Dominique Moïsi (1998), "The World Moves On," *Financial Times*, 8 June, p. 14.
11 Josef Joffe (1984), "Europe's American Pacifier," *Foreign Policy* 54(Spring).
12 Ole Wæver (1997), "Imperial Metaphors: Emerging European Analogies to Pre-Nation-State Imperial Systems," in Ola Tunander, Pavel Baev and Victoria Ingrid Einagel (eds), *Geopolitics in Post-Wall Europe: Security, Territory and Identity*. London: Sage, p. 71.
13 "Wider Europe – Neighbourhood: A New Framework for Relations with our Eastern and Southern Neighbours," Communication from the Commission to the Council and the European Parliament, Brussels, 11 March 2003,

COM(2003) 104 final. Internet: http://europa.eu.int/comm /external_ relations/ we/doc/com03_104_en.pdf (30 January 2004).
14 Ruggie, "Territoriality and Beyond," p. 159.
15 Peter van Ham and Przemyslaw Grudzinski (1999/2000), "Affluence and Influence: The Conceptual Basis of Europe's New Politics," *The National Interest* 58(Winter). See also Harlan Cleveland and Marc Luycks (1998), *"Civilizations and Governance"*, Working paper, European Commission Forward Studies Unit, Brussels.
16 European Commission, "Shaping the New Europe", Brussels, 9.2.2000 COM (2000) 154 final.
17 For a good overview, see Bruno Tescke, "Geopolitik und Marxismus." Internet: http://www.theglobalsite.ac.uk/press/201teschke.htm (20 January 2004).
18 Ola Tunander (1997), "Introduction," in Oba Tunander, Pavel K. Baev and Victoria I. Einagel (eds), *Geopolitics in Post-Wall Europe*. Thousand Oaks, CA: SAGE Publications Ltd. See also Saul B. Cohen (1975), *Geography and Politics in a World Divided*. New York: Oxford University Press, pp. 39–48.
19 Alexander Wendt (2003), "Why a World State is Inevitable," *European Journal of International Relations*, 9(4): 504.
20 Anna Leander (2003), "The Commodification of Violence, Private Military Companies, and African States," COPRI Working Paper No. 11. Internet: http://www.copri.dk/publications/Wp/WP%202003/2-2003.pdf (21 January 2004). See also Kanishka Jayasuriya (2004), "Breaking the 'Westphalian' Frame: Regulatory State, Fragmentation, and Diplomacy," Discussion Papers in Diplomacy, No. 9. The Hague: Clingendael Institute, esp. pp. 9, 15–18.
21 Eugen Weber (1979), *Peasants Into Frenchmen: The Modernization of Rural France, 1870–1914*. Stanford, CA: Stanford University Press.
22 Charles Tilly (1985), "War Making and State Making as Organized Crime," in Peter B. Evans, Dietrich Rueschmeyer and Theda Skocpol (eds), *Bringing the State Back In*. Cambridge: Cambridge University Press. See also Karen A. Rasler and William R. Thompson (1989), *War and State Making: The Shaping of the Global Powers*. Boston, MA: Unwin Hyman. Rasler and Thompson argue, for example, that "[g]lobal wars and global power state making (. . .) are inextricably bound together" (p. 205).
23 Benedict Anderson (1985), *Imagined Communties: Reflections on the Origins and Spread of Nationalism*. London: Verso.
24 Florian Guessgen (2000), "It Fires Back! The Impact of the European Union's Common Foreign and Security Policy (CFSP) on the Evolution of a European Identity", paper presented at The Ionian Conference 2000, 20–22 May, Corfu, Greece.
25 Eurobarometer, no. 59 (Spring 2003). Internet: http://europa.eu.int/comm/ public_opinion/ archives/eb/eb59/EB59_Rapport_Final_FR.pdf (19 August 2003).
26 Burkhard Schmitt (2003), "The European Union and Armaments: Getting a Bigger Bang for the Euro," EU Institute for Security Studies, *Chaillot Paper* 63 (August).
27 Michael C. Williams (1998), "Identity and the Politics of Security," *European Journal of International Relations* 4(2).
28 See the Oliver Stone movie *Wall Street*, where Michael Douglas plays Gekko, a ruthless stockbroker who argues that "lunch is for wimps." That peacekeeping was also considered a wimpish activity was suggested by US Security Advisor Condoleezza Rice, who argued in October 2000: "Carrying out civil administration and police functions is simply going to degrade the American capability to do the things America has to do (. . .) We don't need to have the 82nd Airborne escorting kids to kindergarten." Laura Rozen (2000), "Peacekeeping's Pitfalls,"

Salon.com (22 December). Internet: http://archive.salon.com/news/feature/2000/12/22/kosovo/ index.html (21 January 2004). It is one of history's cruel twists that the US will be involved in nation-building and "peacekeeping" in Iraq for the foreseeable future.
29 Robert Kagan (2002), "Power and Weakness," *Policy Review* 113 (June/July); John Gray (1993), *Men Are From Mars, Women Are From Venus: A Practical Guide For Improving Communication and Getting What You Want in Your Relationships*. (New York: HarperCollins).
30 Gareth Evans (2003), "The Responsibility to Protect: When It's Right to Fight," *Progressive Politics* 2(2): 68.
31 Christopher Hill (2002), "The Geopolitical Implications of Enlargement," in Jan Zielonka (ed.), *Europe Unbound: Enlarging and Reshaping the Boundaries of the European Union*. London: Routledge p. 98.
32 Emanual Adler and Michael Barnett (eds) (1998), *Security Communities*. Cambridge: Cambridge University Press.
33 Peter van Ham (2000), *Identity Beyond the State: The Case of the European Union*, COPRI Working paper No. 15 (July); Ferdinand Toennies (1974), *Community and Association*. London: Routledge.
34 Cynthia Weber (1995), *Simulating Sovereignty: Intervention, the State and Symbolic Exchange*. Cambridge: Cambridge University Press, pp. 18, 19, 27.
35 Forsberg, "The Ground Without Foundation?," p. 14. For the US experience, see Cynthia Weber (1999), *Faking It: U.S. Hegemony in a 'Post-Phallic' Era*. Minneapolis, MN: University of Minnesota Press.
36 Christopher Hill (1993), "The Capabilities-Expectations Gap, or Conceptualizing Europe's International Role," *Journal of Common Market Studies* 31(3).
37 Peter van Ham (2002), "Simulating European Security: Kosovo and the Balkanisation-Integration Nexus," in Peter van Ham and Sergei Medvedev (eds), *Mapping European Security After Kosovo*. Manchester: Manchester University Press.
38 "Reforming Reticence," *The Economist*, 17 January 2004. Emphasis added.
39 David Long, "The Security Discourses of the European Union: A Functional Critique," in Lucian M. Ashworth and David Long (eds) (1999), *New Perspectives on International Functionalism*. London and New York: Macmillan. See also John A. Lynn (2003), *Battle: A History of Combat and Culture*. Cambridge MA.: Westview, esp. pp. 331–341.
40 Erik Ringmar (1996), *Identity, Interest and Action: A Cultural Explanation of Sween's Intervention in the Thirty Years' War*. Cambridge: Cambridge University Press.
41 Michael Billig (1995), *Banal Nationalism*. London: Sage.
42 See the World Values Surveys (WVS) of Ronald Inglehart, where European states whose societies share a clear need "for belonging, self-expression, and a participant role." Ronad Inglehart (2000), "Globalization and Postmodern Values," *The Washington Quarterly* 23(1) (Winter), 221.
43 Friedrich Nietzsche (1967), *The Birth of Tragedy and the Case of Wagner*. New York: Vintage Books, p. 37. The original German text is more poetic: "Jetzt, bei dem Evangelium der Weltenharmonie, fühlt sich Jeder mit seinem Nächsten nicht nur vereinigt, versöhnt, verschmolzen, sondern eins, als ob der Schleier der Maja zerrissen wäre und nur noch in Fetzen vor dem geheimnissvollen Ur-Einen herumflattere. Singend und tanzend äußert sich der Mensch als Mitglied einer höheren Gemeinsamkeit: er hat das Gehen und das Sprechen verlernt und ist auf dem Wege, tanzend in die Lüfte emporzufliegen." Many thanks to J. Peter Burgess for referring me to Nietzsche's work on this issue.
44 Zygmunt Bauman (1997), *Postmodernity and Its Discontents*. New York: New York University Press, p. 3.

45 Chris Hedges (2002), *War Is a Force That Gives Us Meaning*. Oxford: Public Affairs, p. 3.
46 Thomas Diez (1999), "Speaking 'Europe': The Politics of Integration Discourse," *Journal of European Public Policy* 6(4).
47 Ivo H. Daalder (2002), "The End of Atlanticism," *Survival* 45(2) (Summer).
48 Robert Cooper (2002), "The New Liberal Imperialism," *The Observer*, 7 April. Internet: http://observer.guardian.co.uk/Print/0,3858,4388912,00.html (20 August 2003). See also Robert Cooper (1996), *The Post-Modern State and the World Order*. London: Demos.
49 Cooper, "New Liberal Imperialism."
50 Mary Kaldor (1999), *New and Old Wars: Organized Violence in a Global Era*. Cambridge: Polity Press, p. 16.
51 This follows the "anti-geopolitics" stance of critical security scholars, be it from a less theoretical perspective. See Simon Dalby (1992), "Security, Modernity, Ecology: The Dilemmas of Post-Cold War Security Discourse," *Alternatives* 17(1) (Winter), esp. pp. 108–110.
52 Antonio Missiroli (2003), "Euros for ESDP: Financing EU Operations," EU Institute for Security Studies (Paris), Occasional papers, No. 45 (June).
53 Stjepan G. Mestrovic (1994), *The Balkanization of the West: The Confluence of Postmodernism and Postcommunism*. London and New York: Routledge, p. 83. See also Colin McInnes (2000), "Spectator Sport Warfare," in Stuart Croft and Terry Terrif (eds), *Critical Reflections on Security and Change*. London: Frank Cass; James Der Derian (2003), "War as Game," *The Brown Journal of World Affairs* 10(1) (Summer/Fall).
54 Martin Marcussen, Thomas Risse, Daniela Engelmann-Martin, Hans Joachim Knopf and Klaus Roscher (1999), "Contructing Europe? The Evolution of French, British and German Nation State Identities," *Journal of European Public Policy* 6(4): 616.
55 Ole Wæver (1995), "Securitization and Desecuritization," in Ronnie D. Lipschutz (ed.), *On Security*. New York: Columbia University Press, pp. 50–51.
56 Speech on 21 June 1999 at the 26th International NATO Workshop in Budapest. Internet: http://www.nato.int/docu/speech/1999/s990621a.htm (22 January 2004).
57 Elizabeth Pond (1999), "Kosovo: Catalyst for Europe," *The Washington Quarterly* 22(4) (Autumn).
58 Speech by Lord Robertson, Annual Session of the NATO Parliamentary Assembly, Amsterdam (15 November 1999).
59 Van Ham and Medvedev (eds), *Mapping European Security After Kosovo*.
60 Speech by British Prime Minister Tony Blair, "Doctrine of the International Community," at the Economic Club, Chicago (24 April 1999). Internet: http://www.number-10.gov.uk/output/page1297.asp (22 January 2004).
61 "A Secure Europe in a Better World," (June 2003), Brussels, No. EN-SO138/03. See also Peter van Ham (2004), "Europe Gets Real: The New Security Strategy Shows the EU's Geopolitical Maturity", *American Institute of Contemporary German Studies* (9 January). Internet: http://www.aicgs.org/c/vanham.shtml (22 January 2004).
62 Office of the Secretary of Defense (2002), *Proliferation: Threat and Response*. Washington DC: Department of Defense.
63 David L. Altheide (2002), *Creating Fear: News and the Construction of Crisis*. Berlin and New York: Aldine de Gruyter.
64 David Campbell (1992), *Writing Security: United States Foreign Policy and the Politics of Identity*. Minneapolis, MN: University of Minnesota Press, p. 68.
65 Campbell, *Writing Security*, pp. 138–139.
66 Steven Everts (2003), "Iran: The Next Big Crisis," *Prospect* (December).

67 Peter Potman (2003), "Setting the Future Arms Control Agenda: A European Perspective," Paper presented at Wilton Park, 16 December.
68 Seyla Benhabib (2002), "Political Geographies in a Global World: Arendtian Reflections," *Social Research* 69(2) (Summer): 541.
69 Jef Huysmans (1998), "Security! What Do You Mean? From Concept to Thick Signifier," *European Journal of International Relations* 4(2) (June): 241.
70 See Jörg Friedrichs, Chapter 10 in this volume.
71 For documentation, see Internet http://www.europarl.eu.int/comparl/libe/elsj/scoreboard/default_en.htm (21 August 2003).
72 Ken Booth (1998), "Cold Wars of the Mind", in Ken Booth (ed.), *Statecraft and Security: The Cold War and Beyond*. Cambridge: Cambridge University Press, p. 32.
73 Ole Wæver (1995), "Identity, Integration and Security: Solving the Sovereignty Puzzle in EU Studies", *Journal of International Affairs* 48(2) (Winter): 404. See also Daniel Keohane and Adam Townsend (2004), "A Joined-Up EU Security Policy", *CER Bulletin* No. 33 (January). Internet: http://www.cer.org.uk/articles/33_keohane_townsend.html (22 January 2004).
74 Walker, *Inside/Outside*, p. 3.
75 "Final Report of Woking Group VIII – Defense", *The European Convention* (16 December 2002). Internet: http://register.consilium.eu.int/pdf/en/02/cv00/00461en2.pdf (22 January 2004).
76 Pernille Rieker (2000), "Security, Integration and Identity Change", NUPI Working Paper, No. 611 (December), p. 32.
77 Fernand Braudel (1980 [1958]), *On History*. Chicago IL.: University of Chicago Press. See also Andrew Latham (2002), "Warfare Transformed: A Braudelian Perspective on the 'Revolution in Military Affairs,'" *European Journal of International Relations* 8(2).

12 Conclusion
State territoriality and European integration

Michael Burgess and Hans Vollaard

In this edited volume of essays the various authors have each contributed a significant insight into the complex dual relationship between the territorial state in Europe and the process of European integration. In a conceptual vein, we have concluded that the current political fashion to use terms like territorialisation, de-territorialisation and re-territorialisation in somewhat imprecise and arbitrary ways is a mistake and can lead to confusion and misunderstanding about what precisely is happening in the European Union (EU). Our early reference in the Introduction to the five indicators of territoriality furnished us with a much more comprehensive and detailed, yet usefully precise, basis for understanding the complexities and subtleties of state territoriality than previous works have done. And this composite approach, which emphasised the complex interrelationship between the five indicators, imposed an unmistakable modesty in terms of the general claims that we believed we could make regarding this important and fascinating subject.

Despite the conceptual difficulties that inhere in territoriality, we deemed it imperative that we should arrive at a conceptual definition that worked in practice. Accordingly the empirical contributions to this comparative study confirm that *political territoriality* is the most useful conceptual tool of analysis for our purposes and that the most important question for us to address was how far its established significance was changing or had already changed. This had the great merit of taking territory as a given, as we argue below, while acknowledging that its political significance altered at different times according to different contexts.

In combination, the historical, empirical and contemporary chapters have served to underscore certain basic propositions that are empirically verifiable. Clearly context defines meaning. Therefore if we locate political territoriality in different institutional and policy contexts we are able to make certain judgements about the nature, meaning and changing significance of our working concept. At the outset, territoriality has to be taken as a *given* in the sense that it *always* matters somehow in some way for social and political relations. But one of the most striking conclusions is that territoriality must never be construed as a dominant independent variable in every analysis of its place in politics. In practice it exists in an essentially interdependent relationship with other variables in social science analysis. This, in turn, helps to explain why contemporary processes like Europeanisation, globalisation and regionalisation do not herald the end of state territoriality. They merely underline the dynamic nature of political territoriality as a working concept and prompt us to acknowledge its changing significance by reconceptualising and reconfiguring its meaning in different contexts.

Another conclusion that we have drawn from the essays is a matter of revisionist history and refers to the mythical nature of the Westphalian state. It is abundantly clear that historical analysis has served convincingly to rebut the traditional claims and assumptions made about 1648 as the critical turning point in the history of sovereignty and the modern state in Europe. Recent scholarship confirms that the modern state could never have lived up to the intellectual, let alone the practical, expectations and demands that have been imposed upon it by the received wisdom of historians, political scientists and international relations theorists. Consequently if the contemporary state in Europe is deemed to be in some sense either declining or reconstituting itself, it is most assuredly not the Westphalian state.

Furthermore, popular allusions to the so-called 'post-Westphalian' state are now brought into sharp relief. We have to recognise that in successfully unmasking the Westphalian state and repudiating its unwarranted legacies, the implications of the currently fashionable term 'neo-medievalism' for political territoriality seem rather confused and confusing. It is unclear whether or not this attractive term is of any real analytical assistance in helping us to understand the contemporary world. As we have seen in this book, some contributors refute this, arguing that it is actually misleading because it is predicated upon a false reconstruction of historical meaning: Westphalian sovereignty never had any equivalence to modern state sovereignty and the territorially bounded integrity of the medieval polity was always highly ambiguous if not actually disputable. Others, however, claim that there may be a structural analogy between the way in which order was preserved in the Middle Ages and how it is currently sustained in the EU, affording important insights into European integration. Ultimately the intellectual debate about the utility of neo-medievalism for understanding the contemporary EU must be determined by detailed comparative historical analyses. While it is reasonable to suppose that there will always be interesting constitutional and political parallels between different historical epochs, it is quite another matter to claim that we can draw incisive theoretical conclusions from them.

These reflections about the putative Westphalian state, neo-medievalism and notions of the post-sovereign state are also linked to a discernible intellectual discourse most closely associated with mainstream International Relations (IR) theory that has also recently resurrected the following terms: empire (neo-imperial); networks; regimes; multi-level polities; global governance; transnationalism; and a contemporary liberal imperialism. We are now surrounded by a plethora of new terms (along with old ones that have new meanings) and labels that radically alter our conventional perspectives of state territoriality and conjure up vivid patterns of complex images where functional non-territorial imperatives cut across and mingle with different levels of territorial government and governance rooted in different organisational logics. It is a veritable kaleidoscope of competing concepts and contexts.

Moving on from conceptual and historical reflections to contemporary political analysis enabled us to shift our investigation of state territoriality to the area of comparative empirical studies. These suggested several broad conclusions. First, it is important to remember that while the analytical distinction between functional and territorial administration is useful for scholarly purposes, from the practical perspective of the public administration of the state/polity *all* political and administrative activities are simultaneously functional and territorial. They are so interwoven in practice that it is both difficult and dangerous to adopt simple generalisations. Second, the normative principles that underpin the contextual relationships between territorial and essentially non-territorial functional and personal dimensions of state organisation – typically in the form of federal, confederal and decentralised unitary structures – can have unintended consequences in practice.

What works in terms of *functional* efficiency can be highly problematic in terms of equality rights in *personality* systems. In other words, the complex mixture of territorial and non-territorial imperatives in contemporary polities can involve difficult constitutional and political trade-offs that have divisive philosophical implications. The unforeseen outcome is that the normative basis of state organisation is disengaged from its practical operation, opening up the possibility of a legitimacy crisis.

A third broad conclusion derived from the notion of multi-level polities is one that is linked to political imagination and constitutional design. There is a fundamental problem in applying the conventional normative principles of state territoriality and non-territoriality to European integration. It is neither possible nor desirable to use the same assumptions of state-building and national integration that characterised the past in order to build the future. Europe has been constructed according to a logic that must now give way to a new set of priorities. The building of the EU – tantamount to the construction of political Europe – replete with its new Constitutional Treaty (if it is to be ratified) and fifty years of piecemeal, incremental practical experience, has reached the point where national and European political elites have to create new channels of citizen participation and engagement in a new kind of federal model. It is not possible to go back to the drawing board. We have to begin with what has already been implemented. Therefore the contemporary challenge for political elites is to try to fashion the sort of normative federal principles that we see at work in Belgium, Germany and Switzerland and in the EU. A new Constitutional Treaty is an important launch pad for finding a way to build confidence and trust and to communicate that practical relevance so indispensable to an identity formation – however inchoate – that can buttress legitimacy and authenticity.

The enigma that is the EU is enigmatic in many empirical ways and at several conceptual levels. But one of its most difficult and awkward shortcomings is actually characteristic of every multi-level polity, namely, the political distance between different forms of authority. From the standpoint of the individual citizen, the reach of authority seems often to be beyond his or her grasp in the multi-level polity. By definition, citizens' policy preferences are screened and filtered through several layers of political authority structures and processed in ways that both dilute and distend outcomes. This often leads in turn to a deep-rooted systemic discontent and disillusionment that takes the form of a complex critique of representation, accountability and transparency. It is ultimately an authority crisis precisely because it is a crisis of legitimacy. And it is precisely at this point that we need to engage with the concepts of territoriality and non-territoriality. The simple fact is that citizens' loyalties and attachments remain largely with the national territory and are not yet in step with the emerging territoriality of the EU. But this awkward dilemma is not insoluble if both member state governments and citizens come to perceive the EU to be indispensable to their basic needs. Presumably one way to address this difficult problem is to promote and intensify the cooperation of national governments at the EU level. This would serve to enhance public perceptions of the EU as increasingly a necessity in maintaining their predominantly territorial loyalties to the member states and their governments. In this way both the legitimacy of the EU and of the member states themselves could conceivably be rescued.

Clearly existing policy practices in the fields of taxation, socio-economic welfare, law and order and security affairs strongly suggest that while there is practical evidence – and some of it quite strong – of citizens' predispositions and abilities to enlarge their interactive territorial space, it nonetheless remains predominantly within state territoriality. At the levels of both perception and practical policy reality, therefore, the individual citizen's political life experiences in multi-level polities are problematic whether they live in a single state or relate their lives directly to the EU. Accordingly, we might conclude that this is more a question of degree than one of kind or of a qualitative difference. Mindful of the multi-level polity as either a question of degree or kind, then, it is time for us to bring our comparative survey of state territoriality and European integration to an appropriate close. We have raised more questions than it has been possible to answer in the book, but it is at the very least clear that territoriality remains an important concept and a useful heuristic tool for analysing states and other polities as well as the major historical, conceptual and practical policy issues discussed in this volume of essays.

Index

absolutism: capitalism vs 46, 48; defining 51; French transformation to 47–9; and monopoly of force 229; re-definition of sovereignty 55; in Westphalian system 52
Act of Settlement 56
action, worlds of 73, 74, 75, 77–8, 80–1
active balancing 58
administrative reform 72–4
Agnew, John 4
Agricultural Revolution 50–1
Altheide, David 265
Amsterdam Treaty 197, 211, 217, 221, 234
Anderson, Benedict 256–7
Anglo-Dutch Wars 20–1
Anglo-Saxon welfare states 203, 214–15
Annales School 39
area and administration 97
arrest warrant: European 236–9, 267
article 10 EC 186
article 42 EC 191–2
Asscher (C-107/94) 181

BCR (Brussels Capital Region): bilingual policy implementation 135; federal government role 137; governance structure assessment 137–41; institutions 134; local politics 127–33; as meeting place 135–6; overview 120–2, 133–5
beggar-thy-neighbour strategy 201, 212
Belgium: federalism 90; Flemish electoral strategies 132–3; linguistic development 122–4; region/community overlap 126; *see also* BCR
BEPGs (Broad Economic Policy Guidelines) 211
biological determination 53
Black Death 49
Bloch, Mark 41
blue-water policy 56–7
Bodin, Jean 148
borders: territorial 33, 176, 232–3, 234–6, 256, 267
Bosal Holding BV (C-168/01) 187
Braudel, Fernand 39
Brenner, Robert 42, 43, 50
Britain: dependence on Dutch Barrier 25; dual system 90; eighteenth-century conflict involvement 58; multiculturalism 165; new centralism 92; post-1688 foreign policy 56–61; Prussian alliance 30; and SIC 241; and social chapter 210, 216
Brussels Capital Region *see* BCR
Bull, Hedley 40, 231
bundling of territory 147, 149; *see also* unbundling

Campbell, David 266
CAP (Common Agricultural Policy) 155, 166
capitalism: in Britain 58–9, 60–1; defining 50, 51–2; English transformation to 49–52; expansion 59–61; and power balancing 57; relations with territoriality 61–3; and

sovereignty 38, 56, 232; vs absolutism 46, 48
Carolingian Empire 40, 45–6, 66
Castells, Manuel 108
CEEP (European Centre of Public Enterprises) 210
centralisation 7, 48, 49, 51, 81, 84, 91–2
citizenship: awareness of European 157; and confidence 149; EU granting of 154; social 198–9, 201, 202, 206, 223; tests 165
The Civilizing Process (Elias) 229
coercion 32, 42, 48–50, 67, 241, 254
competition law: and social problems 216, 223
condominio 178
conflict rules 182
connectedness: defining 149
conscription: military 164, 169, 170, 262–3
consensus-state 84
consociationalism 34, 72, 83–4, 93, 125, 127, 134, 139–40
constitutional principles: social policy 204
contender states 60
Continental European welfare states 203, 214
Convention on the Future of Europe 114–16
Cooper, Robert 260–1, 268
cooperative federalism 88
cooperative state: institutionalisation 92
COPA (Committee of Agricultural Organisations) 110
Coreper (Committee of the Regions) 110
Cornelissen, Robert 176, 177, 181, 191
CPE (European Farmer Co-ordination) 166
cross-border movement *see* freedom of movement
Cura Anlagen GmbH (C-451/99) 183–5

Daalder, Hans 85
decentralisation 6, 51, 81, 83, 88, 90, 94–7, 222

defensive state: inventors 32
deterritorialisation 38, 58, 151, 164, 164–5, 166, 167, 274; and agriculture 166; discussions about territorialisation and 7–8, 11; indicators 150, 166–8; *see also* unbundling of territories
Dikshit, Ramesh 105
discrimination: and assimilation 165; fundamental right of non- 179–94, 207, 231, 237; indirect 179–80; and language 138; and taxation 176, 180–1
division of labour 82–3, 87, 264
double taxation 182, 192
Dual Polity 90, 92
Duchacek, Ivo 104–5, 106, 120
Dutch Barrier: and the Old System 26–30; Spanish Netherlands transformation into 23–6
Dutch Republic: British alliance 25–6; and European domination 32; French alliance 20, 30; French invasion 22, 30–1; overview 17–18; Spanish wars 18–23
dynastic unions 54–5, 57

EAGGF (European Agricultural Guidance and Guarantee Fund) 155
ECJ (European Court of Justice) 175; and gender equality 212; and the internal market 179–81; and principle of national solidarity 216; principle of territoriality analysis 183–5; scope rules on taxation 182–3; tax legislation criticisms 190–1; treatment of international tax treaties 182–5
economic crisis (1974) 207
economic development: key modules for 77
economic exploitation: fusion of political domination and 42–3
economic internalisation: and the deepening of market integration 208–10
EES (European Economic Space) 217–18
Elias, Norbert 229

EMU (Economic and Monetary Union) 111, 200, 204, 211–13, 214, 216–17; spillover effects 217; symbolic influence 154; and taxation strategies 216; and welfare policy 198, 200, 201, 202, 205, 213, 214
ERDF (European Regional Development Fund) 155
ERT (European Round Table of Industrialists) 110
ESC (Economic and Social Committee) 110
ESDP (European Spatial Development Perspective) 155
ESF (European Social Fund) 155, 206
ESPON (European Spatial Planning Observatory) 155
ETUC (European Trade Union Confederation) 210
ETUC (European Trades Union Congress) 110
EU: evolution of internal market 177–9; policies affecting citizens 153–6; as state in the making 152–3; symbolic shape 152, 159; territorial institutions 157–9
Eurobarometer 59 156–63; attachment/identity 159–62, *161*, *162*, 168–9, *168*, 257–8; on information/knowledge 163, 169–70; institutional interaction 157–9; on security 257, 259–60
Europe: convention on the future of 114–16
European Council: acceptance of mutual recognition 237; and Amsterdam Treaty 216; and EES 218; and OMC 219; and principle of territoriality 234, 246; responsibilities 110, 116, 152, 153, 203
European Parliament: authority 116; elections 157–8, *158*, *159*; motto 152; responsibilities 203, 204, 216
European Union *see* EU
Evans, Gareth 3, 257
extradition 236–9, 240–1, 244, 267

failed states 12, 258, 260–1, 265, 266, 268

federal states: distinction between unitary and 81–2
federal systems: forms of 82–3
federalism: Belgium 90, 125–6; cooperative 88; decentralisation and 81, 83; defining 103; Dikshit on 105; identity under 103–4, 105; Livingston on 104; problems of dual 87; sociological 83; Spain 90; vertical vs horizontal 82–3; Vile on 105; Wright on 80
federation: defining 103
federations: assumption of territoriality in 103–4; and multi-level governance 177
Feudal Revolution 45
feudalism: defining 51; demise of 45–6; in England 46–7, 49–52; in France 46, 47–9; and geopolitics 40–4, 55
fiscal territoriality principle 176
force *see* monopoly of force
foreign policy: de-coupling from dynastic interests 56
Forsberg, Tuomas 258
Forty Years' War 30
four freedoms (EU) 177, 178, 179, 182, 183, 190, 191
Frankish Empire 45–6, 47
freedom of movement 176, 179–80; and border controls 234–6; compensatory measures 239–40; and non-discrimination provision 186
French Revolution 49, 59
French system: impact of institutional reforms 96
Futura Participations (C-250/95) 188

gender equality 203, 207, 212, 220, 223
geopolitics: absolutist 55; and feudalism 40–4, 55; in medieval Europe 40–5; postmodern relevance 255, 257–8
Geopolitik 39
Gilly (C-336/96) 182
globalisation 1–6, 10, 37–8, 73, 107–9, 111; and capitalism 232; EU as response to 113–14; media 170; protests against 166; and territoriality

100, 101, 147, 232, 275; and
  terrorism 252
Goldsmith, M. *see* Page and Goldsmith
Gottman, Jean 147
Gramsci, Antonio 59
Grand Alliance 23–4
Great Britain *see* Britain

Habsburg Empire 17, 22, 23, 24, 26,
  27, 31, 34
Haushofer, Karl 255
health and safety 207, 209, 220
Held, David 107
Hertz, John 106–7, 117
Hill, Christopher 257
Hobbes, Thomas 229
Holy Roman Empire 52, 102
Hood, Christopher 75–6, 77
horizontal principle: vs vertical 82–3,
  89–90, 92
hot pursuit 239–42

identity: and borders 256; in Brussels
  140; definition of territorial 151;
  development of European 114, 268;
  Eurobarometer 59 159–62, *161*, *162*,
  168–9, *168*, 257–8; loss of cultural
  112, 161; and pillarisation 85; under
  federalism 103–4, 105
IGC (intergovernmental constitution)
  81–9, *81*; forms of federal system
  82–3; unitary systems 83–9
IGM (intergovernmental management)
  93–6
IGR (intergovernmental relations)
  89–93
Industrial Revolution 51
institutional complementarities: social
  policy 204–5, 219–23
institutionalisation of territory 148–9
intergovernmental systems 78–96;
  IGC 81–9, *81*; IGM 93–6; IGR
  89–93
intergovernmentalism: term analysis 80
internal market: four freedoms 177,
  178, 179, 182, 183, 190, 191
international relations: inter-dynastic
  marriages and 54; key principle 61;
  medieval 41, 43, 53, 54; Realist

theories 37, 261; territoriality in 102;
  transition to modern 56, 61; and
  Westphalia 40
INTERREG 155
interwovenness 78, 87, 89, 90–2, 276
intra vires 87
Ipsen, Hans Peter 177
Iran 266

Jacobite rebellion 28
jus soli 165

Kahler, Miles 3
Keating, Michael 112–13
Kellner, Douglas 107
kin-based systems 102
Kiser, Larry L. *see* Kiser and Ostrom
Kiser and Ostrom 74–5
Kjellén, Rudolf 255
knowledge-based economy 77
Kosovo 263–4

Laeken Declaration 114
language laws: Belgium 123, 124,
  125–7, 131, 139
Lebensraum 62, 63, 252, 255
Lega Nord 150
Leviathan (Hobbes) 229
Lijphart, Arend 83–4
Livingston, William 104

Maastricht Treaty 111, 210, 211
Maier, Charles S. 117
Marx, Karl 42
means of production 42, 43, 50, 51
means of violence: and feudalism 40,
  41–3, 48–50; public monopoly 52; *see
  also* monopoly of force
medieval Europe *see* Middle Ages
Middle Ages: feudal geopolitics 40–4;
  and sovereignty 148; system analysis
  231–2; territorial strategies 148;
  understanding post-Westphalian
  Europe through 231–2, 275
migrant populations: cultural isolation
  164, 165; discrimination 179–80
migrant workers: and social security law
  191–3, 207; and taxation 182,
  185–7, 189–90

military conscription 164, 169, 170, 262–3
military intervention 252, 258–62, 264–5, 268
military power: medieval build-up 44
military rivalry 48–9
modern state: vs medieval social order 41
monopoly of force: effects of European integration 229–31; and feudalism 44; influencing factors for internationalisation 243–5; operation levels 228–9; *see also* means of violence
multi-level governance 151, 203–4; Brussels *128–9*; definition 121; discovery of importance 73; federations and 177
multiculturalism 137, 165
mutual recognition principle 208, 237, 238

NAP (National Action Plan) 217
national identity *see* identity
negative integration 200, 201, 212–14, 216, 223
neo-medievalism 40–1, 44, 102, 231–3
New Federalism 94
New Regionalism 77
Nine Years' War 23
non-discrimination *see* discrimination
NPM (new public management) 75

OECD (Organisation for Economic Cooperation and Development) 93
O'Flynn (C-237/94) 179–80
Old System 17, 26, 29, 30, 57
OMC (Open Method of Communication) 218–19
Ostrom, Elinor *see* Kiser and Ostrom

PA (public administration): analysis 74–8; appropriateness of different value systems 77–8; collective choice values 75–6; constitutional values 76; positive/normative analysis 74–5
Paasi, Anssi 148

Paddison, Ronan 101
Page, E.C. *see* Page and Goldsmith
Page and Goldsmith 94
passive revolutions 58–9
patrimonialism 41, 47, 48, 53, 55
Peace of Aix-la-Chapelle 21–2, 29
Peace of Nijmegen 22
Peace of Rijswijk 23
Peace Treaties of Westphalia *see* Westphalian system
peacekeeping 257, 258, 262
Peasants Into Frenchmen (Weber) 256
Perfidious Albion 57
permanent war-state 48
pillarisation 84–5; Dutch model 78, 84–5; territorial dimension 86; vs direct intervention 93
political accumulation: definition 43
political fragmentation 112
political restructuring: implications 101
political territoriality: variability 39; *see also* territoriality
politics: and territorial segmentation 233
poll tax 92
pre-emptive strikes 258, 260, 261
primitive accumulation 49–50
production: means of 42, 43, 50, 51
proportional representation 83
proprietary kingship 52–5
protests: EU targeted 158–9, 164, 166–7
Prussia: British alliance 30
Putnam, Robert 121

Reagan, Ronald 94
Realpolitik 254, 257
Reformstau 87
regionalisation: BCR 126–7; of Brussels 127, 137; pillarised systems 78, 86
regulatory policy 220
reterritorialisation 4, 5, 6, 7, 9, 11, 96, 101, 147, 151, 274
retrenchment 92, 201, 212
Ringmar, Erik 259
'Rise and Demise of the Territorial State' (Herz) 106–7
Ross, George 113

Ruggie, John G. 7, 102, 178, 190, 253

Sack, Robert 6, 147
Scandinavian welfare states 202–3, 215
Schengen agreements: on external borders 234–5, 267; and hot pursuit 239–42
Schumacker (C-279/93) 181, 185, 186
scope rules 175–6, 182–3, 189, 192, 193
SEA (Single European Act) 111, 154, 176, 208, 209–10
SEM (Single European Market) 111, 113, 199–200, 234; and national welfare policy 209–10
serfdom 42, 45, 46, 47
SIC (Schengen Implementing Convention) 240, 241, 242
significance of territory 147–51
single currency 154; *see also* EMU
SIS (Schengen Information System) 235, 267
Social Charter 221
social dumping 201, 209, 221
social policy: British opt-out 210, 216; Europeanisation 202–5; historical perspective 205–14; institutional complementarities 204–5, 219–23; and integration 197–8
Social Protocol 21, 210–11, 221
social security: migrant workers' rights 180, 207, 220, 221; and territoriality principle 175–6, 191–3
social services 11, 96, 127, 202, 203
sociological federalism 83
Sonderwege 60
Southern European welfare states 203, 215
sovereignty: absolutist re-definition 55; concept introduction 148; erosion of 201; and intervention 258; modern vs Westphalian 38; parcellised 43; proprietary kingship 52–5; taxation and 176, 180–1; transference 203–4
Spanish Netherlands: Dutch Barrier 23–6; Dutch defence role 20–3
spillover 197, 200, 206, 217
Spinola, Ambrogio 19

Stability and Growth Pact 200, 201, 213
Succession Wars 18, 19, 26, 27, 31, 54, 58

taxation: carry forward 188; and deterritorialisation 179–81; double 182, 192; and migrant workers 182, 185–7, 189–90; noble exemption 48; of peasantry 53; progress 216–17; scope rules 182–3; and sovereignty 176, 180–1; and territoriality principle 187–8; of vehicles 183–5
Taylor, Peter 150
territorial borders 33, 176, 232–3, 234–6, 256, 267
territoriality: Chryssochoou on 177; concept analysis 100–3, 175–6; consequences of case law for 181–91; contemporary challenges 106–9; definition 6; dynastic 52–5; embodiment of 165; in federalist/ federationist literature 103–6; function in globalised world 170–8; indicators 6–7; and power 38–9
territory: etymology 253; institutionalisation of 148–9; significance 147–51
terrorism 228, 236–7, 243, 252, 266–7
Thatcher administration 92, 95
Third Barrier Treaty 24, 26
Thirty Years' War 49
three worlds of action *see* worlds of action
Tilly, Charles 32, 33, 49, 256
Treaty of Amsterdam 197, 211, 217, 221, 234
Treaty on Europe 111, 154, 221
Treaty of Maastricht 111, 210, 211
Treaty of Münster 20
Treaty of Rome 107, 206
Treaty of Utrecht 24, 57
Treaty of Vienna 26
Treaty of Westphalia *see* Westphalian system
Twelve Years' Truce 19

UK *see* Britain

ultra vires 87, 90
unbundling of territoriality 7, 164–5, 190; litmus test for 150; and powers of arrest 235, 240–6, 243–4; Ruggie's examples 7, 178–9; *see also* bundling
UNICE (Union of Industrial and Employers' Confederations of Europe) 110, 210
unitarianism 72, 80, 84, 88
United Kingdom *see* Britain
United States: and EU security 254, 257, 260, 261, 262–3, 264, 265, 267; PA debate 80; pre-emptive policies 260
use of force *see* monopoly of force

van der Pijl, Kees 60
Vauban, Sébastien le Prestre de 22, 33
venal offices 47, 48, 49, 51
vertical principle: vs horizontal 82–3, 89–90, 92
Vile, Maurice 105
violence: means of *see* means of violence
voting behaviour: Belgian communities 126; EU citizens 157–8, *158*, *159*, 168

Walker, Robert 268
war: as border-drawing concept 256; and development of the state 49; EU policies 257; and recognition 259

Wars of Religion 49
wars of succession 18, 19, 26, 27, 31, 54, 58
Weber, Cynthia 258, 262
Weber, Eugen 256
Weber, Max 1, 39, 41, 48, 229, 261
welfare policy issues: and Single Market 200–1
welfare state: constitutive elements 199; development of European 198–9; economic modernisation and expansion of national 205–7; public nature of European 222; territorial foundation 199; types 202–3, 214–15; *see also* social policy; social security; social services
Werner plan 207
Westminster/Jacobin unitarism 83–4, 87
Westphalian system: and Dutch Republic 34; and dynastic territoriality 40, 52–5; fundamental characteristics 1
Wielockx (C-80/94) 181
Wirtschaft und Gesellschaft (Weber) 229
WMD-proliferation 265
worlds of action 73, 74, 75, 77–8, 80–1
Wright, Deil S. 80–1

Zweckverbände (special-purpose associations) 177, 178–9, 200